CHICAGO JOURNALISM

CHICAGO JOURNALISM

A History

Wayne Klatt

McFarland & Company, Inc., Publishers
Jefferson, North Carolina, and London

Small portions of this book appeared in *Catholic Digest* and *Nostalgia Digest.*
Illustrations are from the author's collection unless otherwise noted.

LIBRARY OF CONGRESS CATALOGUING-IN-PUBLICATION DATA

Klatt, Wayne.
    Chicago journalism : a history / Wayne Klatt.
        p.   cm.
    Includes bibliographical references and index.

    ISBN 978-0-7864-4181-5
    softcover : 50# alkaline paper ∞

    1. Journalism—Illinois—Chicago—History—19th century.
    2. Journalism—Illinois—Chicago—History—20th century.
    I. Title.
    PN4899.C37K53   2009
    071'.77311—dc22   2009030264
British Library cataloguing data are available

On the cover: Wrigley Building and Tribune Tower, Chicago, 1930

Manufactured in the United States of America

McFarland & Company, Inc., Publishers
  Box 611, Jefferson, North Carolina 28640
  www.mcfarlandpub.com

Table of Contents

Preface

I entered journalism the same way Jonah became an authority on whales, I fell into it. From the day I was hired as a copyboy, I admired the humor, resourcefulness, and energy of news people.

Such men and women live in a world of their own. My first bosses helped cover the 1929 St. Valentine's Day Massacre, even though they never talked about it. As a rookie reporter, I sometimes shared the police headquarters with George Murray, the impish chronicler of the Hearst papers in Chicago, and Pat Leeds, the first woman in America permanently assigned to a police headquarters. Not many years later I helped train Jack Fuller, who would win a Pulitzer Prize for editorial writing and become president of the Chicago *Tribune* publishing division.

When I became an editor at the City News Bureau and helped prepare young reporters for work at the newspapers or broadcast stations, I came to feel that no one had even tried to portray the breadth of the rich journalism history in America's greatest news town, at least not with any historical objectivity.

Long out of print are two fairly good books about Chicago newspapers up to the 1940s, *An American Dynasty* and *Battle for Chicago*, but both are limited in scope. The first is about the McCormick-Patterson families, who owned the *Tribune*, and the second is largely about the city's wealthy and the major papers.

The *Tribune*'s accounts contain numerous omissions and distortions. In addition, an adoring biography of James Keeley takes the editor at his word and overlooks his role in the circulation wars that killed nearly thirty people. The autobiography of Melville Stone, founder of the Chicago *Daily News* and later an executive at the Associated Press, avoids the human element and occasionally skips over the truth. Even at their best, these books convey little of the day-to-day excitement reporters and editors feel whenever a story breaks.

Less serious books such as Ben Hecht's autobiography *Child of the Century* and Murray's *Madhouse on Madison Street* shamelessly fictionalize events. A.A. Dornfeld's account of City News, *Behind the Front Page*, contains various inaccuracies.

And so, no one seems to have conducted full-scale research into life at newspapers, and no one has ever shown the parallel development of broadcast news, even though their histories are entwined.

Whatever the medium, reporters in Chicago were generally more aggressive than their counterparts elsewhere in America, even reckless, and yet the city was far from unique. It is just that this was where the glories and failures of American journalism were written large.

But is news truly history close-up? When you lay newspaper coverage over conditions and events in the city, you see a startling disconnection when editors ignored or covered up circumstances to glorify themselves, satisfy advertisers, or avoid offending readers. Such abandonment of responsibility also plays a part of this largely anecdotal history.

Several editors and retired reporters gave me encouragement as they helped me understand the news behind the news. They are identified in the chapters unless they have asked not to be. At the Chicago History Museum, I found that its most useful materials in the field were unorganized files called scrapbooks: some on just newspapers and others, the "Harpeal Scrapbooks," covering various subjects. The museum also has several master's and doctor's theses giving specific insights into local journalism in the 1930s and 1960s.

By nature I have not tried to maintain a historical distance. Since I love being around reporters, I wanted to share this feeling with readers and make them feel as if they are in the news business during all of its shifting periods.

Partly because newspeople often go from one employer to another, the entire field operates as a family, with all its quarrels and dysfunctions. And so here you will find glimpses of the black press, wire services, news photographers, and even newsboys and office boys. Along the way you will find step-by-step accounts of changes in communications, which have turned a blessing for the news media into their greatest threat.

Somewhere in the evolution from obsessed publishers a century ago to the glamourcasters of today, news has come to mean less in our lives. Some of this can be blamed on unwise business decisions at the papers and the fair pursuit of profit over public service at broadcast stations, but, as you will see, most of this marginalization is inevitable. It is all part of the continuing story.

Introduction

Long ago a *New York Times* newsman told Edward Doherty, one of six Chicago reporter brothers, that "we in New York do not know your kind of journalism, we merely dabble at it."[1] In 1950, U.S. Senator Estes Kefauver, head of a racketeering investigation committee, remarked in Chicago that "This is the most competitive press I have ever encountered."[2]

The news has always been part of history and cultural life, but its fleeting nature has made it seem unimportant. Yet before news organizations became "the media," people from Fyodor Dostoyevsky to Ernest Hemingway read daily accounts of mayhem for enjoyment and inspiration. That was when editors sensed news by impulse and plunged headlong into stories, nowhere more fervently than in Chicago.

Without old-line wealthy families, the city lacked sophistication or a history that would have given its patchwork of ethnic neighborhoods a sense of continuity. Instead, this was where the farmer and the rancher stood at the foot of skyscrapers, and naiveté and corruption met on an equal plane.

Whether the news came from the city's slums, its Gold Coast, or the suburbs, it was told with such energy that Eastern papers commonly hired Chicago reporters and editors when needing a boost. Yet this field of vigor and sometimes riotous creativity has been overlooked in general histories of Chicago, even though the local news business provided entertainment, ousted crooked politicians, shaped political events, and served as the public conscience for a century and a half.

For a hundred and fifty years, a Chicago reporter or editor was somehow involved in many of the defining moments in American history. The *Tribune* changed the course of the nation with its long-shot support of Abraham Lincoln, and the circulation wars of the early twentieth century led not only to nearly thirty murders, but also paved the way for the bootleg violence that gave the city worldwide notoriety. Yet it was at Chicago papers that Gilded Age reporters began exposing unscrupulous conduct in major industries.

New York had seen its journalistic high point earlier in the nineteenth century, and the period after 1890 was Chicago's. One of the most famous photos in the annals of American criminal justice, the 1928 execution of Ruth Snyder in New York, was secretly snapped by a Chicago news photographer. Henry Luce co-founded *Time* magazine after gaining experience at the Chicago *Daily News*, and the radio voice carrying news of the heart-wrenching destruction of the *Hindenburg* was that of Chicago announcer Herbert Morrison. Chicago radio station WGN broadcast the "Scopes monkey trial" live from Tennessee, and the city also advanced not only the national wire services but the black press as well.

Reactionary entrenchment and racism wore no mask in the Windy City, and for former newsman James B. Simpson, Chicago was "the most theatrically corrupt" city in the United States.[3] Its citizens were amused rather than shocked by corruption, but this rawness at times stirred consciences into liberal action. Muckraker Lincoln Steffens had considered Chicago beyond reform, and was surprised by how much had changed in a few years through the efforts of private citizens with the help of newspapers.

Reporters and editors in the golden period were part detectives, thieves, and con-men who enjoyed prying into the lives and business of others, and a few had the touch of a poet. These motley people were sometimes the only ones who heard the tree falling in the forest. Even then, digging up the information involved hunches, luck, legwork, and both competition and cooperation among rivals.

In 1930, Chicago *Daily News* managing editor Henry Justin Smith remarked that "Some day, perhaps, there will be written, with a degree of completeness, a history of Chicago newspapers."

This is only a partial response, but it is the only book that carries the account through the development of broadcast news and into the world of corporate takeovers and media barons. But rather than being an impersonal chronicle, here is history as it was lived on the inside, including blunders, falsifications, and larceny. You will see editors who chose not to tell the facts or altered them out of fear of losing advertisers, incurring lawsuits, or infuriating the police. In the 1960s, such newspaper omissions gave broadcast crews a way to command public attention. In catching up, the papers became more answerable to their readers.

Here too are some of the news people who could turn streets into literature, including poet Carl Sandburg, novelist Theodore Dreiser, and grumpy columnist Mike Royko, voice of the common man.

To some extent, this is also a look at the news industry across America even though the focus is on the city where scandal, inhuman acts, and reform were so often splashed across the front pages and topped the newscasts.

Since there were so many newspapers in the city's early history, and news, by nature, passes quickly, it might be easy to miss the point of some portions of this book. A running theme will be how the news business changed over the years, along with the city whose pulse it felt.

Only a few of the journalists who gained renown elsewhere after experience in Chicago are profiled here. Instead, this is a look at many of the photographers, reporters, and editors who pursued and shaped local news. As Martin Mayer noted in his study of modern American journalism, "The tradition of the scoop has been cultivated more jealously and single-mindedly in Chicago than anywhere else."[4]

Spouses seldom understand why journalists work terrible hours or have such dedication, and yet the joys and stresses of digging for facts bound newspeople together as a family until decades of foldings and layoffs reduced the camaraderie.

Newsgathering by its nature draws extraordinary things from ordinary people, and for years reporters had an advantage if they were a little different. After laughing over a bit of journalism lore, Bernie Judge, who had served as an editor at the *Sun-Times* and *Tribune,* said a few years ago, "God help the newspapers if they ever stop hiring eccentrics." They have.

In fact, times have changed so much that Chicago *Tribune* editor Clayton Kirkpatrick in the 1970s called that delightful portrayal of reporters, *The Front Page,* a libel on the profession. If some of the quirkiness has been lost in the trend toward respectability, which Lord Macauley referred to when he called reporters the fourth estate, perhaps so has some of the personal involvement.

In downsized news offices, the better reporters are still trying to do their best even though newspaper publishers and station managers may seem to stand in their way. In the last few decades, various executives with backgrounds in business or showmanship have introduced "happy talk," lied to advertisers, and even looted a Chicago-based news conglomerate out of millions of dollars.

Newspapers tell us about other people, but nothing about reporters or editors. For a close look at the workings of a newsroom we sometimes need to pick from among the stories reporters have left behind more for the amusement of their colleagues than for our information. This book has weeded out the less likely anecdotes and will warn the reader when something appears embellished. As Shakespeare put it, "This news, which is called true, is so like an old tale, that the verity of it is in strong suspicion."[5]

The rivalry games that made Chicago reporters famous continued even as newspaper readership declined and local television news started realizing its potential, only to forsake it. But the boundary between the two media in our Internet age is disappearing, and this may be the time to see how all this has come about. For the sake of clarity, "publisher" and "editor" will be used rather generally since the titles for persons in higher positions changed with the times and from one paper to another, and often did not explain their duties.

Today's journalists may be less colorful than those of a hundred years ago, but they are more professional and the news is more reliable even though the standard forms of reaching the public are in trouble. Electronic advances have made news faster, but have not changed the nature of fact gathering, which always begins with knowing which questions to ask.

As with any general history, this book has an unconscious bias in its emphasis and interpretation. If news people ever become truly objective, what would be the point? News and history should never be just stenography, and reporters are moralists at heart.

Part 1: The Editors

ONE. A Bucket of Ink

The world of nineteenth-century Chicago journalism is one of great promise and quick demise.—Richard Digby-Junger[1]

Strong opinions were the entertainment of the mid-nineteenth century. Although the earliest newspapers in Chicago were either opposed to slavery or were active supporters of the South, their underlying concerns were the political interests of the states from Ohio to the Mississippi.

Despite all the abolitionist editorials written across northern Illinois, only a few publishers really believed in the equality of the races. One was Elijah Lovejoy of the Alton *Observer,* who gave his life for the cause. Townspeople had recently smashed the printing presses inside his offices, and on November 7, 1837, Lovejoy tried to save the one kept in a stone warehouse and guarded by volunteers. A mob that believed in state's rights or felt that the region needed Southern commerce torched the roof, and Lovejoy was cut down by gunfire when he ran outside to douse the flames.

Most papers in what was then the West were being published by scribblers who profited only as long as theirs was the only broadsheet in town. An enterprising publisher named John Calhoun started the Chicago *Weekly Democrat* four years before Lovejoy's death as the only paper between Detroit and Galena, Illinois, a promising city near the Iowa border.

No one had thought the settlement at the site of Fort Dearborn known as Chicago would amount to anything because of its drainage problems. But with the Black Hawk war ending the Indian threat in the area, Calhoun was sure the marshy frontier town with the Gallicized Indian name (derived from the Algonquian word *chigagou* meaning "onion field") would grow rapidly. Some time after founding the paper in 1833, he had one hundred and forty-seven subscribers, which probably meant virtually every literate household in the city.

In 1835 publication was suspended for five months when Calhoun ran out of paper. After a shipment finally arrived by lake schooner, Thomas O. Davis challenged him by founding the Chicago *Weekly American* to support the Whig

Party, which was interested in furthering the interests of Northern and Southern states beyond Pennsylvania.

One of the largest men in Chicago history, the six-foot-six John Wentworth, son of a New Hampshire storekeeper, walked from Detroit to this unlikely town of mud and dreams the following year to see if he could forge a career. Not long afterward, local Democrats arranged to have the ailing Calhoun run for county treasurer, leaving his paper in the hands of several supporters, including the brother of a friend of Wentworth. While the nominal owner remained in the East, the Chicago backers, impressed by the ambitious giant, named "Long John" its editor.

Wentworth brought life to the paper on South Water Street, its name showing that it was a block south of the river. He invented the masthead motto PRINCIPLES, NOT MEN, and used his size as well as occasional threats to intimidate city officials into awarding him printing contracts that supplemented money from subscribers. Unable to match Wentworth's zeal and untrained intelligence, the *Weekly American* ridiculed him as nothing but a "Bread and Butter Gawky."

His decision to remain as politically neutral as the backers would let him must have seemed strange. Before western expansion divided the country over slavery, Democrats were split between the Jacksonians, who preferred a strong federal government, and those who wanted to retain an almost colonial concept of state sovereignty.

Within three years of taking over the Jacksonian sheet, Wentworth borrowed money from friends and bought Chicago's first newspaper from the controlling syndicate. He leased offices on Clark Street, wrote the news and editorials in his straightforward style, inked the rollers, cranked the single press, and folded the papers by hand. His day ended only after he distributed copies of the *Weekly Democrat* door to door and carried the rest to the post office for out-of-town subscribers. As he said, "Let me have a chance to go my length and I will go beyond any man. All vanity is excusable in editors."[2]

In the eyes of Edwin O. Gale, a later rival editor, Wentworth's overbearance made him seem "Often unjust to those of a different political faith, cruel to men he did not fear, vindicative where the justice of another's cause won for him success ... [and he] oft times used his power to curse the enemies of his own creation and to carry out some selfish aim." In other words, Long John Wentworth was typical of his times.

Chicago, which had grown to more than forty-four hundred residents, saw its first newspaper war in early 1840. That was when the now twice-a-week *American* was succeeded by the Chicago *Daily Express* and Wentworth was forced to turn his sheet into a daily, even though this led to equipment breakdowns, supply shortages, and occasional suspensions of publication.

Over time, bulky Wentworth became the leading Illinois Democratic voice outside of Springfield and Washington. In 1847, he moved his equipment into a new three story brick building on Lake Street and named it "Jackson Hall" to please supporters of the late President Andrew Jackson. One of his political goals was securing federal money for a major canal and bringing conventions to Chicago-even though investors, thinking only of riverboat traffic, considered Galena more suited as the metropolis of the prairie state.

The city's third significant paper, the *Journal,* had come out in 1844 as a four-page, poorly printed sheet carrying news that arrived by stagecoach from Baltimore, Washington, and New York, but it was ambitious. This second Whig newspaper campaigned for draining the marsh north of the river and electing Henry Clay president.

The *Journal* was fair-minded, a bit lofty, and had a succession of intelligent, inerratic editors who would make it the oldest surviving newspaper in Illinois by the end of the nineteenth century. The paper managed to do this without a single major editor, reporter, or crusade to give it distinction.

A year after the *Journal* gave Wentworth's *Democrat* some competition, Long John installed the first Adams press ever shipped across Lake Michigan. The steam-operated flatbed contraption could print up to a thousand sheets an hour by using straps that carried paper over a form when the bed rose and brought it forward to a sheet flier.

When telegraph lines reached as far west as Michigan City, Indiana, both the *Democrat* and the stolid *Journal* promised to be the first to print President James Polk's annual address to Congress. The two papers held a spirited stagecoach race carrying copies of the speech across the state line, and, when the horses stopped in a dead heat editors at both papers accused the other of bad sportsmanship.[3]

The growing diversity of America led to changes within the industry. When the New York–based Associated Press began in 1846, its founders embraced objectivity not from any noble concept, but to make its news equally usable by Jacksonians, southern Democrats, and northern Whigs.[4] Jacksonian politicians, however, were losing their influence now that the addition of states across the Mississippi was threatening to split the country. These developments cried out for a fresh kind of paper in the growing city.

While towering Wentworth was as prominent in publishing as he was in a crowd, the transformation of what would become the Chicago *Tribune* from populism to abolitionism drew little initial notice. Since the *Tribune* would later call itself the world's greatest newspaper, this early period deserves some attention.

Thomas A. Stewart and John Kelly, a New York leather merchant, published *Gem of the Prairie* as an essentially literary weekly. When Kelly withdrew after a month, Stewart sought ways to turn the paper into a daily. With investors John Wheeler and Irishman Joseph K.C. Forrest, who had been Wentworth's assistant on the *Democrat,* Stewart ran off the first edition of the renamed Chicago *Tribune* on June 10, 1847.

Their single room office was on a third floor at Lake and LaSalle Streets. This was when Lake Street shops served boats harbored at the mouth of the river. Forrest claimed it was he who had provided the new name, presumably after the New York *Tribune,* but he soon pulled out because of doubts that the venture would last.

The initial run was for four hundred copies on a flatbed press, and each copy was sold over the counter for three cents. The paper itself was not the newsprint we are familiar with, made largely from trees, but came from pressed rags. The first page was taken up by advertising, and most of the rest was devoted to such contributions as letters and poems, and whatever news the editors stole from eastern sheets.

The first editorial promised "we shall at all times be faithful to humanity—to the whole of humanity—without regard to race, sectional divisions, party lines, or parallels of latitude or longitude." But this munificence of intent was doomed as Congressional compromises kept raising sectional tempers, and papers across the country were taking sides.

There was still no concept of local news. Instead, a well-dressed, educated man with a pencil would greet arrivals stepping off steamboats or stagecoaches and ask about recent events in their cities, so accounts could be third hand and two months old.[5] It hardly mattered because news was little more than filler between the political commentary and advertising, though this was already beginning to change.

John Locke Scripps, a descendent of English philosopher John Locke and grand-uncle of the founder of the Scripps-Howard news wire, bought a one-third interest in the new paper. Not content with waiting for telegraph messages and stagecoach interviews, Scripps spoke daily with merchants for the city's first distinctive market review.

As a lawyer and former mathematics teacher, Scripps' distinguished appearance and demeanor raised newspaper standards in the city while bossy *Democrat* publisher John Wentworth still resembled a ruffian in dirty boots. Locke also had better news sense. Along with Mayor William Ogden, he was instrumental in bringing the Galena & Chicago Union Railway to the city.[6] Despite its name, the line stopped at what is now west suburban Oak Park. This rerouting crushed Galena, and within a few decades the western Illinois city would be virtually forgotten.

In 1849, the *Tribune* became the first Western paper to receive important news on a continuing basis from an early telegraphic wire service called O'Reilly's Line. This allowed Chicagoans to read about debates in Congress and wire their reactions to Washington in time to influence voting. By then, the paper had about one thousand paid subscribers in a city of nearly thirty thousand.

A fire the *Tribune* blamed on its enemies placed it in temporary quarters over a grocery at Lake and Randolph Streets. The loss was insured, and William

Bross' bookshop donated a new directory, since lists of names and addresses were essential to every news organization. In time, the *Tribune* relocated to Lake and Clark Streets, and in May, 1850, it took up a space in the Masonic Building at 17 Lake. Equipment replaced after the fire allowed the publishers to modernize the paper with wider columns.

Two years later, Whig editor Edwin Gale took over the small Chicago *Express* and turned it into the *Evening Journal* (as opposed to the *Journal*). In his reminiscences, Gale, as if reluctant to admit he had supported a defunct party, said he ran the paper only on behalf of its "high minded" literary editor, Benjamin Taylor.

As the newspapers were growing with the city, up-and-comers were calling for a political organization to succeed the Whigs and push the goals of Ohio, Indiana and Illinois. Demographics were against them, since few railroads served the scattered towns. What the organizers needed was someone from this West who could rapidly gain national prominence.

Congressional hopeful Stephen A. Douglas of Chicago's South Side stepped into the *Democrat*'s office one day and asked Wentworth about printing circulars promoting a speech he was about to deliver in the city. The giant publisher immediately liked this finely dressed gentleman who was little over five feet tall. Douglas slid off his coat, rolled up his shirtsleeves, and prepared the type while Long John readied the press. In time, the ink ran out, and Wentworth had to send a boy all the way to Michigan City, Indiana, to buy or steal another bucketful.[7]

Evening rallies such as Douglas' were becoming more common now that sidewalks were being raised on planks to reduce mud tracked into stores, and gaslight was making streets safer. Eastern investors were starting to sense Chicago's destiny as the major transfer point at the Great Lakes. But the *Tribune* still carried little more than market news and serial fiction.

Wanting to become a political force in this exciting period, Scripps sold his one-third interest to a Whig syndicate and founded the Chicago *Daily Democratic Press* (not to be confused with Wentworth's Chicago *Democrat*) with bookseller Bross, later an important partner in a revived *Tribune*. The new Whig partners of the *Tribune* stooped to popular prejudices for circulation, including the informal, hate-mongering "Know Nothing party," then wondered why major advertisers would have nothing to do with them. The partners let it be known that their paper was up for sale.

Before long, abolitionist physician Charles Ray, former publisher of the Galena *Jeffersonian*, and Ohioan Joseph Medill met over the possibility of buying a paper in the rapidly developing lake city of approximately eighty-five thousand. Dr. Ray, whose prominent jaw and assured bearing gave him the appearance of determination, said that if they purchased the ailing *Tribune* they might sway its readers gradually away from anti-foreign leanings.

This was on their minds as they looked over the facilities on the third floor of a building housing a shop selling out-of-town newspapers and a post office, where every resident picked up his mail because there were as yet no deliveries. We are told that Ray impatiently puffed on a cigar as the handsome thirty-two-year-old Medill, more interested in details, walked about inspecting the equipment.

He did not come back smiling. Medill said the operation needed a new press to replace one powered by an old blind pony turning an overhead driveshaft by trudging in a circle hour after hour. After jotting down figures and working out the math, the two men concluded they would need more investors.

On June 18, 1855, Medill, Ray, and others—including Alfred Cowles, who had worked with Medill at the Cleveland *Leader*—finally bought the nearly bankrupt paper. Once the contract was signed, Medill and Ray took their chairs in the long bare room and must have talked over ways of challenging Wentworth's Chicago *Democrat*, now the largest broadsheet between Cincinnati and St. Louis.[8] The new owners were listed not as Medill and Ray but as Medill and Timothy Wright, owner of the Adams press Medill had ordered.

Medill filled the role of *Tribune* general manager, a position that would later be called managing editor, and this placed him in charge of news. The investors agreed that Ray would write the anti-slavery columns, the soul of the paper. Not that the two principal owners could be considered liberals. Medill detested the foreign-born poor and would call the Irish "the great unwashed," and Ray venomously assumed all Catholics supported slavery.[9]

The city they had adopted still resembled a pioneer town, with some roads built along Indian trails. As the nearby river mouth was being dredged to accommodate more ships, many of them carrying lumber, crews were shoveling cartloads of mud and wet sand into the deepest holes in the unpaved streets.

The two men tested their readership with an initial campaign for alcohol prohibition. German, Scandinavian, and Irish workers marched in front of the office while holding a black banner and a band boomed

Joseph Medill founded the Chicago *Tribune*, pushed Lincoln into the White House, and wanted his final words to be "What's the news?" (Chicago History Museum, photographer—Brisbois, ICHi-51968).

a death march. The next day's editorial proclaimed "The Chicago Tribune is not dead.... The Almighty has ordained it."[10]

The red-haired Medill and Ray ignored trends set by wealthy, rude, and often drunk James Gordon Bennett at the New York *Herald,* such as sports coverage, feature interviews, police court reports, and sensational trials.[11] In fact, Bennett had invented the modern American newspaper. But their national vision raised the *Tribune* above the brash sectional oratory of rival papers, especially infamous Wilbur Storey's Chicago *Daily Times.*

Medill's personality was so strong that Carl Sandburg would call him "terribly alive," and his presence at the paper would be felt for more than a hundred years.[12] Yet little in his background suggested his driving personality. He was born in the largely Irish port city of St. John, New Brunswick, Canada, and studied law in Ohio until entering journalism. When he merged his small Ohio paper, the Coshocton *Republican,* with the Cleveland *Leader* in 1853, he retained the name *Republican,* perhaps liking its strong, embracing sound. As a young man, Medill kept his face clean-shaven in an age of beards—as if using his fine features and determined chin to his advantage. The intensity of his eyes seemed to expect that everyone share the same high standards demanded by his Calvinist upbringing.

The Whig Party at the time was losing its influence, as it largely represented the interests of states lying between the original thirteen colonies and the Mississippi. The scope was too restrictive for an era of western growth, and many of its southern members joined the Democrats, reducing the northern Whigs to a rump faction.

Publishers across northern Illinois were rethinking their politics as new states were being admitted to the union. Dr. Ray and twenty-three-year-old Paul Selby of the Jacksonville, Illinois, *Journal* led an anti-slavery movement among newspaper publishers in the state and called it the Anti–Nebraska Party, referring to the unsatisfactory Nebraska Compromise. But similar clusters of ex–Democrats, ex–Whigs, and ex–Know Nothings in what was still called the West were avoiding the fighting word "abolition" by naming their statewide organizations the Republican Party, and Medill may have been the one who suggested that this body do the same.[13]

As with Wentworth, the Missouri-born Scripps initially looked to Douglas, a Northerner with a Southern wife, as someone who could end regional battles. But his feelings changed when Douglas quashed the planned westward route of the Illinois Central railway so that trains now chugged between New Orleans and Chicago rather than bringing wealth to his adopted city of Galena.

Medill felt that Douglas, the "Little Giant," was supporting too many appeasements and he thought Abraham Lincoln might be a stronger voice in Washington. The editor had met Lincoln when the Springfield lawyer walked up the stairs of the *Tribune* office and bought a subscription while in the city on court matters. In letters and private meetings, Medill started encouraging Lincoln to campaign against Douglas for the U.S. senate.

Lincoln was not a confirmed abolitionist, but he saw slavery as a cancer that must be removed to save the country. The question was, could a homely political unknown lacking in assurance pull it off? This leads to perhaps the greatest example of the adage that when you want to cover an important event, never send an editor.

After a fanfare of *Tribune* editorials in 1856, Lincoln rode to the first Illinois Republican state convention in Bloomington to deliver what would be one of the most important addresses of his life. A Chicago train crammed with lawyers and politicians arrived at two A.M. on May 29. The men meeting to shape Illinois' response to John Brown's recent carnage in Kansas must have felt they held history in their hands.

Among the trained observers waiting in Majors Hall later that day to see the birth of a political party were huge John Wentworth of the Chicago *Democrat,* clamorous Charlie Wilson of the Chicago *Journal,* and Scripps from the Chicago *Democratic Press.* Medill represented the *Tribune.*

With the advantage of being one of the last speakers, Lincoln addressed the delegates for what seemed like an hour and a half in the late afternoon. He had begun shrilly and bent over, but as he went on his tone grew more emphatic and he slowly straightened to his full awesome height. As daylight faded and Lincoln reached the heart of his largely extempore address, Medill joined the cheering and stamping, so carried away that he failed to notice that he had stropped taking notes.

After the speech Medill, probably with some embarrassment, walked over to his rival editors one by one to borrow any quotations they might have. But they, too, had lowered their pencils once Lincoln began electrifying the air. There was always the candidate himself, but, according to one story, Lincoln told Medill he had kept his notes in his hatbox and could not find it in all the confusion of delegates rushing out for destinations across the state.

Medill found himself with just a few notations from the introduction, none worth publishing, and Scripps covered his own lapse by telling readers that "I shall not mar any of the proportions or brilliant passages by attempting even a synopsis of it."

This speech is known as Lincoln's lost speech, although papers did carry scattered phrases from memory, such as "We say to our southern brethren, 'We won't go out of the union, and you shan't!'" and that unless the conflict was settled by the ballot rather than the bullet, "Blood will flow and brother's hand be raised against brother."[14]

Creating a politician out of Lincoln was just part of what Medill and Dr. Ray were doing to turn the country around to their way of thinking. They also sought a post in every committee opening up in the new Illinois Republican Party to prevent others from assuming control.

As this was happening, Wentworth was looking for another way of strengthening Chicago. He found it in the Illinois Central Railroad. Seven months after the convention, he worked behind the scenes to overcome Mayor Walter Gurnee's objection, and saw to it that aldermen allowed the Illinois Central to build tracks on supports across the tip of Lake Michigan. This meant only Illinois Central trains could reach the row of warehouses at the river mouth. Once the city council approved the contract, Wentworth's *Democrat* became the unofficial paper of the Illinois Central. Since the publisher was more interested in buying land than in civic affairs, one wonders whether he had been approached by the railroad interests. Next year, Long John Wentworth became mayor.

Taller than Lincoln, weighing over three hundred pounds, and not versed in law, the new mayor did whatever he pleased. On April 20, 1857, after barely a month in office, Wentworth staged a dog fight in the swampy North Lakeshore red light district called the Sands, and, in the name of preserving order, used police wagons with hooks and chains to tear all nine shacks down. As the piles of wood were set on fire, the smoke may have drifted past his property.

Influential New York *Evening News* editor Horace Greeley had been partly responsible for Medill's teaming up with Ray by giving the physician a letter of introduction, but now Medill was keeping Greeley out of Illinois politics. One of the famed editor's suggestions was that Lincoln gain attention in the senate race by debating Douglas. Medill expanded this into a proposal for a series of debates across the state, and in editorials suggested that Douglas would be a coward if he refused.

Next Medill sent "floating voters" downstate so that southern districts might elect legislators pledged to Lincoln. No wonder Lincoln said in a letter renewing his *Tribune* subscription that he owed the paper "a debt of gratitude which I fear I shall never be able to pay."[15] The two men had become so close that one day, while Lincoln visited the newspaper office, Medill grumbled, "Dammit, Abe, git yore feet off my desk."[16]

The *Tribune*'s unrelenting promotion of Lincoln continued even after July 1, 1858, when Medill's enterprising paper merged with Scripps' *Democratic Press* to become the *Press and Tribune*. Medill gained Scripps as an editorial manager and Alderman William "Deacon" Bross, the former bookseller, as a moneyman.

The talkative Bross let the others make the decisions, but he enjoyed being a back seat partner because of his interest in teaching. He was born in a New Jersey log cabin and worked on a canal before beginning his formal education at nineteen. His Presbyterian convictions were stiffened by arrogance. As Bross would say in future years, "The course of the *Tribune* was the result of four independent thinkers [Medill, Ray, Scripps, and himself], and hence it was always right."[17]

On August 27 of that busy year, Medill, now covering part of his strong face with a beard, detected that Lincoln's confidence was lagging as he was about to debate such an accomplished speaker as Douglas. At a time when verbal aggression was admired, the publisher goaded Lincoln "to give him hell" and even hold him up "as a traitor and conspirator, a bamboozling demagogue."

But, as always, Honest Abe stayed moderate even though he always listened to his political guides. Once when he stepped onto a platform while a stenographer from the paper was still on the way, Bross called out: "Hold on, Lincoln.... There is no use of your speaking unless the *Press and Tribune* has a report."[18]

Of course, Bross had a fair idea what the candidate was about to say. Lincoln would stop at the *Tribune* with a copy of his remarks a day before each debate, then Medill and Ray would go somewhere to rework the pages for several hours. They gave the new draft a final look before Lincoln picked up the revision in the morning.

Medill's other crusade at the time was to lure businesses to Chicago. His boosterism was so blatant that the Cleveland *Plain Dealer* parodied him as boasting, "Lake Michigan is situated on Chicago. The principal productions of Chicago are corner lots, statistics, and wind. The population of Chicago is about sixteen million and is rapidly increasing."[19] Actually, it was about one hundred thousand.

The combined *Press and Tribune* was making up for resources spent on political involvement by stealing news. Like all local papers, it paid a bonus to the first person coming in with a bundle of New York journals. Once someone hurried through the door with a stack, the two editors attacked the editions with scissors. They pasted the chosen articles into mockups for the printer so they could bring stories to their readers within forty hours of when the fresh news left New York presses, without, of course, crediting their sources.[20] The practice faded only after the Associated Press expanded its local bureaus into what was becoming known as the "Northwest" in the 1860s.

Lincoln lost his bid for the senate, but the debates made him more widely known and medium savvy. To prepare readers in other states for his 1860 presidential race, he published his words in the debates as re-edited by the *Press and Tribune*, and for Douglas's portion he used the Chicago *Daily Times*'s more accurate but pedestrian version.[21]

Medill, Ray and Bross called in all the favors they could to bring the first Republican national convention to the city. To seat so many delegates, an army of carpenters spent five weeks hammering together a two story wooden meeting hall at what is now 333 West Lake. The structure was called the Wigwam, a regional word for any convention center.[22]

Local Republican donors who paid for the construction were leaving nothing to chance. On May 18, the building was packed in more ways than one, with as many Lincolnites filing in as Medill could print up tickets for in his capacity as seating manager.[23]

Lincoln remained in Springfield during the convention and told Medill he would not permit any dealmaking. But as the editor sat with old friends in the Ohio section, he became uneasy at the third ballot-counting. Leaning over, Medill whispered to a delegate, "If you can throw the Ohio delegation for Lincoln, [presidential hopeful Salmon P.] Chase can have anything he wants."

The delegate rose and changed four votes from his state, and this ripple turned into a tide. As wire service telegraphers sent the news across the country, a man leaning over the skylight of the Wigwam signaled the results to the crowd below. Bells clanged and thousands of Lincoln supporters cheered and hugged one another. Cincinnati reporter Murat Halstead wrote: "Imagine all the hogs ever slaughtered in Cincinnati giving their death squeals together, and a score of big steam whistles going...."[24] No one may have imagined the consequences of what had just happened.

As the only major political organization not splintered over slavery and national expansion, the Republican Party swept the election. Medill, by now hobbling from spinal rheumatism, left the daily operation of the *Tribune* in the care of his partners and followed Lincoln to Washington. Tempers were so heated there that Congressman William Kellogg of southern Illinois knocked Medill down in the National Hotel and beat him for criticizing a desperate proposal that would have limited but not abolished slavery.[25]

As Medill and his partners were helping the Lincoln administration handle the growing threat of war, *Press and Tribune* circulation reached eighteen thousand, and on February 18, 1861, the hopeful owners incorporated as the Tribune Company.

The same month, Dr. Ray let Lincoln know through U.S. Senator Lyman Trumbull of Illinois that he and his fellow editors expected him to appoint Scripps as U.S. Postmaster. Ray said at another time that the request was "not wholly for the money there is in it, but as a means of extending and insuring our business, and extending the influence of the *Press and Tribune*." Medill was blunter in claiming the paper had spent two thousand dollars to sway the legislature on Lincoln's behalf, a very large sum, and that the debt must be repaid.

Scripps' appointment gave the *Press and Tribune* an advantage over every other paper in the country by letting him authorize special rates and promote national distribution. But once the editorials reached their goal with the election of a pro–Northwestern president, the *Press and Tribune* relaxed its political meddling and let Democrats take over the state. That did not stop Medill from demanding the expulsion of recently arrived French troops in Mexico, saying "We shall permit no nation to abuse Mexico but ourselves."[26]

Shortly after the attack on Fort Sumter, Medill's unambitious brother William put on the epaulettes of a cavalry officer and twenty of his troops enlisted in the offices of the newspaper, which after November 1860 was named the *Daily Tribune.* An armed guard was posted outside the building when Confederate sympathizers threatened to set it on fire.

However far off the battles were, the war was in one way or another close to every man and woman in Chicago. Investors were concerned about continually shifting battle lines, families with loved ones in the military wanted to follow the progress of the army and navy, and soldiers longed for news from home. The *Tribune* offered special rates allowing them to read the paper in their camps as soon as a train arrived.

In September, 1861, the government opened a recruitment center on Douglas's Oakenwald estate on the South Side, and the next year converted the property into a prison camp. At least eight thousand Confederate soldiers captured in Tennessee climbed out of train cars nearby. Those who could walk marched to Camp Douglas at 31st Street and Cottage Grove Avenue, and the many sick and wounded were taken there by wagon.

The ragged prisoners included Englishman Henry Morton Stanley, who fought for the South before becoming a journalist, and who would later find missionary David Livingston in Africa with the greeting, "Livingston, I presume?" Stanley wrote of his internment in Chicago that "we were soon in a fair state of rotting while still alive."

Tribune circulation rose phenomenally during the war, leading the partners to turn out three editions a day. About ten thousand people were buying copies on the street daily and thirty thousand were having theirs delivered by two-wheeled handcart. When no one else was available, Medill served as one of his own paperboys.[27]

Despite the success, there were a number of quarrels between Medill and "Deacon" Ray over various things. The friction increased when Ray became depressed over the death of his wife in 1863, and the energetic Medill could not understand at all. Ray sold his stock and speculated in real estate.

Wentworth had been accused of printing more news about himself than about his chosen city, and his abandonment of the divided Democratic Party in favor of the Republicans just before the war made his publishing the *Morning Democrat* an embarrassment. He also was being sued for a quarter of a million dollars over a political cartoon that lampooned banker Jonathan Young Scammon, a future newspaper publisher.

Not wanting to invest more money in modernizing his equipment to handle all the war news, Long John settled out of court in 1861, sold the facilities to the *Tribune,* and became involved in state politics. The purchase let Medill's paper become a factor in national issues, a goal his grandchildren would pursue with even more determination.

The seven New York papers owning the Associated Press were still keeping their Eastern focus even though its stories were being printed by subscribers across the country. Medill was so dissatisfied with these hand-delivered stories about the war that he sent his own men to report whatever news they could pick up.[28]

After a number of early losses, Ulysses S. Grant was less than gracious when the straitlaced Bross sought an interview with him. In revenge, the paper irresponsibly carried rumors of Grant's intoxication without proof, and relaxed its criticisms only when he started winning. No wonder all the generals regarded war correspondents as mosquitoes. When General William Sherman heard that an artillery shell had killed three reporters near Vicksburg, he remarked, "Good! Now we'll have news from hell before breakfast."[29]

2

Just two blocks from the *Tribune*, Wilbur Storey was using the Chicago *Times* to wage a war against the Union army. On June 3, 1863, with four boys feeding ten-thousand sheets an hour into a huge steam press, the leading editorial announced that "If the reader shall find this paper, it will have been printed before the arrival of threatened military force."

As the Chicago leader of the peace Democrats, Storey matched Medill's drive but lacked his rival's discipline, and spent all he could for scraps about battles and strategy. "Telegraph freely all the news," he instructed his correspondents, "and where there is no news, send rumors."[30]

Storey was born in Vermont forty-four years earlier and, as a journeyman printer, picked up a hatred for blacks along with his newspaper skills. After taking over the Detroit *Free Press* in 1853, he teased the public's taste by printing accounts of executions, scandals, and love-suicides. When he purchased the Chicago *Daily Times* eight years later from harvester developer Cyrus H. McCormick, he brought most of his old staff with him and proclaimed, "it is a newspaper's duty to print the news, and

Wilbur F. Storey. His philosophy of "print the news and raise hell" forced the Union Army to shut the Chicago *Times* down. But one of his reporters withheld news of General Grant's drinking binge near Vicksburg (Chicago History Museum, ICHi-21288).

raise hell." To get more people to buy his penny paper, Storey encouraged merchants to hold ninety-nine-cent sales.[31]

Medill regarded all such Southern sympathizers in the North as "deformed, diseased and the lowest type of human ever belonging to the rotten guild of politics."[32] Even Storey's long-time assistant, Franc Wilkie, referred to this six foot tall, prematurely gray publisher as "the awful ogre, the *bete noir*, the terror that ravaged the jungles of the great West," which still meant the Midwest.[33] He must have seemed especially fiercesome to Wilkie, a small, balding man with a little mustache. Storey operated with impunity because the mayor and most of the aldermen were fellow Democrats.

After Lincoln freed slaves in Confederate states with his Emancipation Proclamation, Storey was so afraid Republican citizens might lay hands on his newspaper offices that he had his employees store guns in every spare room. He even found a way to drive vandals away with steam from the press.[34]

Like other Copperhead sheets, the *Times* relished atrocity stories about Union soldiers and urged them to go home to their sweethearts, outraging General Ambrose Burnside. He had recently been removed from command because of severe losses and now, from a desk in Cincinnati, was in charge of all military paperwork from Ohio to the Mississippi. Infuriated by the *Times*, Burnside came up with a way to redeem himself in Lincoln's eyes.

The president had recently ordered that pro-slavery former Ohio Congressman Clement Vallandigham be turned over to the rebels. His crimes included suggesting that the U.S. be split into four countries. But Vallandigham broke away from his escort and returned to his home state by way of Canada. In a reckless editorial, typical for a time of war, Storey wrote that he hoped the dissident would reach New York so he would be free of Burnside's control and stay where "military lawlessness does not raise its hideous crest."[35]

That did it. Burnside ordered General Joseph Sweet of Camp Douglas to shut the *Times* down for the "expression of disloyal and incendiary statements."[36]

All Storey thought about was the next edition. He hired scholarly attorney Wirt Dexter to stall the action with a federal restraining order. Then he discussed taking bundles of the banned edition to several hiding places until the soldiers left. Next he sat down and wrote an editorial calling Burnside "the beast of Fredericksburg." A Storey spy who had been waiting just outside Camp Douglas came galloping up to the newspaper building at around two o'clock in the morning to report that "Lincoln's hirelings" were on their way. Word quickly spread, waking some Democrats in their beds and sobering others. They gathered in the streets and shouted that "if the *Times* is not allowed to publish, there will be no *Tribune*."[37]

After the four-mile march, federal troops arrived downtown shortly after three A.M. and stood with fixed bayonets along both sides of Randolph Street. When the first *Times* delivery wagon rattled away two hours later, the bluecoats burst through the rear door and ordered that the young printing crew stop the press. Its four barrel-like, steam-driven cylinders hissed into silence. The ink-blackened "printer's devils" climbed down from their narrow platforms and backed away.

Although gaunt Storey sometimes pummeled his opponents and would later push a man threatening him with a gun out a window, he met this pre-dawn intrusion without a curse. The officer in charge deputized a civilian to stay in the office and notify the troops outside of any attempt to lift a block of type. Other soldiers hunted down bundles of the proscribed edition and flung them into the street, where an officer supervised their shredding.

A crowd of angry Democrats and free speech supporters, wildly estimated at twenty thousand, rallied outside the stone city hall and courthouse building, and soldiers were sent to protect the *Tribune* building at Randolph and Clark. According to Carl Sandburg, Chicago came the closest in its history to mob rule.

Republican Congressman Isaac Newton Arnold, a close friend of Lincoln, pushed his way through the swarm and sent a telegram imploring the president to revoke the Burnside order. Not wanting to favor one side over the other, Lincoln decided to wait until local leaders of both parties agreed on the action he should take.

Shortly after sunrise, Democratic and Republican lawyers and politicians met in an empty courtroom to mull over ways of defusing the situation. Senator Trumbull, a Medill confidant who hated the *Times* but thought military action should not suspend due process, suggested that he wire Lincoln in the name of both sides about revoking the order.

Outside the windows, the crowd was incensed by rumors that violent abolitionist Charles Johnson, a follower of John Brown, might be hiding snipers in lofts around the *Tribune* building to keep anyone from smashing windows or flinging torches. Attorney Wirt and former mayor William Ogden, a Democratic businessman, quieted the mob by holding up a copy of the telegram. Faced with this and guns from the troops, the crowd broke up.

When Lincoln telegraphed Burnside in Cincinnati that he was lifting the order, the general responded that he had just rescinded it himself at the request of the War Department. After the *Times* had been in army possession for thirty-seven hours, the civilian guard was dismissed and the paper was, in the view of the *Tribune*, again allowed to "belch out its treason."

Although the *Tribune* had put Lincoln in the White House, it now turned on him for upholding the freedom of the press. An editorial complained that "Better a thousandfold in such times as these, an occasional exercise of arbitrary power, if directed to the preservation of the Constitution and enforcement of its laws, than a timid vacillating policy...."

The military suppression made the *Times* known well outside Illinois. Out-of-town subscriptions increased and shortly after the war, the expanded paper could even hire a night reporter to handle accidents and crime, a novelty for the time. Storey's assistant, Franc Wilkie, said that when he saw Burnside in Indianapolis sixteen years following the shut-down, he shook the old man's hand and thanked him for his "great service" to the paper.[38]

3

Although many editors still acted like children, a new species, the investigative reporter, was showing both daring and restraint. Since these men needed to be educated in order to speak to politicians and travelers, even those covering the battlefields generally came from well-to-do families. But the breeding of at least one newsman posed a dilemma: what do you do when your paper is critical of the Union army and you witness something that could topple its command?

A little before troops shut down the Chicago *Times*, Grant was staying in a tent five miles outside Vicksburg, Mississippi. He turned moody, and left camp on the pretext of inspecting the situation along the Yazoo River. For this he was accompanied by Charles A. Dana from the *New York Times* and Associated Press, who had just been appointed assistant war secretary.

The two men hailed a steamer that happened to have Chicago *Times* reporter Sylvanus Cadwallader aboard. Storey had hired the gentleman away from his family's Milwaukee paper when the *Times'* war correspondent was thrown in jail for overstepping his bounds.

Disgusted by the attitude of other reporters in the field, Cadwallader was helping to elevate war coverage. Only in later years would he write that Grant had "made several trips to the bar room of the boat in a short time, and became stupid in speech and staggering in gait. This was the first time he had shown symptoms of intoxication in my presence, and I was greatly alarmed by his condition...."

Cadwallader said he used a ruse to bring Grant into the general's suffocating cabin, then locked the door and "commenced throwing bottles of whiskey[,] which stood on the table, through the window, over the guards into the river." He added that he had Grant take off some clothes and fanned him to sleep. By the time they reached the village of Satartia, the general had sobered up, but Cadwallader persuaded him not to go ashore because of the danger of sniper fire.

Cadwallader said he learned the next morning that the general later ignored his advice, somehow obtained whiskey ashore, and went partying. Riding a horse named Kangaroo because of its wild habits, the tipsy Grant plunged past everything in his way. Cadwallader said he rode after him until he could seize Kangaroo's reins and have the general lie on the grass. As Grant rested, Cadwallader asked someone to summon an ambulance. Once Grant and the reporter reached headquarters, the general sat up and seemed to have recovered.

Cadwallader added that out of admiration of Grant's ability, he kept the two-day bender a secret. But several Grant supporters denounced this account, including Dana, who explained it away by claiming the general had simply been ill aboard the steamer and that the inspection trip lasted only one day. Perhaps, and perhaps the respected journalist was covering up a slip that occurred while he was a war department official.[39]

As the two armies clashed at Gettysburg, *Tribune* reporters rode forty miles to Joliet for an ecclesiastical hearing on allegations that the Rev. E.W. Hager had enjoyed intimate relations with several women from his parish. Church officials should have known that barring the press would only transform their work into a game. Finding equipment from an abandoned fire station below the hearing room, the reporters lowered a hose down a chimney flue to eavesdrop on testimony. Their editor coyly gave the byline to "Invisible."[40]

As the war dragged on, Storey learned of a planned typesetter strike. He furtively set up a composing room in a Randolph Street loft and had a staff member show forty young women how to do the men's job. As soon as the males stormed out, Storey escorted the women to the loft and watched as they slowly put out his latest attack on the president.[41]

4

A year after the war ended and Lincoln was assassinated, the *Times* moved into the first Chicago building ever specifically constructed for a newspaper, on Dearborn Street between Washington and Madison Streets. The larger space and new equipment allowed the paper to double its news and advertising from four to eight pages.

Dearborn soon became the city's newspaper row since it was close to the post office, although mail was now being delivered door to door. You could practically shoot peas from the *Journal* on Dearborn at Lake Street and hit the *Tribune* on Dearborn opposite the Sherman House hotel at Randolph Street or the influential German-language newspaper *Staats-Zeitung* on Madison just past Dearborn.

With newspapers now hiring reporters for court coverage and night police news, a jargon was emerging. "Deadline" apparently came from the Civil War. Prisoners were told they would be shot if they crossed a certain line, and so the word was used for the last minute a story could be submitted for inclusion in the next edition. A "beat," a steady assignment such as the court beat or the police beat, could have come from a British term for the distance an army picket walked back and forth until relieved.

Chicago newsmen may have invented the word "scoop" for an exclusive story. At least they thought they did.[42] The word might have evolved from someone's mispronounced "coup." In the nineteenth and early twentieth centuries, reporters ended their stories with "-30-," possibly adapting a telegraphic sign-off code.

Since there were as yet no telephones, night reporters wandered the streets looking for news and stopped by a few police stations per shift. The nearest one was half a mile from newspaper row. When there was no hard news, reporters tried to pick up a human interest story, a vignette reminding people in the increasingly industrial and expanding city what life was still like.

One such new reporter, Ferdinand Cook, has left us a brief glimpse of the excitement. One night, he saw a bloodied man being helped into the police station and ran the four blocks to the *Times* headquarters. He arrived just as Storey and city editor Charles Wright were leaving. After Cook breathlessly told his boss what he had seen, Storey said, "You can have twenty minutes. Cut your cloth accordingly." That is, do not overwrite. To the press foreman, Storey called out, "Hold what men are left. I'll see to the heading."

With a stick of type in hand, the publisher composed a snappy headline. Whatever it was, Cook regarded it as a "corker." After all, this was the editor said to have captioned a Southern hanging "Jerked to Jesus."[43]

As Cook sat down, Wright told him, "Start with the facts; I'll attend to the introduction." This meant the novice should put down as plainly as possible what he saw and had been told, and the more experienced Wright would compose what would later be called the "lead" or "lede," a first sentence that draws readers into a story.

The edited item was rushed to the composing room, and in ten minutes was set by a typesetter who could pick up blocks of letters and fit them into words while tossing any damaged type into the "hell box" below. Fifty years earlier such men could handle only about four hundred letters in an hour, but improved methods now allowed them to place that many in four minutes.[44]

Storey enjoyed publishing stories about social misfortunes more than crime, even though his building was so near the gambling district that when his people heard gunfire they dismissed it as "target practice." With no crusades such as pestering Burnside to absorb his energies, Storey was having fun writing or approving such headlines as "Death's Debauch" and "Sexual Skullduggery." His scandal-searching sometimes left him with as many as two dozen libel suits at the same time.[45]

With his rambunctiousness, the *Times* continually beat the *Tribune* in circulation, even though its working-class tone made sure the paper trailed in advertising profits. Storey's prejudice against African Americans and the Irish poor at least led his paper to address community issues, such as exposing the despicable conditions of potato-famine immigrants.

The quickening pace of transportation, business, and news gave Chicago all the bustle New York had had a generation earlier. Thinking there was room for a third major paper, tobacco-chewing banker Jonathan Young Scammon and businessman John V. Farwell hired some of Storey's best people away from him. On May 13, 1865, the partners ran off the first edition of the Chicago *Republican* from a building at Dearborn and Washington. Its four pages were crammed with ten columns each.

The role of publisher was an odd one for Scammon, the man who had pushed Wentworth out of the news business with a libel suit. For their editor, he and Farwell eagerly hired Dana, considered one of the most intelligent men in the field.

As the first professional news editor in Chicago at a time of eccentric amateurs, the New York journalist made sure the *Republican* was the city's first modern sheet. By November, he was putting out a paper that was eight pages long, each page with just six columns, and with all advertising kept in the back. He even lured Medill's lackadaisical brother Sam from the *Tribune* sports desk and made him city editor to capitalize on his knowledge of the city.

But this period of energetic experimentation was too good to last. Dana resigned when narrow-minded stockholders demanded that the *Republican* renounce Lincoln's successor, Andrew Johnson, during his Reconstruction quarrel with Congress. Dana took the paper to court and won a more than ten thousand dollar judgment.[46] He returned to New York, gained fame editing the *Sun,* and Chicago's hope of emerging from its journalistic regionalism went with him. Farwell gave up publishing and concentrated on land speculation, in later years becoming one of the secret developers of Lake Shore Drive.

With Storey out of touch with the mercantilian times, rival sheets were drawing more of his staff away. Making do with whatever he had left, the former fire-eater never told his reporters to fake news, but allowed them to use their imagination as they burrowed into dens of vice for "copy." His goal was still to raise hell.

5

A newspaper in this vigorous time of competition needed a strong personality behind it, a Lovejoy, Wentworth, Storey, or Medill, and the more unconventional the better. The papers these men ran chased stories aggressively, setting them apart from all the others. With so many political and economic slants in the press, educated people would read two or three rival papers a day to understand issues in a city that kept shucking off one paper after another as it grew.

Medill may have lacked vision, but his editor Horace White, like Wentworth before him, was demanding federal money for expanding Chicago's capacity for commerce. Business leaders in the crossroads city still had not decided which direction to look toward: to the East, where culture and the moneyed interests lay, or to the raw West, where thousands of miles of wilderness posed a century of promise. But White knew.

The prematurely balding newsman, with a wide-eyed look of energy and independence, felt that now that the war was over, Congress should make Chicago a transfer point for rail lines and Great Lakes shipping, linking businesses in the East and the recovering South with all the towns going up on the other side of the Mississippi. Although it no longer had the busiest harbor in the land, the city was becoming the railroad hub of America.

The *Tribune* was already losing step with such modern trends as crime stories and full-page sports coverage, and in 1867 Medill attempted to set education back to pioneer days. He privately printed an "Easy Method of Spelling the English Language" for his staff. Omitting a collection of accent marks he felt were easier to memorize than silent letters, the pamphlet states:

> A wurd now with editors. Without their cooperashon the advocasy ov orthografic reform iz a discourajing labor. But with ur (your) ad (aid), this grat (great) impediment in the pathwa (pathway) ov educashon can be remuvd in les tim (time) than it wil tak (take) tu pa (pay) of (off) the nashional debt.

Since his editors had more sense than he did, only a few Medillisms were actually used, such as "frater" for freighter.[47]

The accounts we have of the man do not reflect the mercurial nature that his contemporaries mentioned without elaboration. Medill attributed most sicknesses to sun spots and derisively called sports sections "gambling pages." Although he could be jovial away from his paper, like many self-propelled people he had few close friends.

His staff knew desktops had to be cleared before he came through the door each morning with clippings from other papers and mail from old friends. Medill would dump the letters on the desk of his managing editor, telling him to yank news from the next edition to make space for them. An editor thinking news was more important would later say he had misplaced the correspondence, and Medill would accept the lie good-naturedly. When editors and reporters left for the day, he would put a little water in their glue pots to save a few cents. Yet even his rivals admitted that Medill brought out the best in his employees and often came up with two ideas for every one of theirs.

His amiable brother Sam, before and after his stint at the *Republican*, would often help some newsman or printer down on his luck. He also liked occasionally being in charge. Before going home, Joseph Medill would say something like, "Sam, eight pages tomorrow morning, big type, minion," referring to standard type. But Sam liked a big paper despite the added costs. So when Joseph went on a trip, he would instruct the press foreman, "Twelve pages tomorrow and all nonpareil," the smallest type in general newspaper use.

As a frontier-style publisher heading a modern paper, his two-fingered grasp of events left Medill without a purpose now that slavery was abolished and the Midwest was a powerful factor in Washington. But his support of state candidates allowed him to dabble in politics behind the scenes, and acquaintance Edward Beck said the Illinois state constitution of 1870 "was largely Medill's handiwork."[48] He also went after wire service reform.

Medill had been calling the New York–dominated Associated Press a "monopoly of the worst sort" because it fed outside subscribers only a portion of the information it gave to papers in the Empire State, and these stories were tapped out only between six P.M. and ten P.M. He spoke to disgruntled editors in other states, and after several meetings they chartered the Western Associated Press in Louisville in 1865, and the two wire services co-existed without actually being rivals.

Since newspapers necessarily reflect their times, they evolved in Chicago and elsewhere without any heavy thinking about changes. Starting around 1870, as America was entering its gilded age, women—from shopgirls to the influential wives of industrialists—began reading newspapers in larger numbers. The male publishers were unclear what women wanted to read, and so they started hiring female editors (writers) who had no journalism experience and were sometimes offended by uncouth colleagues with their cigars and spittoons.[49] Under their influence, the papers were no longer purely political and no longer went after a single cause.

In 1871, the first successful transatlantic cable was laid, the New York and the Western AP's were grudgingly cooperating with one another, and all seemed right with the world. But Medill and a few others were worried about what might happen if an uncontrolled fire broke out in Chicago. He was sure the *Tribune* building, completed in 1868, would be safe because it was made of a kind of stone locally called Joliet marble. But most downtown buildings were still wooden.

Two. Ashes to Ashes

"Reform? Chicago?" I laughed.—Lincoln Steffens[1]

On September 10, 1871, the *Tribune* warned readers about miles of firetraps, and that some substantial-looking buildings were nothing more than "sham and shingles." A long drought continued into the following month.

On the unusually sultry Sunday evening of October 8, a wind raking off the parched prairie reached flames on the property of Patrick and Catherine O'Leary at 112 DeKoven Street. This was before pasteurization, and like many families the O'Learys kept a barn with a horse and six cows, which provided milk for their boys. A peg-legged wagon driver named Daniel Sullivan was known to sleep in the barn, and the next thing we know it was about nine-thirty that night and Sullivan was shouting "Fire!"

Fire alarm 342 would be struck only when there was little left in the main part of the city to burn. Wind decided the path of the blaze. First went the shanties, then stucco houses, and next came the limestone sidewalks. Walls were turned into lime and powder and granite paving blocks cracked. Only the few sandstone structures could withstand the heat.

The *Times* staff tried to work as if nothing unusual were happening, although the nighttime darkness had turned a hellish red. Wilbur Storey's final report was to be "The entire business portion of the city is burning, and the Times building is doomed," but the rooms had to be evacuated before the story could be run, and no one was around to watch the edition melt away.

Still standing was the recently opened four-story *Tribune* building, guaranteed fireproof. But reporters and pressmen knew that destruction was inevitable once the flames leaped across the street. The fire swept under the wooden sidewalk and began crawling up the walls of a first floor barbershop. *Tribune* editor Horace White took a kerosene lamp into the basement and emptied the oil into a drain rather than leave anything to feed the inferno. Others put all the matches they could find into the company safe.

Fifteen to twenty men Medill had rounded up helped him fight embers landing on the roof with buckets of water, shovels, and flat pieces of wood. During breaks, Medill went back to getting out another edition even though there soon might be no one in the city to read it. As this was happening, his friends and neighbors were burying their valuables or sitting on chairs in Lake Michigan with water up to their necks.

William Bross, a part owner of the paper, watched a hotel he owned burn to the ground and went home. But when he heard that the fire was intensifying downtown, the fierce-looking man with a long dark beard sprang into action. He jumped on a horse and managed to ride through the flames as glowing cinders dropped like hail around him. Bross found the newspaper departments operating as usual even as windows were cracking from the unbearable temperatures. Around this time, Sam Medill was trying to take a nap in an office so he would be fresh later.

As soon as the city room sent down a paragraph updating the disaster, Bross told the press gang to let the Hoe cylinder presses roll. By then, fire was shooting up the full height of buildings across the street. A gas main ruptured and the newspaper offices went dark. The basement press crew lit candles so they could feed more sheets into the machines, but the presses stopped once a water main exploded. There was nothing more Bross could do, but the anti-union financier was thinking of a way to avoid extortionate pay demands by laborers during what was sure to be at least two years of the city's reconstruction.

Joseph Medill was still battling embers on the roof when a pressman told him the rollers were liquefying and pressmen were choking on the smoke. After ordering an evacuation, the editor and his roustabouts came down from the roof blackened by soot and made sure no one remained behind.

As a tug boat was helping hundreds of people flee across the river, H. W. Farrar of the Chicago *Journal* was riding a train for a Cincinnati business trip. Once he learned of the fire, he bought a four-cylinder press, had it dismantled, and sent the parts home so his own paper could resume publication as soon as possible.

With only two hours of sleep, Medill wandered around with a hell behind him until he found a surviving print shop. He used its crude press on October 10 to roll off the first post-fire edition, with a column head reading CHEER UP. He let the *Journal* use the same equipment for an extra, covering only one side of the paper.

The roofless, empty walls of just the First National Bank, the Post Office, the Tribune building, and the east wing of the Court House stood as ugly towers above miles of disaster. The only downtown structure that remained whole was the sandstone water tower north of downtown. Among the more than three hundred dead was Joseph Stubbs, a Canadian who had recently come to Chicago to work for the *Republican*. He may have died trying to cover the greatest story of his career.

Above and opposite: Chicago in ruins after the Great Fire of 1871. The shell of the Chicago *Tribune* is one of the few partial buildings remaining. *Tribune* publisher Joseph Medill had warned of such a catastrophe but no one paid attention to him (Chicago Public Library, Special Collections and Preservation Division, CCW 1.1156).

The fire ended in a belated rainstorm, and wherever businessmen gathered in the first hours afterward there was incredible optimism about how they would recover their losses. But Franc Wilkie and other *Times* men who returned to the rubble of newspaper row found Wilbur Storey looking old at fifty-two and sitting in a daze on a pile of charred timbers, all that remained of his five-story building. "The *Times* is dead," he told them. "Chicago is gone, and I'm all through."

Wanting to bring him out of his depression, they searched the ruins until coming across a small old press, and on this they cranked out the next edition of the *Times,* ten days after the fire.[2] It was the last major Chicago newspaper to resume publication.

Knowing that the Chicago *Tribune* had nothing to rebuild with, Murat Hubbard of the Cincinnati *Commercial* sent it boxes of his old type. Medill telegrammed Baltimore for a rotary press, and when sections arrived by wagon a new foundation was already being dug at the old location. At least Medill himself was fortunate—his brick house on Washington Street was one of the few homes standing.

Workers hoping to jack up their prices for clearing away debris were surprised to see carloads of young men jumping off trains and eager for work. Ahab-looking Bross had gone from city to city holding rallies and urging, "Go to Chicago now! Young men, hurry there! Old men, send your sons! Women, send your husbands! You will never have such a chance to make money!"[3] New York City officials arranged a relief effort out of compassion and to resume commerce with some of the Midwest's largest manufacturers.

Mounds of rubble hid all that remained of the Chicago *Legal News,* which issued weekly court reports for lawyers keeping track of judicial rulings. Myra

Colby Bradwell of Vermont had established the publication a short time earlier to crusade for zoning laws, court improvements, and women's suffrage. Undeterred by the devastation, she had her periodical run off in Milwaukee and sent to Chicago until she could rebuild. Bradwell was held in such esteem in her two worlds that she became the first woman admitted to the Illinois Press Association and also to the Illinois Bar Association.[4]

The fire had been too great a disaster to be comprehended without casting blame. Fanciful tales arose from the fact that Mrs. O'Leary's home was left intact. *Journal* newsmen Michael Ahearn, James Haynie, and John English noticed a broken kerosene lamp in her barn and came up with a plausible account that a cow had kicked it over during milking. Unable to interview Mrs. O'Leary, the *Times* invented a variation that had her say in a fictional interview that the cow kicked the lamp over after she left the barn, and a legend was born.[5]

Talk came around to how such catastrophes might be prevented. Although Medill delighted in playing politics behind the scenes, friends suggested that he run for mayor under the one-time-only Fire Proof Party. Once elected, he insisted that all new buildings in the main part of the city be made of brick or stone. In 1872, he presided over Chicago's amazing reconstruction, which involved laborers from as far away as Canada and numerous wooden derricks for hoisting lumber. However, accustomed to playing an autocrat at his paper, Medill was unprepared for the frequent battles he had with aldermen who wanted to maintain the tradition of a weak executive.

Although the city's population remained lower than the 1870 census, hundreds of educated young men arrived by boat and train to try fresh ideas, especially in architecture. Necessity forced businesses to centralize, leading to the world's first eight-story skyscraper, constructed on an inventive underground platform rather than bedrock. Within a few years of the disaster, Chicago was the newest major city in the world.

After the flames destroyed the Marder, Luse and Company building, one of the largest type foundries in the nation, a manager suggested rebuilding its molds according to a point system. This introduced standardized newspaper type across the country, and the American press at last caught up with Europe.[6]

Papers imitating Storey's search for social evils never had far to go. During a saloon brawl, a drunken policeman slugged a reporter, and repercussions compelled Mayor Medill to replace ineffectual Police Superintendent William Kennedy with former Joliet prison warden Elmer Washburn.[7]

Medill had found it easier to criticize the city council as a publisher than to work with it as mayor. Overcome by the pressure of leading the massive rebuilding, he abruptly gave up in 1873 and sailed to Europe for a respite. This gave the gambling and saloon interests the opportunity to front their own mayor, Harvey Colvin of the People's Party, with the result that crime was just winked at.

When Medill returned, he found that he could not just walk through the door of his paper as if nothing had happened. The new editors sitting in their five-story sandstone building had drifted into more moderate editorials and saw no place for this antebellum holdover.

Borrowing a sizable sum from department store mogul Marshall Field, possibly at ten percent interest, Medill bought majority stock control of the *Tribune*. Appointing himself editor-in-chief, he once again turned the paper into an extension of his aggressive personality, but some believed they saw Field's influence in the shamelessly pro-business stance.[8]

2

Unlike the cutthroat competition among New York entrepreneurs, rival businessmen in Chicago had learned to cooperate for their mutual benefit. In 1873, they rustled the cattle market from St. Louis by persuading three major railroads to rebate fifteen dollars of the one-hundred-and-fifteen-dollar standard charge for shipping a carload to New York.[9] This "Evaners Combination" not only led to the sprawling Union Stockyards on the South Side, with its cowboys and seemingly endless rows of cattle pens, but also created new problems for the city in terms of stench, spoilage, and labor troubles, since racial violence broke out whenever Southern blacks were brought in by the trainload as strikebreakers. In fact, the ruthless business precedent the railroad covenant had set helped trigger the muckraker movement of investigative journalism.

Banker and lawyer Jonathan Young Scammon, a founder of the Chicago *Republican*, had been out of town during the great fire and was spared the sight of losing everything. He rebounded in 1872 and turned whatever remained of his paper into the Chicago *Inter-Ocean*, whose motto was "Republican in everything, Independent in nothing." Scammon had been a political foe of former newspaper publisher and mayor John Wentworth for forty years, but it was time to put resentment aside. Publicly, Wentworth praised the new paper, but privately admitted he never read it.[10] Under editor William Penn Nixon its reporting was stolid and more interested in explanations than revelations.

Eager to try new things and increase subscriptions, Scammon sent reporter William Curtis on the Black Hills expedition of Lt. Col. George Armstrong Custer. The stated mission was to explore the barren lands of South Dakota. But we now know its real purpose was to manipulate public opinion into opening protected Indian lands though a bogus gold find during a national economic depression. The initial information about gold was splashed across the front page of the *Inter-Ocean,* but subsequent stories retreated from notice.[11]

The newspaper brought Scammon prestige rather than riches, and after selling off his holdings one by one he died insolvent.

So many immigrants had arrived to rebuild Chicago that any person who stayed sober and could speak and write fluent English was assured of a decent job. In addition, many young women left Midwestern towns to become sales clerks and secretaries in the city.

Chicago was expanding too fast for any traditions to take hold. "The town of ours labors under one peculiar disadvantage," wrote novelist Henry Fuller, "it is the only great city in the world to which all citizens have come for the avowed object of making money. There you have its genesis, its growth, its end, its object...."[12]

The bustle and quiet desperation noted by travelers made the city prone to contradictory bursts of righteous indignation and overreaction to labor unrest at a time when there were many outspoken workers from Germany, Hungary, Bohemia and Moravia. They called themselves communists even though they were closer to socialists. They demanded an immediate end to abuses arising from all the cheap labor available to manufacturers and slaughterhouse kings, and Medill mistook their inflammatory talk and occasional walkouts for insurrection.

"Judge Lynch," from whom he believed the word "lynching" was derived, "is an American, by birth and character," Medill editorialized in the autumn of 1875. "The Vigilance Committee is a peculiarly American institution. Every lamp post in Chicago will be decorated with a communistic carcass if necessary to prevent wholesale incendiarism...."

This was the year Myra Bradwell of the Chicago *Legal Journal* and Franc Wilkie of the *Times* successfully campaigned to release Mary Todd Lincoln from an insane asylum in Batavia, Illinois. Her only surviving son, Robert Todd Lincoln, had been keeping his mother there because her uncontrolled spending and continual talk of needing money had humiliated him. As an attorney and assertive businessman, he had insinuated himself onto the boards of some of the largest concerns in Chicago, and naturally was supported by Medill's *Tribune.*

Being the railroad center of the country, Chicago had more tramps than any other city in America. Some were hoboes by nature, but many were wretches who had lost their homes and were looking for a job. When Medill heard that some suburban women were feeding beggars who came to their door, he offered this recipe: "...put a little strychnine or arsenic in the meat and other supplies furnished the tramp. This produces death within a comparatively short time, is a warning to other tramps to keep out of the neighborhood, (and) puts the Coroner in a good humor...."[13]

The *Tribune* had lost its navigation points after the war and was using competition tactics without setting its one-sidedness aside. In a history of the owning families, John Tebbel said that "It tried lawsuits in its news columns, used everything short of gutter language in assailing its enemies and stopped at nothing when it advocated a cause."[14]

Wilbur Storey was never the same after the Great Fire, and he was now losing his hold on the *Times*. Some said he was suffering from syphilis. The sheet was kept vibrant only by young reporters who would rather work for a paper that, unlike the *Tribune,* put local news over editorials. One reason there were fewer papers in the city was that political sheets were gradually becoming passé. As Paul Selby said in the *Illinois State Journal* in early 1879, "The greatest danger to the liberty of the press in this country is from itself.... It cannot be true to itself, so long as its managers use it for purposes of mere personal or political defamation."[15]

Although newspapers were less fervent than before the Civil War, they performed a public service by carrying the harangues of politicians and industrialists in the form of front page interviews, with little editing to make the paragraphs more interesting for the casual reader.

The proliferation of papers elsewhere across the country was giving rise to a new breed of newsman, the "boomer." At least, that was what they were called in New York—the term does not seem to have caught on in Chicago. Papers hired extra talent whenever they expected big stories such as a political convention, and fired drifters when the need was over or budgets were tightened.[16]

These men learned to live by blather and sporadic energy, and had a reputation for drinking on the job. Out of work boomers sometimes warmed a reception room bench for days until an opening, or else they let editors know the saloon where they could be found. Since they were paid space rates rather than a salary, boomers were tempted to embellish minor stories and attribute information to imaginary sources. The colorful lot was the primary cause of journalism's negative reputation through the 1950s, long after the last of them had settled in or moved on.

Another reason for drinking on the job was that newspaper people worked such long hours they were denied a normal social or family life. Reporters carried flasks in their pockets, and printers and columnists were known to keep a bottle stashed away. As later Chicago *Daily News* publisher Melville Stone said, "every competent journalist was expected to be a drunkard." Editors would rouse one of the best *Tribune* reporters at the time, George Lanigan, from a stupor in his home, and as soon as he turned in his assignment he took another drink.

Former Union Army surgeon Leslie Keeley, unrelated to future *Tribune* editor James Keeley, was promoting the novel idea that chronic inebriation was a disease. As an experiment, Medill sent six drunkards on his payroll to a facility seventy-six miles away, in Dwight, Illinois. As he commented afterward, "They went away sots and returned gentlemen." After a similar place, the Washingtonian Home, was set up in Chicago, Stone said "it was a poor week for the institution when I did not have one or more of my staff imprisoned there."

3

The advent of the telephone and the typewriter at last gave local news the immediacy of telegraphic dispatches. But it really was not until the founding of the *Daily News* at about the same time that Chicago became America's greatest news town. And yet this newspaper came close to folding in only its second year.

The force behind the paper was Melville Elijah Stone, son of a Methodist minister. He was perhaps the most contradictory of the city's great newspaper publishers. His various phases saw him as a liberal crusader, a dangerous conservative, a seeker of truth, a fabricator, a person of character, and a con man. Despite his faults, journalism was indebted to him.

Whatever was driving Stone, he grew up in Chicago and lost a foundry in the fire of 1871. His news experience came from working at Scammon's *Republican* and the Chicago *Post and Mail*, founded in 1874 by the consolida-

Melville E. Stone founded the Chicago *Daily News* through ambition and deception. He gave authorities a way to prosecute the Haymarket "conspirators" and afterward modernized the Associated Press (Chicago History Museum, photographer—Brisbois, ICHi-51970).

tion of two small papers, the *Evening Post* (founded in 1865) and the *Evening Mail* (founded in 1870).

With a friend, reporter William Dougherty, Stone operated the Chicago *Daily Herald* (unrelated to the later suburban paper by that name) a short distance from the Dearborn Street newspaper row, but the paper folded in only four months. Never one to admit failure, he explained in later times that they had run the paper only as an experiment and did not expect to succeed.

Bursting with ideas and eager to make a name for himself at twenty-eight, Stone used the Philadelphia *Star* as a model for an independent sheet that would make no attempt to sway the reader's opinions. To start the Chicago *Daily News*, he and Dougherty used whatever funds they had left and an inheritance they swindled from visiting Englishman Percy Meggy.

The equipment was carried into the four-story building housing the *Skandinaven*, a Norwegian-language daily. The high peak and large clock of its facade were like those of a Scandinavian town, in contrast to the narrow, flat-roofed brick buildings flanking it. A shop occupied the first floor, and writing initially had to be done on packing crates for desks. The walls at 123 5th Avenue (later renumbered 15 North Wells Street) must have shaken during each run of the shared press.

After an introductory issue on Christmas Day, 1874, the smudged and off-centered first edition of the *Daily News* aroused curiosity on January 1 in the midst of a financial panic that would see the end of the Chicago *Courier* (1874–1876) and would plunge the *Post and Mail* into permanent debt.

The *Daily News* printed whatever local news its few reporters could dig up and extensively used wire services. But Stone rejected the common practice of gaining advertisers by threats of turning the paper against them. He distributed a barrelful of pennies he had ordered from the Philadelphia mint to merchants who would lower the price of goods by a cent, since his paper was one of the few things besides candy that could be bought with the change.

After its first year the paper was turning out two editions a day, and was giving the city's final market reports and steady coverage of the Chicago White-stockings baseball team. What *Tribune* subscribers read on Tuesday morning, *Daily News* buyers had been discussing since Monday night.

Stone hired a small army of boys around sixteen years old to peddle his paper in the streets. Tired of hearing "*Daily News!*" called out at every corner downtown, rivals grumped that Stone was a "Daily Nuisance." Hoping to draw more advertisers, Stone boastfully printed the paper's sworn circulation figures on the inside page, but major stores stayed with the friendly *Tribune*.

The hoodwinked English backer, Meggy, put his time in at a do-nothing office until buying up Stone's and Dougherty's shares, spending eighty-five hundred dollars for the title of publisher. When Stone indicated the paper was near collapse, Meggy sailed back to England and seems never to have heard from his former partner again. Meggy complained later that Stone had not once publicly acknowledged his former ownership or ever repaid him.[17] Yet the paper was doing so well it was now running editions at 3 P.M., 5 P.M., and midnight.

The opposite of pragmatic Stone was Henry Demarest Lloyd, an idealistic lawyer from New York who joined the *Tribune* shortly after the Great Fire at the age of twenty-four. Born into comfortable circumstances and untested by life's usual struggles, he was hoping that newspapers would return to the principles they had compromised in their scramble for readers. The slender, nice-looking young man was the son of a minister in the Dutch Reformed Church and, like many men of the new generation, was influenced by Ralph Waldo Emerson and the newly rekindled British Christian socialist movement.

Perhaps not knowing what Lloyd was up to, Medill and Bross hired him as their literary editor in 1872 and soon named him financial editor. What intrigued Lloyd were the profits that industries were making from "combinations" or "trusts," secret rate agreements that kept prices barely within reach for necessities ranging from paper to steel, and from milk to beef. Some of the information was available in business reports, but no one before seems to have linked such data with the social impact of these agreements.

Lloyd at the time was courting—and, on Christmas Day 1873, married— Bross's beloved auburn-haired daughter, Jessie, whose intellect matched her husband's. Although the bridegroom seemed sure to rise further at the *Tribune*, he preferred a forward-looking paper such as the *Daily News*. His solution was to work at both simultaneously.

With Meggy gone, and Storey planning to start a newspaper that would copy the *Daily News*'s content and newsboy distribution Stone needed a new investor. He decided to tap Lloyd's shoulder, since the intense young man's family was well off and his brother worked for a New York paper. Lloyd, the quixotic journalist, audaciously asked his father-in-law for a loan, even though Bross was one of the founders of the *Tribune*. Bross was so taken aback he brought Medill in to help emphasize the word "No," and that meant the young writer was of no use to Stone. Lloyd must have been crushed at being forced to give up his dream of aligning himself with a crusading paper. Stone said the two of them wept as they said goodbye.

At the *Tribune*, Lloyd wrote editorials favoring the new concept of government regulation in major industries, and sometimes clashed with Medill and Bross. Although Lloyd had a personality more suited to a progressive federal judge, he wore himself down in the frustrations of being under the thumb of his father-in-law, a worthy man who was nevertheless unsympathetic to attacks on capitalists. Complaining that Chicago was being corrupted, Lloyd said that honesty in the city "is ordinarily considered a mild or noxious form of insanity."[18]

Stone was still seeking ways to raise two thousand dollars. Bross, never imagining that the *Daily News* would seriously compete with the *Tribune*, lent him the sum at nine percent interest, with the principal to be paid back in just nine months. This provision meant that a default on the loan, and a chattel mortgage on the press, would let Bross take over the paper as soon as it folded. Insiders speculated that he intended to hand it over to his bright son-in-law.[19]

But Stone was determined not to lose control of the *Daily News* even though he was unable to meet a one-hundred-dollar payroll. He made a surprising offer to his twenty-two-year-old landlord, Victor Fremont Lawson. The two men had known each other since high school, and Lawson recently inherited the building as well as a real-estate fortune believed to be more than one million dollars upon the death of his father, publisher of the Norwegian-language paper.

Lawson was a slender, pleasant looking young man with a handlebar mustache too big for his small oval face. He was still living with his mother, and his only working experience had been at a bank. But he sank six thousand dollars into the seven-month-old newspaper and, in July 1876, took command.

That summer also saw the first of two marriages that would determine the future of three publishing families and of the *Tribune* itself. Joseph Medill's elder daughter, Kate, married Robert Sanderson McCormick, nephew of harvester developer and former newspaper publisher Cyrus McCormick.

Less than two years later, Medill's younger daughter, Elinor, known as Nellie, married Robert Patterson, who had been a journalist at Storey's *Times* before switching to the *Tribune*.

The weddings introduced into the tangled extended family a strain of self-destructive behavior blamed in later years on tainted blood. Whether for biological or psychological reasons, the McCormick and Patterson women were independent and outspoken, and the men were given to depression, alcohol abuse, and rash behavior. The mingled bloodlines managed to create one of the greatest newspaper empires in

Victor F. Lawson became Melville Stone's partner in the Chicago *Daily News* and, without experience, turned it into a crusading newspaper and literary force (Chicago History Museum, photographer—C.D. Mosher, ICHi-51969).

the country, yet one wonders what would have happened if the families had expanded their awareness of the times and learned to work together.

Among the *Tribune* reporters at the time was Percy English, who also was an occasional stenographer for Police Chief Elmer Washburn, meaning that he would take down confessions and such. In November, 1876, English learned that the police were going after a forgery gang plotting to steal Lincoln's body from a Springfield sarcophagus and hide it for ransom. English accompanied the officers and saw the two men escape, only to be arrested the following week in a Chicago saloon.[20]

At the *Daily News*, the partnership of Stone and Lawson seemed less than promising. Lawson lacked a news sense, strictly abided by the Sabbath, and abhorred liquor, even though he could be forgiving of others. He thought a paper should enlighten its readers with causes and well-written articles. His partner browbeat him into handling just the business end of the paper, letting Stone live from excitement to excitement in the editor's chair.

Naturally, the muscular journal was emulated by the competition; that is, brothers David and James McMullen were stealing its news for their under-financed *Post and Mail*. To have a little fun with them, Stone printed a bogus item about a Serbian famine in which a mayor issued this proclamation: "Er us siht la Etsll iws nel lum cmeht." The *Tribune* and the *Times* were let in on the joke and informed their readers that, when read backward, the statement was "The McMullens will steal this, sure."

Unable to meet their payroll, the McMullens sold their paper to the north suburban Willard family. The Reverend Oliver Willard edited the paper evangelically, and upon his death it was taken over by his widow and his sister Frances, the respected leader of the nationwide Women's Christian Temperance Union. They were the only female publishers of a major Chicago newspaper, even though it lasted only a few months.[21]

What the *Daily News* needed for attention was some cause or event that it could cover better than any of its half-dozen rivals. The opportunity arose with the railroad strike of 1877. The disturbance had several grounds in Ohio and Pennsylvania before the fighting reached Chicago in July, when the Michigan Central railroad threatened to cut its switchmen's pay. This protest linked up with other walkouts, and unemployed rowdies joined in as strikers pounced on scabs. The mob destroyed two locomotives at a Burlington railroad roundhouse, and police clashed with a crowd on the Randolph Street bridge. John V. Farwell, who had been a partner in the now-defunct Chicago *Republican*, and Marshall Field, whose loan had allowed Medill to retake the *Tribune*, lent the police their delivery wagons so officers in riot helmets could speed from one melee to another.

Medill approved of officers firing on strikers without warning. "Chicago is too far advanced to permit her bad element to interfere with her interests," he sent down to the compositors in his hard-to-read scrawl. Future Haymar-

Railroad Riot of 1877. Federal troops put down violence in Chicago during the first national labor strike. The Chicago *Daily News'* coverage brought respect to the upstart newspaper (Chicago History Museum, from *History of the Chicago Police* by John J. Flinn, ICHi-32336).

ket "conspirator" Albert Parsons—a blacklisted former Chicago *Times* typesetter—told a mass meeting that the *Tribune* was installing machinery that would virtually shackle pressmen to their jobs for ten to fourteen hours a day.

As the only paper supporting the strikers, the *Daily News* sent reporters into the midst of the clamor, some on horseback to cover changing events and others mingling with angry workers even though it meant being arrested with them.

Stone now held only a one-third interest in the paper that he had founded and, in addition, worked on it as editor for just twenty-five dollars a week. He could look outside his office window and see people tossing coins at newsboys and grabbing special editions, each printed on a single side to rush the news out.

Hordes of extra boys were hired to sell the papers, and a business group urged Stone and Lawson to suspend publication until the riots were over. The two men refused. After all, no one was asking the *Tribune* to shut down.[22] Chicago's era of brawny journalism had begun.

4

Two possibly linked opposites enlivened papers at around this time: scandalous reporting and informed, rather than emotional, editorials.

Scandal sheets began in London around 1770, and as early as the 1840s, some appeared in America, such as New York's the *Weekly Rake*. But it took the *National Police Gazette* to make reading about crime, suicide, and sexual scandal part of our culture. The choice of articles may have been considered low-brow, but they were being written by moonlighting successful reporters who were virtually locked up in a large Manhattan room on weekends with plenty to eat and drink.

Although the magazine started publishing in New York in 1845, it was not until the early 1880s that its illustration-heavy pink pages were sold at barbershops, bars, and newsstands near theaters across the country. Newspaper publishers in Chicago decided to attract that same readership by increasing their crime coverage, and at the same time, as if to distance themselves from the new trend, they took their editorials to a loftier plane.

In the view of journalism historian Norma Howard Sims, this elevated tone interested young businessmen who had flocked to the city after the Great Fire and wanted to reach fashionable customers. But most readers preferred the other pages, and in a recent account of the *Police Gazette*, Gene Smith said future Chicago newspaper publishers William Randolph Hearst and Colonel Robert McCormick admitted their debt to it.[23]

Storey's imitation of the *Daily News*, called the *Daily Telegraph*, finally came out in 1878. Around the same time, Stone and Lawson bought the foundering *Post and Mail* to frustrate the competition, improve their own press, and acquire the Western Associated Press franchise. Only after circulation reached fifty thousand, surpassing that of Storey's paper, was Stone confident the *Daily News* would last.

There were so many reporters in the city by 1880—whether they were covering the streets, city hall, hotels, or the courts—that they founded the Chicago Press Club. A year later, it moved into space above a North Clark Street pool hall. Its membership list would grow until by 1920, the club was the largest of its kind in the world. Those forty years would see the heyday of freebooting reporting, as encouraged by a few editors with an eye toward circulation or being offered a larger salary elsewhere

Against this riot of snooping, Henry Demarest Lloyd was promoted to chief *Tribune* editorial writer in 1880, and saved his investigative work for magazines. The recent railroad strike had led him to believe that *laissez faire* was dragging the country toward social revolt. His 1881 *Atlantic Monthly* piece "The Story of a Great Monopoly" took on Standard Oil and is considered the start of the American muckraking movement.

While Lloyd and soon several other journalists were making their sweep-

ing analyses of industrial abuses, there was a new energy in papers as they laid
bare dangerous or outrageous conditions at the local level. The fashion was
called "detective reporting." At the time, the federal government had neither
the will nor the means to investigate rampant collusion in city and county
departments.

An early *Daily News* scoop hunted down D.D. Spencer, who had victim-
ized hundreds of people who had lost their money in the State Savings Institution. After the paper traced Spencer to Europe, he was indicted for
embezzling, and the case led to federal laws requiring the financial inspection
of savings bank records.[24]

Although Stone was too busy with breaking news to mix with society,
publishing agreed with Lawson. He put on weight and stepped up socially when
he married Jessie Bradley, daughter of the U.S. Court Clerk.

Under Stone and Lawson, the *Daily News* cried out for fair elections.
Everyone knew the about election abuses, such as beating poll watchers and
bringing tramps to polling places by the wagonload, but it took the paper to
send Joseph Mackin, the behind-the-curtain political boss of the First Ward,
to prison.

The First Ward was open to graft since it covered downtown and the near
South Side Levee, a red light district a short walk from hotels serving the railroad terminals. No doubt feeling untouchable, Mackin lived in luxury at the
Palmer House hotel—not bad for a former saloonkeeper who had introduced
free lunches to Chicago. He and his wild First Ward Democratic Club fostered
the city hall corruption epitomized by Bathhouse John Coghlin and Michael
Hinky Dink Kenna in the days when each ward was represented by two aldermen.

The *Daily News* learned that Mackin, strutting about with his Chesterfield
coat and lapel carnation, disliked the way an election for state senator was
going, so he went into the county clerk's vault and removed an Eighteenth
Ward ballot box. He replaced those votes with forgeries for Rudolph Brand.
Brand was so outraged that he helped the newspaper expose the plot, and
Mackin was sentenced to serve five years for election fraud.[25]

By 1878, telephones had been installed at only three papers: the *Daily
News*, Storey's *Daily Telegraph,* and the plodding *Journal*, with such lowly business publications as the *Northwestern Lumberman* and the *Furniture Trade
Journal* beating out the *Times* and the *Tribune* in adopting the new technology. With these early telephones, a bell-shaped transmitter hung on a wall next
to a wooden box with a crank for reaching "Central." The caller told an operator what exchange he wanted, then put his ear to the transmitter.

After a rocky start, the *Daily News* had now established itself as possibly
the city's most effective newspaper, and gone were the days of sharing a press
with a foreign-language sheet. The fourth floor held heavy printing equipment,
five hundred pounds of body type handled by six compositors (typesetters) and

an apprentice. Reporters and editors took up space in the composing room and scribbled on a table set against a wall. Tired of seeing people getting in each other's way, Stone tore down a partition to gain four feet.

Newspaper equipment eventually filled the building from the basement to just under the roof, and in time overflowed to three stories of a second building on the block and two stories of a third. Everyone involved worked seven days a week for a while—even the usually drunken editor Nate Reed.

In 1881, James W. Scott, a third-generation newsman from western Illinois, turned Storey's short-lived *Daily Telegraph* into the two-cent Chicago *Morning Herald,* unrelated to a former paper with a similar name. Like most nineteenth century newspaper publishers, Scott was a little larger than life. The hardy and daunting man was born in Wisconsin and worked at newspapers in several cities before coming to Chicago from Galena after the Great Fire. He talked big in the manner of the time, claiming that before he died he would own a bank, a newspaper, and a railroad, but this was said with a wink that made him beloved by his staff.

So cramped were conditions in his building on 5th Avenue (Wells Street) that two reporters might be seen fighting for a chair, and yet some people considered the *Morning Herald* one of the best-written papers in Chicago. The city editor and copyreaders worked out of cubbyholes, and by nightfall the main room shared by reporters waiting for assignments was a haze of cigar and cigarette smoke.

The boxes of pencils were still there, but the *Herald* had two or three typewriters. "Typing machines" had been perfected in 1874 with the Remington No. 1, but only a single staff member, Charlie Steger, had mastered the keyboard. Steger might be heard pecking away as Fred Rae came down from the composing room in slippers and straw hat to announce, "Well, the baby is born."

One day, county commissioner Buck McCarthy stormed into the *Morning Herald* office, pounded on a table, and demanded the retraction of an article about his beating someone.

"Isn't it true?" editor John Ballantyne asked with his Scottish burr.

"True, hell," McCarthy exploded, "what's that got to do with it?"

The commissioner backed down when staff members came in with baseball bats that had been lying around the office for a team the paper sponsored.[26]

When the *Daily News* put out an early edition in 1881 to challenge the *Tribune,* Lawson called it the *Morning News.* Movers hauled the equipment into the main building to put out the two-cent paper. The two staffs worked overlapping shifts and at times tripped over one another.

An early editor at the *Morning News* was former Civil War surgeon Frank W. Reilly. He tried to make the public aware of health problems arising from unsanitary conditions that increased when, on August 2, 1885, a heavy rain befouled the water supply for the city of more than half a million. After Dr.

Reilly took part in founding the Chicago Sanitary District, his paper continually protested the waterway agency's political hacks.

Largely through Reilly's campaign, the city performed the engineering miracle of reversing the Chicago River so that its water flowed backward, away from Lake Michigan and toward the Mississippi, somewhat purifying itself by aeration along the way. Buildings in the business district and some neighborhoods had to be raised on jacks.

After two years, Lawson renamed his morning paper the *Morning Record* to reduce reader confusion with the evening paper, the *Daily News.*

Also in 1883, Ernest E. Lehman, head of The Fair discount department store on State Street, accepted a settlement in his twenty-five-thousand-dollar libel suit against Scott's *Morning Herald.* Technically, the well-written paper folded. But banker and railroad investor James R. Walsh purchased all the stock being released as part of the dissolution, and Lehman waived his claim provided that management gave three thousand dollars to charity. Scott, who had not been accused of taking part in the libel, was kept on as publisher.[27]

Walsh made the *Herald* an unexceptional business-oriented paper rather than one that reflected the investigative spirit of the era. As will be seen later, there may have been a reason why he did not embrace reform. In 1885, Walsh also set up the penny *Chronicle,* little knowing that over the years he and that paper would ruin each other.

Another repercussion of the Lehman settlement was the end of seven-day work weeks at the *Daily News.* The older paper was able to grab some of the *Herald*'s best talent, including reporter William Knox and managing editor David Henderson, a Scottish liberal. The staff increase also let *Daily News* editor Nate Reed grab his top hat and go off for what was then known as The Cure, a detoxification regimen at a rest home. Being a sot did not mean Reed was ineffective. In fact, he may have saved one of the most famous quotations of the muckraking era.

On October 8, 1882, William Henry Vanderbilt, son of railroad king Cornelius Vanderbilt, was riding a private car on the Michigan Central line on his way to Chicago. Youthful freelance reporter Clarence Dresser boarded at Michigan City, Indiana, for an interview that he might sell to one or two papers at the end of the line. That is as much as we can say with certainty.

The simpler and more believable version of what happened next portrays Dresser as a dilettante. The night of the interview, he left the train and went to the *Daily News,* where he outlined for Reed the story he intended to write, and Reed told him to go ahead. As usual, when the reporter handed in his copy the editor looked it over and asked if there was anything more that might be of interest.

"He said one thing but I didn't put in," Dresser replied, according to this version.

"What was that?" Reed asked.

"When I asked him whether he ran his trains for the public benefit, he said 'The public be damned.'"

Reed told Dresser to go back and rewrite part of the story to include the comment. The reporter presented a balanced interview and put "public be damned" matter-of-factly in the body of the article.

For whatever reason, the not-always-reliable Melville Stone gave a contrasting account. He said Dresser was one of those pushy reporters who was always trying to provoke rude remarks from famous people, and that the *Daily News* night editor did not want to make Vanderbilt look uncaring by featuring the remark up high, so he buried the quotation deep in the story.

Dresser sold a second version of the interview, with the same quote, to the *Tribune*. But Vanderbilt's off-handed comment did not cause a stir until it was picked up by the New York *Herald*.[28] The outcry helped create the Interstate Commerce Commission, the first regulatory agency in the nation, although under the Vanderbilts the railroads steadily improved and were even able to provide twenty-four-hour mail delivery between New York and Chicago.

As yet, there was no technology for printing photographs in newspapers. On a trip to New York in 1883, *Daily News* editor Henry Ten Eyck White was struck by the immediacy of graphics in Joseph Pulitzer's *World*. He borrowed the illustration team long enough to show his staff how to reproduce line drawings, over Stone's insistence that they were just a fad. The artists drew outlines on metal plates that had a thick layer of chalk, and this reproduced the uncluttered lines.

But there was no doubt the public held newspapers in lower esteem than in the abolition days. N. K. Fairbank, who had turned a Chicago lard company into a major detergent industry, told Medill of the *Tribune* some time in the eighties that "Our jobs are somewhat similar. I go through the streets raking up garbage and trash to make soap, and you do the same in order to publish a newspaper."[29]

Although some papers had adopted Wilbur Storey's love of sensationalism, the era had passed him by. He relinquished control of the *Times* after paralytic strokes left him talking nonsense, such as claiming he was in communion with a dead Indian girl. He was pitied by a few who knew him and hated by the rest.

"I don't want to perpetuate my newspaper," Storey said late in life. "I am the paper. I wish it to die with me so that the world may know that I was the *Times*." On Oct. 27, 1884, he died blind and insane in his Gothic stone mansion at the age of sixty-four. Everyone had assumed he was in his seventies.[30]

Around the time Vanderbilt had put his foot in his mouth, young German-American Ottman Mergenthaler of Baltimore was tinkering with a device to replace typesetters. In 1885, Stone and newspaper publishers from other parts of the nation formed a company to develop this linotype machine. The name, from "line of type," was suggested by longtime Chicago newsman Will Easton.

When a linotype operator struck keys on a typewriter-like keyboard, brass matrices (narrow blocks with letter impressions) were brought together with a space band to fill out on an "assembly elevator," usually just called "a stick." This framing piece of metal, which could be kept in the palm of the hand, accommodated an average of a hundred and fifty words, which was what editors meant when they told reporters to keep a routine story down to "a stick of type." To eliminate any line containing a garble, the operator struck the first keys in two vertical rows at the left of the keyboard, creating the nonsense phrase "etaoin shrdlu."

Molten metal was pumped into the mold and letter indentations. If an apprentice forgot to pull the clutch when the machine was acting up, a squirt of liquid metal could scar his arm or hand forever. A turn of a casting wheel cooled and trimmed any excess metal so the stick was now ready for printing. The form was used in making forty pound leaden page plates, called stereotypes.

The first twelve linotype machines went to the New York *Times*, the second to the Louisville *Courier*, and the third set was installed at the Chicago *Daily News*. An editor there, Charles Henry Dennis, recalled that the staff laughed at the "clanking contrivances with their comical keyboards and their hot pots of metal."[31] Until then, printers tended to be an independent lot and were usually rovers, like "boomers." The new composing machines gave them a steady career, and they became more dependable, if less interesting.

But nothing stopped the turnover in editors, who expressed their own personalities more than reporters were allowed to. When Henderson resigned as *Daily News* manager to operate a theater, he was succeeded by former *Post and Mail* and *Tribune* editor Henry White, derisively called "Butch" behind his back for "butchering" copy.

The domination of publishers was being replaced by a new spirit among young reporters, who found along city streets adventure in a time of peace. The Democratic (and therefore Irish-friendly) *Times* had Finley Peter Dunne as a crime reporter before he became a humorist and created saloon philosopher Mr. Dooley for the *Daily News*.

Dunne looked like a smart aleck wearing someone else's clothes, and sociability concealed his sharp reporting instincts. He was fascinated by the disappearance of physician Patrick Cronin after a quarrel with Alexander Sullivan of the secret Irish society Clan-Na-Gael, which conducted dynamite raids on British soldiers in northern Ireland. Witnesses said the squabble had concerned a suspected English spy, but a later news report said the real cause may have been that Dr. Cronin accused Sullivan of misusing thousands of dollars in Clan-Na-Gael funds to cover his failed investments.

After once being shot at, Dr. Cronin was reluctant to answer night calls.

Then a messenger boy came to his door on the night of May 4, 1889, and handed him a business card with the address of what turned out to be an abandoned cottage that had been made to look in use with a few sticks of furniture. He never returned.

Not that any of the papers covered the controversy behind Cronin's disappearance: too many tempers and people in high places were involved. Convinced that Cronin was dead, Dunne talked about the case with his friend William Pinkerton, whose famous detective agency operated out of an office a few blocks from newspaper row. "I don't care what you Irishmen do to each other," Pinkerton replied with his accent, "I'm Scotch."

Boys target practicing in a woods came upon an empty trunk with blood-soaked cotton lining. Yet a news silence continued until a sewer crew at Broadway and Foster found parts of Dr. Cronin rotting in a catch basin. John Kelley, working for the *Tribune,* was the first reporter at the scene. He recalled years afterward that newsboys called out the headlines "in all parts of town until midnight."

As it turned out, Cronin had been convicted by a secret committee of seven, and Detective Dan Coughlin of a North Side police station supposedly drew the lot to be the assassin. Dunne was able to trace a horse and buggy Coughlin had rented just before the doctor was last seen alive. The reporter ran into the office of *Times* publisher James West, who had bought the paper from Storey's widow, and realized every reporter's dream when he heard West shout, "Stop the presses!"[32]

Sullivan, husband of future *Tribune* writer Margaret Sullivan, was never charged although he may have been involved. But, after a mistrial, Coughlin was convicted of murder and sentenced to life in prison. He won an appeal and was acquitted in his third trial.

5

In the 1870s and 1880s, a number of men who bankrolled newspapers thought only of the prestige and advertising profits without considering whether the market could bear another paper. The papers that survived could innovate or at least adopt publication advances made elsewhere, and were also able to hire top writers and reporters. For some reason, former Iowa Congressman Frank W. Palmer thought the city needed another newspaper, and in 1881 he attended to the birth of the Chicago *Daily Herald,* the second sheet with that name.

With the new paper barely getting by, Lawson started buying stock in the company and seems to have been waiting for any weakness that would let him take charge. Because Palmer was succeeded by more experienced publishers, Lawson's wait would last more than thirty years.

Sensing a certain phoniness in news writing and editing to keep ordinary information entertaining day after day, reporters became a playful lot. But to journalism historian Norman Howard Sims, their pranks were part of growing pessimism in the business. Hoaxes, he said, kept reporters "from being vulnerable" as they moved among the corrupt, the cheated, and the dead.

On a slow day on the hotel beat, Peter Finley Dunne, then working for the *Daily News*, and his friendly rival Charles Dillingham, who had succeeded him at the *Times,* started concocting interviews with such nonexistent people as a Tibetan explorer and a tiger hunter from India. The *Tribune* fired its own hotel reporter, future banker Frank Vanderlip, for not finding these bogus people. When the truth came out, nothing happened to the talented Dunne but Dillingham was severed from his paper.[33] This allowed him to make a fortune playwriting and producing lavish New York musicals until the Great Depression ruined him in the 1930s.

Lawson's two papers were becoming the most literary in the city, with Dunne doing his humor column at the *Daily News* and Eugene Field whipping up the "Sharps and Flats" column at its early edition, the *Morning Record.* For the general public, including such fans as British Prime Minister William Gladstone, Field penned poetic trifles including "Dutch Lullaby," with "Wynken, Blynken, and Nod." Only his friends heard his bawdy verses.

Behind much of Field's writing was a brooding about the end of life, possibly because of the death of his mother when he was six and of his two sons before their second year. When he arrived in Chicago from newspaper jobs in St. Louis and Denver, he hardly had enough money to buy all the books he had to sneak past his wife. As supposedly explained by his eight-year-old daughter, Trotty, "The Lord will provide because my father can't."

Alone in the small office he shared with nighttime editor Charles Henry Dennis, the gangly more than six-foot columnist would replace his shoes with slippers, put his feet on the edge of the desk, remove his vest and detachable collar, bite off the end of a cigar, and ease into a creative slouch. Probably egged on by his wife, he once decided to ask for a raise he no doubt deserved, considering how important he was to the paper. In preparation, Field put on ragged clothes and hired about six street boys he introduced to Lawson as his children.

Lawson probably was the only one who did not think the stunt was funny, although he at times showed a sense of humor. When the publisher was handing out turkeys for Christmas Eve, Field said he would rather have a suit. As a story goes, the writer later opened a box in his office and saw a striped uniform from Joliet state prison. We are told Field wore the "zebra suit" until Lawson made amends with clothes from his own tailor.[34]

The editing area—usually known as the city room or local room—varied only in specifics from paper to paper. In general, the large room had a rolltop desk or two and a pot-bellied stove. Copy readers, not yet called copy editors, typically had desks by dirty windows. Reporters, often wearing hats, wrote their copy in longhand on desks with tops that slanted to catch the illumination from gas lights around the room. By 1886 every city room in Chicago had a telephone, but some editors were frustrated at being unable to talk and listen at the same time, preferring to have their reporters come to the office for a discussion after covering each story.

The business manager of the *Times,* Austin L. Patterson, unrelated to the Medill-Patterson family at the *Tribune,* wanted to found another energetic Democratic morning paper. In 1888 he set up the *Globe* across 5th Avenue from his old colleagues. Austin Patterson had only one night reporter, but two or three covered general assignments on days, one of them a Canadian woman.

With the *Herald, Globe,* and *Daily News* close to each other along what is now Wells Street, they created a secondary newspaper row. As was common at the time, several editors wore green eyeshades to reduce the lighting glare on pages they edited, and some wore armbands to keep their wrist cuffs from smudging as their blue pencils scratched across a page. The stories were increasingly turned in on typewriters, and summertime insects from the opened windows were martyred on platens being rolled line by line.

In its first year, *Globe* night reporter John Kelley was assigned to cover famed European contralto Adelina Patti at the gala opening of the Auditorium Theatre. All the other reporters were in formal clothes, but Kelley, who came from Pennsylvania, was so shabby a policeman mistook him for a bum and tried to stop him from getting the names of important people arriving.

Impresario Milward Adams assured Patti of glorious reviews with generous servings of champagne to the press corps. After the performance, Kelley had to help an unnamed reviewer into the *Globe* office, where the man wrote one sentence and fell asleep. In a scene paralleling one in *Citizen Kane,* city editor Charley Tuttle read this solitary line—"See Patti and then die!"—and with editor's magic turned this into a warm, detailed account by using the reviewer's copy of the program and his own imagination.

At this time you could often tell the age of a newsman by whether he was bearded, meaning he was an editor; wore a mustache, as most experienced reporters did; or was a clean-shaven cub reporter. Female reporters still wore long skirts and invariably worked days for their safety. But they learned to be canny, such as Nora Marks of the *Tribune,* who simulated fainting spells to demonstrate the need for a city ambulance service.

Socialists were planning a week of rallies and demonstrations in Chicago for early May 1886 for such then-radical goals as an eight-hour work day. The city had been chosen because of the way industrialists had crushed the railroad strike nine years earlier. Organizers would explain that they advocated anarchy only because the papers never printed their moderate speeches. The threat touched off such public paranoia that no newspaper could put them in perspective.

Before his death, Storey, in his typically hotheaded fashion, had suggested using dynamite against labor agitators, and such *Times* columns were quoted in outrage by the German-language newspaper *Arbeiter-Zeitung*. This was one of the most widely read sheets in the city because it informed workers from Germany and across the Austro-Hungarian empire.

The more responsible *Daily News,* which had supported the railroad strikers, now feared a labor Armageddon. "Chicago is the last place on the continent where [socialism] would exist were it not for the dregs of foreign immigration which found lodgment here," a column ran. Lawson's paper later detailed how anyone could make a bomb.

In preparing readers for violence, both newspapers helped bring it about.

A high point of the week was to be a rally in Haymarket Square just west of downtown on the evening of May 4. While speakers delivered inflammatory statements from a wagon platform, Mayor Carter Harrison surveyed the peaceful crowd. In his Kentucky drawl he told the extra policemen to go back to their station. However, after he rode off on his white horse in a light rain, the officers started to break up the crowd instead. In the hubbub someone threw a dynamite bomb at them.

Daily News reporter Paul Hull was nearly shot by frightened officers as they broke ranks and fired randomly. It is possible that in the confusion some of the policemen were hit by fellow officers. Seven officers were killed by the explosion and gunfire, and an eighth would die before the year was out. Sixty-six officers were wounded. Injured rally-goers were carried away by others in a scramble to clear the square, so their number was never learned.

Stone was in his home on West Adams Street when he heard the bomb go off, and not long afterward came the creaking of horse-drawn wagons taking officers to boxlike Cook County Hospital. In the morning he was summoned to a meeting in the courthouse basement with the police chief, the chief prosecutor, and the coroner. The three officials were afraid of general terror unless the bomb-thrower was caught, and they wanted his advice on what they should do.[35]

Stone told them the bomber had been acting in a conspiracy with rally organizers, who had told the crowd that when the law went against them they should "Throttle it. Kill it. Stab it." That the organizers may have never met the man was irrelevant, he said, nor did it matter who he was because the man could have been anyone inflamed by such rhetoric.

The officials could not understand this approach, so, as Stone boasted in his autobiography, "I finally went to a standing desk in the room and wrote out what I considered to be a proper verdict for the coroner's jury to render." Stone's behavior would astound a modern reporter.[36]

Henry Demarest Lloyd, now the *Tribune*'s chief editorial writer despite his muckraking sympathies, personally appealed to Governor Richard Oglesby to save the lives of all eight organizers convicted of conspiracy. He must have known that his stand would forever alienate him from his father-in-law, William Bross. There was such a heated quarrel with Bross and Medill that Lloyd boarded a ship for England to clear up his "brain fog," and, before returning, he decided to quit the paper.

Not satisfied with the resignation, Bross punished his daughter for marrying such an idealist by cutting her off from a fortune estimated at five million dollars. The couple continued to live in north suburban Winnetka but now had to reduce their living expenses.[37] Freed of office work, Lloyd devoted his time to writing exposés and tracts in favor of organized labor, ending child labor, reforming insane asylums, and giving women the right to vote.

Just months before his death in 1903 at the age of fifty-six, Lloyd joined the Socialist Party. His female descendants were active in social causes for decades, and, ironically, he founded a three-generation tradition of writers and editors at the *Tribune*, the paper that had forced him out of established journalism.

But all that lay in the future. Lloyd's appeal for sparing the lives of the Haymarket organizers failed, and in 1887 they were sentenced to hang in the courtyard between the jail and the criminal courts building, a seven story ripple stone structure that had replaced a gambling den at Dearborn and Hubbard Streets.

On the eve of execution, Louis Lingg detonated a blasting cap in his mouth, fatally blowing his handsome face away. The following day, November 11—the city's "Black Friday"—Parsons, August Spies, Adolph Fischer, and George Engle stood shoulder to shoulder in white robes and faced identical nooses.

The bulletin board in Potter Palmer's posh hotel, the downtown Palmer House, carried this message: "Trap fell. ... the law vindicated." That same day, Stone's *Daily News* sold nearly half a million copies of the complete newspaper, rather than just a one-sheet extra. This was said to have been the most of any English-language paper in America up to that time.[38]

Listening to pleas for mercy, the new governor, German-born Democrat John Peter Altgeld, pardoned the remaining "conspirators" in an act Medill called "an hysterical denunciation of American principles...."

Editors and reporters may have reflected the interests of the common man, but they formed their own world, with their strange hours, their lives of going from one changing event to another, and the fact that they always worked within the limits of deadlines and machines. When excited, editors at times even spoke in headlines. When newsman Charles Chapin left Chicago, he surprised a New York newsroom with such exclamations as "Hurry up with 'Tiny tot with penny clutched in chubby hand dies under train before mother's eyes.'"

For generations, newspeople had been encouraged to write on the order of Charles Dickens, but the *Daily News* was instructing its staff to present facts in cogent short paragraphs, which forced rivals to do the same. As a *Globe* edi-

Execution of Haymarket Conspirators at the Cook County Jail in 1887. These men were regarded as terrorists but are now considered martyrs to the labor movement. One of them had been a newspaper pressman (Chicago History Museum, Creator—Michael Schaak, ICHi-03675).

tor would say, "News is information. People want it quick, sharp, clear, do you hear?" The movement really caught on after the city went baseball mad in 1887.

Since most readers were unable to attend weekday games, Finley Peter Dunne and his friend Charles Seymour, the tubercular brother of *Herald* and former *Times* editor Horatio Seymour, packed their accounts with vivid verbs and broke each throw of the ball or swing of the bat into a separate breathtaking action. Even as late as the 1920s, if an editor wanted lively writing for a court story he assigned the trial to someone from the sports department.

While the literary-minded *Daily News* was respected by its competitors, the paper was having potentially crippling management trouble. We do not know all the infighting between Lawson and Stone, especially since Stone insisted there had been none, but there definitely was a rift between the two men in 1888. The cover explanation was that as a self-made man, Stone felt out of place with his educated staff.

Lawson gave him three hundred and fifty thousand dollars for his portion of the business and added a guarantee of ten thousand dollars a year if Stone did no work at any other Chicago paper for ten years. Stone went on to head the Associated Press of Illinois. The religious Lawson, less interested in the sort of day-to-day news that had preoccupied his partner, now concentrated on causes.

Unlike publishers seeking opportunities for exposures, Lawson asked his reporters to turn in stories that would help the city reach his personal goals of suppressing vice, social assistance to the needy, municipal ownership of city services, and improving local government. Yet he was aware of the numerous obstacles in finding such information at a time when city departments omitted questionable meetings from public reports, and handwritten records were easily falsified or conveniently misplaced.

The city had reached a population of about one and a half million in the last years of the nineteenth century, and it knew how to entertain. Even before Chicago became a center for what the French would call *le jazz hot*, the term "ragtime" for syncopated music used in African American "ragged" dances may have been popularized by an unknown Chicago reporter around 1897.[39]

The name and the music suggest saloons and brothels, but the craze came as the city was blossoming into the form it has now. Mansions were going up on Lake Shore Drive, moneyed families were moving north from the South and West Sides, and streetcars were making a loop around the downtown legal, business and theater district. But the idea of keeping this prime real estate attractive to retail businesses and shoppers seems not to have occurred to anyone.

The liveliest corner in town was Clark and Madison Streets, where gambling houses near city hall abounded and "cappers" (handicappers) solicited customers from doorways. Not surprisingly, pawn shops as well as saloons and "policy shops" lined both sides of Clark from Washington to Harrison Street, and Clark Street was where court personnel looked for jurors.

Charles Tyson Yerkes (pronounced yer-kees)—an average-looking man with a bushy mustache that took attention away from his thinning nest of wavy hair—had come to town in 1882 with money from Philadelphia investors wanting to take over the city's traction (cable streetcar) businesses. As would be discovered later, much of that money was passed out to aldermen and state legislators Philadelphia-style whenever a transportation measure came up.

One of the few people suspicious of Yerkes's methods was Joseph Dunlap, a former managing editor of the *Times* who somehow was familiar with prostitutes and pimps. Dunlap owed his position on the paper to the insistence of Storey's widow, although one of his employees said he never seemed to do anything other than "look disgusting."

Dunlap left Storey's old paper to found the Chicago *Dispatch* and used his shady contacts to specialize in personal exposés. Somewhere along the way he caught a rumor that Yerkes had been hounded out of the City of Brotherly Love because of financial misdeeds. Actually, Yerkes was an able, if corrupt, businessman whose juggling of Philadelphia municipal bonds had collapsed only because of the Great Chicago Fire. Caught short, Yerkes was convicted of misappropriating the bonds but was pardoned and eventually paid everyone back.

After Dunlap edited the piece, he sent a reporter to Yerkes for a reaction, probably afraid of the banker son's influence rather than acting out of journalistic fairness.

"The boss wants you to look it over and see if it's all true," the reporter said.

"You're damn right it's true," Yerkes responded. "And you tell that God damned Dunlap that if he ever publishes a line or tells a soul I'll kill him the first time I see him."[40]

Dunlap's hushing up of Yerkes' shady background left the *Daily News* and the Chicago *Record,* its morning edition, to lay bare his business practices. The full story of how this happened is lost to us, but we know that it started when Indiana reporter Edward Price Bell sent some articles to *Daily News* editor Charles Henry Dennis as an example of what he could do and asked for an assignment anywhere in the world. Dennis was a former street reporter who had covered the Haymarket trial, and he thought there could be no better subject than Yerkes.

Bell, one of the earliest muckrakers, had been encouraged to enter journalism by Eugene Debs, editor of *Fireman's* magazine in Indiana before becoming a nationwide labor activist and presidential hopeful. "No worker does more for the world than the good reporter unfettered," Debs told Bell. "He tells the truth, and the truth is mankind's one ineffable blessing."[41]

Bell was able to track the way Yerkes used local shysters and political insiders to bribe jurors in personal injury cases involving his five hundred miles of street railways. Later disclosures showed that Yerkes gave liberally to Mayor

Harrison and was able to manipulate Governor John Tanner, who sanctioned fifty-year franchises for streetcar lines.

Chicago's numerous papers generally avoided the yellow journalism that was cheapening several New York sheets. But, with the "anarchy" movement afraid to rise again, Windy City papers more than ever concentrated on news as entertainment, and that meant increasingly light treatment of the facts. Reporters and feature writers balking at the chicanery and sham left for respected publications. But those who enjoyed treating their jobs as a game thrived more in Chicago in the nineties than perhaps anywhere else.

The *Tribune* was still putting advertising on the front page in the latter 1880s, and writing at most papers was rather dry except for florid passages and some features. A few papers were still "political rags." As late as 1892, the future chronicler of the age, Theodore Dreiser, watched a *Globe* editor who disliked the Democratic Party write invectives against Republicans for forty dollars a week. Such provincialism seemed out of place in Chicago, which had recently supplanted Philadelphia as America's second largest city.

With passion leaving the newspapers, reporters loved hoaxes, including the Indian rope trick. The story of a boy who climbs a rope thrown into the air apparently originated in a front page article and accompanying sketch in the August 9, 1890, edition of the Chicago *Tribune,* where it was explained as possibly being a mass hallucination. That would have been equally impossible.

The hoaxer who pieced together some Indian and Chinese tricks was former police reporter John E. Wilkie, son of the more serious-minded editor Franc Wilkie. John worked for a while at his father's paper, the *Times,* before moving to the better-paying *Tribune* in 1881. His article claimed to be based on an account by Chicagoan Fred S. Ellmore. Look at the name again and you will see that it spells "Sellmore," a reference to "a sell," a feature article intended to increase street sales.

The *Tribune* was forced into a retraction four months after the story appeared in newspapers around the world, but Wilkie was allowed to stay at his desk. In fact, it was possibly through *Tribune* influence that he went on to head the U.S. Secret Service for fourteen years, gaining a reputation for disreputable conduct and press exploitation in his pursuit of counterfeiters.[42]

As the owner of two sheets, Lawson thought he and all the other newspaper publishers in Chicago were wasting money by sending reporters out for routine news. In 1890, seven of them established a local wire service, the City Press Association, to train reporters while simultaneously handling common shootings and accidents. People worked there for a few months or years hoping for a scoop that would make them noticed, with only a handful of editors staying on for stability.

By dispatching reporters within minutes of when they were hired, City Press helped foster the running, jumping, and sneaky style of journalism that would soon distinguish the Chicago press.

Newspeople had an effect on literature as well as politics. Eugene Field's column inspired Theodore Dreiser from Indiana to try journalism. As the future novelist went from newsroom to newsroom looking for a job he found "the strangest, coldest, most haphazard and impractical of places," crowded with desks and lamps, and with editors talking to reporters while doing such things as pushing a blue pencil through a sharpener. Copies of rival newspapers were on all the desks and lay strewn on the floor.

With no experience, the twenty-year-old Dreiser accepted fifteen dollars a week from the lowly *Globe* when it was increasing its staff for the 1893 Columbian Exposition. The better papers had at least twenty reporters, but the *Globe* employed only eight or nine, and some of its editors landed there only after being ousted by office politics elsewhere.

The naïve Dreiser did not know it, but he was working for a crook. *Globe* publisher Michael Cassius McDonald had sold newspapers and candy on trains as a boy until learning he could make more money with cards and dice. As criminals go, McDonald was fairly decent and was never known to use violence. But with his gift for organization, he formed the city's first gambling syndicate and the Chicago Democratic Party machine, welding crime with local government at the onset.

As could be expected from someone too stingy to join City Press, McDonald paid his staff less than any other publisher in the city and relied mainly on national wire services. Not really interested in news, "King Mike" had bought the *Globe* to defend himself against assaults by other papers, primarily the *Tribune*, and sometimes the other papers attacked him literally.

McDonald was so agreeable he did not mind it when reporters, including Finley Peter Dunne, from time to time were sworn in as deputy sheriffs so they could raid his downtown gambling house for a story. But he was upset when "Deputy" George Weber of the *Daily News* savaged his roulette wheel with an axe in the name of the law and the front page.

On Dreiser's first day at McDonald's haphazard newspaper, he was assigned to eavesdrop on political talk in downtown hotels. The remarks from an editor at the end of the day sound familiar to anyone at a modern paper:

"This is awful stuff," the editor said when he looked over the first page. "You want to try and remember that you're not the editor of this paper and just consider yourself a plain reporter sent out to cover some hotels. Now, where'd you go today? What'd you see? No, no, I don't mean that! That might be good for a book or something but it's not news. Did you see any particular man? Did you find out anything in connection with any particular committee? Very good! You haven't anything to write."

Then, as Dreiser recalled, "He tore up my precious nine pages and threw them into the waste basket."[43]

When assigned to the police beat, he sat on a bench by a precinct station courtroom and waited for victims and witnesses to go inside and put their hand on a grimy Bible. With papers now printing photos through the halftone process (reproducing them in tiny dots), he found himself one of the early picture-stealers in the city. Before the papers started hiring staff photographers, people in bereavement might come home from a wake only to discover the window open and a favorite image of their loved one missing. More often, photos were simply conned away from families. Dreiser at first cringed at this part of the job but found that "I was like the others, as eager to get the news ... lust for the chase would in critical moments seize me and in my eagerness to win a newspaper battle I would forget or ignore every tenet of fairness and get it."

Dreiser accepted an inducement to forget what he had learned about a phony auction shop so his paper could bring a charge of attempted bribery against the owner. This led to a job offer from the St. Louis *Globe-Democrat*. From there he moved to the New York *World*, but his interests were always with the city of his *Sister Carrie* and his trilogy based on Yerkes, *The Financier*, *the Titan* and *The Stoic*. Even though his news experience was ordinary and his style often clumsy, no one grasped the totality of the growing city so well.

As a one-purpose newspaper, the *Globe* collapsed after McDonald's informal wife, Dora, shot her young lover to death, only to be acquitted by a forgiving jury on the grounds of temporary insanity. The fight went out of the gambling king, and his paper would fold in 1895.[44]

Strictly moralistic newspapers appeared stodgy in the exhilarating and challenging progressive era. Yet Chicago papers remained essentially straightforward, even though the *Daily Telegraph* existed on whatever advertising it could sign up from week to week and was rumored to have engaged in minor blackmail after Storey's death. This was nothing like New York, where William d'Alton Mann gathered gossip for *Town Topics* but showed the galley proofs to people who might pay well to keep their indiscretions out of print, or the New York *Post*, which took five thousand dollars a month to avoid exposing the Boss Tweed ring.[45]

Papers in the nineties had an additional attention-grabber with the development of the bannerline, bold letters across the entire top of the front page rather than being squeezed in tiers within a single column. A bannerline lured non-subscribers in the street, and gave reporters something to aspire toward.

In 1892, *Tribune* presses were printing up to seventy-two thousand eight-page newspapers an hour. But even a year later there was still only one telephone in the newsroom, keeping the staff from widening its out-of-town coverage with the limited long-distance service then available.[46]

Telephones, typewriters, photographs, and the spread of wire services were making boomers superfluous, since fewer reporters were now sitting around the city room until needed. If there were sirens in the Loop, the portion of downtown encircled by elevated tracks, or a socialite murdered in a love triangle, extra reporters could now be called in from the court or society beats or even from their homes. Or an editor could just say "Let City Press do it" and wait for the story to come in.

6

After the Western Associated Press, which Joseph Medill had helped set up, merged with the New York Associated Press, Melville Stone became its general manager in 1893. This made it a national wire service, but several papers established a rival, the original United Press. The badly managed UP pilfered news so flagrantly that the AP carried a fake story (probably a Stone prank) about a rebel leader in India named Siht El Otspueht—backward for "The UP Stole This."

The United Press treasurer was "triple millionaire" John R. Walsh, the banker who published both the Chicago *Morning Herald* and the *Chronicle*. There was always something shady about this man whose hearty smile masked a devious mind. In 1894, he abruptly switched from the administrative offices of the UP to a similar position at the Associated Press. Almost immediately, Walsh issued or at least backed an order that its members have nothing to do with any paper holding a United Press franchise. What was called a "newspaper war" at the time saw many sheets forced to drop the UP, including the Cincinnati *Enquirer*, the New Orleans *Times-Democrat,* and the Chicago *Tribune.* No wonder a *New York Times* article from the period snidely referred to Walsh as a "rule-or-ruin man."

As if slowly being strangled, the UP—unrelated to the United Press International of our time—was forced to lock its doors on April 7, 1897. Many of its employees joined the AP but some, led by Edward Wyliss Scripps, half-brother of James E. Scripps of Chicago, formed the Scripps-McRae Press Association. This evolved into the valued Scripps-Howard News Service.[47]

Newspapers were by now always on the watch for conflicts of interest, except when they themselves were involved. For a while, *Tribune* attorney A.S. Trude also represented the Chicago board of education. According to a later allegation, *Tribune* and *Daily News* representatives persuaded the school board at a "midnight meeting"—held without public notice—to grant them ninety-nine-year leases at especially low rates on downtown real estate the board owned, depriving schools of thousands of dollars a year.[48]

Contrary to the impression that women were virtually unheard of in dirty, tobacco-smelling city rooms until World War Two, they had been working for the papers since the earliest days, and not only as society editors. By the year the UP closed, sixteen women worked at the *Tribune*, with Margaret Sullivan writing features and, occasionally, uncredited editorials.

Margaret seems to have been the woman who earlier had worked at the *Herald* and to whom reporter John Kelley gave the fictitious name "Marjorie

Judson." Although the long dresses of other women swept the floor, "Marjorie" wore abbreviated skirts or bloomers and, at times, a jaunty sailor cap. One immediate effect "Marjorie" had was that an employee called "Dirty" Davidson started coming to work with clean collars and polished shoes. Like her male counterparts she chased after stories of murders, fires, and suicides, but she was more interested in features.

Whereas men tended to take things as they were, women brought a progressive tone to papers, yet they were still compelled to work within the societal constraints of their generation. Edna Wooley, later an uncredited editorial writer at the *Journal*, tailed a man of questionable reputation down side streets for an interview but refused to follow him into a saloon. Instead, she paid a newsboy a nickel to see if the man would come out and talk to her. He refused, and she nearly lost her job.[49]

The *Times*—once silenced by General Burnside—was shut down again by Police Capt. Michael Schaak on January 5, 1889. He ordered the presses stopped when the paper was exposing the fact that he was assisting a fencing ring. Schaak jailed both city editor Joseph Dunlap and principal owner James West on charges of criminal libel, and even saw to it that no bailbondsman was available to free them. Their treatment created an outrage leading to Schaak's suspension, but there was an ironic aftermath. The captain was reinstated after a change in administration, but both West and Dunlap went on to serve prison terms for unrelated crimes. Less than a year after the *Times* was briefly interrupted, West had to let go of the paper and was sentenced to five years for over-issuing stock. Then Dunlap was sentenced to prison for two years for letting the classified section of the *Dispatch*, a paper he had started, be used to recruit women and clients for prostitution.[50]

As the century was ending, newsmen were no longer the well-bred gentlemen of the 1850s. According to Dreiser, the impression was that "by and large newspaper men while interesting and in some cases able, were tricky and shifty and above all, disturbingly and almost heartlessly inconsiderate of each other."

Reporters, of course, thought unexpected daily happenings were the soul of the paper, but to editors they were just a part of the makeup. All the dailies by now had managing editors, Sunday editors, railroad editors, news editors, city editors, copy readers, editorial writers, "sporting editors," society editors, drama critics, and political editors, whose legmen nosed about hotels and city hall for gossip.

Dreiser said that before he was turned down at the *Tribune* he noticed an office sign there reading "WHO OR WHAT? HOW? WHEN? WHERE?"[51] These were four of the "five W's" of a lead for the inverted pyramid story form, which placed the most relevant or interesting information at the top of the story, and from then on the story dwindled to minutiae. This structure facilitated casual reading and made articles easier to trim. Since "Why?" was commonly used rather than "How," Dreiser's memory may have been faulty.

Now that newspapers were frequently unveiling corruption in local government, honest politicians were learning to work with them. In 1891, Alderman Salo Roth privately told the *Daily News* that Yerkes had sent someone to approach him with hints of a bribe if he would support a mayoral override of a transportation measure. Roth accepted seven hundred and fifty dollars from the go-between but stashed the money in the *Daily News* vault as evidence. Seven aldermen were charged with taking bribes but were acquitted, raising the possibility of jury tampering.[52]

What readers never realized was that police officers and public officials were not required to give information. A reporter obtained stories by making regular checks on police stations, slapping the backs of policemen who did not mind it, asking about their families, telling jokes, staying out of their way, going for coffee, giving officers a few news tips, and keeping after any unsolved crimes day after day. The type of news a reporter picked up depended largely on his or her personality. According to reporter Charles Washburn, police officers, criminals, and politicians would round corners to do favors for John Kelley, and he was called the boss of the Harrison Street station.

Probably more than in any other city, police in Chicago were so friendly with reporters that they often let them move freely about a crime scene and gave them advance information on raids. Public figures were just as friendly. While Alderman Bathhouse John Coghlin was inviting Kelley to ghostwrite poems for him, the crooked politician said, "Go as far as you like, Kell, I'll stand for anything but murder."

At the *Tribune,* city editor Fred Hall was never known to take a vacation in his twenty-eight years of working up to sixteen hours a day, sometimes seven days a week. But we know about the straw-hatted Hall only because one of his protégés was energetic young reporter Charles Chapin, who in subsequent years would drive himself and his employees relentlessly in New York.

As Chicago *Tribune* maritime editor, Chapin showed his resourcefulness when he raced by train, schooner, chartered tug boat, and finally dinghy to find public hospital warden William McGarigle, who had been Mayor Harrison's police chief and was now escaping a scandal involving large-scale bribery and misused public funds. In the words of a later report, McGarigle "enjoyed the bubbly stuff while patients in his Cook County Hospital rotted." As a stepping stone to Canada, the fugitive headed for the area where two of the Great Lakes meet.

While Chicago police and other reporters waited for McGarigle to show up at the Straits of Mackinac, Chapin found him hiding in a livery stable near Lake Huron. With no arrest authority, the reporter interviewed him for a five thousand word scoop. McGarigle did not stay around to read it and remained at large for two years. He surrendered, paid a sizable fine, and returned to Chicago to open the Round Bar, one of numerous downtown press hangouts.[53]

One day in 1890, amiable career reporter John Kelley stepped into

McGarigle's saloon while on the "justice shop" (police court) beat for the *Morning Herald*. Kelley was no stranger to violence and even owed his career to it. He had been unable to get a job at any of the papers until the *Globe's* society editor was shot to death by her jealous husband. As Kelley would say, "I stepped into a dead woman's shoes." Two weeks later he was put on general assignment, and the next year was working for the paper next door.

On this day, he heard "Bad Johnny" Connerton calling dapper Michael "Doc" Haggerty (from a nearby gambling house) a blackmailer, and the men began shooting. Kelley reported that all the "diners" ducked under tables, and one assumes he was among them. Both bleeding combatants fought off anyone who tried to intervene and carried their shootout into Clark Street. Haggerty died of his wounds two or three days later, but "Bad Johnny" lived for another year.

Despite the cold, sneering stereotype of reporters, many were softies. In November, 1891, Kelley took a horse-drawn cab to a middle-aged woman's home without explaining why he was there. He saw that her stove was empty, and so he and a policeman he found climbed a coal yard fence and brought back two buckets full of coal. The officer kept the mother company while Kelley made the three of them dinner with whatever food he could find. Only then did he tell the woman that his editor had seen her daughter jumping to her death in Lake Michigan and that he would like to know something about her.

"Well," the mother said, "her troubles are over."

When copyreader Billy Lewis finished checking the spelling and commas of Kelley's account, he appeared to have been crying. He came out of the local room and said, "John, I think we had better go downstairs and have a wee little drink."[54]

The three German-language papers in the city tried to compete with the major dailies in crime and accident news, but it was said their reporters would arrive at night from their day jobs as dishwashers in restaurants and beer gardens. Many other reporters were Irish, and several of the best city editors came from Scotland or England. They included one of the fastest rising and most famous in the late nineteenth century, James Keeley.

Despite his little education growing up in London's East End, Keeley in later years tried to pass himself off as a scholar. After the desertion of his alcoholic father, his stern schoolteacher mother strongly encouraged that the bothersome adolescent leave home. To wish them out of his life, Keeley would make up the fiction that he had been orphaned.

With a valise containing only clothes and the equivalent of fourteen dollars when he arrived in the United States, the fifteen-year-old boy moved in with maternal relatives in Kansas. Before long his mother wrote something derogatory about him, we do not know what, and James struck out on his own.

Looking older than his age, the long-faced teenager worked on a Kansas City paper, and this leads us to one of his apparent fabrications. Keeley said he chased a murderer into an Arkansas swamp and held a gun on him with one hand while writing the story on a dry log with the other. As a young man he worked on papers in Memphis and Louisville, where, he claimed, he wrote the "Jerked to Jesus" headline Storey later used. Because Storey wrote or authorized a number of similar headlines and Keeley did not, there is no reason to believe him.[55]

By the time Keeley reached Chicago in 1889, most papers were keeping three night police reporters, one for each side of the lake-bound city. With so much competition, every newsman longed for a good scoop, called in those days "a pippin," and, perhaps two or three times in a career, "a bell ringer."

Keeley started carrying a walking stick—not for protection, but to give him individuality with the police, much as some pass out business cards today. For his first "pippin," the overachieving newcomer seized upon what would be known as "the Johnson County war" in far-off Wyoming.

Stockmen had hired gunfighters to stop small ranchers from rustling cattle or, in another view, grabbing their land. Some of the "regulators" arrived by rail in April, 1892. Reports coming in were so confused that Keeley's editor gave his night reporter three hundred dollars and said, "Go to Johnson County and get the facts." Three days later, his first report was about two alleged rustlers who were killed and some African American troops who headed for the scene. Imagine the excitement of *Tribune* readers when they saw the headline BIG BATTLE IMPENDING.

Keeley reached the troops as they escorted forty-eight regulators to Fort McKinney. The soldiers said the men had been rescued, but the cowboys told him they had been arrested to keep them out of trouble. The reporter said that when a stagecoach failed to arrive, he rented a horse and buggy and hired one-eyed cowhand Dick Tate as his guide. They purportedly rode through a thunderstorm that became a snowstorm and lost their way. Every few miles, Keeley averred, he would tie a stone to a lasso and throw it over a telegraph wire to drag it down.

He made this seem as if he—or, more probably, Tate—had done this to find their way to the nearest town, but it certainly would have kept the competition from contacting their news offices. But perhaps the whole story was made up, since the stockmen's cowboys as well as the rustlers often downed wires to forestall reinforcements. We do know that when Keeley encountered a lineman working on one of the cables, he encouraged the man, which probably meant that he bribed him, to prolong his work for four days.

Keeley's breathless and exaggerated dispatches supplied the *Tribune* with eleven front-page stories over two weeks and often beat a Chicago *Herald* reporter following the cattlemen. The epicmaking by such reporters turned the Johnson County conflict into a staple of Western fiction, and helped Keeley rise to become *Tribune* managing editor in eight years. One longs to hear his British accent as he said his ultimate goal was to turn the *Tribune* into "the world's greatest newspaper." While city editor, instead of leaving at five or six o'clock in the evening he often remained at his desk until midnight to "put the paper to bed," which involved laying out the stories and checking the general format and headlines.[57]

It was the spirited *Daily News*, however, which enjoyed the highest circulation in the city, and it moved into a new four-story building at 12 5th Avenue (Wells Street) three months after the failed Yerkes trap. The top floor housed the editorial and composing rooms. The third floor held the library, including reference clippings from all the papers, as well as the line-drawing etching room and the linotype section. On the second floor were supply rooms, a large hall for newsboys, and a lunchroom that encouraged employees to stay out of free-sandwich saloons. Below were the mailroom and subscription area.

All the papers were increasing their staffs for the 1893 Columbian Exposition, which would make Chicago world famous. The *Tribune* hired pretty and independent Gertrude Small, the only female at the Boston *Post*, and made her the Sunday editor in all but job title. James Keeley, then the assistant city editor, wooed her by sending back edited copy with notes such as "May I ask forgiveness?" and later addressing them to "dearie." As a result, Keeley gained a wife and the *Tribune* lost an educated and promising writer.

Although not a writing editor, Keeley was quick to sense the possibilities of a seemingly ordinary story. He would have reporters follow up additional angles over the next few days, and had the sense to let it go rather than milking the feature dry as other editors might have.

On the first week of the fair, a legislative hearing was held in Chicago on suspicions that building Lake Shore Drive by the independent Lincoln Park Board over the tip of the lake and across a worthless marsh was a land grab by a few secret investors who saddled taxpayers with the construction bill. The Republican-hearted *Tribune* and *Journal* ignored the days of testimony, perhaps because the event was a Democratic Party show and such notables as John V. Farwell, N.K. Fairbank, and real-estate magnate and hotelier Potter Palmer were involved.

It took the *Times, Daily News,* and even the lowly *Globe* to report the disclosures and insinuations of collusion by the park commissioners in authorizing the project without public notice. But since these papers had little influence in the city council and Springfield, no public protest followed.

The Columbian Exposition showed the world Chicago, and showed Chicagoans the future. Fairgoers marveled at the newest inventions and sights, especially the giant Ferris wheel. During its closing days, friendly Mayor Harrison returned to his West Side mansion and soon heard Patrick Prendergast knocking. The disturbed young man believed he should have been appointed chief city attorney. He shot Harrison to death at the threshold, then ran down the steps and surrendered at the nearest police station.

One visitor who made a lasting impact after the fair was British editor and reformer William T. Stead. He had exposed a male prostitution ring catering to some of London's best families and now wanted to see what he could do with what he regarded as the wickedest city on earth, a reputation gained from diligent newspaper work in the news-mad town.

Stead believed the only way to expose tolerated vice and various kinds of cheating in Chicago government was by approaching the problem systematically. He rented downtown office space and used assistants beyond reproach, including some wives and daughters of the city's leading men. He also compared the county tax laws with the tax rolls and proved that buildings owned by the privileged few, including the *Tribune*, were taxed at only a small percentage of what they should have been. The title of this thick muckraking document also revealed Stead's religious fervor. Instead of something comparable to Jacob Riis's *How the Other Half Lives* or Lincoln Steffans' *Shame of the Cities*, he called it *If Christ Came to Chicago.*

Later reporter John McPhaul has left us an account of what happened next. Stead gave galley proofs of his book to *Tribune* editor James Keeley with the understanding that they would be published in the newspaper only after he returned to England. But *Herald* editor Horatio Seymour was eager for a copy. He learned that one of Stead's sources, Edmund Browne, known as "king of the bums," happened to have a key to Keeley's suite in the Auditorium Hotel. Browne let friendly reporter John Kelley and Seymour's brother, Charles, sneak in and take notes.

McPhaul said that in a rage over being scooped on its own scoop, the *Tribune* tried to minimize Stead's work by claiming the newspaper had already disclosed many of the abuses—certainly not the tax oversights—and that the rest was little more than a guide to gambling halls and houses of ill repute.

The outrage must really have been over disclosures of the paper's illegal tax break and bargain lease. Governor Altgeld charged that the *Tribune* should be assessed three times the twelve thousand dollars it was paying annually for its downtown site. But administration-friendly courts eventually upheld the lease.

After Stead left, Chicago banker Lyman J. Gage and Bertha Palmer, wife of Potter Palmer, followed his example by setting up the Civic Federation to study crime and social problems in the city, and their work inspired other reform groups. Lawson of the *Daily News* contributed five thousand dollars toward establishing the Municipal Voters League, which uncovered corruption and supported honest candidates.

When Steffens at last arrived in town in 1904 to lay open the rampant bribery for *McClure's Magazine*, he was bewildered at the improvement since the "King" Mike McDonald days. He did not credit the newspapers for this, but they had been instrumental in pointing the way and driving good people into action.

With so many nineteenth century editors filled with self-importance or believing they were guided by divine calling, it may be refreshing to glimpse the career of the happiest and least successful news publisher in Chicago history, Herman H. Kohlsaat.

Kohlsaat was a sort of Horatio Alger figure who grew up poor in Ohio and at fourteen came to Chicago, like many others, by way of Galena. After making a little money hawking the *Tribune*, the Episcopalian young man hit upon the idea of opening a chain of bakeries and "stool and counter" restaurants serving lunch to workmen and reporters for fifteen cents. With the romanticism of an early financial success, Kohlsaat wanted to run a paper. By 1891, the blond young man with horn-rimmed glasses and a pleasant, open face had enough courage and capital to buy into the respectable but rather unexciting Chicago *Inter-Ocean*. The paper had begun publishing at Wabash and Congress, site of the Auditorium Theatre, but then moved to the same Madison Street building as a burlesque show office and one of the pool halls reporters frequented.

Feeling unwelcomed by the staff at his own paper, Kohlsaat gave editor William Penn Nixon, a former firebrand from the abolition days, sixty days to buy him out. Not caring where he got the money, Nixon took a loan from Yerkes, who used this leverage to gain control of the "I-O" so that he could publicly answer his critics, as gambler Mike McDonald had done with the *Globe*. The "Traction King" eventually fled to Europe under repeated disclosures by other papers, and Chicago was left without any flamboyant villains for political cartoonists to have fun with.

Herman H. Kohlsaat, the most experienced amateur among newspaper publishers in the city. Among the ailing properties he bought and ran for fun was the respectable but unexciting Chicago *Inter-Ocean* (Chicago Public Library, Special Collections and Preservation Division, GP-Smith 357).

Kohlsaat was surely rich enough to retire in comfort in his forties, but he loved newspaper publishing more than money. He dreamed of buying the Chicago *Tribune* or even the *New York Times,* but what he could afford was the Chicago *Times*. The paper had lost its bite once Storey died and for a while had been published by Mayor Carter Harrison because no other paper would back him. Upon Harrison's murder, his sons, Preston and Carter II, took over and renamed it the *Evening Dispatch*.

The brothers were not really

newsmen but sincerely tried to act like ones. The Harrisons usually ended their workday at around four in the morning, bought a bundle of rival papers at a stand and, despite their wealth, caught a horse-drawn streetcar at Madison and Wells. On the ride to their home at Jackson and Ashland they studied their competition by the streetcar's oil lamp.

The *Evening Dispatch* remained sympathetic to the working class even during the strike by Pullman sleeping car company workers. The turmoil came at a time of financial reverses. Because of tourism during the World's Fair, Chicago was spared an economic panic that had hit New York and other cities in 1893, but when winter came the panic struck all the harder, nearly wiping out some leading businessmen, including industrialist N.K. Fairbank. Hundreds of homeless people were allowed to sleep in city hall on the coldest nights.

Where some editors saw a threat from the swarm of unemployed, reporter Ray Stannard Baker from Wisconsin sensed a social necessity. The intense young man with a spinal defect that made one shoulder higher than the other, worked from one P.M. to midnight for fifteen dollars a week at Lawson's morning paper, now called the *News-Record*. With permission from managing editor Charles Henry Dennis, he slept in a newspaper office until *Daily News* start-up noises awakened him at around nine o'clock each morning.

Baker's hours made it easier to detail life in flophouses and soup kitchens, and he hoped the pieces could spur civic leaders into finding a remedy. He turned out to be too good at what he covered, such as interviewing Jacob Coxey in Ohio during a march of the poor and Stead before the reformer returned to England—only to go mad, recover, and die on the *Titanic*. Editors trimmed Baker's copy considerably, and one told him, "We can't make it look as though everyone in Chicago was starving and homeless."[58] He left the city and eventually won a Pulitzer Prize for an eight-volume biography of Woodrow Wilson.

Things were going so well for the owner and the publisher of the Chicago *Morning Record*, John R. Walsh and James W. Scott, that, in 1886, they started the Chicago *Evening Post*. This was printed in a separate building and was unrelated to the Civil War–era paper by that name. Internal trouble began when Scott started making a number of bold decisions on his own, such as firing Horatio Seymour when the popular editor had a mental breakdown in 1893, and replacing him with someone less skillful but easier to work with.

The wedge between the two men came the following year, when railroad car factory workers in the company town of Pullman, later a South Side neighborhood, walked out because of firings, jacked-up rents in company-owned homes, and increased prices at company-owned stores. All this was in response to the panic on the New York Stock Exchange. In sympathy, unionized employees at two dozen railroads also refused to work. This first nationwide strike involved walkouts in twenty-seven states and halted all mail going by train. The turmoil gives us a look at how smaller newspapers had nothing to do with truth.

As *Morning Herald* owner John Walsh had suddenly switched from the United Press to the Associated Press to cripple his former employer, he abruptly went from long articles praising Eugene Debs' newly formed American Railway Union to demanding that his editors and reporters "show the strikers no quarter." The mystery behind the vicious turnabout was explained shortly after federal troops set up tents downtown and quelled the strike.

Debs said that a *Morning Herald* representative, who may have been Scott, had repeatedly hinted to him and others at a pre-strike convention that if union funds were deposited in Walsh's Chicago National Bank the newspaper would remain friendly. After the union refused and Debs objected to the sudden editorial attacks, the unnamed representative told him that "you have yourself to blame for it."

Scott bought out Walsh in 1895 and merged the *Morning Herald* with the newly acquired *Times*. But just a month later he died of apoplexy on a New York vacation.[59] Walsh took over the *Times-Herald* but found that he could not keep it going by himself. When the staunchly Republican Kohlsaat paid one and a half million dollars for the Democratic morning sheet, Walsh threw in the *Evening Post*, but this was more of a liability than an asset.

On his first day as publisher of the *Times-Herald*, the former baker good-naturedly slapped the employees on the back and said, "This paper is going to be strictly independent, except that it will be for [trade] protection, for William McKinley, and for anything he wants." Yet everyone liked the bespeckled new publisher, who still looked young in his forties.

Kohlsaat sank his real-estate fortune into the *Times-Herald* and the evening paper, running them mainly for his enjoyment and what he considered the edification of the city. Under him, the *Evening Post* snubbed the trend toward playing up sordid crimes and called itself the paper for "the man with [only] three minutes for murder."[60]

Reflecting Kohlsaat's easygoing nature, on Thanksgiving Day, 1895, his *Times-Herald* sponsored what may have been America's first organized auto race, or "reliability trial." The cars rumbled and shook from Jackson Park on the South Side to near north suburban Evanston and back. A Mercedes-Benz won by making the trip through snow in just under eight hours.

A couple of years afterward, some cost-cutting policies at the newspapers stirred up labor unrest. *Daily News* managing editor Charles Faye suggested to Lawson, who was vacationing in Europe, that every department operate as an open shop to head off trouble. Lawson balked at the idea, to his regret.

The scores of reporters the dailies had on the police, court, railroad, sports, and society beats were useless for three days in 1898 when a citywide printers strike shut the presses down. Police officers guarded all the newspaper buildings, and there was no violence. Lawson kept his presses running with scabs.[61] When the pressmen returned to work, everything was back to normal.

The *Tribune* had increased its size to thirty-six pages on some days and enjoyed a circulation of seventy thousand. That was still behind the *Daily News* but well ahead of it in advertising dollars.

Victor Lawson knew that a paper had to keep exploring areas to stay ahead. With twelve English-language dailies in the city, the competition was "never so keen as now," he noted in a letter. As Medill had been so fed up with the New York–based Associated Press that he helped found the Western Associated Press, Lawson co-founded the Illinois Associated Press and served as its president in 1894. He also started thinking about establishing the first independent foreign service outside New York, one that would do more than just cable articles from the London morning papers.

His European correspondents turned stories in only to his morning paper, but Lawson dropped the idea of expanding the service to newspapers in other markets because he felt that such events as the Boer War would not sufficiently interest Americans. The foreign service was transferred to his main paper when Lawson sold the *News-Record* in 1901.

Papers nationwide were turning more toward yellow journalism toward the end of the nineteenth century. News gatherers were less like the gentlemen of forty years before and more like Charles Washburn, who joined the *Tribune* as a copyboy at fourteen, rose to reporter, and somehow became an expert on the city's red light district. Washburn came up with what should be every journalist's motto: "Success is having the right [telephone] number." No wonder such eager and thoroughly unprofessional reporters scrambled all over Chicago's first legendary murder.

Police searching for young, moderately attractive Louise Luetgert in 1897, examined the defunct sausage factory of her once-wealthy husband and found vats of potash with chemical lye and, nearby, fragments of bone, some teeth, and tissue that might have been human. Even without a body, authorities charged Louise's stocky, German-born husband with murder. Rumor had it that the middle-aged Albert Luetgert was a crazed butcher who had melted his former love to destroy all evidence. Newsmen from across the country stood on roofs surrounding the criminal court building to watch deliberations through telescopes and binoculars. But it took a few locals to show them tricks. Chicago *Journal* reporters and Fred A. Smith of the suburban Palatine *Independent* sneaked into the courthouse attic with a rope. The Chicago reporters lowered Smith on a chair through an airshaft to a register vent and held him there as he used a speaking tube to call out the shouting of the deadlocked jury. A detail that may be fable said he learned the jurors turned away a sausage lunch.

No one seems to have doubted that Luetgert was guilty of dissolving his marriage and his wife at the same time. Besides, the defendant was such a large man he looked capable of the unthinkable. Yet no one at the time could prove that the physical evidence came from his wife's body. With a single juror refusing to vote guilty, the case ended in a mistrial. But Luetgert was convicted on retrial and sentenced to life in prison.[62]

7

At the *Inter-Ocean*, Herman Kohlsaat was thoroughly professional in manner, devoid of the inner push that made Medill and Storey so idiosyncratic and hard to get along with. Kohlsaat even took advice from his staff. Like all worthy news publishers, he occasionally embarked on causes, such as denouncing Republican political boss William Lorimer, a Scottish-born former newsboy and streetcar conductor who became a U.S. senator while keeping his hand in Yerkes' pocket. In fact, Kohlsaat and the *Tribune* separately helped oust Lorimer from office only a year after a bipartisan majority of the state General Assembly elected him to the Senate.

In 1910, *Tribune* editor James Keeley startled readers with this under a "five column box," a headline covering five columns:

> The Chicago Tribune has in its possession and will submit to the proper authorities. ... a sworn statement made by Charles A. White, a [Democratic] member of the lower house of the Illinois legislature from the 9th district, charging that William Lorimer was elected to the United States Senate last summer by bribery and corruption; ... that he (White) received one thousand dollars for voting for Lorimer and that he also received nine-hundred dollars as his share of the "jackpot," a term applied to the general corruption fund distributed at the close of each session.[63]

The *Tribune* had paid Representative White thirty-five hundred dollars for the whistleblowing, but denied speculation that the lawmaker might have gone to the paper only after trying to elicit a bribe from Lorimer to keep quiet.

The *Inter-Ocean* was believed to have been the last daily in the city with a large number of "rum pots." In this later period, reporter-writer Robert J. Casey said, it was common for the head of the copy desk to go down to "the Sewer," a basement tavern next door, and find which copy readers (copy editors) could stand up.

"I-O" reporters would fabricate absurd stories just to see if they could slip them past managing editor William Moore in the big barn of a city room, such as one of an Indiana farmer who supposedly put green glasses on his cows to make them think their waste was edible. One hopes that Moore endured fewer pranks when he became managing editor of the New York *Post*.

Yet Kohlsaat was never easygoing with copy, at times quoting Samuel Butler's remark that "I can forgive a liar but I hate inaccuracy." A comma in the wrong place could lead to a day's suspension. Anyone who misspelled a name might be suspended for a week.[64] Kohlsaat also kept his staff so accustomed to rushing to assignments that hardly anyone took his hat off or sat upright.

With reporters enthusiastic about grisly stories, it was little wonder that those on the police and court beats were a rough lot. But the *Tribune* assured readers that the paper could obtain details of society divorces because "the gentlemanly reporter is indigenous to Chicago. Nowhere else do travelers find the calm repose, the insouciance, the neatness and elegance of attire, the quiet, unassuming manners, the soft, smart, smooth voice, the graceful gait that conspire in the construction of the Chicago reporter."[65] Perhaps the writer was thinking of Walter Rice, a poet and literary man who wore a top hat to work and spoke with what the staff took for a Harvard accent.

Turn-of-the-century reporters would often channel their unappreciated intelligence into practical jokes. The most elaborate was the informal Whitechapel Club. The group, similar to the Clover Club in Philadelphia, met in several locations near the *Daily News* building, especially the back of Henry Koster's pub, at 173 West Calhoun Place. This alley-like street was a gathering place for newsboys and employees of papers along what is now Wells Street.

The club began in 1889, when Charles Seymour of the *Chronicle* and a few other newsmen were tipping glass steins somewhere while mulling over names and themes for a social establishment. The club got its name when a newsboy dashed in yelling "All about the latest Whitechapel murder!"—referring to a murder by London's Jack the Ripper. As the story goes, they raised their steins and said, "Here's to the Whitechapel Club!" Its members would celebrate death and the outrageous, and as a courtesy also admitted a few police officers, clergymen, and persons considering themselves philosophers.

Mimicking Dante's *Inferno*, the motto above the door of the one-room club read: "Leave Everything Behind, Ye Who Go Hence." Each of the grotesqueries inside was a nose-thumbing at decorum. The tubercular Seymour set the tone when he dragged in a skeleton and Indian memorabilia from the Western wars he had covered. Next came a hangman's noose from the county jail and a coffin-sized coffee table, possibly replaced later by a real one. Skulls came from a doctor at a mental hospital.

Curious visitors included William Stead, champion boxer John L. Sullivan, and author Rudyard Kipling. This was where Eugene Field read his bawdy poetry, and sometimes the members sang "Then stand to your glasses steady, and drink to your comrade's eyes; Here's to the dead already, and hurrah for the next who dies."

The largest event in the club's short history was its farewell to migrant Texas poet Morris Allen Collins, who had been found in a Loop hotel dead from a possible suicide. On the night of July 16, 1892, thirteen Whitechapel members, probably including some who had mocked Collins' writing, accompanied his body on a train to Miller's Station, Indiana, and walked through tall weeds to the sand dunes rimming Lake Michigan. The corpse, in Grecian robes (one guesses it was a bed sheet), was placed atop a supposedly twenty-foot pyre of tar and kerosene-soaked cotton, and the mourners were warmed by the crackling flames as they read aloud the poetry of Percy Bysshe Shelley, who also had died young. All expenses were paid for by Charles Seymour's brother, Horatio, who had bought the rights to the exclusive story for the *Herald*.

The club closed down when the Whitechapel moneyman, *Herald* partner James W. Scott, passed on and none of the members cared to take on the responsibility. Besides, by then many newspeople had been lured away by New York papers hoping to capture the Chicago spirit.[66] They never did.

8

Although Wilbur Storey had wanted the *Times* to die with him, aging Joseph Medill longed for a successor at the *Tribune*. Now a walking legend with a Moses-like beard, he quickly raised his intelligent but unexceptional son-in-law Robert W. Patterson through the ranks as telegraph news editor, assistant night editor, Washington correspondent, editorial writer, and finally managing editor. Patterson showed so little initiative in these positions that the official history of the paper would attribute to him several major stories he had nothing to do with.[67]

Just before the seventy-five-year-old Medill died at his winter home in San Antonio, Texas, on March 16, 1899, he predicted that his last words would be, "What's the news?" He had helped buy the *Tribune* when it was in danger of extinction, believed he had saved the Union by pushing Lincoln into the White House, lived to see the circulation reach two hundred thousand, and rejected an offer of four million dollars for his paper.[68]

But when Patterson took over the *Tribune*, circulation was still behind not only that of the *Daily News* but also of the *Morning Record* and the *Journal*, which published from near Dearborn and Madison. Despite having a top editor in Keeley, Patterson ignored labor concerns and the need for regulating major industries. Instead of putting in twelve-hour days at the office, as Medill had done, he moved out of his Astor Street home and settled in Washington, D.C., where his wife loved mingling with society.[69] He must have felt that hands-on publishing was passé.

Patterson's paper did just as well without him. *Tribune* reporter Winifred Black and settlement founder Jane Addams showed readers that thirty thousand children arrested in the city each year were in danger of being corrupted and sexually abused because of having to share cells with adults. In response, Cook County opened the nation's first juvenile court in 1900.

In 1901, Kohlsaat, still with the glee of a child emptying a toy box, borrowed ten thousand dollars to meet a payroll and sold the *Evening Post* to John C. Schaffer, publisher of the *Rocky Mountain News* in Denver, for two hundred thousand dollars. He now had enough operating cash to take over Lawson's *Morning Record*. Kohlsaat merged it with his *Times-Herald* as the *Record-Herald*, one of the better newspapers in the city's history.

The paper would have such a complex financial history that the following is only a summary. For some time, Victor Lawson had invested in property owned by the *Times-Herald*, which had roots in Wilbur Storey's Chicago *Times*. He apparently intended to take it over, but could not as long as Kohlsaat was the principal stockholder.

Running the combined newspaper in addition to the *Inter-Ocean* became too much for Kohlsaat, and he sold the *Record-Herald* in 1902 to Frank B. Noyes. The Washington, D.C., native had been the director of that city's *Evening Star* and had recently become president of the Associated Press, where he strove to improve its reputation for thoroughness and accuracy. Under Noyes, the *Record-Herald* was a thoughtful paper that did not try to compete with the crusades and entertaining columns of the *Daily News* or the features and financial coverage of the *Tribune*.

Kohlsaat retired from publishing for a decade, but on December 31, 1910, Noyes announced that the former baker, now his friend, was buying the paper back from him. To save money, Kohlsaat ran his editions off the *Daily News* presses rather than in the cramped but fortress-like Record-Herald building, at 165 West Washington, with its twelve-foot bronze statue of a herald sounding a trumpet. He was able to keep the paper running with profits from land speculation for only two years, and in 1912, Lawson finally acquired the sheet after what may have been thirty-one years of waiting.

During this busy period of acquisitions and foldings, and with competition being waged in the streets rather than with improved or fresher content, all the managing editors looked the other way at abuses involving influential politicians. By 1902, a political machine created by one-time *Globe* chief Mike McDonald was too powerful for any publisher to challenge, and the cruel silence was keeping the public innocent of death traps in the form of run-down buildings around them whenever they went downtown.

The local Democratic Party had entrenched itself partly through an ethnic formula for public office. This meant putting well-meaning Peter Kiolbassa in the city treasurer's seat as the first Pole to hold an elected municipal position in Chicago. Poles at the time were teeming into the city by the thousands, many of them crammed into apartments along Milwaukee Avenue. Kiolbassa established a reputation for civic responsibility by ending the practice of putting interest on public funds into his own pocket. Party bosses Bathhouse John Coughlin and Hinky Dink Kenna decided to exploit his honesty by having him appointed building commissioner, a great potential source of "boodle" for the two downtown aldermen.

This made Kiolbassa worse than a dupe; he owed the Party a debt. As soon as he assumed the office, inspections at First Ward hotels and theaters slowed down or halted. The danger became so severe that the city decided not to publish the number of major fires that broke out during Kiolbassa's single term, 1902–1903, suspiciously creating the only interruption of this practice in Chicago history.[70]

Since the Chicago Architects' Business Association could not compel Kiol-

Chicago. *Chicago Record Herald Bldg.*

Chicago *Herald* building. This fine paper failed to catch the progressive spirit of the 1890s, and under James Keeley it abandoned news in favor of "feel good" features.

bassa to take action against an alarming upsurge in downtown fires, the group brought its pleas to pompous and hypocritical Mayor Carter Harrison II in July 1902. He dismissed the problem even when ten people were killed that same week at St. Luke's sanitarium in a run-down former hotel at 21st Street and Wabash Avenue. Among the charred remains of alcoholics still manacled to their beds were those of blind former alderman Billy Kent.

That December, fourteen people died in a fire at the Lincoln Hotel in the Loop. Still, city inspectors refused to clamp down on First Ward code violators. The *Daily News* came closest to warning the public of the danger by pointing lightly to possible explanations for the hotel fire, in a newspaper's way of quoting without comment. But Coughlin denied using his office to forestall an expensive fire escape, and Kiolbassa would not remark on seventeen instances of shoddy inspections at the same hotel in two years. Before the month was out, the Haymarket Theatre became the second Loop stage venue gutted by fire that year.

On November 23, 1903, the opening day of the Iroquois Theater two blocks from the Marshall Field department store in the Loop, the audience was awed by upholstered seats, scarlet decorations in the boxes, a roof high above the main floor, and a splendid hall with tinted marble pillars. The premier production was a traveling costume musical fantasy, *Mr. Blue Beard*, with Eddy Foy providing comic relief to the romance.

The holiday family matinee on Wednesday, December 30, was a sellout with sixteen hundred people. Foy remarked that he had never seen so many children in an audience. No one seems to have noticed that the wiring was incomplete. During the performance, a short-circuit ignited some papers. Foy, who had been speaking in a squeaky voice during the play, stepped out in costume and said with his beloved lisp, "Please keep your seats. The asbestos curtain is being lowered, and everyone is safe."

However, the fire curtain snagged, creating a whoosh of flame. The first people to run up the aisles found that the fire doors had been locked to keep anyone from sneaking in. Other exits were blocked by construction debris. Men, women, and children were fatally trampled or were trapped under others and unable to escape the smoke and flames.

Legend carried as fact in several books has it that Walter Howey—later the most animated city editor of the "Front Page" era—had been on a routine assignment for a newspaper when he saw a manhole cover pop up. Out came frightened children or, in one account, a costumed actor, saying something about a fire. Unfortunately for the romance of Chicago journalism, Howey late in life wrote a third-person account that replaces myth with a look at an ace, or unethical, reporter in action. Working for eight dollars a week at City News rather than for a newspaper, he was on his way to city hall when he heard bells clanging and saw a fire wagon horse colliding with a laden delivery truck. Down the block, firefighters were rushing into an opening they had smashed into a glass door. Howey quickly found an injured firefighter who told him that at least twenty-five people lay dead inside the theater. The reporter rushed into a saloon next to the Iroquois, pressed a button for a telephone operator, and gave a City News editor all that he had picked up. But how could he keep rival reporters from using the lines once the small local wire service flashed the

The Iroquois Theater Fire. A City News Bureau reporter scooped the newspapers on a 1903 disaster that killed more than 600 people. The papers had declined to expose the graft that would make the fire possible (Chicago History Museum, ICHi-02591).

news? He rushed to the back of the saloon, where there was a bookie with a rolltop desk and a phone with an open line. Howey offered the bookie all the money he had saved, about twenty dollars, for the exclusive use of the phone through the afternoon.

Although only a reporter, Howey instinctively acted like an editor. He called the head of City Press and advised him to send all available men to the saloon for further instruction. Howey then dispatched one of them to a store for a paper of pins and told him to go around to all the public telephones for several blocks "and stick a pin into the shielded wires of each telephone." The newspapers saturated the hospitals and the morgue, but the fastest news from the scene kept coming from City Press. One imagines rival reporters going from one phone to another angrily wondering why they could not reach an operator. Howey saw his salary jump to twelve dollars a week.

An early estimated body count was six hundred and one, far more than those who had died in the fire of 1871. Many of the victims died in heaps behind locked or blocked doors. Since there was never such a thing as a deadline for a major story, the presses at all the papers were operated around the clock as editions were replated with every block of fresh developments. That is, only one or two pages were changed to avoid composing an entirely new edition.

Needing to cover up the evident graft responsible for the tragedy, Mayor Harrison proclaimed that "the Iroquois disaster was due to fate."[71]

The *Tribune* scrambled to carry the names of the dead on its six pages of fire coverage in the December 31 edition.[72] Now would have been the second-best time for one of the papers to suggest that bribery must have turned what would have been a minor fire into the city's greatest loss of life up to that time. At least the *Daily News* on January 2 pointed out the obvious—that city laws had been violated and that "the innocent dead speak for the enforcement of the law." Then the paper dropped the story.

With the smaller and rather old-fashioned papers now dying away, the story of Chicago journalism would primarily be concerned with the gaining strength of the *Daily News,* internecine discord at the *Tribune,* and what happened to the ethics and circulation at both these papers when brash newcomer William Randolph Hearst breezed into town with the new century.

Part 2: The Reporters, Newsboys, and Photographers

THREE. Anything Goes

The press is a blind old cat yowling on a treadmill. —Ben Hecht[1]

The reason hulking San Francisco millionaire William Randolph Hearst launched a Chicago newspaper was not because the city needed one more but because he was determined to occupy the White House by the time he reached forty. Hearst's ambitions were given a lift in 1900 when the National Association of Democratic Clubs elected him its president, with the understanding that he would start a Democratic paper in the Windy City to offset the staunchly Republican *Tribune*. Hearst's business manager, Solomon Carvalho, warned him about Chicago newspaper competition by saying, "It's a tough town. We'll have to shoot our way in."

The staff rushed production of the *Evening American* in just six weeks. On July 2 of that year, Hearst-supported orator William Jennings Bryan, of the 1896 "Cross of Gold" speech, interrupted an Indianapolis visit to sit down at a telegraph key and with one touch start the presses for a new kind of Chicago newspaper.

Hearst was not interested in advertisers or integrity, and editors who had followed his battle with Joseph Pulitzer in New York knew what to expect. "The modern editor of the popular journal does not care for the facts," Hearst wrote privately. "The editor has no objections to facts if they are also novel. But he would prefer novelty that is not fact, to a fact that is not a novelty."

With his arrival, the friendly rivalry among newspaper publishers was through, and the nine established English-language papers remaining threatened to shut out any department store advertising in the *Evening American.*[2]

In those early days, Hearst personally presided over his newest paper. Now that he was closer to his goal, he put away his checkered suits and donned a black slouch hat or fedora that contradicted the impression given by his reticent manner, high voice, and icy blue eyes.

Hearst's wealth was spent freely on scoops, but it was not bestowed on the *American* offices in the old building at 216 West Madison, where his staff rushed to put out multiple editions. As the most impulsive news publisher in the city, Hearst was known for running outside on a big story and giving a coachman a sizable tip to whip horses through downtown congestion. Once, when a makeup editor told him there was no time to reset the paper for a breaking story, Hearst shoved the form off the table and said as it crashed to the floor, "Now there is time to reset. There is always time to make a thing better."

Hearst found himself competing not only with Victor Lawson of the *Daily News* and the Patterson and McCormick families of the *Tribune*, but also with his former right-hand man, John Eastman of Ohio. After Eastman helped Hearst settle in Chicago, he borrowed sixty five thousand dollars to buy the Chicago *Journal* from a Detroit family.

For crimes and accidents, the writing-reporter of the 1890s had been replaced by reporters who called in notes to rewrite men or women. These were former reporters who now directed others to possible additional sources and sometimes made a few calls of their own to tie up loose ends. They then put the story together, often adding background from memory or from the clippings morgue, and the best of them could do it with style.

This system allowed newspapers to hire people with more street smarts than education. Their errors at Chicago papers over time included "new miracle order" (numerical), "his leg was decapitated at the knee," and that strippers taken into custody were wearing only "a little cheesecake on their breasts" (make that "cheesecloth"). Bill Doherty of the six Doherty brothers said one reporter called in a story in which a car "went off the road and struck a cul-

The six Doherty brothers at an undated event. All six boisterous men worked at various Chicago newspapers, but two of them became priests (Ed Baumenn collection).

prit." He meant culvert. More recently, newsman Ed Baumann said longtime reporter James Murray asked him how to spell "cyanide" because he was doing a story about "Mount Cyanide Hospital." Baumann made it "Mount Sinai."[3]

As a sign of things to come, reporter William Salisbury's first story at the newly founded *Evening American* was about the sinking of an old Lake Michigan tugboat. He made the mistake of turning in only the facts, with the result that a rewrite man hunched over a typewriter and had his way with them. "I didn't recognize my story, at first," Salisbury recalled. In convincing but imaginary detail, the piece was transformed into a tale of tugboat crewmen risking their lives to save their drowning cat. Salisbury was later laid off for turning in a fire story that failed to mention details carried by another paper—a rescue by firefighters forming a human ladder.[4] Since the fire had been in a one-story building, Salisbury understood the Hearstian message: use fiction if you must, but never let yourself be outdone.

Rather than relying on just reporters, Hearst's staff regularly paid off at least one nurse in each hospital, one bellboy in each hotel, one policeman in each precinct, nine of the eleven deputy coroners, and several chief telegraph operators. These people received a dollar or two a month as retainers and would call in anything of interest for a bonus. This was nothing new, Hearst was just doing it on a larger scale.

Eager for even more readers, "The Chief" started a morning paper in 1902, the Chicago *Examiner*, and seemed unconcerned that it usually lost money. Despite frequent hangovers, its first editor, Sam Chamberlain, always wanted to hear the clacking of Underwood No. 5's. During a lull, he would call out, "Get excited, everybody!" Over the next two decades, *Examiner* reporters would be among the most aggressive and creative in the city.[5]

Reporters eager for a sensational story sometimes forgot to check their facts, such as when George Pratt of the *Evening American* claimed in August 1903 that admired sharpshooter Annie Oakley of Buffalo Bill's Wild West Show had become a cocaine addict and was jailed for stealing clothes. The *Examiner* also carried the item, as did forty-three other papers across the country. But the story turned out to be a libelous "cover" to a scoop by Amy Leslie of the *Daily News* saying that Oakley had been scalded at a health resort bath. The cocaine user turned out to be a burlesque performer who had taken the name "Any Oakley." In possibly the most extensive litigation up to that time, the sharpshooter sued in numerous state courts and won judgments against all but one of the papers.[6]

Despite a mistake that might have ruined someone else, Pratt remained the *Evening American's* kind of man. He was clever, energetic, and, unlike older reporters, knew the value pictures added to a story. Hearst papers flaunted photographs of the sort that other broadsheets declined to use because they felt that they smacked of sensationalism.

In the winter of 1904–05, an editor assigned Pratt, cub reporter Jack Lait, and two others to look into the death of a man from a good family who had shot himself behind the steering wheel of his car. Autos were so new that the suicide was shocking. Lait, an ordinary-looking but energetic young man with glasses, stopped one of the deputy coroners outside his home and persuaded him to give an interview in the warmth of a saloon. With two reporters attending to his glass, the two other Hearst men lifted his briefcase with its photos and love letters. Victor Lawson of the *Daily News* accused Coroner John Traeger of selling out, and Traeger hurried to the *Evening American*'s office to demand an explanation. All the people he spoke to assured him that they never had the pictures and suggested he look for them in his own office.

The *Evening American* embarked on campaigns only when it suited The Chief. One of Hearst's campaigns was to unseat Circuit Court Judge Elbridge Hanecy for opposing the election of Hearst-supported Carter Harrison II to fill the shoes of his murdered father. The judge further set The Chief against him by ruling that an *American* commentary cartoon criticizing his judicial decisions amounted to contempt of court.

Hearst knew that Hanecy owed his office to West Side Alderman John Brennan. To get something on Brennan for his boss, in May 1904, Lait—later of the New York *Daily Mirror* and co-author of the spicy *Chicago Confidential* and *New York Confidential* books—grew a straggly beard and went to the Madison Street skid row district a short stroll from the Loop. Claiming to be from Kansas City, Lait found himself being encouraged to vote under four different names for fifty cents a ballot at each precinct he visited, with reporter William Stuart staying close to him as a witness. After Brennan tossed Lait a coin, the alderman was arrested, and the shaggy reporter was put under guard by Pinkerton detectives as a Hearst publicity stunt. Brennan went to prison, Hanecy was defeated, and the *Evening American* gained civic legitimacy.[7]

Also in 1904, Catherine O'Leary's son James equipped a large building near the stockyards as a bookie joint catering to bettors arriving on three "gambler special" trains from downtown. The police were bribed into not noticing the action, which was guarded by at least twenty dogs. "Big Jim" thought nothing could shut him down, but the *Journal* kept embarrassing public officials until he was arrested and fined seventeen hundred dollars.[8]

The stolid *Journal* under Eastman seems to have been read more as a supplement to livelier sheets such as the *Tribune* and *Daily News*. His facilities increased when he acquired George Booth's Chicago *Press* (formerly the *Mail*, 1885–1895), which ran news in short takes for busy readers—a forerunner of the tabloids. In keeping with this trend, Hearst editors imposed a rule set down by Arthur Brisbane, Hearst's language authority in New York: "If you don't hit the reader in the eye with the first sentence, don't bother to write the second."

Energetically keeping numerous papers going across America, The Chief was unaware how soon his presidential hopes would crash. When an assassin turned President McKinley into a martyr in 1901, readers remembered Hearst's vehement denunciations of McKinley's administration and turned against him. From then on, he generally ran his papers aloofly from his spacious California estate.

As for why a reporter dedicated to accuracy would join one of his journals: Hearst sometimes doubled the wages of people who crossed over. He also hired people with no experience, such as William Berns. As a boy, Berns ran away from home and was found sleeping between the huge *Evening American* newspaper rolls. He was taken on as a copyboy and was put "on the street," that is, made a crime reporter. He later founded a successful corporate coffee machine business.[9]

Because of funding limitations, the *Evening American* would send reporters to breaking events by streetcar instead of cab, and rather than deliver fresh news, would turn an exclusive from a rival paper into another kind of story, a practice called "covering" a scoop.

By now, the molds for reporter and city editor were completed, and their experiences were similar to what reporters would go through more than fifty years later, except that in the early days of the twentieth century they lived in an unplanned city overwhelmed by one and half million people.

The incorporation of several suburbs had left Chicago with thirteen streets named Washington. There were even eight 42nd Streets—and yet no street signs had been installed. Since the city administration had done nothing about the problem, in 1901, salesman Edward Brennan launched a thirty-year movement to standardize street names and establish State and Madison as base lines for address numbers. This was called "the world's busiest corner" simply because *Globe* managing editor Charlie Tuttle had claimed it was in the 1890s, after he and a reporter had studied pedestrian and vehicle traffic for several hours.[10]

Larzer Ziff, in his book *The American 1890s*, noted that since reporters worked for editors who steered clear of anything that might involve advertisers, they lived in a maze of suppressed and half truths. This, according to Ziff, led them to develop the twin defenses of cynicism, to prevent honest feelings from affecting their work, and sentimentality, to keep from losing their interest in human nature. Surely many news people seemed to enjoy their cynicism. As an editor told Theodore Dreiser, "Life is a God damned stinking, treacherous game, and nine hundred and ninety-nine men out of every thousand are bastards."[11]

When the century was young, reporters enjoyed the vicarious adventure of spending part of their days with police officers and firefighters, and seldom wondering whether what they did for a story was right or wrong. After all, an absence of ethics seemed outweighed by the good the papers were doing in civic reform, such as a disclosure following the death of artist's model Marie Denbach in a Chicago boarding house after five days of intestinal agony. An investigation into why her body was cremated so hastily showed that her physician and her fiancé had taken out five life insurance policies on her. Curious about why the coroner's jury had not suspected poisoning, the *Daily News* learned that Deputy Coroner John Weckler's inquest had been conducted before "six empty chairs." The paper reported this on June 2, 1901. His villainy exposed, Weckler disappeared and editor Henry Justin Smith—a slender man of quiet strength—sent reporters to find him. They learned he was hiding in his brother's cabin amid the Indiana dunes. Reporters also discovered that he had been conducting such non-inquests regularly so he could collect a one-dollar fee for each juror's name he invented.

2

Newspapers were just getting away from their political bias when something in a Newfoundland cliffside hut touched off a sequence of events that more than half a century later would challenge the papers' command of the public's attention. Holding an earphone against the side of his head on December 12, 1901, Guglielmo Marconi could make out only an "s" in words spoken to him through a microphone in England, but radio was born.

Unchallenged by the invention, papers might go all out on a story they considered their own, as the *Evening American* did in pursuing the "Car Barn Bandits." On August 30, 1903, an accountant and two clerks at the City Railway Company were shot to death with a new kind of weapon, an automatic pistol. Around Thanksgiving, minor criminal Gustav Marx aroused suspicion by carrying an automatic into a bar and flashing a roll of bills. During his arrest for being part of the gang, Marx was wounded as he drew his pistol. A few days later, detectives persuaded the bandaged suspect to re-enact his arrest for an *Evening American* photographer. But a short time later the lensman called his city desk from a police station phone and said, "This place has gone nuts!" Officers were scrambling out the door. A moment later an Illinois Central tipster notified the *American*'s wire chief that for some reason a special train was being put together at a downtown station on orders from city hall.

What was about to turn a good story into a great one was the touch of magic that some newspeople had. Wondering what all this bustle could be about, city editor Moses Koeningsberg remembered reading in the *Tribune* that Chicago police had spoken to some hoboes on the dunes about something and let them go. Why would Chicago police talk to people in an Indiana scrubland?

For Koeningsberg, news judgment meant gambling. He sent a telegrapher and every available reporter, regardless of his beat, to "Get on that I.C. train and keep us informed." He gave them the paper's entire emergency fund of nine hundred dollars.

Deputy Police Chief Herman Schluetter was upset when he learned that reporters were jumping onto the secret train, but he must have assumed they could do no harm since there were no telephone lines in the marsh and sand hills. Apparently only after arriving more than an hour and a half later did the *American* team learn that the robbers had just killed two detectives in Chicago, and that was why the station had "gone nuts."

The newspaper telegrapher climbed a pole and attached a wire for his Morse code key. After that, there was nothing to do but wait in the cold for something to happen. Suddenly, the surrounded bandits shot their way through a cordon of officers and fled into the wilderness. Clicking over the wire provided fresh headlines for each edition of the November 27, 1903, *Evening American* until the men were captured.[12]

The hellbent style of Chicago journalism coincided with the muckraking movement. Since the papers dared not disclose revolting and dangerous goings on at the Union stockyards on the South Side, it took the respected British journal *Lancet* to run articles exposing them. Amiable twenty-six-year-old writer Upton Sinclair of Baltimore and New Jersey visited the area long enough to take notes for his novel *The Jungle*.[13] "I aimed at the public's heart," he said after its 1906 publication, "and by accident I hit it in the stomach."

The *Tribune*, always protective of major business, tried to portray the book as a fraud, only to back away when its own investigator found that Sinclair could have made even grosser disclosures. The conditions that the Chicago papers had chosen to ignore led to the creation of federal pure food and drug laws.

But the most outrageous journalistic avoidance was an era of circulation wars that lasted on and off for a dozen years.

Not having the resources to cultivate a steady readership, the *Evening American* decided to use muscle. In 1902, Max Annenberg, one of two former newsboy brothers from the German state of East Prussia, went from the *Tribune* circulation department to similar work at the *American*. Soon bullies and ex-boxers pummeled newspaper sellers with blackjacks and brass knuckles. The thugs warned that unless all rival papers were put out of sight, their bundles would be hauled away and burned. If a news dealer asked what he was to do with stacks of the *American*, he was told, "Sell 'em or eat 'em." Newspapers were even sometimes pulled from the hands of streetcar riders.

The early fights were between the *Evening American* and the *Daily News*, with holier-than-thou Victor Lawson lying about not being involved. Out of professional courtesy, even competing sheets kept silent. Pedestrians seeing newspaper sellers being beaten apparently mistook the fights for private quarrels because nothing about them appeared in print.

The police virtually sanctioned the drubbings because of the political might of the two papers. Should the tactics sound familiar, some of these toughs, including Dion O'Banion and Mossy Enright, would take part in the bootleg wars that would make Chicago notorious in the twenties.

At twenty-five, barely-educated Annenberg was sharper than some executives at the *American*. He showed them how to publish the equivalent of today's local editions simply by changing the headlines on some press runs to emphasize a neighborhood angle, even when that story was on page seventeen. Despite his savvy, Annenberg was still a thug. When the city's leading department store, Marshall Field's, withdrew its ads from the undignified *Evening American*, Max led bruisers in shouting at terrified shoppers, "Marshall Field's is closed!" The ads quickly returned.[14]

In time, Max was aided by his tall, younger, and somewhat less violent brother, Moe, who would go on to earn a fortune with the *Daily Racing Form* and the Global News Bureau, a Chicago-based sports wire. One day, after being slugged by someone from the *Daily News*, Moe went inside Lawson's building, insisted on speaking to the circulation manager, and warned him that the next time he would take it out on him personally.[15]

Murder was not supposed to happen in this first stage of the circulation wars, but at least once it did. Moe Annenberg was trying to take over newspaper sales in a black neighborhood by bringing in a boxer already on the Hearst payroll and hiring eight rough men from the stockyards, where Southern blacks were routinely employed as strikebreakers. A man from Moe's team then called Lawson's circulation manager claiming to be the son of a well-known blind newsstand owner, and said that *American* ruffians had destroyed all his copies of the *Daily News*, so he needed replacements. When a delivery truck showed up with its own African American guards, one of them, named Clark, jumped down and made a menacing gesture. Someone from Moe's truck hit him and another shot Clark in the head. Moe's neighborhood circulation chief, Lawrence Finn, was indicted for murder but was acquitted after a defense by Clarence Darrow, who had made Chicago his home but had not yet become "the attorney for the damned." From then on, the area around 39th and State belonged to the *Evening American*.

During this time, the major dailies were ignoring the problems and interests of thousands of African Americans who had come to the city as factory workers, coal haulers, counter clerks, maids, doctors, railroad porters, and businessmen. The papers did not even notice when Robert Sengstacke Abbott of St. Simons Island, Georgia, son of slaves and stepson of a German-American merchant, founded the Chicago *Defender* on his landlord's dining table on May 5, 1905, "with," as legend has it, "twenty-five cents in his pocket."[16]

Lacking funds for reporters, Abbott made a weekly round of "Bronzeville" bars to pick up news even though he was not a drinking man. The paper was widely distributed by railroad porters and, in the South, by newsboys. At least one of them was arrested.

Once the weekly became a daily, it was the most widely read black newspaper in the country. Early editorials encouraged readers to help Southern migrants adjust to the hostile city, and this unofficially Republican paper slowly became a political force.

In November 1905, a sudden divorce allowed adventure writer Jack London of San Francisco to marry Charmain Kittredge while touring in Chicago. Promising exclusive coverage, London had the *Evening American* city editor use his contact book to wake up the license clerk and send him downtown to prepare a special license for a Sunday morning marriage, despite an Illinois law barring post-divorce quickies.[17]

A month later, James Walsh, the banker who sank large sums into the *Chronicle*, was about to make headlines. He had the sense to hire ace police reporter Frank Carson from City News but, once again running into financial difficulties with his paper, juggled the books of his other businesses. This led various financiers to hold an emergency meeting on December 17, 1905, over the impending failure of Walsh's two La Salle Street banks.

Tribune editor James Keeley, who had distinguished himself with his coverage of the Johnson County war, was leaving work that night when he became curious about lights still burning in the office level of the First National Bank building. A policeman guarding the door told him a business session was going on. Keeley slipped in, and when the financial experts recognized him he indicated that someone had sent for him. Once Keeley had enough for an exclusive, he yawned and went to the washroom. There he took off his coat and picked up a bucket as if to go for coffee. As soon as he was outside he sprinted to the *Tribune* building while wagon drivers were awaiting the final edition. He stopped the presses and turned in a story that drew the outrage of the U.S. attorney. As a result of the revelations, the *Chronicle* folded on May 31, 1907, and Walsh was eventually convicted of misappropriating funds. He was sentenced to five years in federal prison.[18]

The major papers in Chicago were trying to reflect society in general rather than embracing yellow journalism. The practice of scandal-seeking and ducking behind freedom of the press to make insinuations had started with Hearst's circulation battle with Pulitzer's New York *World* in the late eighteen nineties. The name came from "The Yellow Kid," a cartoon character appearing in both papers.

The *Evening American* was not very serious about its forays into sensationalism; its goal was merely to entertain readers with a sparkling first page, occasional contests, a galloping style, and color cartoons. The management of its more energetic sister paper, the *Examiner*, remained chaotic. Often-drunk Sam Chamberlain was only the first of what would be twenty-seven city editors there in a few years. One reason for the hectic turnover was that Hearst was using Chicago as a proving ground for talent, and would send the best employees to his other papers across the land.

This opportunity sometimes led reporters and city editors to toy with the facts, and authorities usually let them do it at a time when crime news had become even more important than at the turn of the century. One might think reporters would be an annoyance to investigators, but the relationship between them was generally friendlier than what it seems to have been in New York and Boston. Here is just one example:

An unknown *Examiner* city editor was complaining that his supervisors were not interested in the murders of several Italian immigrants near the Levee red light district, so reporter Charlie Johnson decided to make the crimes more intriguing. In those days when the police let favored newsmen do whatever they wanted with evidence, he supposedly planted an inside straight flush of spades in the limp hand of one victim, and let a rewrite man assume that this and several future killings were by the Black Hand, a feared early form of the Mafia.[19] The deceit may have happened, but colleagues were so fond of telling Charlie Johnson stories that one wonders how many of them were true.

Flamboyant as the Hearst papers were, The Chief was timid with strangers and needed to dictate relationships with his few friends. With the evaporation of his political dreams he was in Chicago only occasionally and might not have had much to do with the intermittent beatings between circulation crews. One thing we do know, however, is that he did not stop them.

Because of the *Evening American*'s support of city and county Democratic officials, the paper was so influential that it arranged some jail hangings in the afternoon instead of the morning for the convenience of its reporters. These events were usually well covered because they were held just outside the Loop. Since no telephones or telegraph keys were allowed, each paper had its own signaling system involving one reporter inside the jail, at 440 North Dearborn, and a second employee near an office phone. An *American* reporter perched where he could see the cell door swing open would wave a blue kerchief at a window. A reporter sitting by a "candlestick" phone in the state's attorney's room would see this and call his paper. No more than ten minutes later, the inside man would wave a red bandana, meaning the prisoner had entered the past tense.

On February 23, 1906, Chicago "Bluebeard" Johann Adolph Hoch was waiting in his cell probably thinking unkindly about the *American*. The already married man had wedded two more women and poisoned both for their money. Hoch might have gone on marrying and poisoning had city editor Moses Koeningsberg not been scanning burial permit notices. Koeningsberg thought the man's name seemed familiar, and asked a reporter to find out why. The reporter soon picked up neighborhood gossip that Hoch had come home with one bride after another. The paper turned this over to the prosecutor's office, leading to Hoch's capture in New York.

On the winter afternoon of his execution, the entire *American* staff was poised for action. A large blue bandana flashed at the jail window, and the presses began churning out seventy five thousand copies of a special edition, many destined for Milwaukee and other cities with a large German population. Amid the roar of getting out the extra, Koeningsberg wondered out loud, "What happened to the red handkerchief?"

A reporter in the city room snatched a phone and called the state's attorney's office. Just then a wire service announced that a writ of habeas corpus had been filed before U.S. District Judge Kenesaw Mountain Landis because Hoch had been tried for murder although he was extradited on a bigamy charge. Koeningsberg, who had sharpened his skills at Walsh's *Chronicle*, took a chance and said, "Keep 'em rolling."

What had happened was that there was no way the reporter covering the hanging could signal a last-minute stay, so he hurried out of his perch and followed the news instead. He learned that Hoch had been taken by carriage to the federal courthouse, only for the judge to turn down his appeal. The returned prisoner marched to the gallows accompanied by two ministers, cheating death by two and a half hours.[20]

A year after Illinois farm boy Edward Wyllis Scripps founded the reawakened United Press in 1907, the wire service opened a two-room Chicago office across Wells Street from the *Daily News*. One room was for telegraph operators sending and receiving dispatches from other parts of the country, and the other had a few old chairs and desks for writing and editing local stories.

But no wire service could match the energy of the papers. Reporters of the golden age were snappier than their counterparts in the era of political sheets. With the country enjoying a long peace, newspapers were the place to go for excitement and opportunities to use intelligence and competitive instincts. Consider the career of Walter Howey, the young man who had scooped the competition on the Iroquois Theatre fire.

At sixteen, Walter did odd jobs at his hometown paper in Fort Dodge, Iowa, and took charge as editor at nineteen. Shortly afterward, an anarchist shot President McKinley in Buffalo. Howey immediately called the private home where McKinley lay near death on September 6, 1901. Unlike other reporters, he knew that the owner's family would never consent to an interview and so he asked to speak to the butler instead. "The moment the President dies," Howey said, "I wish you would telegraph me collect." The teenager added that he would be wiring him ten dollars as a retainer as soon as he hung up. As Howey waited, he wrote up an obituary with background material on Vice President Theodore Roosevelt, who would succeed the president. On September 14, the excited butler forgot to telegraph and called Howey about McKinley's last moments, several hours before the White House announced the death. Wire services credited the teenage Iowa editor with the scoop.

Such enterprise might have won Howey a newspaper job anywhere else, but not in Chicago. When he went to the *Daily News* he tried to bluff about his knowledge of the city. The editor sent him to "the intersection of Jackson and Washington Boulevards." After running around, Howey came back saying those streets ran parallel. With a laugh the editor recommended that he gain experience at City Press first.

The City Press Association, which would be renamed the City News Bureau in 1910, operated like a mini-newspaper and was powered by cardboard quart cylinders of coffee. The rewrites labored on waxed sheets, which were edited with a stylus rather than a pen. Instead of presses running off thousands of copies of stories, copyboys mimeographed just enough for house reference and one for each of the ten newspapers then represented on the board of directors, including, for a time, the *Staats-Zeitung*, the German-language sheet.

The wire service had delivered copy by hand until 1898, when it started to send stories in canisters through pneumatic tubes running under downtown streets. City News editors could be as exacting as at the papers, but, because salaries were so small, they were more forgiving. Not that they sounded that way. A City News "graduate" usually could jump into newspaper work without much additional training.

After scooping the papers with the Iroquois Theatre fire, Howey left City News for a major opening at the *Inter-Ocean.* At twenty-four, he was one of the youngest editors of a full-sized American daily. But the paper was limping toward a demise. Felonious Charles Yerkes had operated the "I-O" until all his traction legislation was approved, and then handed it over to managing editor George Hinman.

With Hinman's takeover came an electric light plant in the Loop to pay the cost of running the paper. The gift drew the ire of power company magnate Samuel Insull and Mayor Fred Busse, a supporter of the *Tribune*. Not giving up the plant without a fight, Hinman had Howey dig up the dirt on Busse to make him back off. What followed were two months of what a later *Time* magazine article called "burglary, bribery, and tireless sleuthing." When Howey had all he needed, he took the notes from his black suitcase and filled his articles with city hall shenanigans, possibly contributing to Busse's unexpected death from natural causes not long afterward.

Howey was too good for the *Inter-Ocean*, and the *Tribune* snatched him up at four times his salary. There he exposed venereal disease quacks by sending them a healthy reporter with a planted bank book in his pocket. Each doctor he visited snooped into his clothes during a physical examination and charged the "patient" whatever was listed as his savings.

Wherever the diminutive Howey went he seemed to be hiding behind a scowl, but he could tap out stories rapidly. To save time, he might write up a planned event before it happened and add details afterward.[21]

On some slow evenings Howey and *Tribune* reporter John Kelley dropped by the Everleigh Club, the most elaborate brothel in the Levee. The place had a floor of mirrors and three separate string orchestras. Both newsmen told colleagues they went there to hear the music. An assistant *Tribune* city editor once needed extra help when a major fire broke out in the early morning, perhaps the deadly stockyards fire of 1910. To round up a staff, he dialed the Everleigh Club at Calumet 412.[22]

3

A new police reporter usually started his night at the First Precinct station, in the former Sands red light district across the river from downtown. After about three hundred thieves, robbers, and hookers jammed into the station daily during the Columbian Exposition, William Stead described the building as a "reeking, filthy place." Newsmen serving their time there included humorist Finley Peter Dunne, editor James Keeley, future U.S. Secret Service chief John Wilkie, and respected journalist Henry Barrett Chamberlain, who would head the Chicago Crime Commission.

Cub reporters spending an hour or two at the crumbling building kept an eye on the hundreds of jottings in the desk sergeant's complaint book, then phoned anyone who might be involved in the more interesting cases, or they called their editor for permission to visit the neighborhood if the story was more promising.

Reporters went to police headquarters in the former P. W. Peck home, at LaSalle and Washington, at around seven o'clock at night because that was when the "press book" was usually ready. This was a log of each day's crimes and accidents, as turned in by the precincts. But every precinct kept a "squeal book" not to be shown to reporters because it listed crimes still under investigation, such as premeditated murders and major con games. Kelley said his colleagues would steal the information by inviting the desk sergeant to have a drink and then slipping a cigar to whoever took his place.[23]

When people bought a newspaper in this period to learn about a shameful crime, check the stock market, or look for jobs, they had no idea of the bruising competition for their attention. After hostilities with the *Daily News* eased, the *Evening American* opened a second circulation war when Hearst gunmen hijacked a *Tribune* delivery truck in 1907 and hurled its hundreds of pounds of newspapers into the Chicago River. This began two years of scuffles between hooligans from both papers, but no stories of major attacks have come down to us.[24]

Behind the upsurge was Hearst's longtime San Francisco friend, Andrew Lawrence, an expert at using newspapers to extort favors. While Lawrence was working in Chicago, the *American* looked good because it was disclosing minor public fraud, but Lawrence was actually reminding price-gouging utilities and sticky-fingered politicians what would happen to them unless they delivered favors for his paper. The juiciest stories dug up by *American* reporters were said to have remained in Lawrence's vault.[25]

The year of Lawrence's arrival, (Joseph) Medill McCormick, elder brother of future long-time *Tribune* publisher Robert R. McCormick, gave up his interest in the Cleveland *Leader* and returned to Chicago to head the family paper even though his eyes were on the U.S. Senate. The good-looking, slender, and prematurely balding man considered himself a progressive despite views reflecting the general conservatism of the Medill-McCormicks. The Medill-McCormicks were not suited for the real world, and their forays into public service never lasted long or meant anything other than to themselves. These descendents of publishers Joseph Medill and Cyrus McCormick had come to regard one of the largest papers in America not so much as their birthright as something they were raised to protect against anything that might challenge or weaken it.

With alcoholic (Joseph) Medill McCormick losing control, stronger minds began to take over the *Tribune*, and they were eager to challenge Hearst. How this came about has become clear only recently.

(Joseph) Medill McCormick, who never used his first name, was showing what Richard Norton Smith, a biographer of his brother, Robert, regarded as possible manic-depression, but it may have been just a failure of certainty. He was, after all, caught between infighting at the board of directors and the dictates of his mother, Kate McCormick, whose determination and business sense were but incompletely copied in her sons. His idea of leadership was an avoidance of confrontation. He suffered his first breakdown in 1906, and Kate immediately thought not of him, but of the fate of the paper. Smith observed that the *Tribune* was "perhaps the only thing that coldly manipulative woman was truly capable of loving."[26] No doubt that at this time it would have been stronger in the hands of the women of the family.

While (Joseph) Medill McCormick was away, Robert Patterson, the late Joseph Medill's son-in-law, was in charge of the paper, but usually had authority conflicts with his strong-minded editor, James Keeley. Whenever Patterson made a suggestion, Keeley would reject it simply for the sake of refusing to be dominated. Patterson died from "apoplexy," the cover explanation his family gave for an overdose of Veronal (hypnotic barbital), in Philadelphia just hours after the death of his mother, and Keeley took over without a change in job title. His contributions are a little unclear because references to him were obliterated or falsified after his defection to a rival paper, but Keeley managed to keep the *Tribune* robust at a time when the owning families were stumbling about and sneering at one another. His management style was so aloof that he was never known to speak directly to his reporters, choosing instead to address them through an assistant.[27]

Keeley probably never knew what would happen next in the office amid conflicting egos and families. This can be seen in the case of the Little Red Book. In 1909, (Joseph) Medill McCormick decided to make public the names of leading citizens receiving rents from brothels, as had been done in England. This slender volume, with names supplied by the state's attorney's office, was to be padlocked in the city editor's desk until (Joseph) Medill gave word to print it. But then he and Keeley squabbled over something and Keeley went on a vacation, supposedly to Japan.

In Keeley's absence, (Joseph) Medill decided that he and his more confident brother, Robert Rutherford McCormick, should no longer be affiliated with the same paper. The board of directors offered (Joseph) Medill thirty thousand dollars a year to take a long vacation, and in response he had another breakdown. When Keeley returned, (Joseph) Medill greeted him in an opera hat, gave him a manly hug, and walked out with the Little Red Book— apparently to keep his brother from claiming the scoop. The names were never published.[28]

(Joseph) Medill had insinuated that he might leave the paper for good, claiming that Eastern investors were trying to win him over. Sensing instability at the advertising-rich paper, Victor Lawson of the *Daily News* tried to scare the company into a ten-million-dollar merger by intimating he might drop the price of his two-cent *Record-Herald* in order to compete with Hearst. The effect on the two-cent *Tribune* would be devastating.

At a secret meeting, John Schaffer of the Chicago *Post* told (Joseph) Medill that he wanted majority interest in the *Tribune*. This would have been better than giving in to Lawson, but Kate McCormick urged her younger son, Robert, to leave the sanitary district and come to the rescue. Robert agreed, if only because running a paper would let him play politics without risking defeat. As editor, he successfully campaigned for his mentally erratic brother's 1918 bid for the U.S. senate, where (Joseph) Medill did little more than keep a chair warm.

While stockholders dithered, two dissimilar cousins in the family—Robert McCormick, who had been called "Bertie" since childhood, and Joseph Patterson, the often-brooding son

Robert R. "The Colonel" McCormick stabilized the management of the Chicago *Tribune* and made the paper a national conservative voice. Like his grandfather Joseph Medill, he unsuccessfully tried to reform English spelling (Chicago History Museum, ICHi-14792).

of the late Robert Patterson—acted on good terms as they jointly took over. But unlike Kate McCormick, Robert's aunt, Elinor "Nellie" Patterson, felt no obligation to speak kindly about anybody. "The two owners are the weakness of the property," she grumbled.

Despite this fragility, editor Keeley, perhaps encouraged behind the scenes by Kate McCormick, decided that the paper was strong enough to renew its circulation war against Hearst, and this time would play dirty.

As the first step, in late 1909 the *Tribune* offered Walter Howey, then making eighty dollars a week at the *Evening American*, eight thousand dollars a year to cross over. Next, it tantalized *American* circulation director Max Annenberg with a twenty thousand dollar salary if he could guarantee increased *Tribune* circulation. He apparently was given a free hand.[29] In late February or early March 1910, Keeley was named chief managing editor of the *Tribune*, which he pretty much had been for some time. The understanding was that he would only be keeping the spot open for someone from the Medill-Patterson-McCormick families. Yet, he would later insist under oath that during this time "My authority was absolute."[30]

When Hearst eventually sued the defecting Annenberg for breach of contract, a court would declare that the *Tribune* agreement with him had been invalid because it was a compact to commit illegal acts.[31] But it was under this pact that the *Tribune* declared war on Hearst in October 1910 by dropping its price to a penny, matching that of The Chief's morning paper, the *Examiner*.

With Annenberg gone, sporty Hearst henchman Andrew Lawrence assured his bosses that he could round up men who were just as rough as those of the *Tribune*. Both papers budgeted approximately one million dollars for the battle, expecting to recoup their expenditures through increased circulation and therefore advertising money.

The *Tribune* called its tavern toughs its "wrecking crew." Annenberg handed out guns for self-defense, and they drove around in what was then called "an automobile truck," the equivalent of a modern van. After *Examiner* circulation workers were shot at, they staged an ambush by using a decoy truck and then firing at *Tribune* men about to attack it. One battle was said to have involved about sixty men.[32]

The usually non-crusading *Inter-Ocean* demanded indictments, but nothing was done because State's Attorney Maclay Hoyne, a former police chief, answered to the *Tribune*, and Police Chief John McWeeney was beholden to Hearst. Reporters were never involved, except that they could not turn in stories on the increasingly violent sluggings.

Also never involved was the small City News Bureau, which competed on major local stories with its newspaper-owners. But its primary purpose was to save them from wasting resources on matters of only passing interest. One of its daily duties was to supply them with lists of people who had died under unknown or unexpected circumstances. A City News reporter would pick the

names up from the coroner's office and then make calls on the more interesting cases.

One day when Edward Doherty was still a copyboy, switchboard operator, and writer at the City News Bureau for six dollars a week, Leroy F. "Buddy"
McHugh phoned in.

"Hello, Edward," Buddy said, "here's the stiffs." Actually, there was only one
name this time, which was unusual. "Got your pencil ready? Lucy Doherty. Three
years old. Daughter of Lieutenant James E. Doherty of the East Chicago Avenue
station. Died at Saint Elizabeth's Hospital. Burns. Edward, this little girl was getting up in a chair to light the gas. Her home, 1425 North Central Park Avenue.
The match fell on her cotton dress. They put out the fire, but I guess the kid swallowed some of the flames. The coroner says her lungs were burned out."

"O.K., Buddy," Doherty said and hung up. What else could he say upon
learning of the death of his baby sister? He wrote the story and was excused
for the day.[33]

Doherty, destined to become one of the city's best-liked reporters, learned
that writing was just as important as reporting after he settled in at the *Record-
Herald.* On April 21, 1910, he saw reporter Jack Lawson ponder over a lead for
a local obituary on Mark Twain, who had just died in his Connecticut home.
Jack not only had a leonine head, he paced the floor like a caged lion while
searching for an arresting opening sentence. Then he had it: "Tom Sawyer and
Huckleberry Finn are orphans."[34]

At around 5 A.M. that December 22, Edward Doherty was working in the
detective bureau, which had been jerry-rigged into a seedy former hotel at 179
LaSalle Street. An alarm at the stockyards came in from Fire Marshal James
Horan, who would sign off every message with the signature code of one ...
one ... one. Soon came the code for a three alarm, followed by a signature code
of one ... one ... two.

"Call your office, you little fool," old-timer Ray Beckman told Doherty,
"tell 'em Horan's dead."

"How do you know?"

"Didn't you hear that signature? That wasn't Horan. That was Sayferlich,
Horan's chief assistant. He wouldn't dare sign that message if Horan were on
the job."

Indeed, Horan and twenty-one of his men had just perished battling
flames from a loading dock. Debris from an exploding building had fallen on
them in what remains the Chicago fire department's greatest loss of life.[35]

(Joseph) Medill McCormick returned to his family's paper and was named
president of the Tribune Company on March 1, 1911. This made him personally responsible for continuing the circulation war now that it had reached the
killing stage. But he would later swear under oath that he held no position on
the paper that year.

As if raising a flag over a castle, the *Tribune* copyrighted "The World's

Greatest Newspaper," a phrase James Keeley had already been using in advertising, and the motto first appeared on the masthead on August 29, 1911.[36] That also was the year the *Tribune* opened a paper mill in Canada to compete with the discount Hearst was receiving for buying huge amounts of newsprint for his papers nationwide.

Even if Keeley had encouraged the brutal competition over street sales at the start, he was growing tired of the intrafamily bickering of the owners. Just an hour or so after he reluctantly signed a new contract with the *Tribune* that year, Lawson's news editor, Charlie Faye, showed up with an offer to work at the *Daily News* or its sister paper, the *Record-Herald*. Keeley learned only later that he would have been notified in time to switch allegiance if only "Pop" Faye had not stopped at the Chicago Athletic Club to play billiards.

The only paper daring to cover the renewed war between the *Tribune* and the *Examiner* was the Chicago *Daily Socialist*. Referring to these accounts, Ferdinand Lundberg stated in *Imperial Hearst* that the acts included kidnapping newsboys off the street to beat them in private, and shooting up the Wellington Avenue elevated station to frighten a female anti–Hearst newspaper seller. No one was arrested for any of the serious beatings or shootings. But not even the supposedly independent Associated Press reported what was going on, because it had become dominated by Chicago editors. Outside papers pretended not to notice.

The attacks started appearing in the papers only after the circulation wars began to ease in 1912 and 1913, and too many people were wondering why the violence they had seen was not carried in the news. Even then, the circumstances were falsified to blame a fictitious union dispute.

At least a few details came out when the Chicago *Journal of Commerce* sued the Tribune Company for interfering with its newsstand sales. In 1921, Robert R. McCormick hesitantly testified that from 1910 through 1912 about twenty-seven men and newsboys had been killed in the unpublicized clashes. This did not include the earlier killing of a man named Clark.

Murdered circulation department employees included "Dutch" Gentlemen of the *Examiner*'s wrecking crew. Petty gangster Maurice "Mossy" Enright of the *Tribune* circulation department had walked into a State Street saloon, put a gun to Dutch's abdomen, and fired point blank. Another wrecking crew member, Nick Altman, was killed in cold blood at the bar in the Briggs House hotel, a Hearst employee hangout.[37] *Tribune* officials were unable to explain why the paper carried nothing on the murders if, as they said, unions were responsible.

4

With the Hearst papers featuring full pages of photos of crime scenes and victims, good picture-thieves were the envy of their papers, and not even an attempted presidential assassination could stop them.

As Teddy Roosevelt was leaving a Milwaukee hotel to make a speech on October 14, 1912, fanatic John Schrank shot him in the chest, ostensibly to stop him from seeking a third term. The slug came near Roosevelt's spinal column. The crowd pounced on the gunman but the president asked that the man be brought before him. "Poor creature," Roosevelt said and then insisted on continuing to the meeting hall for his address. But at a Chicago stopover on his train ride to New York, the wounded Roosevelt was given an escort to Mercy Hospital.

Examiner reporter Kent Hunter lurked around the institution but could not get past the building guards. He went outside and noticed the flickering bluish light of an X-ray lab in use. Hunter crept up a fire escape and waited until a doctor left, then slipped inside and took a plate from a drying rack. He sneaked out of the room, hurried down the fire escape, and cut his pants hopping over a wall, but the X-ray picture caused a sensation. Later writer-reporter Robert J. Casey offered a post script to the story. He said that two months later a doctor friend told Hunter the X-ray probably showed a six month fetus.[38]

Tribune editor James Keeley was saying "the day of 'fine writing' is past," referring to the Victor Lawson tradition of magazine-style composition. Keeley, whose own writing was stiff, added that the modern emphasis was now on accuracy rather than expression. What had been foisted on readers as fine writing in the lesser papers had included some dreadful phrasing, such as when Walter Wardrop of the *Inter-Ocean* supposedly described firefighters as conducting "an aqueous assault on the igneous outbursts."[39]

In November 1912, the *American* moved a block down from its old headquarters to a ten-story building purchased from the Marshall Field estate at 326 West Madison Street. This officially became the Hearst Building. But when in Chicago The Chief, no longer dreaming of the presidency, spoke to his reporters at nearby Union Station.

One of the few Toddlin' Town reporters ever killed getting a story was agreeable Jim McCabe. The *Examiner* had suspected that a county official was engaged in fraud, so "Sunny Jim" hid in a county building storeroom to eavesdrop on a private conversation. He somehow came in contact with an exposed wire and died instantly.[40]

A startling disclosure about the *Tribune* in these rough-and-tumble times came when U.S. Senator William Lorimer was under attack by the paper. He persuaded the Congressional committee investigating him to look also into the criminal element of his accuser. Keeley was called to testify because he had taken over after Robert Patterson, Jr., committed suicide in Philadelphia.

Keeley, hailed by his biographer as the city's greatest reporter, conceded the cover-up of a vicious assault that was not directly related to the circulation war. His backtracking testimony suggests that the attack may have been even more serious than he was admitting.

A fired circulation department employee returned to the *Tribune* at Dearborn and Madison in a pay dispute sometime around 1913, Keeley said, but he could not be specific. Using the word "we" to mean the Tribune Company rather than himself or any other individual, the British Keeley said, "we killed a man, or a man was killed, in an elevator shaft five or six years ago." A few sentences later he amended this to say "not killed," but "He was beaten up, thrown down an elevator shaft, and shot at.... I say, he was on the mailing floor, the first floor below the street level, and he was thrown to the pressroom floor, the second floor below the street level.... I left Chicago that day.... Not because of that, Judge, no."

When asked to elaborate, Keeley said: "Some pressmen or stereotypers picked up this man and took him over to the big washbasin there, and started to wash the blood off him; and the fellow who was after him came down after him with a gun and shot at him," but, the editor added, the bullet missed.

"And no prosecution of any kind was made against him by complaint, indictment, or otherwise?" Judge Hanecy of the Congressional committee asked. "By either the *Tribune* or any of its officers or employees?"

"No, sir."

Keeley then denied that competition among the papers was behind any previously disclosed deaths, and he took the line probably advised by company lawyers that organized labor was behind them. There was never a circulation war, he would have the judge believe.

"(V)arious unions in one trade have been split, one side has been fighting with the other," he maintained, "and as a matter of fact, in the last year, they have had gangs of murderers out. ... and they have been killing on both sides."[41] He did not name the unions.

Keeley may have personified the company line, but privately he chafed at the continual power struggles between conservative Robert Rutherford McCormick, yet to be called "The Colonel," and his somewhat more liberal cousin, Joseph Patterson.

An acquaintance described Patterson as a "clear-eyed, well-mannered, intelligent, unaggressive, eager-to-learn young man," and pictures show someone with good features even into early middle age. He was an idealist and never a realist. Patterson grew irritable when he could not carry out reforms, and to distance himself from other privileged sons he sometimes picked fights in bars.[42]

Both of these grandsons of Joseph Medill brought their petty grudges to the paper when it was at its weakest point since 1850. But they pretended to have common interests and drafted what they called an "iron bound agreement" pledging to work together. That is, with a few strokes of a grease pencil, an early form of marker, they declared themselves free of Kate and Nelley's control.[43] The only lasting result was an expansion of the Sunday edition with an emphasis on family features, short stories by popular authors, and—Patterson's specialty—comics.

As the Chicago population surpassed two million by 1910, the *Tribune* grew with it. The paper, which had begun in a single room above a pony powering the press, now had fourteen hundred employees, including guest columnists. Celebrated actress Lillian Russell was hired in 1911 to submit beauty tips. When she mused about life in general, as the *Inter-Ocean* had allowed her to, an editor wired Russell: "Write less about soul and more about pimples." Whether because of this or some other slight, she harrumphed that the paper was hostile to women, and from then on sent her advice to the *Record-Herald*.[44]

Starting on May 1, 1912, previously overlooked organized labor at the papers asserted itself with a dispute over the number of men working on the eight large presses in the Hearst Building. The company locked out the *Examiner* pressmen and called it a strike. As the stoppage spread, the strikers were joined by members of the Newspaper Delivery Drivers', Newsboys', and the Stereotypers' unions, and the Chicago Publishers Association refused to let labor leader Samuel Gompers intervene. Rather than hamstring his paper, Hearst broke the long deadlock by recognizing the Chicago Pressmen's Association, and soon Lawson led negotiations that would improve employee relations for years at the *Daily News*.[45]

As an outsider at the *Tribune*, Keeley must have felt his quarreling bosses stayed awake nights thinking up ways to pry him from the city editor's chair. The three-way tug of war ended after someone apparently whispered in Robert R. McCormick's ear and "Bertie" sprang on the stockholders some proxies slyly obtained from Bostonians whose predecessors once owned part of the *Tribune* before Medill and Dr. Ray took over.[46]

With no longer a way of remaining in charge, Keeley wrote a glowing appraisal of his value, left it in his typewriter, and stamped out of the building just before midnight in the spring of 1914. A few steps led him to the Washington Street offices of Lawson's neglected paper, the *Record-Herald*. There must have been rejoicing because the vastly experienced Keeley had arrived not only as its editor but as its future publisher.[47] That story, however, will have to wait.

Joseph Patterson returned to the family paper after accompanying the Marines on a slow chase after revolutionary Pancho Villa in Mexico, and took over the editorial office Keeley had deserted. Patterson surely was out of place in the city's most conservative paper. He admired the writings of left-leaning Jack London and went to the opera in a lumberman's shirt. But hardly a true liberal, he editorialized that the infirm and unfit should be killed to eliminate the burden on others.[48] Patterson also could act like an angry child when thwarted, and, in one snit, fired all the people he had hired.

Who would think that Hearst would be the better publisher? While the *Tribune* continued the "write like Charles Dickens" tradition, The Chief thought nothing of bringing in outsiders such as James Arthur Pegler of Minneapolis, father of future influential columnist Westbrook Pegler, as an authority on modern newspaper phrasing.

Pegler could have been mistaken for a financier with his cane, gloves, and cutaway coat. This beanstalk of a man was just as hard inside as he looked, and he seemed to dislike—that is, not understand—anyone outside the news business. Pegler's main task was to teach the locals Hearst's "trick style" of terse factual writing blended with descriptive phrasing. This was nothing more than journalese asking to be mistaken for literature, and in time would be absorbed by crime noir fiction. Eventually Hearst and Pegler had a falling out, and the Twin Cities man was glad to amble over to the Chicago *Journal*.[49]

As always, the behavior of some newspaper executives was unworthy of their reporters, who at times were exhausting themselves with eleven-hour days, six days a week. Readers never remembered their everyday stories, but Edward Doherty has given us a glimpse of how such events were covered in his ten years at various Chicago papers:

—As the son of Police Lieutenant Butch Doherty, Edward was allowed to ride in a wagon as officers chased robbers on the run. The horses galloped over a wooden sidewalk and into a vacant lot, where Edward was pitched into the tall weeds. When he climbed to his feet and asked why the wagon driver had made such a reckless turn, the Irish officer replied, "Sure it wasn't myself I thought of, nor was it Biddy and the kids, it was the horses."

—Edward, who had entered journalism from a monastery, put a gun in his pocket before helping the police search Clark Street gambling dens and "sporting houses" for a man who had wounded an officer. Unsuccessful in his hunt, he went to the hospital to interview the dying victim's guard, and a little later his own father showed up. "None of my boys [officers under him] ever went like this," Butch Doherty sadly told him. "They got it the easy way. Thank God." Edward said it was the only time he saw his father cry.

—Racing against a deadline, Edward hired a cab to take him twenty miles to north suburban Lake Forest for the names of the dead and injured in a train wreck. By then it was just past midnight and everyone was gone. Needing to speak with someone in authority, he stood on the street and shouted, "Help! Police! Murder! Fire!" An officer came running with beer foam on his mustache, and Edward asked to be taken to the lockup for the night. After being fined ten dollars for disturbing the peace, Doherty learned that the newspaper would not reimburse him. "A real reporter doesn't get arrested," Howey told him.[50]

In modern eyes, newspaper tactics in the early years of the twentieth century entailed unconscionable acts. But reporters viewed them as part of a game as they competed with their friends and rivals, just as the papers were competing with one another. The more experienced reporters learned ways that worked better for them than for others, such as women who wept with relatives of victims or men who posed as salesmen, canvassers, and even beggars. Another ploy was speaking quietly when interviewing people who had too much to drink, because concentration helped them sober up.

Handsome Wallace Smith (real name Schmidt) of the *American* once obtained a confession by using details from police reports to reconstruct events mentally, something other reporters never bothered with. When Smith went over with one prisoner how the crime must have occurred, the man admitted everything.

Smith was one of the few reporters who apparently not only looked but also wrote and acted liked an ideal member of the profession in the days when laws were commonly flouted—such as the way he scooped his friends after a verdict was reached in the trial of a man accused of killing a woman in a graveyard. He went to the roof of the stone criminal courthouse, held onto the overhanging eaves more than fifty feet above the sidewalk, and leaned upside down to the jury room window as Edward Doherty stood behind him. Smith laughed so hard when a Civil War veteran shouted at the other jurors "You are eleven of the stubbornest sons of darkness I ever met in all my life!" that he lost his balance and Doherty had to grab him, probably becoming the first news anchor.

Edward's talent for features won him a promotion to rewrite. "You're off police," an editor told him. "You'll miss that. Well, kids grow up. And adventure dies."[51]

It was Smith who cautioned Doherty against letting work overcome him just because he had a mortgage and a wife. "Be careful, or you'll lose your enthusiasm," the older man said. "You'll be reaching into the old mental files and pulling out lead number seven or lead number twenty-nine, or whatever lead you need for each new story. That's fatal, Irisher. You're not getting any fun out of life."[52]

Smith had plenty of fun in his own life over the next few years. He went on Pershing's expedition against Pancho Villa, quit the news business, and helped his friend Ben Hecht write the hit MGM movie *Viva Villa*.

At the time Smith left Chicago, Doherty came under the wing of Walter Howey at the *Tribune*. The little editor could be a hellion inside the office, but outside he seemed unthreatening with his polka-dot bow tie, pressed suit, shiny shoes, and dabs of cologne. One day he told Doherty to tighten his articles, which meant snipping parts and rearranging others. "Edward," Howey said, "you'll write your best story with a pair of scissors and a bottle of paste."

Sometimes Howey would have a copyboy take a City News story and its many unconnected inserts (later additions) for Doherty to rewrite "in fifty words or less." Another time the dapper editor might advise, "Play it up. That story's good for a column," meaning just over a thousand words.

A pattern was emerging that the *Tribune* hired some of the best talent in the city only to lose it because of a lack of local news focus. For two years the paper had the energetic team of short city editor Walter Howey and tall associate editor Frank Carson. Reporter-politician Dwight Green, who would work under both men, said, "There was a combination! As a team they were the most terrific thing that happened to Chicago since Mrs. O'Leary's cow kicked over the lamp." But dissatisfied with his salary and bosses, Carson left for the *Examiner* in 1914.

The streets saw only sporadic fighting between newspaper wrecking crews that year, but burly circulation chief Max Annenberg remained the *Tribune's* cock of the walk. He was courageous, a little uncouth, and aggressively friendly, thumping female stenographers on the rump as he strode toward his carpeted office. Wanting class, he wore turtleneck sweaters and kept his checkered cap at a tilt. He also learned to play golf just like the newspaper executive he practically was. (In the nineteen eighties, his family established the Max Annenberg Foundation to support nonprofit groups in the United States and other countries.)

When Keeley walked over to the *Record-Herald* after deserting the *Tribune* in the spring of 1914, he considered the publication only half a newspaper. His plan was to expand the capacity of this sheet with presses from the financially crippled *Inter-Ocean*. The outward transactions involved suggest that a number of private meetings were held beforehand. But rather than attending bondholder meetings for the two papers, Keeley sailed to Algeria.

Former owner Herman Kohlsaat had been appointed receiver of the I-O in March, letting editor George Hinman, as holder of a majority of its six hundred thousand dollars in bonds, assume control while creditors worked out some kind of arrangement.

At the same time, Lawson, who had three million dollars invested in the *Record-Herald,* was eager to get rid of the paper before it incurred even greater losses. The *Daily News* publisher met with creditors in Keeley's absence and they agreed to sell the paper to him.

In the next step, Hinman immediately appeared in federal receiver court in the late afternoon of May 8, 1914, and bought the *Inter-Ocean* for a token price of fifty thousand dollars. He immediately cabled Keeley that he could have the paper for an undisclosed sum, which involved some way of liquidating its assets.

The actions had been approved by the I-O bondholders, including the Marshall Field estate, and the money was provided by three powerful men: Lawson, Ogden Armour of the meatpacking family, and a personal friend— electricity tycoon Samuel Insull. According to Keeley, he managed to purchase both ailing papers free of debt.

The I-O presses were moved into the *Record-Herald* building on Washington Street, and the once-worthy but now exhausted *Inter-Ocean* ceased to exist. The revivified paper was named simply the Chicago *Herald*. Although the city was brimming with news talent, Keeley chose as his editor W. W. Chapin of the *Seattle Post-Intelligence* and the *San Francisco Call.*

But Keeley's news sense had been blunted by years of *Tribune* backbiting, and in the four years that he headed the *Record* it drifted into such soft content as friendly editorials and poems for children. His excuse was that he was rejecting yellow journalism.

Kohlsaat was finally out of the publishing business but he would live until late 1924, the last few years in failing health. As he awaited death he spoke most fondly of counting Teddy Roosevelt, William McKinley, Howard Taft, Woodrow Wilson, and Warren G. Harding among his friends.

The outbreak of the Great War in August 1914 had no immediate effect on the city. But Lilian Bell, a former Chicago reporter living out West with her Army major father, had a disturbing thought only a few days later: "Oh, God, what about the children?" She envisioned a ship bringing Christmas and Hanukkah toys to families in all the warring countries from England to Russia.

When no one took her seriously, Bell sent her idea to Keeley at the Chicago *Herald*, and, as she was darning a sock, a Western Union boy arrived with a telegram reading: "Can you get on a train?" Bell leased an apartment in the city and wrote a front page editorial seeking donations. Keeley persuaded President Wilson to offer a coal ship, and the *Herald* formed a syndicate of papers wanting to carry Bell's running account. The effort by then had come under the auspices of the Red Cross.

People across the country either bought toys for the mission or, as was the case with inmates at Joliet state prison, made them. More than thirty railroads offered to carry the freight for free, and Wells Fargo and American Express lent their delivery trucks. In all, at least five million gifts crammed the hold of the *USS Jason*, and around the deck were numerous Christmas trees to be handed out. The ship sailed from New York on November 14, flying a white flag featuring a golden star and the word "Inasmuch" (from "Inasmuch as ye have done it unto the least of these brethren, ye have also done it unto me").[53]

The *USS Jason*. The United States Navy donated this coal ship in 1914 to a Chicago *Herald* charity to deliver holiday toys and Christmas trees to families overseas during World War I (courtesy United States Navy).

It was ironic that a city which produced such humanitarianism had just seen murderous circulation wars. The violence had been over a single penny, the lowered price of the *Tribune*. But by the time the street fights ended in 1915, the paper had the highest readership in the city, and additional features and comic strips helped keep it at the top for years.

Also in 1915, *Tribune* editors had a tiff with newly elected Mayor William "Big Bill" Thompson, a fellow Republican. From that day on they printed the worst photo of the tall, homely man they could find every time he made news.

Despite all Keeley had done to head his own paper, the *Herald*, he could not stay interested in it. Hearst bought the paper from him on May 1, 1918, and combined it with his own *Examiner,* creating possibly the most vigorous broadsheet in the city at the period between the world wars.

5

Without doubt, Floyd Gibbons was the most adventuresome of all Chicago reporters, as well as one of the best and most versatile news writers of his age. As a newsboy for the Chicago *Tribune* in Milwaukee, he patterned his dreams after dashing turn-of-the-century war correspondent Richard Harding Davis, and after Gibbons moved to the Toddlin' Town his career suggested someone living out a child's fantasy.

He covered part of the Mexican Revolution for the *Tribune* from a railroad boxcar in 1915, and the next year accompanied Pershing's expedition after Villa. Instead of returning with the Marines, he went along with the *villaistas*, eating their meager stew and watching untrained soldiers in sombreros and white tunics being cut down by machine-guns outside strands of barbed wire.

While the United States remained neutral in the Great War, Howey put Gibbons on a British liner to gather news about German submarines over British face-saving censorship. As if hoping the ship would be sunk, the paper supplied him with flashlights, a bottle of water, a special life preserver, and a flask of brandy to help him recover from hypothermia.

After the ship was torpedoed in the Irish Sea on February 25, 1917, Gibbons cheered up fellow passengers in a lifeboat, distributed cigarettes, kept a lookout for survivors in the icy waters, and offered to man the oars. Two hours after landing in Queenstown, he cabled his account of the disaster and apologized for taking a break to dry off and warm up. The article was read in Congress as proof that despite its promises, Germany was waging unrestricted U-boat warfare. And what a story it was, reading in part:

> It is now over a little more than thirty hours since I stood on the slanting decks of the big liner, listened to the lowering of the lifeboats, heard the hiss of escaping steam and the roar of ascending rockets as they tore lurid rents in the black sky and cast their red glare over the roaring sea.

Too excited about world events to rest, Gibbons reported the arrival of the American Expeditionary Force in France and put into the mouth of General "Black Jack" Pershing the words "Lafayette, we are here." Pershing declined to embarrass anyone by correcting the account; besides, he must have known it was what he should have said.

Among the intelligence officers who had come off the ship with Gibbons was his boss, Robert R. McCormick. The publisher was growing a narrow mustache and telling people his minor polo injury had come from football, and his practiced arrogance masked the shyness of a man belittled by his mother all his life. McCormick by now was married to a rather plain divorcee older than he by a few years and felt his family nickname of "Bertie" seemed too juvenile. Soon after winning a promotion he asked to be called "The Colonel" forevermore.

His duties did not bring him close to the action, but he endured days of shelling as the landscape turned into charnel. Gibbons was wounded twice and then lost an eye to machinegun fire at Belleau Woods. He came back from the hospital with a black eye patch that gave more flair to his good features. He excitedly reported the American advance on Amiens.

Staying in Europe, Gibbons was appointed head of the *Tribune*'s fabled Paris Edition as well as all of the mother paper's European correspondents. The Paris Edition was published on the fifth floor of a building at 21, rue de Berri, near the Avenue des Champs-Elysees, using reporters recruited from Pershing's press section and perhaps nearby Harry's Bar.

Their rather laid-back work was augmented by carbons of stories from the *Tribune*'s Foreign News Service, which operated out of a twelve-foot-square telegraph room receiving cables from several correspondents. When the nightly traffic of up to ten thousand words in cabelese shorthand was "dressed," that is, condensed and rewritten, the output reached up to seven thousand words for subscribing papers from Canada to South America.[54]

The Paris Edition was established to provide news for American soldiers stationed in Europe, although cynics said the six-foot-four Colonel McCormick hoped it would make him General McCormick. In its greatest coup, managing editor Spearman Lewis negotiated for weeks before obtaining a copy of the Versailles treaty, which ended one war and indirectly started another.

Newsman George Seldes said many years later, that while Lewis's taxi was stalled at the Place de la Concorde, the managing editor promised never to reveal his source if the Chinese diplomat riding beside him would smuggle out a copy. The treaty was then "dropped through the letter slot at the Tribune [in Paris], wrapped in a piece of Chinese silk...."

Since Lewis needed to stay in France, Frazier Hunt of the New York *Times* smuggled the treaty through United States customs and had a senator read it into the Congressional record so his paper might publish the text without being accused of treason. According to Seldes, a consequence of the premature publication was the end of President Wilson's dream of a League of Nations, and it broke his heart.[55]

The Paris Edition continued, but the sharp-eyed, one-eyed Gibbons left the outdoor cafes to cover famine in post–Revolutionary Russia, troubles in Ireland, and a Moroccan uprising. He returned to America in 1925 to broadcast news over the *Tribune*-owned radio station WGN (World's Greatest Newspaper) in the Drake Hotel. By then the United States had more than five hundred radio stations, but most were shoestring operations that did not carry advertising.

Too restless to read his own copy in front of a microphone for long, Gibbons led a trek across the Sahara in search of a lost tribe in 1927 and was fired by the *Tribune* for racking up twenty thousand dollars in expenses. Not that Gibbons cared, he was already writing *The Red Knight of Germany*, a bestselling biography of Baron Von Richtofen of Germany's "Flying Circus."

Then an odd thing happened. Gibbons was trying his hand at fiction, when he walked into the Chicago office of the National Broadcasting Company in 1929 to learn how someone might deliver radio dispatches from an airplane. During the conversation he imitated the vivid, excited way a reporter might sound with breaking news, and to his surprise he was hired as the nation's first network radio correspondent.

Gibbons not only wrote well for the radio, he spoke well and could read his copy rapidly. Someone once counted that he spoke two hundred and seventeen words a minute.[56] His fifteen-minute "Your Headline Hunter" was quickly grabbed by General Electric and later the *Literary Digest*. The next few years saw Gibbons filing eyewitness dispatches of the Japanese invasion of China and Italy's war in Ethiopia for the International News Service, which Hearst had founded in 1909. The under-funded wire service had a Chicago office on the fourth floor of a building by the elevated tracks at Madison and Wacker.

Gibbons escaped capture in all his roving reporting, but *Tribune* correspondent Joe Powell was taken prisoner when Chinese bandits overran a train in 1923. He was released six weeks later only after promising to deliver their side of events. The *Tribune* sold the Paris Edition to the New York *Herald* in October 1934, just as Europe was erupting.

When Gibbons delivered his breathless account of fighting near Madrid in the Spanish Civil War, soldiers were stationed inside the radio studio to shoot him if he mentioned anything against the Republic. In the next couple of years doctors told Gibbons his heart was too weak to continue his adventures, but he was preparing to cover the outbreak of World War Two in 1939 when he died at fifty-two.

A good reporter awoke every day to the possibility of excitement, and Chicago in the twenties was alive with newsmen eager to do anything for a story. One of them was Walter Trohan of Pennsylvania, who was hired at the City

News Bureau to work nine A.M. to eleven P.M. with every other Sunday off for eighteen dollars a week.

A man's decomposing remains had been found in an automobile on a country road after a bank robbery shootout, and painstaking rewrite man Joe Lavandier told Walter to learn from the morgue whether the victim had been shot by bank guards or the robbery gang. "(B)ecause a coroner's physician had no taste for it," Trohan would write years later, "I grasped the slimy hair ... and sawed off the top of his head...."[57]

Newspapers were the greatest source of mass information the world had ever known, but rivals were on their way. Thousands of families had bought radios or built crystal sets from mail-order kits, and the Pathé company of France began producing United States newsreels in 1910. These grainy silent films were the forerunners of television news.

In 1924, brothers H. Leslie and Ralph Atlass moved from Lincoln, Illinois, to North Sheridan Road in Chicago and set up radio station WBBM in their basement. Five years later, the station, then owned by the Columbia Broadcasting System, operated from the newly built Wrigley Building across the river from downtown.

6

"The iron bound agreement" of cooperation between Colonel McCormick and Joseph Patterson was working only because the cousins no longer shared the same part of the country. Patterson had adopted New York in 1925 and was involved only marginally with the family paper, such as heading the Tribune Syndicate, which sold features and cartoons to more than two hundred publications. Comics were no longer mere diversions, and they assured a steadier readership than changing headlines could.

At the *Tribune*, Colonel McCormick discovered a family more rational than his own. And, as with the army, he found in its plush offices a place where he could move about with the importance he felt he merited and without his judgments being criticized. McCormick bragged that he and Patterson were "the most vital single force at the center of the world," but the *Tribune's* influence beyond the Midwest was simply self-delusion.[58]

His grasping for prominence only bared his commonplaceness. Even when he became the master of six thousand employees, some of them in other parts of the globe, the Colonel never matured in anything beyond proficiency. Yet, just as Patterson was adept at building circulation with features, the Colonel had a wider vision than most contemporary newspaper publishers outside New York, such as starting Sunday regional editions in 1925.

As with his struggle for appreciation over the attention that had been given to his sharper older brother, (Joseph) Medill McCormick, the Colonel was determined to make Chicago the best regarded city in the country. But his dictates and editorials—written on months alternating with Patterson since 1924—showed that he was merely trying to sound meaningful. There was no consistency in the opinions. Consider his wrongheaded resurrection of Grandfather Medill's eccentric spelling in 1934, burdening the paper for decades with such shorn words as "jaz" and "iland" (island).

Some reporters at the time had more nerve than education. This description would include Harry Reutlinger, who had a deceptively cherubic face and gentle manners. He was never known to read a book or write a news story, although that did not stop him from becoming a hard-nosed editor at the *American*.

This Jewish teenager started as a four dollar and fifty-cent-a-week office boy. He had just been promoted to reporter in 1915 when he was sent to Columbus Hospital on the North Side to speak to a man who had killed his wife and shot himself. Columbus Hospital had been founded by Francesca Xavier Cabrini of the Missionary Sisters of the Sacred Heart because, like William Stead, the Italian immigrant believed Chicago needed spiritual uplifting. The other nuns thought she looked emaciated from malaria, which she had contracted as a result of her work in New Orleans, and at sixty-five she was barely able to walk but continued her menial duties at the hospital.

Reutlinger entered the six-story brick building and, rather than giving himself away by asking directions, wandered around in hopes of finding where a police officer was guarding the wounded man.

"Do you want to see one of the patients?" a wrinkled nun in a thick habit asked in an Italian accent.

"Mother Cabrini sent me," Reutlinger said.

"I think you are fibbing," the nun told him, readying her mop as a weapon. "I'll ask you to leave the way you came in."

The nineteen-year-old reporter tipped his hat and left, but only to go down an alley, climb a box, and grab the fire escape. Once back inside, he stepped down a corridor until he slipped on soapy water and saw the same old nun scowling over him. She raised her dripping mop and said, "Young man, you get out of here the same way you got in. Down the fire escape, now!"

Not moving fast enough, Harry tried to duck the swinging mop but felt a slap of dirty water across his face, and caught on that only Mother Cabrini herself could be so formidable.

Reutlinger left without his story, but this was one time a city editor did not say, "You should have tried harder." On the editor's desk was a photo of Mother Cabrini, and if Harry had been raised Catholic he might have known how feisty some nuns could be.[59] Mother Cabrini died in Chicago in 1917, and twenty-nine years later was canonized as America's first saint, which will lead us to a later story.

John Eastman of the *Journal*—who had helped found the *American* before breaking with Hearst—may have been the last of the eccentric editors in the city, even though his idea of journalistic license meant being ill tempered. Since Eastman saw to it that people he disliked were never mentioned in his paper, he sent them long, mean-spirited messages by way of a reporter who would read the message to the subject's face for a response.

"That's swell," Mayor Thompson allegedly told reporter Robert J. Casey in 1915 in response to insults over his closing saloons on Sundays. "John is getting better every day. Ask him to send me an autographed copy of that thing in six-inch perforated squares."[60]

News people of the time were a mixed lot. Joseph Weil was a math whiz who went from City Press to the *Chronicle* but was caught embellishing. The offending article told of how an opened copy of the King James version of the Bible was found in a dead woman's hotel room. But other reporters learned that she knew no English. Giving up journalism and taking the name "Yellow Kid" Weil from the same comic strip that gave us the phrase "yellow journalism," he became a fabled con man, and his autobiography may have inspired the hit film *The Sting*. Yet even after swindling people out of an estimated ten million dollars over his career, Weil became a charity case until he died in 1976 at the age of 100.[61]

Baltimore curmudgeon H.L. Mencken found in the Windy City "the mysterious something that makes for individuality, personality, charm; in Chicago a spirit broods upon the face of the waters" and, he might have added, provoked newsmen and authors to write in a peculiarly American voice.[62] Consider that during this time newspapers in the city employed four future famous biographers: Francis Hackett (*Henry VIII*), Marquis James (*Andrew Jackson* and *The Raven*, about Sam Houston), Lloyd Lewis (*Sherman, Fighting Prophet*), and poet Carl Sandburg (the six-volume *Abraham Lincoln*).

After coming from New Orleans, Marquis James worked for the Chicago *Tribune* while his young wife, Bessie—who earlier had walked toward a shotgun to get an interview—wrote for the *Herald & Examiner*. When the couple moved to New York they lugged with them their only earthly possession, a Remington typewriter.

Hackett arrived from Ireland in 1904, sensed an "impenetrable melancholy" of the lake and Lake Shore Drive in winter, and was told to speak like a gentleman and keep in mind that "The policy of the *American* is to please as many as possible." He never forgot Arthur Brisbane's defense of what some considered the indefensible. "Yellow journalism is real journalism," Brisbane had said. "Yellow journalism is war on hypocrisy, war against class privileges, and war against the foolishness of the crowd that will not think and will not use the weapon it holds, the ballot."[63] Hackett floated to the Chicago *Evening Post* before moving on.

While Lloyd Lewis was growing up in Indiana, he imagined Chicago as an Emerald City from what he learned about the Columbian Exposition. He started at Keeley's lazy *Herald* in 1915 and one of his first assignments would be the catastrophic capsizing of the *Eastland* in the Chicago River. Not really interested in reporting, Lewis served as the *Daily News* drama critic and amusement editor under Henry Justin Smith. In 1929, they wrote *Chicago: the History of Its Reputation.*

Sandburg had been hand-printing his poems in the railroad town of Galesburg, Illinois, before boarding a train for the mysterious metropolis by the lake. He took his first paycheck from the *Daily News* in 1917 but was never fully a street reporter. Instead, he was sent on some labor stories and did whatever suited him, a rare exception granted by Smith, the literary-minded new editor. When Sandburg was on the court beat, he used the corridors of justice as just another space for writing his turgid free verse.

Sandburg never outlived the thrill of living in a bustling city. Instead of staying at his desk in the long and narrow local room, he would turn up at odd times with copy he had written in some suburb or Bronzeville or even Milwaukee. This tall, lean son of Swedish parents, with a mop of hair indifferently parted in the middle, sometimes would look out a news room window and see images and energies no one else had sensed before in the "Stormy, husky, brawling/City of the Big Shoulders."

Ben Hecht told a story to illustrate the dreaminess of Sandburg, who sometimes worked with him on the courts beat. In this fable, the poet was sent to a Minneapolis labor strike that was turning increasingly brutal. No dispatches came in, but the AP kept reporting arsons and gunfire. Exasperated, Henry Justin Smith wired Sandburg to come home. Carl wired back: "Dear Boss. Can't leave now. Everything too important and exciting."[64]

The story is good for a laugh but had been told of several other reporters. John McPhaul of the *Daily News* relayed a similar story. Some reporter was sent to a mine disaster and telegraphed an account beginning "God sits on the hills here tonight brooding over the stricken community." The city editor wired back: "Forget mine story. Interview God."[65]

One more journalism misfit who added to American literature was Vincent Starrett, whose *Daily News* experiences included a ride with Pershing's men in Mexico. Among his friends were Ring Lardner, who straddled the worlds of sports and literature, and the writing team of Hecht and Charles MacArthur. Starrett's best-known contribution was an earnest 1930 "biography," *The Private Life of Sherlock Holmes.* In 1986, a headstone in the form of an opened book was placed over his grave in Graceland Cemetery in Chicago after contributions were sent by Holmes fans as far away as Nairobi and Australia.

Among the others for whom the news business was just a phase was Charles Cecil Fitzmorris, who left the *American* in 1912 to work as a secretary to Mayor Carter Harrison II. Fitzmorris became the police chief in the turbulent twenties.

Most newspapers in the early twentieth century preferred sentiment to literature as a reaction to old fashioned political sheets. Nearly every paper in the nation had a "sob sister," such as Hearst's Adela Rogers St. John in California. Since male reporters tended to come off as unfeeling, sob sisters found ways to be emotionally close to witnesses, victims, and relatives of people in the news, sometimes doing errands for them if not actually joining their weeping. Newsmen may have mocked them, but these women introduced emotion to the once-dry news.

When men tried writing such stories, they usually forgot that less can be more. Edward Doherty was writing his second sob story in as many days when Walter Howey told him, "This isn't that kind of story, Eddie, it's straight news. Write it that way. And don't try to break my heart. It isn't that kind of heart."[66]

7

The first news of the city's worst disaster in terms of lives lost began with a phone call to the *Journal* at about seven-thirty in the morning on Saturday, July 24, 1915. Managing editor Richard J. Finnegan sent inexperienced features reporter Lowell Thomas to the Clark Street bridge to report on a boat accident. This was long before Thomas became a traveling journalist and radio personality whose steady baritone would be heard by millions.

The large excursion boat *Eastland* had been built for speed, but years of increasing safety requirements made her topheavy. Employees counted the tickets of passengers swarming aboard, more than half of them for a Western Electric company picnic, but some may have been overlooked, and children were allowed on board without tickets. Many passengers went to the top deck to wave goodbye to friends and co-workers as the gangplank was pulled up.

By the time Thomas reached the capsized boat, the first few bodies were being laid along the riverbank in a placement suggesting there would be many more. What was so eerie was that the boat lay on its side in just fifteen feet of water—in the Loop, the heart of the city—and emergency workers were walking across planks to reach the exposed portion of the hull.

"I clambered aboard and joined those trying to haul the living up portholes and the drowned and drowning from the river," Thomas would write. "I supposed I'd have a real scoop if I'd rush back to the office with the story, but I stayed on the *Eastland* and finally got back at around noon, wet and dirty, my face no doubt reflecting my emotions at having been there when 812 souls met their deaths. Dick Finnegan looked up and said, 'Go some place and forget it, Tommy! See you tomorrow.'"

The papers were sending to the scene a battery of messenger boys for running copy, as well as everyone who could be called up or not needed in preparing the next edition. To accommodate them all, the phone company strung

The *Eastland* capsizing in 1915 killed more than 800. The newspapers sent every available employee to the accident, including future radio and television news commentator Lowell Thomas (Chicago History Museum, photographer—Jun Fujita, ICHi-32987).

lines from South Water Street, just off the river, to the concrete walkway lining the bank. *Herald & Examiner* day city editor Frank Carson kept ahead of the competition by putting stenographers to work as telephone reporters and mimeographing questions for them to ask the shocked families of the known dead, freeing journalists to take down every available fact about the rescues.

One of the least experienced reporters at the scene was Louella O. Parsons, who penned the *Herald & Examiner* movie column before becoming a catty Hollywood gossip queen. Edward Doherty was so upset by the disaster that, after turning in his account, he went home and his policeman father gave him something to settle his nerves.[67] *Herald & Examiner* reporter Webb Miller kept by the boat for twenty hours straight to write continual updates.

Around this time, Finnegan gave Lowell Thomas a slip of paper with "Carlton Hudson" written on it and asked why the name kept popping up in people's wills. Thomas learned that no one in the families of the deceased seemed to know much about Hudson except that he seemed cultured, was affiliated with a favorite cause of Victor Lawson, the Moody Bible Institute on the North Side, and spoke with "an Eastern accent." On a hunch, Thomas wrote to every college president in New England, describing Hudson and saying that the man had just inherited a gold mine. A letter from Vermont stated that the heir apparently was Carlton Hudson Betts, who had gone to New York some time before.

Two hours after Thomas saw this, Finnegan gave him an envelope with a train ticket and a hundred dollars for expenses. The fledgling reporter found his way to the New York *World* and, as a professional favor, was allowed to go through its morgue clips. These were articles folded, and sometimes folded again and again, inside alphabetized envelopes about six inches wide. The file cabinets for these envelopes were kept in their own room.

The articles told him Betts had been arrested for wooing ladies out of their money but that he had vanished after posting bail. That would be enough to satisfy Finnegan. But since his paper was paying the expenses, Thomas boarded a train for Albany and told the governor, "I have something the people of New York State want. In exchange, I want something for the *Evening Journal*."

Thomas phoned his story in, and when Betts stepped out of his Chicago office the following afternoon "the police were waiting for him," Thomas recalled. "So were the newsboys, with our extra edition."[68]

The next year, Leroy F. "Buddy" McHugh was helping homicide Sgt. John Quinn search for evidence in the home of a lovely widow who had died a bloody death. Buddy had risen from newspaper copyboy to City News drone and then reporter for Hearst's *American*. Like Frank Carson, he was a policeman at heart. He and Sgt. Quinn came across a hatchet, and McHugh went door to door asking about its owner. Neighbors told him it belonged to a shopkeeper with a simpleminded son, Edward Nettinger. After the police questioned the suspect for some time to no avail, possibly employing physical intimidation, McHugh used psychology. Approaching Nettinger as a friend he asked, "Did she scream when you hit her, Edward?"

"No," he said, and in those pre–Miranda-warning days that was considered a confession.[69]

Also showing resourcefulness was droopy-faced Bill Bockelman of the *Tribune* circulation department. Scampering to put a bag of newspapers aboard a train pulling out of the Polk Street station in 1916, he drove onto the tracks and in his excitement rammed the back of the rear car. Bockelman jumped out of the truck, ran faster than the departing train, and flung the heavy bag into the mail car.

Howey enjoyed his *Tribune* job so much that he turned down an offer to work at the *Herald & Examiner* for thirty-five thousand dollars a year. Yet he chafed under the weak and meddling leadership at the World's Greatest Newspaper. The last straw came in 1917, when he accused Joseph Patterson of wanting only yes men and took Hearst up on his offer.

The Chief's not entirely ethical right-hand-man, Arthur Brisbane, made Howey's mission simple for him: "Beat the Trib. That's your only job. First beat the *Tribune*." But, rather than scooping his former employer, Howey preferred making a fool out of him. As lifelong crime reporter John Kelley noted, newsmen most admired hoaxes that covered up all earmarks of a rib. Before his first week went by, Howey planted in the *Herald & Examiner* some nonsense about an Indiana woman who was in town to spend a million dollars that had come her way. The article even warned readers that this might be a press agent fake, since the Hearst chain was currently promoting one of his motion picture serials about a suddenly wealthy woman.

Howey set up an attractive actress in the downtown Blackstone Hotel and waited for Patterson to take the bait. When an editor sent a reporter to interview her, Howey pulled the bogus feature from the later editions and wrote an editorial thanking Patterson for promoting the serial.[70]

Howey's spies at the *Tribune* routinely called him an hour before each edition came out to read him the headlines and front page, giving him a head start over the other papers in recovering any scoops. Not only that, the white telephone in the city desk bank of otherwise black phones was a direct line from the police headquarters switchboard, where certain operators on his payroll called in fresh tips. Detectives sometimes wondered how Howey's reporters reached the scene before they did.

As *Time* magazine would describe him, Howey was "a profane romanticist, ruthless but not cruel, unscrupulous but endowed with a private code of ethics. He was the sort of newsman who managed to have hell break loose right under his feet, expected similar miracles from his underlings, rewarded them generously. Undersized, unprepossessing, he was afraid of nothing."[71] Yet Howey's unending drive to stay on top in what may have been America's most continually competitive field was turning him empty inside.[72] It was as if he were seeking to recapture the excitement of scooping all other papers with McKinley's death or the Iroquois Theatre fire. He came to object to his reporters' having any emotional interests beyond their work, as Ben Hecht and Charles MacArthur would hilariously portray in *The Front Page*.

Howey also loved putting a little con in his personal anecdotes. Whenever reporters got around to asking why he had a glass left eye, the unathletic Howey blamed it on the circulation wars. The truth, disclosed years later, was that some chemicals had exploded during one of his frequent home experiments. Howey's tinkering might have seemed quaint, but his news-related inventions won several patents, including one for Soundphoto, a telephone picture transmission system that was leased to Hearst's International News Service before the Associated Press came out with Wirephoto.

As American troops were arriving in New York Harbor in the autumn of 1918, Chicago was one among the cities stricken with the "swine flu," the most virulent pandemic in world history. Before the influenza virus evidently mutated into a harmless strain, streetcars were filled with office workers coughing, breaking into sweats, and shaking. Movie theaters were closed and city officials urged clergymen to shorten their Sunday services. Hundreds died, but nothing stopped the newspapers. Every absence meant someone in that department moved up a step for as long as needed.

Out-of-work servicemen and neighborhood gangs posed another kind of problem. Former *Record* editor Henry Barrett Chamberlain persuaded the Chicago Association of Commerce and Industry to finance a private crime commission to make the public realize how hooliganism was affecting everyone. The resulting Chicago Crime Commission was established in 1919, just ahead of the bootleg era.

Perhaps the *Herald & Examiner*'s splendid coverage of the *Eastland* capsizing made *Tribune* executives realize how much they had lost when Frank Carson resigned, and they offered a higher salary to lure him away from the Hearst Building. Carson swallowed his pride and switched over. But in August 1919, Howey was determined to drag him back even though Carson was not interested. So Howey employed comedy actor Frank Tinney to drop by the *Tribune* offices and invite him to come backstage that night. Anticipating the outcome of all the liquor that was being ordered for the event, Howey wrote up an insulting resignation for his former assistant and waited out events.

When Carson was so groggy he had to be bundled into a cab, the driver took him to Howey's home. Carson awoke the next morning in strange surroundings and picked up the continually ringing phone only to hear Howey telling him to report for work at the *Herald & Examiner*.[73]

8

This is how former Chicago *Herald & Examiner* copyboy Harry Romanoff secured pictures of a flood devastating Pueblo, Colorado, in March, 1919: his editors sent him to acquire photos that would accompany wire service copy. Romanoff took an overnight train and gave a Denver *Post* photographer on his way there three hundred dollars for a copy of everything he would shoot. However, after seeing the extent of the flood's destruction, the lensman wanted to give the money back because the pictures would be worth more to another paper.

"Romy" told the *Post* managing editor, "I spent the last twenty-four hours with your man and I'm familiar with his work. I'll pay three-hundred dollars for reprint rights to the pictures he gives you."

He attended to the development of the photos, put the contact prints in a shoebox, and gave a train conductor twenty dollars to deliver them to the Hearst Building in Chicago. Next he telegraphed his notes and lied by saying he had spent six hundred dollars for the pictures. Two dozen other papers paid the *Herald & Examiner* for using them, and Romanoff was jubilant with a three hundred dollar bonus as well as the three hundred dollars he had tricked out of his boss.[74]

Among the things Chicago newspapers were clueless about, including the emerging black press, was the potential for a race riot such as the ones that had broken out in Tulsa, St. Louis, and Florida. The *Defender* recognized the dreadful conditions in the city for black workers, but continually urged that they leave the South with all its hatred and move to Chicago, where there were plenty of (low paying) jobs.

Defender Publisher Robert S. Abbott may have been thinking largely about increasing black political strength, but what has been called the Great Migration meant there were more arrivals than could be assimilated. Real estate covenants confined African Americans to the city's South Side "Black Belt," though there were a few areas where they came in close contact with whites.

With temperatures in the nineties on Sunday, July 27, 1919, a white boy at 25th Street Beach threw a rock at a black teenager swimming past the invisible racial boundary. The act might have been nothing more than a prank or a warning, but a hush spread across the lakefront when the swimmer failed to surface, and people quickly grabbed their clothes and headed home. Intermittent fighting broke out when the police declined to arrest anyone for the fourteen-year-old's death. Primarily Irish gangs such as the Colts—which had supplied thugs for the circulation wars—came in and set black-owned homes on fire. No taxicabs would go into the riot area, and so Hearst's *Herald & Examiner* provided feature writers with motorcycle sidecars and drivers to take them through police lines. One of the writers, Edward Dean Sullivan, has left us this account:

> A shot exploded at my ear, fired by my driver, who was gazing intently on a roof. ... [where there was] a Negro, his eyes on us, struggling with a giant Negress, dressed in white. He had a rifle, and was trying to turn it on us.... "One side's enough to worry about," said the driver, who, automatic in hand, eyed the buildings opposite us as we drove along....

This motorcycle driver was Dion O'Banion, one of Max Annenberg's thugs in the circulation wars—destined to be gunned down six years later by mobsters presumably sent by Al Capone.

After three days, the riot toll was at least fourteen whites and twenty blacks killed, and more than five hundred people injured or wounded.[75] Chicago had become one of the most dangerous cities in the country at the dawn of the bootleg era, and the shame of the nation was about to become the playground of police reporters.

Carson's mischievous nature showed up when the *Herald & Examiner* sent a relief truck to tornado victims in southern Illinois. The *Tribune* used a picture with the truck in it but airbrushed out the rival paper's name. Feigning outrage, Carson sent a copyboy to the *Tribune* offices to demand an immediate correction, no doubt hinting legal action. But following instructions, the boy waited to do this until it would cause the most damage, after the replate was rolling off the presses. Carson then sat back with a grin.[76]

Disputed tradition has it that Chicago was called "the windy city" because of its many political meetings, and one held in June 1920 gave rise to an even more common phrase. Republican Party leader George Harvey of New York was meeting with other GOP officials in Suite 404 of the downtown Blackstone Hotel to decide on a candidate to endorse for the presidential nomination, with U.S. Senator Warren Harding mentioned only as a dark horse. At sunrise. Associated Press reporter Kirke Simpson turned in that "Harding of Ohio was chosen by a group of men in a smoke filled room today."[77] A reporter's inclusion of a telling detail gave the press a lasting catchphrase.

With its early combination of bootleg gangs and openly corrupt officials, speakeasy-era Chicago was possibly the most vibrant city in the land, and reading newspapers from the period is a joy with all their disclosures and enthusiasm. But innovations in delivering the news were starting to be made elsewhere.

An experimental radio station underwritten by the Detroit *News* made the first known newscast in September 1920. By 1923, a Newark, New Jersey, station was pioneering fifteen-minute news programs, and aristocratic newscaster and commentator H. V. Kaltenborn was the darling at a couple of New York stations. But his scripts were still just a rephrasing and condensing of newspaper stories.[78]

Probably because there were so many dailies in Chicago, the papers were modernizing equipment rather than branching out into the new medium. The *Tribune* in the twenties started operating a line of more than two dozen high-speed Goss presses interspersed with folding machines.[79]

In 1921, Colonel McCormick donated funds to Northwestern University to establish the Medill School of Journalism, based on an idea from Edward Doherty. While the *American* and the "Her-Ex" (*Herald & Examiner*) were still hiring one-of-a-kind people from off the streets, graduates of Medill and other "j schools" were professionalizing local coverage. Yet some established broadsheets were adopting "jazz journalism," featuring stories of sex and violence to keep pace with the times but written with more restraint than the yellow journalism of the recent past.

One of the many educated people who fell into journalism only temporarily was Dwight Green, just another "Hey, you!" reporter at the *Herald & Examiner*. His triumph came in August 1921 when Carson sent him to the huge Edgewater Beach Hotel on the North Side. Green's assignment was to obtain the only known picture of beauty Madalynne Obenchain. Her jealous estranged husband, Ralph Obenchain of Evanston, had just fatally shot Belton Kennedy in Los Angeles. The press took to calling the seductively lovely femme fatale "The Tiger Woman." The portrait Green needed was in plain sight on an easel in an artist's gallery at the hotel but, since this was a Sunday, the room was locked, and the gallery owner would not authorize the manager to open it.

Green gave an assistant janitor two dollars to borrow a ladder and squeezed through the transom. He must have flushed with pride when he arrived at his paper with the picture and Carson told him he was now a real reporter. But the hotel manager, under threat of a suit by the gallery owner, stormed into the *Herald & Examiner* office to complain, and Carson fired Green on the spot. Two days later the editor called him at home and said that "the heat's off and everybody's happy. Let's get back to work."[80]

Carson was friendlier than Howey had been, and less burned out. But that likability turned cold whenever he set his eye on a good story, and then it was anything goes. He was the first Chicago editor to use air mail for stories, and John McPhaul provides a second-hand account of how flattery and fakery might have led the post office to rush him photos of the July 1921 Jack Dempsey–Georges Carpentier heavyweight bout in Jersey City, New Jersey.

The only man who could approve such a flight was President Harding. Carson remembered that when Harding ran an Ohio newspaper he had published a list of lofty standards. Carson resurrected a photo of the statement from the *Herald-Examiner* files, had it blown up, and directed a photographer to take a picture of his staff looking upon the document in feigned awe.

And so Chicagoans were the first outside the Eastern seaboard to see the battered Frenchman lying on the mat after a fourth-round knockout. But radio programming was already catching up with the papers in covering sports. Less than three months before the bout, stations were broadcasting sporting events with an immediacy newspapers never tried to equal.[81]

The size and equipment needed for newspaper offices made them a world onto themselves. As just a small example, an October 1922 accident in the *Tribune* ink supply line flooded the pressroom with hundreds of gallons of liquid black. Company plumber Joe Christophe sped from home by car and dived in. By the time he had fixed the problem a small patch of the Chicago River had turned black, and the rough-looking Christophe had to scrub for weeks before his pores cleared.

Just when the city was about to reach its frantic heyday with glittering movie palaces, apartments turned into casinos, and merciless gangsters, the zesty period of police reporting was starting to fade like a sunset too gradual to notice. For the next forty years, the reporters doing anything for a story were individually inspired more by the Howey-Carson phase than by their own editors. Sometime in this golden twilight there supposedly was a conversation in the Chicago Press Club bar, as set down by Edward Doherty:

Sam Blair (*Herald & Examiner*): "The things we do for our papers! We lie, we cheat, we swindle and steal. We break into houses. We almost commit murder for a story. We're a bunch of lice."

Marquis James (*Tribune*): "Maybe we are, so it is my time to buy a drink."

Jack Lawson (formerly of the *Record-Herald*): "We'll even die for a story, if we have to, like Sunny Jim McCabe."

Gil Parker (whose affiliation is lost to us): "We'll say we had a good time, didn't we. Yeah. And we'll work our heads off. We'll go without sleep. We'll freeze our ears off at fires. And when we're too damn old to go after stories any more, and some whelp of a city editor throws us out in the ashcan, we'll say, 'Well, we had a good time, didn't we?'"[82]

FOUR. A Valentine for the Age

Socially, a journalist fits somewhere between a whore and a bartender, but spiritually he stands beside Galileo. He knows the world is round.
—Sherman Duffy of the Chicago *Journal*.[1]

One late December around 1914, the North Side apartment of jobless Richard Hanlon was cold. He had been promised a job at the unexciting *Inter-Ocean* if he could bring in a good story. As reporter-raconteur Robert J. Casey tells us, Hanlon thought to interview a neighbor who was a novelist. When she greeted the stranger with unexpected buoyancy, he asked how she could stay so happy. The unnamed novelist replied that she had thrown her husband out a few nights before and was expecting him back with an apology. While Hanlon was still speaking with the writer, her anguished husband burst in, shot her to death, and fatally turned the gun on himself. Although aghast, Hanlon decided not to get scooped on his own story by notifying the police.

He locked the bloody apartment and headed for the *Inter-Ocean*. On his way there, however, he decided to take his story to the better-paying *Record-Herald* as a passport to a career.[2] He fit right in, because the *Record-Herald* under James Keeley had frowned upon improper behavior. Colleagues at other sheets regarded his reporters as no more than grocery clerks and ribbon salesmen.

Casey said he could not recall a single interesting story Hanlon worked on afterward. And yet, he had the one trait a good crime reporter needs: he could distance himself from a situation and think of human misery as a commodity. As later reporter Gera-Lind Kolarik would say: "Your adrenaline goes up, and it's not a body any more."[3]

Such exuberance might extend to newspaper offices, where the police were at times summoned because of furniture bashing during a celebration over a major scoop, just as nowadays papers hold a sedate party when a staff member wins an award.

When a new reporter took a seat in the local room to await an assignment, his peers might pull his leg by resurrecting the sinking of the steamboat

Lady Elgin off suburban Winnetka before the Civil War. Someone would make an unseen call to the city desk. Next, a rewrite man would pick up the receiver and exclaim just enough for the novice to beg that his editor send him to the scene. The supervisor would reply with a bored scowl as the old-timers laughed.

After the old First Precinct station was torn down in 1911, neophytes often started their nights at police headquarters, where they were normally allowed to read teletyped lists of crimes printed on a paper roll after they were tapped out by secretaries in the precinct stations. The teletype machines—installed by order of Police Chief Fitzmorris, the former newsman—were four-foot-tall keyboard devices that punctured letter codes into a narrow strip of yellow paper. The raised dots, reminiscent of Braille, activated all receiving machines.

The papers gave their new reporters badges that the more enterprising would flash as they passed themselves off as a detective or assistant coroner. By the mid-twenties the badges were replaced by cards reading: "All courtesies extended the bearer will be appreciated by Charles Cecil Fitzmorris, Chief of Police," or his successors. Reporters kept the cards safe in their pockets and not protruding from their hatbands, where they could be snatched. But with evidence-gathering becoming a science, by the mid-thirties, officers were keeping newspeople back as if they were bystanders.

Reporters with moderate experience were usually assigned to the detective bureau on LaSalle Street, with its bare and windowless interrogation rooms. Detectives were said to apply the third degree only to suspects who had an arrest record and were therefore presumed to be lying, and they would inflict each blow where marks would not show, such as above the kidneys.[4] The press room table was used for pinochle and short-order meals, and sometimes as a bed for reporters who liked to kick off their shoes for a nap.

This might be where you would find Walford "Buddy" Lewis, not to be confused with older reporter Buddy McHugh. Lewis looked as if he had slept in his clothes, and with his glasses resembled Mr. Average Joe, only a little shorter. Lewis put himself through Northwestern University's school of journalism at night while working days at the *Daily News*. Like many career crime reporters he had little imagination. Lewis would ask a slew of questions because he never unconsciously assumed anything.

Although the city was motorcar crazy by 1921, the *Tribune* still had sixty-eight horse-drawn wagons to augment its forty-eight trucks. The trucks needed twelve thousand gallons of gasoline a month, and in the same time the horses required thirty-three hundred pounds of hay and twenty-eight thousand pounds of oats. Wagon drivers seldom had to flick their reins because their horses knew where to stop. The last was retired in 1928.

All the news rooms in the city at this period were half modern and half old fashioned. All had large rooms shared by city editors and reporters, and a small electronic bell tinged whenever the AP or City News sent a bulletin, one or two sentences of a breaking story demanding immediate attention. Otherwise, each paper maintained its own tempo and approach to the news.

The *Tribune* had just installed one hundred phones and fifty-seven linotype machines in its location at Dearborn and Madison, yet as early as 1919 the editors were discussing the need for a new building. The fifth floor local room (actually, a suite of offices) was a warren of editorial department offices: the Sunday edition room, the telegraph room, and several rooms for graphics and photo development, along with spaces for the managing editor and the clippings morgue, later called the library. Typewriters, still usually Remingtons, were sunk on a platform a few inches below the desktop level for easier pecking. You could tell how long newspeople had been on the job by how many fingers hit the keys.

Near Lake and Wells, *Daily News* windows rattled with every elevated train crossing the river. In a rolltop desk, copyboys regularly dumped routine wire service copy, and the staff filled pigeonholes in the upper portion with reports, statistics, and ghostwritten speeches yet to be delivered. At any moment an editor might be standing over the shoulder of a telegrapher whose hand was laying out a story as it came in letter by letter. In the composing room the head compositor and his assistant would be "breaking up the paper," getting equipment ready for the next edition while shouting over the steady clicking of linotype machines.

Printers in shirtsleeves chewed tobacco while their blackened fingers moved as if by themselves. Type lay in bundles of lines about the printing "stone" (plate), and long galleys were stacked like logs. Everyone in the building looked forward to Tuesday, the payday Lawson had set to keep his people out of check-cashing saloons on weekends.[5]

Both of Hearst's Chicago papers continued to be printed in the "madhouse on Madison Street." Because the small "Her-Ex" staff needed to get out multiple editions, the newsroom was "keyed two notches above hysteria," Casey said, even though he worked for its sister paper, the *American*. "Nobody moved even to the water cooler except at a dead run," he added. "Every story ... was a big story and greeted with quivering excitement by everybody who had anything to do with it."[6] The pace quickened after the U.S. Supreme Court ordered Hearst's International News Service in 1918 to stop stealing Associated Press stories, contending that the events themselves were not exclusive but that the means for learning about and covering them were. This, in effect, ended most news piracy nationwide.[7]

One Howey protégé at the *Herald & Examiner* was Sam Blair, a heavy drinker and smoker who was the wit of city hall. When one of his lungs was removed, he said, "If the Good Lord had wanted me to have two lungs, he would have given me three." As Blair was about to take his third drink at a downtown saloon, he rejected a suggestion that he have lunch instead. "What," he replied, "and walk into city hall with food on my breath?"

Former Chicago *Tribune* reporter Charles Chapin—the man who had raced by train, schooner, tug boat, and dinghy to interview fugitive William McGarigle—became a holy terror when he was hired away by the New York *Evening World*. Who would have imagined that this exacting fop shouting in headlines with a pince-nez, double-breasted suit, and pearl tie pin was seething inside? He had risen to his position when *World* editor Ernest Chamberlain went mad, and now Chapin was planning to kill himself and take his beloved wife of thirty-nine years with him.

The Chapins were living beyond their means at the Hotel Plaza, and in his mental confusion Charles could think of no way to pay their one thousand dollars in bills. In the early morning of September 18, 1918, he shot Nellie behind her ear as she slept. As he cradled her thrashing body for two hours, Charles realized that he wanted to live, after all. When her death finally came, he prayed for forgiveness, dressed as smartly as ever, and went to his barber. He aimlessly rode subway trains rather than going to work, and then gave himself up. While serving a twenty-year to life sentence for second degree murder, he edited a house publication for fellow Sing Sing inmates.

Joseph Medill Patterson returned from the Great War as an artillery captain and in 1919 used *Tribune* capital to start the New York *Daily News* as the country's first tabloid. He was aided by his wife, Mary King, who had been his assistant when he was the Sunday editor at the Chicago paper. No one thought her influence unusual because the period after the war saw women kicking their heels at college dances, opening speakeasies, and joining newspapers in larger numbers.

With frequent water cooler banter between young men and women at the papers, and reporters of both sexes sometimes covering the same story or meeting socially after work, romances were inevitable. As Mildred Frisby of the *American* exchanged sweet talk with Edward Doherty's brother James of the *Tribune,* everyone knew what would happen.

Not long after their wedding, Mildred was assigned to the July 21, 1919, test flight of a Goodyear blimp, intended to demonstrate the convenience and beauty of graceful flight. Admittedly this was little more than free advertising for Goodyear. So Mildred and Jim went off somewhere—chronicler John McPhaul said they took a stroll—and she missed the airborne departure from the White City amusement park at 63rd Street and South Park Avenue. When Mildred returned to her office, editor Edward Mahoney gasped, "Good God! We've got you among the dead!" While she had been away, the dirigible's ninety five thousand pounds of hydrogen exploded and the huge flaming bag hit the roof of the Bank of America building, at 231 South LaSalle, in the city's financial district. A witness said the scene looked like "a blast furnace raining hell." Thirteen people either from the blimp or in the bank building were killed, including the photographer who was to have accompanied Mildred on the flight.[8]

You cannot count on falling dirigibles to attract readers, and there was no end of corruption to expose. At the *Herald & Examiner* city desk, Walter Howey developed a way to twist exclusives out of city hall. After his reporters found incriminating information he would call the official with such threats as this: "I do not intend to use this material now. I want your resignation, written and signed but undated. I will not publish it unless and until the day comes when you do not cooperate with me."[9]

Reporters needed to be as devious as their bosses. Harry Romanoff, who would become perhaps the last of the Chicago newspaper legends, was working for Howey when the police locked up graying janitor Thomas Fitzgerald for the murder of six-year-old Janet Wilkerson in July 1919. "Romy" wondered how molesters lured children, and told himself that it was probably with candy and dolls.

He bought a large doll and went up to Fitzgerald as the suspect was being released on bail. Putting the plaything in front of him, Romanoff said, "Yes, it's little Janet's doll. Her mother wanted to get it out of the house. Don't you think it's time you got this off your conscience?" Fitzgerald clutched the doll, and in time signed a paper in front of detectives stating that he was giving his confession exclusively to the *Herald & Examiner.* [10]

And yet sports sold more papers than crime or political news. We can imagine the excitement as the Chicago White Sox headed into the 1919 World's Series against Cincinnati. Ballplayers Swede Risberg, Fred McMullin, Lefty Williams, Edward Cicotte, Happy Felsch, Chick Gandil, Buck Weaver, and common-looking Shoeless Joe Jackson were citywide heroes. Nationwide interest was so intense that hundreds teemed into New York's Times Square to watch numbers change on a mechanical scoreboard.

For some time, leading *Herald & Examiner* sportswriter Hugh Fullerton had been submitting articles about gamblers trying to muscle in on baseball, but his editor kept crossing out details. Then, while watching the final game in Cincinnati on October 9, Fullerton heard from a gambler that he was about to behold the strangest inning of the series. Also astounded by what he was seeing was John Eastman, Hearst's one-time right-hand man in Chicago who now headed the *Journal.* What followed proves that editors should listen to the inner little bell that rings whenever something does not seem quite right. Eastman telegraphed Casey in Chicago: HAVE INCONTROVERTIBLE EVIDENCE THIS SERIES FIXED (STOP) WHAT ABOUT IT (QUESTION). Never an energetic sports reporter, Casey wired back: SUCH THINGS ARE NOT DONE IN THE BIG LEAGUES. Both then dropped the story.

Undeterred by his editors, Fullerton dug up information that small-time Eastern bettors had approached flashy New York gambler Arnold Rothstein about making an investment. Events would indicate that Cicotte and Gandil then told the rest of the team what they should and should not do. This was the greatest investigative story of Fullerton's life, but once again an editor eliminated names, places, and even dates either to avoid a libel suit or at the request of team owner Charles Comiskey.

Since the *Herald & Examiner* would not print the full account, Fullerton sold his information in the form of a serialized feature to the New York *World*, and readers were shocked when the first installment came out in December. But some gaps still needed to be filled in.

Harry Reutlinger—the man who had been mopped by Mother Cabrini— asked the staff at Hearst's *American* to name the dumbest Sox player, that is, the person most likely to be fooled into telling all. The consensus was Felsch. Reutlinger got him on the phone and said, "Look, the other guys are going to confess and leave you holding the bag. They say you're the brains of it."

"Naw," Felsch said, "I ain't the brains. But I got mine."

Reutlinger pulled some details from him and eagerly told editor Edward Mahoney, who was not impressed. "Call me with it later," Mahoney said.

"Call back nuts! I'll call the [*Daily*] *News*!" Then, so the story goes, Reutlinger actually headed for the rival paper, presumably when his shift ended. This made Mahoney realize the importance of the story, and he jumped on the phone to keep the circulation trucks from delivering the latest edition. Next, we are told, he ran out and stopped Reutlinger as the reporter was about to enter the *Daily News* building.[11] The story seems too dramatic to be factual, but it might have happened.

By then the Chicago team was labeled the "Black Sox" and eight players were put on trial, following pressure from Fullerton, Ring Lardner of the *Daily News*, and James Cuisenberry of the *Tribune*. Fullerton improved history by having a boy tell Jackson, "Say it isn't so, Joe," and Shoeless Joe replying, "It's so." The quote must be bogus in that no witness ever confirmed it, Jackson denied the story, and the ballplayer always insisted he never did anything wrong.

Some time between booking and the trial, the signed confessions of three other players disappeared and so did all records and minutes of the grand jury hearing. Then for possibly the first time in a Chicago court, the defendants invoked the Fifth Amendment against self incrimination, leaving prosecutors without a case.

By the time all eight were acquitted on July 18, 1921, major league owners had chosen hatchet-faced Chicago federal judge Kenesaw Mountain Landis as America's first baseball commissioner, something Fullerton had been pushing for. *Herald & Examiner* reporter Alan Hathaway was curious about how Landis would deal with the scandal, so he cozied up to the commissioner's secretary and read over her shoulder as she typed the pronouncement. Hathaway beat everyone to the news that Jackson was being banned from baseball for life.[12]

James Doherty of the Doherty brothers said of the few years after the 1918 armistice: "You didn't have to seek news in those days. You just had to keep up with it."[13] This includes a double murder known as the Case of the Ragged Stranger.

On June 21, 1920, minor war hero Carl Wanderer killed a hobo who supposedly had just murdered his wife, Ruth, in a street robbery. The police thought Wanderer had once again proven his bravery, but at the *Herald & Examiner* Howey was suspicious. He telegraphed the Colt Arms Company and was able to trace the stranger's gun to Wanderer himself. Howey sent Harry Romanoff to accompany detectives driving to the home that the supposedly grieving husband still shared with his mother-in-law.

While Wanderer gave plausible answers to the officers' questions, Romanoff scouted out a publicity-seeking police lieutenant who let him search the apartment. "Romy" discovered photos of another young woman and scraps of a torn-up love letter. Austin O'Malley of the same newspaper used a skeleton key to sneak into the apartment after Wanderer's mother-in-law left. He found taped to Carl's shirt drawer fifteen hundred dollars Ruth had withdrawn from a bank to buy a house, and the reporter found additional love letters in a boot. O'Malley had the letters copied at the newspaper office, and only after publication did he turn them over to the police.

When Wanderer received a prison term of only twenty years for murdering his wife, Howey waged a campaign to execute him. Wanderer underwent a second trial, for killing the "ragged stranger," and this time was sentenced to death. He sang a popular song while the noose was fitted around his neck, leading hefty New York critic Alexander Woollcott to comment, "From the crowd of reporters watching came the audible comment that Wanderer deserved hanging for his voice alone."[14]

Howey never lost a chance to get back at the *Tribune* for the way it had treated him, and he might have been snickering behind his sleeve when he sent *Herald & Examiner* reporter Eleanor "Cissy" Patterson, sister of Joseph Medill Patterson and cousin of Colonel McCormick, to cover the 1920 Republican National Convention in town. There was a fondness between the short, average looking Howey and the pretty, lively red-haired woman with a butterfly heart but, for whatever reason, Walter seemed incapable of tender feelings.

This neglected daughter of social climbing Nellie Patterson should have been snapped up by the *Tribune* if only for her qualifications. But the Colonel was against it. Biographers have speculated that he did not want her to learn business secrets that she could use to obstruct him, or, more likely, that Kate McCormick would not have it. Certainly not after Cissy accused her of ruining her sons *and* the paper.[15] Cissy responded to the rejection by leaving town. She so relished journalism that within twenty years she edited Hearst's Washington *Herald*. Cissy then bought another D.C. paper and combined them as the *Times-Herald* to cover the capital city around the clock. Her novelist daughter, Felicia, who hated her, briefly married future influential newspaper columnist Drew Pearson. Cissy's niece, Alicia, founded the *Newsday* newspaper in Long Island.

Things were going so well in Chicago that Hearst made the mistake of thinking its raucous style of journalism was transferable. He dispatched Howey to resuscitate one ailing paper after another, including ones in Boston and New York. Howey even helped start the New York *Daily Mirror,* Hearst's tabloid answer to the *Tribune* family's New York *Daily News.* But the bantam-sized editor was never happy after being uprooted, and he could often be seen drinking brandy and talking about the old days in the Windy City.

More than any other person, Frank Carson typified the outrageous period of Chicago journalism. When he replaced Howey at the *Herald & Examiner,* he had fewer restraints than at the *Tribune.* Whereas Howey had been adept at playing the system, Carson encouraged his people to use whatever means they could think of for a story, since he was sure the friendly police would not bother them.

Carson's praise was as frequent as his anger. When he sent copyboy John McPhaul to steal a photo for a murder story, the future reporter overdid it and brought back everything he could snatch, including letters, laundry bills, and even a piece of wallpaper. Only the picture was usable but Carson gave him a five dollar bonus and was delighted, as McPhaul put it, to be at "the birth of a new burglar in his flock."

The new editor's first chance to show what he could really do came when Ruth Randall fatally shot her lover, adman Clifford Bleyer, and then herself in their apartment in March 1920. After portions from her diary were read to a coroner's jury, Carson declared that the entire book was now public record and was determined to get it. The journal disappeared from a precinct station a minute after officers rushed to the staged collision of two "Her-Ex" circulation trucks outside.

To sell this blatant sensationalism to more sensitive readers, Carson prefaced each daily excerpt with a comment from one society matron or another and the words "Crime Does Not Pay." Unless, of course, you were in the news business.[16]

Carson was nearly six feet tall, slender, and rather plain with his dark-rimmed glasses. But his undistinguished appearance concealed his antic heart and amazing memory. He not only seemed to know all policemen in the city and members of their families, he also had enough phone numbers in his head to reach everyone who frequently appeared in the news. He worked from four P.M. to six A.M. on slow nights and would stick around longer when a good story came in. He also never stopped looking for chances to shove a thorn in the side of his former employer. If a "Her-Ex" reporter stole a photo from a wrong address, Carson would send it back by a messenger saying he had picked the picture up at the *Tribune* lobby.

As described by McPhaul, who had served as his chief copyboy, Carson "had the small boy's delight in playing cops-and-robbers." To make sure a suspect did not return while his home was being searched for letters or diaries, Carson would have him "arrested" and taken to the "station," the Hearst Building. The editor kept a desk full of blank court forms, such as search warrants, for when his reporters showed up with their prisoners. After lulling them into a confession with enough to eat and drink, he turned the criminals over to the real police, destroyed the bogus documents, and tossed the phony badges back into his desk.[17]

In his first September on the job, Carson sent Austin O'Malley to the house of Harvey Church, a railroad brakeman from Wisconsin who was the last person known to have seen car salesmen Bernard Daugherty and Carl Ausmus. Church had seen Daugherty and Ausmus when the three of them had gone on a demonstration drive. Daugherty was later found dead and Ausmus was still missing, and so was the Packard sedan, and so was Church. Among the trash in the brakeman's basement, O'Malley found two bloodied hats. When he phoned this in and Carson did not say a word, O'Malley asked, "Do you feel it, too?" He meant that tingly sensation of sensing something dreadful.

At Carson's direction, O'Malley went to the homes of the two salesmen and had the hats identified as theirs. The editor himself called the police chief in Adams, Wisconsin, and learned that Church was back home and his family was proud of him because he was driving around in a new Packard.

Carson and O'Malley gave their evidence to the police and, rather than await extradition, made the long drive to Adams in a chauffeured touring car with a pair of burly circulation employees. Along the way they checked with investigators by phone and learned that Ausmus's body was found buried near where the reporter had nosed around in the unfinished basement.

Interrupting a family dinner, O'Malley and the circulation toughs introduced themselves to Church, his sister, and their parents as police officers, and Carson said he went along with them because he was certain of Church's innocence. Carson promised that if Harvey consented to being taken to the *Herald & Examiner* office, the suspect could explain to the "officers" how he had paid for the car.

At the state line, Carson faked car trouble and had Harvey and "Detective" O'Malley cross on foot, with the two circulation men as backup. Once their feet touched Illinois, Carson made a citizen's arrest, and the brawny men kept the double killer still while O'Malley found a phone and called a rewrite man.

Church's execution was as unusual as his arrest had been. While in jail he went into a coma and had to be carried to the gallows strapped to a board. Then he was moved to a chair and plunged sitting down.[18]

Reporters who knew how to turn stories in quickly, with human interest details enlivened by spry wording, and how to twist the facts according to the publisher's political outlook, might be put on the city hall beat. Two large desks in the day press room were reserved for "guests," that is, reporters between jobs who dropped by for a nap. Another press room in the building was for night reporters covering after-hours meetings.

Politicians would reward "the boys" at Christmastime with thank-you bottles in the main press room, leading to the term "City Haul." The grandest event ever held there was a holiday bash awaiting reporters once when they returned to the room from making their rounds. The feast was supplied by the German-language papers, and the master of ceremonies was *Globe* city editor Charley Almy of the former Whitechapel Club. Almy would claim he could afford to eat nothing but beans since entering the news business. He told the gathering that when he arrived from Grand Rapids, "I found the Long John Wentworth style of journalism still in vogue. I introduced a dashy, breezy style of composition which has been likened to that of Guy de Maupassant. Far be it from me to accuse Guy of plagiarism."[19]

Newspapers of course saw an intermittent stream of cranks who evidently were unaware they were cranks. Drop-ins during the twenties included a man who insisted he was Jesus Christ, and still apparently virginal spinsters who declared they had been violated. Perhaps as religion was being de-emphasized, and as living in a city of two-million narrowed everyone's personal contacts, these people thought being mentioned in the newspapers would make their unexceptional lives worthwhile.

On December 11, 1921, the resident of Cook County Jail cell 427, cop killer Tommy O'Connor, was not worried about the noose he was facing. When he and a few other inmates were being let out for exercise one of them jumped a guard. At the elevators they overpowered a second guard and some trustees, locked them in closets, turned a stolen key in the lock of a steel door, and scaled a nine-foot wall. "Terrible Tommy" jumped into the car of an unwitting city light inspector or, according to another account, a knowing law student. An investigation led to the firing of several jail guards who should have prevented the breakout.

Since O'Connor had been sentenced to hang, when Illinois switched to the electric chair the gallows were dismantled in 1927 and kept for him at the new jail. Cold-hearted Tommy became a legend as the lookout for him continued for more than half a century. The rotting boards of his gallows were sold to the Seven Acres Museum in Union, Illinois, the same year as his last reported sighting, 1977. Ripley's Believe It Or Not Museum bought them in 2006.

Before turning O'Connor's escape into the play *The Front Page*, Ben Hecht was widely known in literary circles for his *Daily News* column, "1001 Afternoons in Chicago," playing upon the *One Thousand and One Nights* collection of Arabian tales. Doing uncredited snooping for him in 1921 was Henry Luce, who was born in China twenty-three years earlier while his father was answering his calling as a Presbyterian minister.

The Yale-educated but struggling reporter had come to Chicago earlier that year and was agape at what he saw. His duties amounted to walking the streets and picking up anecdotes for Hecht to transform into vignettes and get the credit. Luce wrote home that his salary was about ten cents a day more than his carfare to and from work.

One story in the column concerned a former sailor who had to keep his rooming house quarters brilliantly lighted because he was afraid of a nameless Thing that came in with the dark. Before long Hecht fired Luce as being too naive.[20] Perhaps that meant his legman wanted the stories to stay factual. The setback was fortunate for Luce because he found real newspaper work in Baltimore, eventually co-founded *Time* magazine, and become a national opinion-maker.

Also in 1921, Texas-born salesman David Stephenson, a Ku Klux Klan Grand Dragon, sent a recruiter from his Indianapolis headquarters to transform Chicago into the hate center of America. The *Tribune* fell into Stephenson's plan for using the group as a step toward the White House. Not only did the paper feature a full page Klan ad on April 16, an August 27 editorial promoted the initial movement in the South as a "romantic" response to "the danger of Negro domination." The paper also gave fawning coverage to the hundreds of motorists who massed at a Chicago park on their way to a Klan rally, and sent a photographer and a reporter to every church where hooded members would be distributing food.

Just two months after recruitment began, a suburban torchlight meeting attracted ten thousand Klansmen to watch two thousand new members receiving their white robes. A *Tribune* editorial favoring the group claimed that lynching is "seldom justifiable" but "has its roots in our national character and derives from qualities essential, we think, in the American scheme."

Muckraker Edward Price Bell wrote against the Klan in a *Daily News* series. But none of the other major Chicago papers dared to go after the movement, which had a Loop chapter for just attorneys and several across the city for businessmen. The organization already controlled Indiana state politics and was beginning to influence voting in Springfield.

Blacks in the city still lacked an effective political organization and could not counteract the group, but not so another Klan target, the Catholic Irish, Germans, and Slavic people whose families had flocked to the city. Several of them stole and published a membership list that was distributed to all parish churches in the archdiocese. Business boycotts quickly put the movement into retreat.

The northern branch of the KKK completely gave way when Stephenson was arrested for causing the death of his secretary after he abducted and raped her aboard a train from Chicago to Indiana. When the Klan-influenced Indiana governor responded to public pressure by refusing to pardon him, Stephenson took revenge by opening his private files to Illinois and Indiana reporters who should have been going after him all along.[21]

The year of the mass Klan recruitment, Chicago police opened a little-known satellite office, nicknamed "Scotland Yard," in a former precinct station at 2075 South Canalport for undercover operations and intensive interrogations. This was one of the few places where reporters were barred.

In an attempt to overwhelm the Hearst papers, the *Tribune* expanded its popular features. In 1921, it filled the back page with photos and in 1924, along with its sister paper, the New York *Daily News*, increased its circulation with the *Little Orphan Annie* comic strip. The *Tribune* even received a bomb threat when production problems kept Annie from appearing for a couple of days.

By now radio had gone beyond its experimental stage and was turning into a major industry. Station WGU, owned by the *Daily News* and the Fair Store, started broadcasting from the Loop discount department store on April 13, 1922. Before long, the newspaper bought out the Fair's share, moved its microphones to a downtown hotel, and invited U.S. Commerce Secretary Herbert Hoover to provide new call letters. The future president chose WMAQ—We Must Ask Questions.

In 1925, the station carried the first local broadcast of a baseball game. In 1931, it moved to the huge, newly completed Merchandise Mart across the river from downtown, greatly boosted its power, and, as the flagship station of NBC,

Merchandise Mart. This huge building was the national headquarters of NBC radio. The station aired the first national newscasts, written and delivered by adventurous reporter Floyd Gibbons.

would originate two of the most popular comedy shows in the medium's history, "Amos 'n' Andy" and "Fibber McGee and Molly." In the early thirties the local station would use a mobile radio unit with a beach umbrella for an antenna. But, as at other stations, its newscasts were brief, stale, and written off newspaper copy.

In 1923, Robert S. Abbott of the Chicago *Defender* hired ten-year-old Willard Motley to edit a children's page. Encouraged as an author, Motley would later write the top-selling crime novel *Knock on Any Door* with its motto of "live fast, die young, and have a good-looking corpse." Since his characters were white, most readers were unaware he was African American.

For people coming from small American towns and Europe, bootleg shootings offered something exciting to write home about. The public seldom felt threatened because, as a common phrase went, "they only kill their own." In 1924, with the Chicago rate of violent deaths twenty-four percent higher than for the rest of the country, weekday editions of the *Tribune* carried a stylized clockface with three hands to show the current death tolls for autos, guns, and "Moonshine."

On the basis of a coy letter by an inexperienced job applicant, the *Tribune* that year hired petite Maurine Watkins to put a feminine slant on the courts beat. When cute Beaulah Annan shot her lover to death and was jailed with another murderess, plain-looking singer Belva Gaertner, Watkins broke tradition by using a light touch. After both women were found not guilty, Watkins wrote the play *Chicago* loosely based on their cases, adding snappy dialogue to the premise that in the Toddlin' Town women were seldom convicted of murder. Rather than delighting in her transient fame, Watkins was haunted for years by the possibility that her tongue-in-cheek articles had led to the acquittals.[22]

Eclipsing public interest in Annan and Gaertner that year was the shocking murder of fourteen-year-old Bobby Franks, whose body was found in a South Side culvert. What was then called the "Crime of the Century" involved wealth, social class and, as the *Tribune* put it, "mystery beyond belief."

Daily News cub reporters Alvin Goldstein and James Mulroy were assigned to do just legwork for seasoned newsmen, but they were determined to beat the veteran reporters. As a result, the two young men shared a Pulitzer Prize for helping detectives put the pieces of the Franks mystery together.

First, Goldstein and Mulroy sent the missing boy's uncle by taxi to where the body was found so the boy could be identified. An investigation showed that Bobby had been struck on the head with a chisel and suffocated on a gag shoved down his throat. Questioning everyone who could possibly know something about the crime, the two neophytes narrowed the list of possible suspects to someone at the University of Chicago.

After committing the "thrill murder," one of the killers had typed a ransom note to throw authorities off. The young reporters in their thick suits of the day obtained copies of student papers and saw that Richard Loeb's matched the typing on the ransom note. A crucial paragraph in their prize-winning article on May 30, 1924, stated:

> Leopold had been insisting all through a night and day of questioning that he owned only one machine, a Hammond. The friend produced examples from two typewriters, one the Hammond and the other apparently a portable. ... [and] a slightly off-line "t" and a minutely twisted "i" seemed to make the comparison still more intimate.[23]

Authorities would learn that Loeb and fellow teenager Nathan Leopold were linked by a strange bond, with Loeb an active homosexual and Leopold possibly just going along. Out of this relationship between two young men too bright and too rich to feel comfortable in the real world, had grown the fantasy of a random *folie a deux* murder for no more conscious reason than to baffle authorities.

Trial preparations received unrelenting coverage, and even today newspeople admire the way reporter George Wright scooped everyone on weeks of secret grand jury testimony. The *Tribune* always claimed that Wright was one of its employees at the time. The truth is that he had been working for City

Former Cook County Criminal Court building. The trials held here included the Loeb and Leopold "thrill kill" case. The press room is the setting of the newspaper play *The Front Page* (Chicago History Museum, photographer—Copelin, ICHi-00462).

News since he was fifteen and was hoping that bravado would land him a job at one of the papers.

The official story is that while on the court beat one day, Wright idly tossed keys into the air and heard a hollow thud. "Maybe the ceiling is a fake," he supposedly thought. "Maybe I could get in there."

His *Tribune* obituary says the chief janitor told him, "Sure, George, there is a five-foot opening above every ceiling in the building." The false ceiling apparently was installed to keep the rooms warmer in winter.

But the keys story must have been untrue, since Wright would have had to toss them idly more than eight feet in the air. Perhaps Wright simply wondered why some ceilings were fourteen feet high and others were nineteen feet. But why fib about it? More likely, he was covering up a bribe to the chief janitor, who either suggested using a board or at least showed him how to do it. The janitor might even have supplied a painters' board and possibly set it up for him.

Certainly it seems unlikely that with or without help, Wright could not have lugged a twenty-foot plank into a public building without someone seeing or hearing him. If the plank did come from the outside, then he and the janitor must have set it up sometime after ten o'clock at night to avoid being seen by jurors and lawyers moving about during late deliberations. Wright's City News editors had to have known what he was doing because he would be incommunicado during his entire shift and for some time afterward.

The plank he left up there allowed Wright to creep close to the area above the witness stand without danger of falling into the grand jury room. "At first I got scared stiff but later I got accustomed to this balancing act," he said. With a hand drill he made an opening in the false ceiling for a stethoscope that would act as a headset.

Wright remained silent each day and jotted down the secret grand jury testimony "in shorthand." One imagines it was the kind of abbreviations reporters make up for themselves. He brought his sweat-limp notes each night to the City News office at Clark and Randolph for someone to transcribe into news copy, probably with his help. Everyone at the papers wanted to know how he was obtaining testimony. As he said, "I drove them wild." The scoops of course were an illegal violation of the defendants' rights.

After Wright was snatched up by the *Tribune*, he continued using a plank for all major court cases. After all, as his obituary noted, his court scoops "were obtained in a period of intense and often hazardous competition." These exclusives lasted until trials were moved to 26th Street and California Avenue. Wright continued to be a good reporter, but less inventive.[24]

Any sentence other than death for Loeb and Leopold seemed unthinkable, but Clarence Darrow took the case because he opposed executions. One of Frank Carson's last triumphs before he went on to lesser accomplishments at the New York *Daily News* came when he sized up Judge John Caverly and hazarded a guess on the outcome.

Carson ordered fifty thousand copies of the *Herald & Examiner* printed in advance with a bannerline declaring that the two men's lives had been spared. If he was wrong, he would have to burn all the copies and answer to The Chief, but the editor was excited by a chance to beat the other Hearst paper, the *American*. When the bannerline became fact, he ran outside the newspaper building for the pleasure of watching delivery crews racing downtown and stopping just long enough to toss bundles of *Herald & Examiner*s near the news stands. McPhaul assures us he "wore that cat-that-ate-the-canary grin" of his.[25]

In the year of Bobby Franks' murder, U.S. Senator (Joseph) Medill McCormick was found dead in a Washington, D.C., hotel room of a "heart attack" (suicide by barbiturates). He might have been a better leader for the family paper than the Colonel if he had not been afflicted by the family curse.[26]

Victor Lawson continued operating the *Daily News* without consulting anyone up to his death in 1924. His will specified that the paper be run by a banker on behalf of the Congregational Church. That lasted until Lawson's nephew, Walter Strong, raised six million dollars and pledged eight million more in 1926 to buy the paper and wipe out its debts. Strong was neither a financier nor a newsman, and the paper from then on went into a respectable decline.

But Chicago-style journalism was still going strong, and was being ennobled by fiction in the way that *Morte d'Arthur* turned the barbarism of knights into inspiring legends. But instead of a round table at Camelot, the focus of *The Front Page* was a long table in the press room of the criminal courts building at Dearborn and Hubbard. At the wooden chairs sits a 1926 cross-section of reporters playing cards as they await the execution of a mousy cop killer. The authors tell us that there is not one of these coarse men who is unfamiliar with the European writers of the day, and several might be acquainted with the tangles of German philosophers.[27] As the curtain rises they appear to be just smoking and laying down grungy cards, but a shrewd observer might sense expectancy and readiness.

Little needs to be said about the more famous author of *The Front Page*, Ben Hecht, because much of what he told about his Chicago years can be disproved or is unverifiable. He arrived from Racine, Wisconsin, at the age of fourteen and, through the influence of an uncle, was hired by Chicago *Journal* editor Richard Finnegan as a picture stealer. Hecht claimed he obtained the photo of a suicide by blocking the family's chimney and sneaking in after the relatives ran out to escape the smoke. Perhaps.

After making a name for himself at the *Journal*, he jumped to the *Daily News* in 1914 while editor Henry Justin Smith was creating a Chicago force in literature. Fellow newspeople knew Hecht as being "short and stubby with sharp blue-gray eyes and stringy black hair." He was assigned to post-war Berlin at the end of 1918 and came back with some European ideas, including an interest in psychoanalysis.

Hecht was essentially a paragrapher and vignette writer rather than a news-man, and was never associated with a major story, apart from the fiction that he broke the Carl Wanderer case. As Henry Justin Smith said, Hecht's approach to newspaper writing was that "just under the edge of the news. ... lay life; that in this urban life there dwelt the stuff of literature ... walking the downtown streets, peering in windows from skyscrapers, sunning itself in parks and boule-vards."

Hecht presented himself as outgoing and sociable, but those close to him knew of his fits of depression and occasional abrupt changes in behavior. When he was smitten by Rose Caylor, a pretty yet earnest actress who was also work-ing at the *Daily News,* he thought nothing of leaving his wife and daughter for her.[28]

His writing partner would be Charles MacArthur, who was one of nine children of a fundamentalist minister growing up in Scranton, Pennsylvania. His future insurance magnate brother and sister-in-law would found the John D. and Catherine T. MacArthur Foundation "genius grants." Charles was also a distant relative of General Douglas MacArthur. But the only thing the anti-authoritarian "Charlie" shared with his relatives was a sense of independence and a streak of romanticism.

His father wanted Charles to go through a school for missionaries, but at seventeen he struck out on his own. On his eighteenth summer, MacArthur worked at his family's *Oak Leaves* newspaper in the Chicago suburb of Oak Park. He said he once put on a cassock and entered a cell to hear the confes-sion of a man who had killed his wife and her lover.

Restless, romantic, a prank-puller ... there was only one place for him, Chicago in the twenties. He worked for a while at City News, but at Cousin Douglas's suggestion joined the Army. He took part in the last major action involving a horseback expedition, the futile pursuit of Pancho Villa.[29] After service as a doughboy in the Great War, he was hired by the *Herald & Exam-iner* and relaxed by socializing with columnist Hecht at the Corona cafe, and by mixing with news writers including Carl Sandburg at Schlogl's restaurant. As if by intent, he had become everything his father detested: someone who craved excitement, neon lights, women, and liquor. But inside, MacArthur was simpler and more easily hurt than he let on.

Just after kindred spirit Gene Fowler arrived in the city from Denver, he was jailed due to a misunderstanding. When word quickly spread that a news-man had been locked up, the Chicago Press Club dispatched a delegation of Hecht, MacArthur, and a *Journal* sports writer to bail him out. For the rest of their lives Hecht, MacArthur, and Fowler would be more open with one another than they may have been with their wives.

Fowler regarded the tall, slender MacArthur as having been "born with the spirit of a wild colt." The reporter whom pals called "the Scotsman" reveled in satirizing the phoniness of others. MacArthur fell in love with

Herald-Examiner columnist Carol Fink and followed her on a train to New York.

MacArthur would claim that in an attempt to keep him, Howey ordered the train stopped because "That son of a bitch stole my watch!," the famous last words of *The Front Page*. But from accounts available to us, Howey had used deception only to grab Carson as his assistant and was never determined to retain any reporter, certainly not one whose main talent lay in buddying with friends. We should remember that after MacArthur died, his widow, actress Helen Hayes, remarked that "My Charlie used to find the truth unchallenging and quite candidly created the most amazing tales to displace it."[30]

While still married to Carol, MacArthur met Helen at a Long Island party such as the ones that drew Irving Berlin, Harpo Marx, and violinist Jasha Heifitz. In a case of opposites attracting at first sight, the curly-haired Protestant ex-reporter went up to the tiny, shy Catholic actress while holding a bag of peanuts. Pouring some into her hand, he said, "I wish they were emeralds."[31] Although both MacArthur and Hecht were now living in New York their hearts still beat for the Toddlin' Town, with all its narrow-mindedness and criminality. As Hayes would say at a talk in Chicago, "This is where they fell in love with life."[32]

Inspired by the success of Watkins' play about the city, the men discussed writing one centering on the escape of Tommy O'Connor ("Earl Williams") and likewise basing the characters on real people. Walter Howey's doing anything to get Carson to switch papers was turned into three lively acts with editor "Walter Burns" trying to keep reporter "Hildebrand Johnson" from marrying and leaving for New York.

Real-life Hilding "Hildy" Johnson was a blue-eyed lightweight from Sweden with a subtle sense of humor or, if you prefer another description, "a brooding giant." He would never think of accepting a bribe and enjoyed playing news games, such as assisting Howey in abducting witnesses on the pretext of being a police detective. From the day City News made Johnson a court reporter, the ripple stone criminal courthouse adjacent to the jail was his real home, and his *Herald & Examiner* checks were mailed to him there.

Although accurate in his stories, Johnson had little interest in details. Writing about his own newspaper days, William Moore parodied the way Hilding would turn a story in to a rewrite: "Now, you understand all this is horseshit [an insignificant story], Art. It's about a guy named Rogers. You can get his first name out of the clippings. Well, he's up in court today.... You'll have to look up the charge in the morning paper.... You can get everything out of the afternoon papers. I've lost my notes. Anyway, Art, it's all horseshit." End of story.[33]

Johnson would go out of his way to break in new reporters but also was a tough competitor. In the 1919 trial of J. Norman Cook for the fatal shooting of William Brodway, he slipped into the jury room after the late-night verdict was put in the judge's vault to be announced in court the next morning. Johnson rummaged through the discarded ballots and mentally reconstructed the way the "not guilty" verdict must have been reached.

To assure himself of the exclusive he pocketed enough ballots from the wastepaper basket so that the *Tribune* reporter sneaking in after him would report that Cook had been convicted. After the mystified judge read the *Herald & Examiner* story in the morning, he demanded to know who had unlocked his vault.[34]

Other reporters would shrug off inaction by authority figures, whether because of politics, cowardice, or payoffs. But Johnson would bring the subject up in public, such as when aggressive Assistant State's Attorney William McSwiggin was sprayed with bullets from a Thompson submachine gun on April 27, 1926. All means of identification had been removed, but a reporter recognized the body at the morgue intake room. A short time earlier, McSweeney had won a rare conviction in a gangland murder and said he would next "blow the lid" off the city. Some believed he was building a case against Capone for the demise of hijacker Joe Howard.

No one doubted that State's Attorney Robert Crowe knew who killed McSwiggin, but the official refused to concede a link between crime and county government. So the *Herald & Examiner* ran the headline WHO KILLED MCSWIGGIN AND WHY? Each morning afterward, Johnson would drop by Crowe's office and ask the same question until the official started keeping his door locked. One day Johnson shattered the door glass with his walking stick, reached in for the knob, strode in, and asked, "Who killed McSwiggin and why?"

Crowe at last issued this statement: "It has been established to the satisfaction of the state's attorney's office and the detective bureau that Capone in person led the slayers ... [and] that Capone handled the machine gun, being compelled to this act in order to set an example of fearlessness to his lesser companions." But no action was taken until tax evasion sent Scarface Al to Alcatraz.

Hilding Johnson's outspoken nature sometimes immersed him in trouble. A chance remark turned brawny state's attorney's aide C. Wayland Brooks on him in court. This lawyer and ex-marine knocked the skinny reporter down and kept beating Johnson until bailiffs and fellow reporters pulled him back. Johnson climbed to his feet and said, "Turn him loose. I haven't finished with him yet."[35]

To Johnson's unrelenting spirit, MacArthur and Hecht added a little of MacArthur himself and a pinch of competent but unexciting court reporter Enoch Johnson, who apparently was of no relation to Hilding.

The City News character, "Buddy McCue," was patterned after Buddy McHugh. And then there was the severely diabetic Sherman Duffy ("Duffy"), who lived in far away Ottawa, Illinois, and could tend to his precious garden only on weekends. After working as a Springfield political stringer and sports editor at the *Tribune,* the real Duffy held a similar job at the *Journal,* where he served as a mentor to his assistant, Ben Hecht. Robert J. Casey said Duffy "was the architect's model for all the literate lads who have come to clutter up his profession since."[36]

For their relentless, unfeeling editor Walter Burns, the authors used Howey sprinkled with traits from their Broadway producer, Jed Harris. But the poet-reporter "Bensinger" hardly seems made up. Later Chicago *American* columnist Jack Mabley said he once worked with the real person, Roy Bensinger, and found him no different from the way he was portrayed.

The part of the stupid Sheriff Peter Hartman came from rather stupid former Cook County Sheriff Peter Hoffman, and MacArthur shamelessly modeled Mrs. Grant, the shrewish mother of Hildy's fiancée, on Helen Hayes's mother.

And yet the two friends did not regard reporters of their own time as equaling ones they had known or heard about from the period of 1900 to 1919. In the prologue to the printed edition, Hecht called *The Front Page* a valentine for a time gone by.

With Hecht's flair for colorful writing, he was assured of a steady income even if the play flopped. But MacArthur, going through a divorce, was staking the rest of his life on whether New York audiences would appreciate Chicago-style journalism. He did not want his second marriage to be one in which his wife was famous and he was a failure.

Too edgy to sit in the Times Square Theatre for the premier on August 14, 1928, Hecht and MacArthur waited on the fire escape while Hayes took a seat near an exit so she could give them a running account of the response. The actress playing Molly, who jumps out a window to take attention away from the fugitive hiding in the *Daily News*–style rolltop desk, was "greeted to one of the wildest ovations I've ever heard," Hayes would say after a life in the theater. "I raced out [to the fire escape] at the end of the act. The heroes of the night were huddled on the iron steps, all pinched and white in the half-light," she added. "Reaching Charlie's arms in two bounds over the rickety fire-escape grating, I babbled wildly about the audience's reaction." That moment, on the fire escape, Charlie looked into her eyes and asked, "Helen, will you marry me?"[37]

The ovations for *The Front Page* came while bootleg violence was making Chicago a national scandal. Thugs who had armed themselves with brass knuckles and guns in the war between the *Tribune* and the *Herald & Examiner* now joined punch-drunk fighters and alley toughs in beating shop and restaurant owners into buying their boss's liquor. The gangs were such good copy that not even the self-righteous *Tribune* expressed outrage at the public corruption that obviously was letting them thrive.

Freebooting Chicago mobster Frank McErlane entered criminal history when he tried to kill Spike O'Donnell on September 25, 1925, in the country's first documented gangland use of a Thompson submachine gun. Capone's team picked up some of them to be on equal terms. McErlane was later seen killing a lawyer at an Indiana speakeasy. He drove back to Illinois and was protected by the governor for two years until Indiana authorities demanded extradition.[38]

The newspapers exposed laxness at the Cook County Jail after McErlane attended a hearing intoxicated. The judge ordered an investigation into how liquor had been secreted into the cell of one of the country's most dangerous gangsters and learned that the guard in charge of McErlane had likewise been drunk.

In the nation's first killing of an FBI agent, Martin Durkin shot Edwin Shanahan in Chicago on October 11, 1925, during an investigation into an interstate auto theft ring. With newspapers following his every step, Durkin was arrested on a train near St. Louis the next January and tried in the Toddlin' Town. While in jail he imbibed so much that he appeared before the judge half-soused. Yet reporters never dared to write about how the county administration had become a mockery, because their editors wanted to keep official sources friendly.

It seemed like shootings were everywhere, even in the Loop and the Near North Side entertainment district. On November 10, 1924, Dion O'Banion was killed in his flower shop across from Holy Name Cathedral at State and Chicago. On October 11, 1926, O'Banion's successor, Earl "Hymie" Weiss, and his chauffeur were cut down at almost the same location, and local lore has it that some pits in the cathedral stones are from the gunfire. Top mobster Tony Lombardo and his bodyguard were gunned down on September 7, 1928, at State and Madison, long considered the world's busiest corner. Yet the papers were still pretending each killing was isolated instead of part of mob power struggles protected by the police and prosecutors.

Chicago mobsters enjoyed having newspeople around them like pets. Union racketeer Big Tim Murphy, who often gave advice to Italian mobsters, would phone Peggy Doyle of the *Herald & Examiner* with updates on underworld doings. Vern Whaley, writing a boxing column for the *American*, was never without a cigar after Capone introduced them to him. Reporters were generally freeloaders, and gangsters were always good for a meal. "But we never really thought about it," Whaley said. He and other sports writers were often invited to Capone's table at his Club Metropole on South Wabash for drinks "and a lot of unclean stories."

Only newsman Robert St. John risked his life to expose Capone. St. John had been hired as a *Daily News* reporter after serving in the Navy during the war, but he left to serve as the "boy editor" of the small Cicero *Tribune* at the age of twenty-two. His brother, Archer, ran the *Beacon* in nearby Berwyn.

A reform administration forced Capone to take his operation to the adjacent western suburb of Cicero, and St. John made it clear he was not welcome.

Daily accounts of gang beatings and murders appeared on the front page, and denouncements of the gangster and the suburban political candidates he supported filled the editorial page. In the hottest story the paper ever ran, Robert St. John personally investigated a Capone brothel near the Hawthorne Race Track and found what he concluded to be its death chamber.

Archer St. John was about to start a special edition attacking corruption as the Berwyn polls opened for the 1925 mayoral election. Capone's men forced him into a car, blindfolded and handcuffed him, and held him captive until the balloting ended. That same day Capone's brother Robert and another mobster jumped Robert St. John and severely beat him in front of two policemen.

As the battered editor was being released from the hospital a week later, he was told a husky gentleman with a scar on his cheek had paid his bill. Capone then furtively acquired the paper to silence it, and the St. Johns had no choice but to leave town. Robert completed his career at the Associated Press.[39]

Whether because the papers had exhausted themselves with more than a decade of Prohibition after a decade of circulation wars, or because too much news was breaking across the city, the sense of competition among reporters was letting up. The *Tribune*'s John Kelley believed that "The old 'dog eat dog' spirit is gone" because the papers were putting out so many editions to beat their rivals that readers no longer remembered where they had seen a story first.

No amount of newspaper coverage could match the force of hearing the "Scopes monkey trial" over the radio as it was happening in Dayton, Tennessee. Science teacher John Scopes had been arrested in 1925 for introducing evolution to the classroom. He was defended by Clarence Darrow and prosecuted by dying orator William Jennings Bryan. The presence of these two powerhouses turned the minor proceedings into a clash of free-thinking and long-held beliefs.

Scopes was convicted and fined one hundred dollars, but it was a clear victory for radio news. The *Tribune*-owned WGN had been allowed to rearrange the courtroom to suit its microphones and cables, and newscaster Quin Ryan maintained a running commentary for gavel to gavel coverage. The phenomenal cost for these uninterrupted broadcasts was one thousand dollars a day.[40]

The daring coverage was just one sign of prosperity at the *Tribune* in the twenties. With its popular combination of popular features and detailed treatment of local and national events, the paper had outgrown its quarters in just fifteen years. While other newspaper publishers were happy in ordinary office buildings, McCormick sponsored a one-hundred-thousand-dollar worldwide architectural competition for a headquarters that would be built just across the river from downtown, facing the soaring new Wrigley Building on North Michigan Avenue. The design judges unanimously chose a plan by New York architects John Mead Howells and Raymond Hood for a thirty-story Gothic tower emphasizing vertical lines and links to the European past.

The Tribune Tower, winner of a national design competition, replaced a building where a former employee was beaten and thrown down an elevator shaft.

When two years of construction ended in May 1925, the building truly looked as if it could be the site of the World's Greatest Newspaper. The seven levels below the street formed a maze of presses, heating and cooling plants, and storage spaces for huge paper rolls of newsprint. These came down on barges from the *Tribune*-owned paper mill in Canada, the St. Lawrence River, Lake Michigan, and finally the downtown stub of the Y-shaped Chicago River.

The outer walls of the tower were limestone in variegated shades of gray, and a cathedral-like entrance arch rose more than twenty feet from the sidewalk. The revolving door led to the impressive walls of a wide lobby carved with inscriptions about the freedom and responsibilities of the press.

McCormick gave the paper plenty of room to grow as if offering it a fresh start, and turning his back on a time when someone could be beaten nearly to death and thrown down an elevator shaft in a building his family owned. The Colonel at this time even rewrote history, attributing the circulation wars to individual scuffles between native-born newsboys and adult immigrants trying to take over their corners.[41] Gone was the supposed union violence James Keeley had perjured himself about.

Rather than exposing the graft that had made Capone seemingly invincible, the *Tribune* may have used the mob to crush a delivery drivers' strike, as Capone himself told Cissy Patterson. Colonel McCormick, of course, denied it. The former head of the newsboys union, Daniel Serritella, claimed that in

Above: Entrance of the Tribune Tower still impresses passersby. *Below:* Lobby of the Tribune Tower. The history of the newspaper does not always live up to the high ideals carved into the walls.

Stones on the walls of the Tribune Tower include these from the Great Wall of China, the Berlin Wall, and Martin Luther's Wurttemberg, Germany. Colonel McCormick regarded "The World's Greatest Newspaper" as a culmination of history.

1927 Max Annenberg summoned a scarfaced "Al Brown," an alias of Capone's, to sit in on talks between circulation manager Louis Rose and Joe Duello, head of the drivers union. There was no strike. Capone also averted a newsboys strike, Seritella said. He might have been lying—after all, he once was indicted for cheating taxpayers out of millions of dollars as city sealer—but his account is convincing.[42]

Capone's influence on city government was seen in Chicago's ban on performances of the 1927 play *The Racket* by former *Daily News* reporter Bartlett Cormack. The cynical drama, which starred Edward G. Robinson on Broadway, portrays how the state's attorney's office was secretly involved in rampant bootleg bloodshed.

Maintaining a sense of ethics was difficult for newspeople working long hours for low pay in a city where organized crime was chic. A clever *Journal* reporter identified only as Murphy arranged for an extra sheet to be included in every police accident report in the city, and sold these sheets to ambulance-chasing lawyers. Reporters needing a good lawyer for a divorce could get one for free by mentioning him favorably in stories and waiting for the phone to ring.[43]

People outside the profession might not realize how much a family the newspaper world could be. A short, wiry former office boy for the New York

Sun, James Cagney, was in Chicago in the late twenties and wanted to wire a friend, so rather than pay Western Union he stopped by the *Tribune* and asked the telegraph desk for a professional courtesy. By coincidence, it was John Bright of the Chicago *Evening Post,* and former Ben Hecht copyboy at the *Daily News,* who helped make Cagney a star a few years later.

Bright and soda shop owner Kubec Glasmon had an idea for a crime picture, but they needed money to get to Hollywood. Glasmon reportedly hired two men to set fire to his shop for the insurance. After he and Bright sold their story to Warner Brothers for the grapefruit-in-the-face film *Public Enemy,* they pressured the producer to feature Cagney because they liked the tough energy he showed in his early film roles.[44] Bright and Glasmon stayed on in L.A. and in time would help found the Screen Writers Guild.

Chicago had no topographical features apart from a chain of manmade beaches, and a lakefront protection law kept the shoreline free of amusements, and so a number of large passenger boats would sail across the lake every summer. One of them, *The Favorite,* went down on July 28, 1927, off Lincoln Park in a sudden late afternoon storm.

City News reporter Arnold A. Dornfeld, who had started his watch at around four P.M., was sent from the detective bureau to help cover the tragedy. Most new reporters would just turn in a story about the bodies, the survivors leaving boats that had rescued them, and the trucks taking fatalities away. But Dornfeld wanted to watch the recovery of the dead. The lifeguards who had been taken out by motorboat to bring back the twenty-seven bodies in that terrible late afternoon included Johnny Weissmuller before his Tarzan days.

Dornfeld climbed aboard the yacht of Zenith Radio Corporation president Eugene McDonald and asked the millionaire to take him out. "Dorny" shouted developments through a megaphone to a cub reporter on shore. Eventually McDonald asked to take his yacht back. Dornfeld wanted to return to the detective bureau to finish his shift, but his editor made him stand through the night at Municipal Pier and report the vessel-raising by scow and tug boat. The pier—now the Navy Pier entertainment center—was a pair of long, narrow exhibition halls jutting in tandem five-eighths of a mile into the lake.

At dawn, Dornfeld went to the City News office to wrap up the story, but a new shift had come in and the day editor sent him out again to cover the aftermath. When Dornfeld phoned in his final report from the county morgue at four-thirty in the afternoon, more than twenty-four hours after he had started, the editor coming on wanted to know why he was not at the detective bureau. "The day man is yelling for his relief," the editor griped. "Get over there right away!"[45] So "Dorny" worked there until midnight.

During his thirty-two-hour watch, radio listeners could feel close to the scene because announcer-reporter Quin Ryan provided an eyewitness account from the WGN studios in the Drake Hotel.

One of the City News desk men at the time was Larry Mulay, a small but animated man who seemed to live for work. His having been orphaned as a child may have been one reason the news business was the only family he knew. As a reporter he had put a match to newspapers on a front porch in a missing persons case so he could follow firefighters inside, where he found a woman and three children dead in a suicide and triple murder.[46]

In later years the prematurely bald Mulay was obsessed with cleanliness. Every midnight editor needed to wipe germs off the desk phone before he arrived, and each Monday ignite a coating of benzene on the large metal desk from the defunct *Herald & Examiner* to destroy bacteria. Even so, Mulay would vigorously wipe the desk with a cloth as he spoke to his staff. This continued until he moved into the general manager's office of the two-room news service in the sixties.

Walter Trohan, the reporter who had sawed off the top of a shooting victim's head, was on rewrite when well-dressed U.S. Senator James Hamilton Lewis showed up for someone to interview him in 1928. Trohan asked the politician to wait a few minutes because he was working on an important story.

"That's quite all right, young man," the orator replied, "I used to work here myself."

He picked up a stack of the stencils editors used instead of pencils, wrote a longhand interview with himself about an international problem, then had Mulay edit it and send copies to the half dozen dailies that owned the wire service. On his way out, Lewis tipped his hat and gave the editor a little bow.[47]

That year, McCormick was outraged that a rapist had attacked a nurse who had answered a help wanted ad in the *Tribune*. The Colonel was sure that if anyone could bring the man to justice, it was Mose Lamson. The reporter had no schooling and had joined the paper as a newspaper delivery helper. Perhaps he took part in the circulation wars. After being made a police reporter at the suggestion of James Doherty, Lamson learned the value of making contacts, presumably by paying police officers and gangsters a few dollars for good tips. Many tipsters enjoyed being helpful to reporters or the police, and money they received was just an added inducement. But officially reporters and city editors never gave money to sources.

Over the next five months, Lamson spent six thousand dollars of the *Tribune*'s money and traveled through nineteen states, wearing out two autos. After Lamson at last found the ex-convict in suburban Kansas City, the man pleaded guilty in Chicago and was sentenced to serve sixty years in prison. McCormick gave Lamson a one-thousand-dollar bonus.[48]

In late 1928, the *Tribune* and WGN installed the city's first police radio system at a cost of forty thousand dollars. During regular programming, a secretary would walk quickly to an announcer—usually Quin Ryan—with an emergency report, and the announcer would sound a gong before reading the message to all forty of the touring cars in the detective squad, as well as to the general public. As an audience builder, WGN advised people to "listen to the gong." But the police complained that the messages drew disruptive crowds to scenes, and many listeners were annoyed by interruptions of their programs, and so the expensive experiment was abandoned even though it was a forerunner of modern police communications.[49]

Jimmy Durkin, an orphaned copyboy who rose to *Tribune* city editor, died of a heart attack after coming home from work on December 30, 1928, six weeks shy of the story that would do more than the Columbian Exposition in making Chicago world famous.

Hoodlums said to include Fred Burke and friends from East St. Louis, Illinois, were provided with blue uniforms and autos resembling police cars to raid a repair garage Bugs Moran was using as a liquor loading point. On St. Valentine's Day, February 14, 1929, the murder squad caught six gangsters in the garage as well as a mob hanger-on. The two "officers" with their long coats concealing Tommy guns and two "detectives" with pistols drawn from their topcoats ordered the seven to face the brick back wall and cut them down without mercy.

Eighteen-year-old Walter Spirko was the first newsman with the story. As he did every day, the "City News kid" had been putting together death reports at the coroner's office on the fifth floor of the county building when Deputy Coroner Bill Baumann came over and said, "Walter, you better call your office."

"I just stood there," Spirko recalled in an interview. Not long before, City News editor Isaac Gershman had warned the nice-looking, lanky former newsboy that people would try to fool him with false tips. Could this be one?

When Spirko followed Baumann to his cubicle, the deputy coroner quietly said, "We just got a call. Seven men were shot to death at 2122 North Clark Street."

Walter immediately phoned city editor Mulay and then "Gersh," and both told him it had to be a prank. "See, I warned you about stuff like that," Gershman said.

But on the chance the story might be true, Gershman called the City News reporter at the detective bureau, seventeen-year-old John Paster, and asked him to check into it. Paster was on his first week as a reporter after serving as a sixteen-dollar-a-week copyboy, and he already was admired for the way he could turn in breaking stories fast and accurately. The teenager telephoned the police station closest to the address, but the officers said they had not heard anything about a shooting, a ploy to keep reporters from flocking to the scene while the evidence was still fresh.

Still thinking the story could have some basis because of the source, Gershman, a future general manager at City News, told "Johnny" to keep on it by phone. Paster was able to get hold of Coroner Herman Bundesen as the official was putting on his derby and coat. Stammering with excitement, Paster phoned the desk with confirmation.

"Gersh" personally dictated to Trohan this cautiously toned-down bulletin: "Six men are reported to have been seriously injured in a fight in a pool room at 2122 N. Clark St." Seven became six, dead became injured, and the scene became a pool hall, possibly because the editor could not imagine why seven men would meet violence in a repair garage.

When Trohan finished typing, he told his boss, "I'm going up there. Can I take a cab?'

"Take the Clark Street streetcar," Gershman said, "it runs every five minutes."

Then they heard sirens as South Side police rushed to reinforce North Side officers keeping back onlookers and searching for the killers. When Gershman learned the enormity of the crime he had twice hung up on, he snapped at Spirko, "Walter, why didn't you convince me!"

Everyone in the Chicago news business through the sixties knew at least one person who claimed that he or she had been the very first on the scene, even TV host Virginia Graham, who at the time was a *Tribune* stringer. Trohan said the only reason he arrived first was that other reporters "were all tied up in their City Hall rackets," that is, wheedling favors from lawyers and politicians. Perhaps the first couple of reporters reaching the garage had not seen one another, since the gunfire and sirens had drawn such a crowd.

Abraham Lincoln Mahoney of the *Daily News* jumped out of a cab and passed himself off as a deputy coroner to get through the police line. Seeing Coroner Bundesen taking paper from his pockets and jotting notes, Mahoney did likewise but made sure the esteemed doctor did not notice him. He had known some of the victims and was able to get the other names from people standing around, while also making note of the grimy floor of the garage, the unwashed windows, and the cars in disrepair.

Seeing Bundesen, a health columnist for the *American*, hanging his overcoat on a hook, the reporter rifled the pockets and snatched a page of notes when no one was looking. Getting out fast, he hailed a cab without glancing at what was on the page and called his office to prepare the editor for the names. He then put a rewrite man on hold, gave the pilfered sheet to the cabby, and stayed on the line until he made sure the notes were delivered.

The editor broke in and said, "Mahoney, the stuff you stole from Bundesen just came in. You looted the wrong pocket. The message the cabby handed me was written for Bundesen's column." It was about the importance of a baby's second month.

While half a dozen newspeople were busy being the first one on the scene, the job of Vern Whaley was to "kidnap" photographers from other papers on their way to the scene so that the *American* would have the best photos. Whaley was nearly arrested, so the story goes, by a policeman suspicious about his driving around the North Side "with several hoodlum looking guys in the car."[50]

After reporters from the six dailies were allowed to walk all over the scene,

City News reporter Willis O'Rourke remarked that "Some of us guys have got more brains on our shoes than we have under our hats."

Trohan always downplayed his own reporting of the St. Valentine's Day massacre, now lost to us because City News needed space, but it led to a job at the *Tribune*, and in the momentous forties he would became its leading Washington correspondent.

With the failure of the court system to return indictments over the massacre, Judge John H. Lyle wanted to call public attention to the horror that Chicago had become. So he cited Capone and a number of lesser mobsters with vagrancy. Colonel McCormick assigned reporters to help compile the names, and former newsman Henry Chamberlain, head of the Chicago Crime Commission, made sure the list went to all the papers.[51] When the infamous vagrants appeared in court, Lyle set each bond at one thousand dollars. This caused a sensation, since the maximum fine was two hundred dollars.

After returning from the war, former airman Dwight Green worked for a spell under Howey and Carson at the *Herald & Examiner* between his law classes, and then entered public office. Green had an algebraic mind, leading-man looks, and political ambition to spare. We can imagine the assistant state's attorney's excitement when Colonel McCormick said the *Tribune* would back him for whatever political position he sought.[52]

When Green was named the U.S. attorney for northern Illinois, the paper made up the fiction that he had devised the "net worth" theory of prosecution, which had already been in use, to convict Capone underlings. The paper's press agent-style coverage of his career contributed to his being elected governor. But as Green continued to behave as if untouchable, *Life* magazine showed him lunching with Mayor Edward Kelly at a time Kelly was promoting a city-operated transit system, and the St Louis *Dispatch* alleged that Green was consorting with criminals. He was defeated in a third run for the office in 1948.[53]

In 1931, the *Daily News* had a new publisher, William Franklin Knox, a tall, middle-aged extrovert from New Hampshire who wore glasses and pinstriped suits, and who changed his first name to Frank. He had served in the Rough Riders with Teddy Roosevelt and rose to colonel while serving in the artillery during the Great War.

Knox had been fed up with Hearst's sensationalism in papers across the country and heard that under the late Walter Strong, Melville Stone's and Victor Lawson's once-proud paper was about to be taken over by the Central Trust Company of Illinois. Knox bought the paper without using any of his own money and insisted on complete editorial freedom.

Like Colonel McCormick, Colonel Knox thought big. For a foreign correspondent he was lucky to have John Gunther, who after World War Two would write popular books about cities in Europe and the Middle East. A little after Knox settled in, he hired Leola Allard as his Sunday features editor based on her work with several papers, or maybe he was smitten. The men on his staff were suspicious when he presented her with a car at the paper's expense.[54]

Although these were the best-known Chicago newspaper people between 1919 and 1932, attorney Samuel Emery Thomason for a while was the highest paid newspaper employee in the land. A friend of McCormick ever since they met at Northwestern University law school, Thomason was hired as *Tribune* vice president and in 1926 was promoted to business manager, eventually receiving two hundred and seventy-five thousand dollars a year. Under this large and likable financial expert, the *Tribune* once again topped the *Daily News* and Hearst's *Evening American* in circulation. Thomason also initiated competitive wages and adopted practices favorable to workers in order to keep unions out.

But after nine years of success he quit and moved to Florida for the benefit of his paralytic wife. Retirement must have made him restless, because not long afterward he became a partner in a Tampa paper. Enjoying the freedom of being a boss, Thomason returned to Chicago and took over the stodgy *Journal*. Intelligent but not creative, he patterned it after the conservative New York *Sun,* but the revamped paper never took hold. Not only that, the two Hearst papers in town were conducting a holier-than-thou anti-monopoly campaign at a time when the federal trade commission was revealing that both the *Daily News* and the *Journal* were partly financed through an illegal alliance with the International Paper Company.

Thomason closed the eighty-five-year-old paper—then the oldest in Illinois—in 1929 and sold the equipment to the *Daily News.* But he retained the AP franchise by running five hundred copies a day of a mini-paper called the *Commercial Chronicle.* This was just to give him time to start a major sheet from the ground up.

With tabloids across the country cashing in on enthusiasm generated by the picture-heavy Hearst papers, Thomason and John Stewart Bryan of the Richmond *News Leader* in Virginia set up Chicago's first reduced-size paper, the *Daily Illustrated Times,* on the sixth floor of the old *Journal* building. He copied the format of the McCormick-Patterson New York *Daily News.*

The basement press crew of the *Times* was awaiting word on September 3, 1929, when the foreman yelled, "Let 'em roll!" At the familiar hiss and chugging of presses, Thomason muttered, "There goes the last of what was three million dollars." The first editorial denounced millionaire power company head Samuel Insull before it became fashionable.[55]

For years the tabloid would be the liveliest paper in the city, but Thomason was far from ruthless. Employees called him "Uncle Emory" and secretaries in the American Newspaper Publishers Association considered him "the nicest president we ever had." He left aggressiveness up to his editors, such as Richard Finnegan.

One day Finnegan was reading the rival *Tribune* when he saw a small item about a man confessing a long-ago murder before dying. The *Tribune* did not follow up its own story, but Finnegan had his reporters question two key witnesses. Both women admitted lying on the stand. The resulting story led to the parole of Jesse Lucas, who had been wrongfully imprisoned for twenty-three years.

The tabloid *Daily Illustrated Times* may have represented the future, but the type of freewheeling crime and court reporter idealized in the fictionalized Hildy Johnson was drifting into legend. "Schools of journalism and the advertising business have nearly extirpated the species," Hecht and MacArthur lamented.[56]

There was every reason for optimism in 1929. Despite the St. Valentine's Day massacre in February, the number of gangland murders in the city of more than three million had dropped sharply from the year before, from seventy-two to fifty-three, and the jazz age was dancing its way out.[57] The Dow-Jones stock average reached an all-time high on September 3, and investing fever seemed everywhere. Chicago radio station WLS, formerly owned by Sears, the World's Largest Store, declared itself the first station completely independent of advertising. The new owner, the *Prairie Farmer* newspaper, satisfied rural listeners by delivering wire service news more plainly and simply than the others. As Carl Sandburg put it, "no gee-whiz."

The Chicago *Defender* in July sponsored its first Bud Billiken Day parade on the South Side, celebrating a mythical African American as a way of treating its newsboys and all other black children in the city.

The *Daily News* moved out of its rickety building at 15 North Wells and set up shop in a handsome twenty-six story art deco office tower at 400 West Madison Street, by Union Station. WGN in time would move its studios to the top of the building. The newspaper presses were moved farther along the river, even though this took some romance out of the profession.

The construction boom that year also saw a new opera house and a new court and jail complex. What could possibly go wrong?

FIVE. Changing Times

"Young man, don't you know you're employed in a shameful business?"
Harold McCormick's housekeeper asked when she refused a bribe to
let John McPhaul steal a photo of the millionaire's new wife.
"Yes, mam," he replied.[1]

"Just because you handle news about those fellows is no reason to share
their emotions," Chicago *Daily News* editor Henry Justin Smith told reporter-
writer Lloyd Lewis as they walked down LaSalle Street a few months after the
stock market crash of October 29, 1929. "There's something more to reporting, and that's shrewdness and honesty—there's a viewpoint!" With this, Smith
bit off the end of a cigar. "You are paid to be independent, and I don't know
anywhere else in the world that a man is paid for that. You are paid a salary
to be in on things but still above them."[2]

Events were changing so quickly that the only constant was Prohibition
violence. Everyday prices were measured in pennies, some newspapers and
radio programs were drifting toward populism, and many movies were shocking or electric in their cynical candor. The more leisurely literary spirit of the
press was eroding, and there seemed to be no heroes any more.

The new court and jail complex, which opened on April 1, 1929, had been
built in the grassy countryside at 26th and California because county board
president and future mayor Anton Cermak owned nearby property. Hilding
Johnson complained about his change of quarters, "Cook County's most
magnificent new edifice is located five miles this side of Keokuk, Iowa."[3]

George Wright could no longer use a plank to eavesdrop on testimony
and had to do his reporting the old fashioned way. A local legend says another
reporter, expecting an indictment, sat inside an air duct to hear testimony and
lit up a cigar. Firefighters found him after grand jurors complained of smoke
coming from a vent.

Press room card games continued, sometimes attended by lawyers and
judges. Relationships were so friendly that some judges would get a signal from
a reporter during a trial and excuse themselves for an imaginary phone call so

that a photographer could rush in and take a picture of the courtroom and trial personnel.[4]

2

The gray, drab new courthouse seemed suited for criminals whom the Chicago Crime Commission in 1930 began calling "public enemies." But not all gang victims were fellow bootleggers. One was ace *Tribune* newsman Alfred Lingle, who looked like the hoodlums he hung around with.

As a boy he had been "police struck," and as a newspaperman was familiar with officers at all forty-one precincts. Wanting to sound tough, he had people call him Jake. Lingle was a bit pudgy and at leisure might be holding a cigar while wearing a messy white shirt and an old tie carelessly worn over an opened vest. But he sported tailor-made suits when making contacts. Lingle was neither a full-time reporter nor a writer. Instead he was a legman, setting his own hours and chatting with bookies and gangsters on the street, in "jazz houses," and at the track for something others at his paper might turn into a story. Some *Tribune* reporters such as Walter Trohan suspected that the former copyboy was "dirty" but did not tell their bosses.

On the blindingly sunny afternoon of Monday, June 9, 1930, President Hoover—who once said that presidents should be allowed to kill two reporters a day—attended the dedication of the Ceres statue atop the lofty Board of Trade Building in the skyscraper canyon of Chicago's financial district. At about one-fifteen, the thirty-eight-year-old Lingle was walking downtown to take an Illinois Central train for the Washington Park racetrack in suburban Homewood. He bought a paper at the large wooden newsstand outside the main public library at Randolph and Michigan and was hopping down the steps a few yards away to the open platform below street level. While he was glancing at the sporting news he was being followed by a blond man wearing a straw skimmer and black silk gloves. The stranger fired into Lingle's neck, sending a bullet through his skull. Outrunning witnesses, the killer left behind the sprawled body of the eleventh Chicago gang fatality in ten days. With hundreds of onlookers being kept back, investigators saw around Lingle's abdomen a diamond-studded monogrammed buckle Capone had given him for Christmas. Insiders knew it as a gangster's emblem.

A *Tribune* editor sent reporter John Boettiger (pronounced bot-igger) to the county morgue. There he found that the victim had been carrying fourteen hundred dollars in one-hundred-dollar bills, which Boettiger assumed came from the track. But instead of leaving the money for Lingle's wife to claim, Boettiger, who would later marry into the Roosevelt family, brought it to the Tribune Tower to keep authorities from disclosing the cash to the other papers.

Scene of a reporter's murder, 1930. Only after offering a large reward did Colonel McCormick learn that "Jake" Lingle was a friend of Capone mobsters (Chicago History Museum, DN-0092194).

Probably with that flushed feeling of being on the tip of disaster, the editors decided to lie that amount down to Jake's weekly salary of sixty-five dollars. When talk went around that Jake often carried large sums, the paper boosted his five-hundred-dollar inheritance from an uncle into fifty thousand dollars. No one seems to have told Colonel McCormick about the falsifications.

Murdering a reporter was outrageous, but a gang slaying in crowded downtown was inconceivable. McCormick called a staff meeting and put Trohan at the head of a team to investigate everything Lingle had been working on and see which of his stories had touched a nerve. A *Tribune* editorial called THE CHALLENGE stated: "The meaning of this murder is plain. It was committed in reprisal and an attempt at intimidation.... [To the list of gang victims] the name is added of a man whose business was to expose the work of the killers. The *Tribune* accepts this challenge. It is war." Strong words from a newspaper that was said to have called in Capone to avert two strikes.

All Chicago papers contributed to a fifty-five thousand dollar reward for information leading to the hit man. But McCormick knew more than he had been telling. In *The Colonel,* biographer Richard Norton Smith reports that the publisher had told the head of the U.S. Secret Service, Frank Wilson, at a meeting in the Tower that "I'll get word to Lingle to go all the way with you," and Jake was killed one day before he was to speak to him.

Lingle's remains were given a hero's procession to Our Lady of Sorrows Church. Trohan's group never learned the name of the gunman but it picked up a lot about Lingle, such as that he had acquired sixty thousand dollars a year, mostly from undisclosed sources, sometimes tooled around in a chauffeured limousine, and had just bought a sixteen thousand dollar summer home in addition to maintaining a suite at the expensive Stevens Hotel, later the Hilton.

More about Lingle's shady dealings was learned when *Illustrated Times* publisher Samuel Emory Thomason checked into bootleg banking transactions through the Chicago Clearing House Association. Unlike McCormick, Thomason owed nothing to Capone and felt free to dig deeper.

On June 30, 1930, the *Tribune* announced that it was "disturbed by the discovery that this reporter was engaged in practices contrary to the code of honest reporters." But the paper added that its investigation had not changed. Capone himself said the police knew who pulled the trigger, and maybe he was right, but no one dared print his name.[5]

Louis Rose succeeded Max Annenberg as the *Tribune* circulation manager. He spoke daily with the city editor, sometimes advising him when extras should be run off, and held meetings with McCormick at least once a week, but not about news judgment. "I have to sell the paper," Rose said. "It's merchandise, like anything else." News was to be determined by the market, the same concept that would debase television newscasts sixty years later.

The advertising-rich *Tribune* had become too large for individual control, and rigid departmentalizing seemed the answer. McCormick's managing editor in the thirties, J. Loy Maloney, who seems never to have disagreed with him, dictated reporter assignments to stenographers and had them type up questions for the newsmen to ask. Better reporters of course disregarded such lists and thought up their own questions, and Maloney's method may have made lesser reporters lazy. Also under the Maloney system, the main job of the day city editor was to give out assignments, leaving the night city editor to handle the copy.[6]

3

The *Tribune* soon had the nation's most famous crime-fighter, Dick Tracy. While cartoonist Chester Gould of Oklahoma was studying simultaneously at Northwestern University in Evanston and the Art Institute of Chicago downtown, he was fascinated by the way the Chicago Crime Commission kept track of mobsters as well as by the world's first scientific crime laboratory, set up at Northwestern to avoid gangland interference.

After Joseph Patterson's Tribune newspaper syndicate in New York rejected an estimated sixty of Gould's cartoon strip ideas, he came up with Detective Richard Tracy. The stylized violence entertained an estimated one hundred million readers after its appearance on a trial basis in the McCormick-Patterson Detroit *Mirror* in October 1931. Seeing that Dick Tracy would carry him through life, Gould settled in suburban Chicago and for a time rode with real police detectives for ideas. Some innovations he imagined became a reality.

At the *Illustrated Times*, publisher Samuel Emory Thomason remained friends with his law school friend Robert R. McCormick, and in his Market Street office even had photos of "Bertie" along with *Tribune* managing editor Edward S. Beck and brass-knuckled circulation manager Max Annenberg, now publisher of the Detroit *Mirror*.

Despite the Depression, the papers raised their prices to increase features and specialty pages. Hearst was disturbing the balance by keeping the *Herald & Examiner* down to five cents, half the cost of the *Tribune* and the *Illustrated Times*. Thomason in early 1932 decided to drop his Saturday edition and start one for Sunday mornings, putting him in competition with the *Tribune*, but only after breaking the news to McCormick.

"Well, that's your affair, Emory," the Colonel said. "But of course I'll do everything I can to protect my circulation. We can't let sentiment stand in the way."

His answer was to remind newsstand operators that copies of the *Tribune* should always remain exclusively on the top shelf and *Herald-Examiners* on the lower shelf, a compromise reached after the bloody circulation wars. With no space left in the open part of the kiosks for Thomason's Sunday papers, he had to hire a number of newsboys to sell them.[7]

Telephone tricks were making *American* editor Harry Reutlinger a beloved character. When aviator Charles Lindbergh's twenty-month-old son disappeared from the family's New Jersey home in March 1932, many people suspected it was a kidnapping for ransom, meaning there had to be a note. Harry grabbed a phone and called the New Jersey state police. After identifying himself as an aide to FBI Director J. Edgar Hoover he said, "The Director wants you to give us the exact wording of the kidnap note, with punctuation and all, so we can give it to our cryptographers."

"Wait a moment," the officer said, "I'll get it from the safe."

Reutlinger's heart must have beat rapidly at the scoop. After having someone type out the sensational story, he called Hearst for clearance at his castle-like California estate. "We can't use it," The Chief decided. "Burn every copy and tell that rewrite man to keep his mouth shut. We don't want to do a single thing that by any stretch of the imagination might endanger the life of the Lindbergh boy."[8]

The wording was published only after the child was found dead. Handyman Bruno Hauptmann was executed for the kidnapping and murder on the basis of a ladder and money found on his property.

In July 1932, the forever complaining Kate McCormick of the extended *Tribune* family became forever lost in memories and died of heart failure in Paris. Richard Norton Smith said her death left the Colonel "richer, more powerful, and more alone than at any time in his fifty-two years."

One of the reporters invigorating the *Herald & American* was former vaudeville song-and-dance man Basil "Gus" Talbott, who was well acquainted with a tavern across the river. When one lunch break lasted three days, Reutlinger asked Talbott, "Where the hell have you been?"

"The bridge was up," Talbott said.[9] With his sense of humor, he made side money by contributing to the *Duffy's Tavern* radio comedy of the forties.

Harry ran "a wild place" with his crew of bold and imaginative rewrites and reporters at a time when his paper sponsored WMAQ's spot radio programming, with large Len O'Connor using a newly perfected wire recorder in 1948 to become one of radio's first street reporters. Broadcasting had to be done from the city room, where Reutlinger seemed oblivious of the chaos around him.[10]

A final Reutlinger story seems incredible, but the news world at the time was so crazy, who is to say? "Harry had sent a reporter (name eludes me) to the nuthouse to do a story," Jack Crandle claimed. "Harry had him committed. And just about that time a big story broke and Harry forgot about the guy at the funny farm. About two weeks later, Harry Munzell, who was on the city desk, asked Reutlinger about the guy. Getting him out was a little more difficult than getting him in. Harry got a judge to issue an order and then Harry remembered he had some vacation plans."[11]

Picture-stealing was less flagrant than in the twenties but was still dangerous, especially if you were only five feet five like one of "Reutlinger rats," Buddy McHugh. At the time some reporters kept burglar tools in their cars, including a hammer covered with heavy cloth for quietly breaking windows. In the autumn of 1930, McHugh's editor demanded photos of a man and wife following their murder and suicide in a forest preserve. Buddy somehow obtained the wife's picture and went to a radio shop where the husband's large brothers worked. The brothers believed McHugh already had the husband's photo and locked the front door on him. "We get it," one of them said, "or you will never leave this place." But they let him call his desk. Bluffing, McHugh asked his editor to return the husband's photo, which of course the man did not have. But the editor had gleaned enough of the situation to call the police and give them the location. When the brothers heard sirens they threw Buddy out of their shop.

Coroner's investigator Francis Donoghue once learned that McHugh was impersonating him for information. Making it easier was that McHugh looked like political figures of the time, with a fireplug build, pasty face, and wire rimmed glasses. Once when Donoghue went to someone's home a man said, "Nuts! Donoghue just left here" and quickly shut the door. A neighbor explained to the coroner's investigator that the man had told people to slam the door on anyone claiming to be Donoghue because "it would be some snooping newspaperman."

The thirties would be McHugh's heyday although he worked until 1972, covering every major local story for sixty-one years.[12] He must have been proud of his son-in-law, attorney Richard LeFevour, who as a judge would head all the local courts in Cook County. Only later did federal investigators learn that LeFevour had systematized corruption in all the courthouses for a share of every bribe.

4

The Chicago *Post,* just across the river from the Merchandise Mart, fell victim to the Depression, and employees at surviving papers felt lucky to have a job—although the local economy was expected to improve with the 1933 World's Fair, the Century of Progress.

Not that the *American*'s perennially grumpy verse columnist Delos Avery

The Chicago *Post* building (center, flag on roof). This stolid paper succumbed to the Great Depression of the early 1930s.

turned cheerful. He seems to have lost the sense of humor he had when he was on rewrite at the *Herald & Examiner* and sent his copy to the editor by way of a wind-up tank from a five-and-dime. In time, Avery would put telephone books on the floor so he could watch the little tank bravely climbing over them. Avery's wallet was stolen as he was taking a woman to the fair. His editor called junkyard owner William Skidmore and said that unless the cash was returned in two hours, the paper would put on the heat. He was well aware that "Skid" had a side business of coming up with bond money for thieves. Within twenty minutes, a messenger showed up with Avery's wallet wrapped in a newspaper.[13]

After revitalizing the local Democratic Party and making an enemy of Capone, Mayor Anton Cermak was mortally wounded at a Miami race track in March 1933. The bullet was possibly intended for his companion, President Franklin D. Roosevelt. Cermak supposedly said, "I'm glad it was me instead of you." But newsman John Dienhart, a friend of his, maintained that the words were an editor's invention, and the mayor really had said something like, "The sons of bitches got me," meaning that Chicago mobsters had shot him in Florida to make it look like an attempted assassination of the President. The truth has never been learned.[14]

Typical of workers in numerous other industries during the Depression, those at the papers were working twelve-hour days. Cub reporters were generally earning twenty-five cents an hour for sixty-hour weeks. Suburban reporters worked from nine A.M. to midnight and received only one day off every two weeks.[15] Half the people at Hearst's two Chicago papers were fired to avoid lowering the salaries of the rest. But the radio business was booming.

The *Tribune*'s WGN and several stations in other states formed the Mutual Broadcasting System in 1933, rivaling CBS and NBC. Heading the new network was former *Tribune* business manager William McFarlane. By then, Americans were listening to eighteen million radios, and in March a rash of bank closings led to FDR's first "fireside chat" radio address. Roosevelt was able to ease the crisis with simple phrasing and a confident delivery the papers could not approximate.

That November 21, police were notified of the death of pretty Rheta Gardner Wynekoop in a basement surgical room at her mother-in-law's West Side mansion. Walter Spirko of City News and Newberne "Shadow" Browne of the *Tribune* arrived not more than fifteen minutes after the police call. All the evidence was in front of them: an empty bottle of chloroform, the body face down on a surgical table in a chemise and covered by a blanket, a bullet wound in her back, and chloroform burns on her face. Her clothes were neatly folded on the table, and a gun wrapped in fingerprint-proof gauze lay by her head. But what story did all this tell?

Rheta's husband was taking up with another woman in Kansas City at the time of death. His ungrieving mother, Dr. Alice Wynekoop, insisted that the body be cremated immediately and told the police a prowler must have shot

Rheta. She showed them a drawer and said that six dollars were missing. The police actually huddled with the two reporters in a "What does this look like to you?" session, but no one could come up with a theory that would account for everything.

At the police station, Dr. Wynekoop claimed her daughter-in-law had died from chloroform during an operation for a pain in her side, neglecting to account for the bullet wound, the wrapped-up gun, and the absence of chloroform in her system. The investigation also showed that Dr. Wynekoop had taken out life insurance policies on Rheta. But what really happened in that basement laboratory remained a favorite mystery to kick around newsrooms as long as the case was remembered.[16]

5

Only aging crime reporter John Kelley and old-fashioned foreign correspondent James O'Donnell Bennett still turned in *Tribune* copy by pencil. Everyone else in Chicago journalism used typewriters. And so there were different staccatos of one, two, and three fingers hitting keys when thirteen dizzying years of Prohibition was approaching its end on December 31, 1933.

At midnight two thousand champagne corks popped in dining rooms at the downtown Sherman House hotel. Thousands of other revelers crammed the Loop, street peddlers sold balloons and noisemakers, and police on horseback tried to keep motor traffic moving.

Drinking at the workplace was no longer winked at. Supervisors at the Hearst Building were sure Frank Devine was imbibing but they could not imagine how. Devine, one of the last boomers in Chicago, had worked at several Southern papers before being hit by his first Chicago winter. Since he did not know enough about the Toddlin' Town to be a reporter, he was put on the copy desk. His secret came out after he passed out in the office, and workers found inside his tailored suit coat a flask with a straw.[17]

At Hearst's *Herald & Examiner,* the latest editor imported from New York was graying Victor Watson, who devised his own coffee percolator. Women in the office hung rain-wet stockings on the coils while avoiding his pinches.[18] The "Her-Ex" also had on its payroll a known falsifier, Harold Cross, whose lack of professionalism came in handy on slow days. He supposedly put himself in trouble at least twice, once when he gave a fictitious account of how a junkman's horse was injured and the owner threatened to sue. In the second instance, which sounds like a fable, the address he gave for a made-up Chinese laundry in upscale suburban Lake Forest was that of a former *Herald & Examiner* publisher.[19]

Future WBBM-AM political editor John Madigan was a copyboy under Reutlinger at the other paper printed in the building, the *American,* and recalled that if you were unable to find some dead woman's diary you made one up. Madigan also said night editor Harry Romanoff used so many phony names on the telephone that by morning he did not know who he was.[20]

For some reason, county officials decided that three electrocutions scheduled for April 20, 1934, should be carried out not at the usual time of midnight but at five a.m., the deadline for the four afternoon papers. Because every second counted, newspaper editors decided to let City News provide pool coverage even though the wire service had always skipped executions.

City News persuaded jail officials to run a direct telephone line to the back of the death chamber witness room. Reporter Dick Henry stood on a table for a better view while holding the telephone. He relayed every detail as it was happening to the City News office on the seventh floor at 155 North Clark Street: the men brought in one by one, strapped in, the juice turned on, the body throes, and the death pronouncement. At the same time, Walter Spirko gathered tangent information and called his notes in from the warden's office.[21]

Prohibition brutality was hardly over when Chicago police formed a forty-man squad to catch notorious Midwestern bank robber John Dillinger, who was believed to have fled to the big city. Reporters sometimes followed police cars going from one tip to another with shotguns, but then Dillinger was captured and taken to the Crown Point Jail in Northwestern Indiana.

At the Associated Press's small Chicago office, desk man Ray Brennan was trying to decide whether to send a photographer all the way there for a routine hearing set for March 3, 1934. Brennan dialed county officials and asked if their star prisoner would appear or sit it out.

"No, he won't be in court," Lake County Prosecutor Robert Estill told him. "He just escaped from jail." While Dillinger was in the exercise yard he had shoved what appeared to be a gun against a guard's abdomen and threatened to shoot everyone in his way, including a national guardsman providing security.[22]

The bulletin struck like a microburst, and the Dillinger squad was instantly reactivated. The FBI agent in charge of the Chicago office, Melvin Purvis, was determined to stop the man who had been blamed for several murders that may have been committed by others in his gang.

Dillinger sat in a white suit that July 22 with two women in the North Side's Biograph Theatre as they watched Clark Gable walk to the electric chair in *Manhattan Melodrama*. The show was only a few blocks from the scene of the St. Valentine's massacre. The threesome left just before ten-thirty. But once outside, the two women went off on their own. As the fugitive approached the alley he suspected that the more than a dozen men standing in readiness were police officers and federal agents. He reached for his gun only to be riddled by gunfire.

John Foust of City News rushed to the alley from the Sheffield Avenue police station on a report of gunfire. When he asked who the dead man was, some of the law enforcement officials pushed him away but one, perhaps Purvis himself, gave him the victim's name. For the scoop, Foust received a two-dollar raise to his salary of seventeen dollars a week.[23]

The morgue pathologist making sure he was the one who examined the body was Charles Parker, who knew he would receive a *Tribune* bonus for exclusive information. Still wearing a straw hat, Dr. Parker attended to the undressing and noted each item removed from the bloody clothes. Sergeant Frank Reynolds of the Dillinger squad went up to the slab and shook the corpse's hand.

The shooting had occurred on the first day of Walter Spirko's vacation. When Shadow Browne called him about it, Spirko, thinking it was a joke, said "Bullshit!" and went back to sleep.[24]

The violence in that alley ended an agreement between the press and radio stations against airing any news before the papers could hit the streets. Staff announcer Norman Ross was broadcasting a dance pickup for WMAQ when he heard shouting about Dillinger's death. He flipped the on-air key and announced the shooting, opening the news to competition between the two media and contributing to a fifty-year war between them.[25]

Scores of people flocked around the Biograph, with many dipping newspaper headlines or clothes in Dillinger's blood. The shooting, and the killing of his accomplice Baby Faced Nelson after a running gunbattle in suburban Barrington that November 27, were the high points of Chicago crime sensationalism. But the satiated city's reputation for violence lingered in the world imagination for more than a generation.

6

With a large German population on the North Side, the city was ripe for Nazi recruitment. In the autumn of 1934, *Herald & Examiner* reporter George Murray was assigned to cover a meeting of the Friends of New Germany at a church near Fullerton Avenue. Swastikas decorated the stage and the mood was as cheerful as an Oktoberfest. Murray, possibly in his usual fedora and blue suit, wanted to slip away and meet a girl. After interviewing the guest speaker, the German consul-general, he told a public relations man named Peter that he would be calling back to learn whether anything unusual happened while he was gone.

"You mean you want me to give you my telephone number?" Peter asked incredulously. "Do you think I am stupid?" As he walked away, Murray felt that more than a kafeeklatsch was going on. Rather than telephoning his girlfriend, Murray contacted his office.

"Better make a dozen phone calls and find out what the mystery is," said the slender, pipe-smoking assistant editor, Jack McPhaul. The result was an early series on the dangers of Nazism in America.[26]

The *Tribune* response to the bund movement was altogether different. The paper that glorified the Klan now gave Nazi vice-consul Wilhelm Tannenberg editorial space on two successive Sundays the following spring. The editorials extolled the glories of fascism, regardless of what the paper's foreign correspondents must have been cabling to the home office,[27] and in spite of the maxim carved into a wall inside the Tribune Tower: "History teaches us that human liberty cannot be secured unless there is freedom to express grievances."

City News people were more raucous when its small office was on Clark Street than in later years on Randolph, and bored night reporters would use binoculars to peer into windows at the nearby Sherman House hotel. Four New Orleans showgirls staying there were invited over to end the loneliness of the midnight watch. Alumnus George Selgret recalled years later that champagne flowed not only in cups, it overflowed onto the large wooden switchboard, spewing alarming sparks. Not being electricians, the panicking newsmen threw water on the problem, shutting operations down since there was no way to receive calls from reporters or make beat checks with police and fire units. The switchboard kept disgorging smoke and flames until one of the men sprayed it with a fire extinguisher and someone called the fire department from a downstairs all night restaurant. The morning shift found the office a mess, but at least the champagne odor had dissipated.[28]

Jargon being used at City News and the papers at the time included "a three-bagger," a baseball reference for a three-eleven alarm fire. The "fire joker" was a fist-sized alarm system that pinged in code for any location in the city. The "squawk box" was a speaker tuned in to the police or fire department radio frequency, and "cheap" meant a story holding little interest for the general reader. This was not a value judgment. When an editor decided not to send out a story on a minor accident or a routine death he "cheaped it out" at the risk of being scooped.

Newspapers and wire services kept a "gang book" containing the private numbers of everyone who might be in the news some day, from gangsters to the governor. New reporters copied relevant ones in their private "beat books" before they worked out of police stations.

Beat books ranged from a new leatherbound notebook TV newscaster Mike Flannerry's sister would give him to a thick three volume set an especially aggressive City News reporter carried with him. Such notebooks were soon filled with phone numbers the reporters picked up in various ways over their careers, including from city hall garbage cans. In time a beat book was loved all the more for its sandwich smears, cross-outs, notations, rips, and outdated numbers.

Universal terms among newspaper people included "a head story"—a story good enough to take up at least a third of a column length. Shorter items were called "four heads," a fourth of a column, and "five heads," a fifth of a column. A "balloon" was an off-chance remark by a suspect or an official that a sharp reporter would remember for possible development without letting his excitement show, as if in a poker game. Add to this each editor's own abbreviations. At the *Daily News*, Bill Mooney would send copy back with "1/2/E" for "Cut it in half. Put it in English."

Stories were typed on "copy books," several flimsy pages lightly held together with carbon sheets in between, for distributing copies to other editors and the national wire services. Copy was triple-spaced to provide room for editing above the lines. One prank was sneaking cap-pistol snaps amid the multiple pages so they popped as they were moved line by line up the platen. Reporters sometimes slipped on carbon sheets that had dropped to the floor.

"Give me half a book" did not refer to a hundred and fifty pages, it meant half a "copy book" page. Each page was a "take." When Harry Romanoff wanted to use a story only as filler he would ask for "half a paragraph." Even then, there was a chance the story would wind up in the "overset," the type taken out of an edition when something more pressing came in.

"Spiked" meant an editor decided not to use a story after it was written. By putting the copy on a desk spindle—what future reporter-novelist Kurt Vonnegut would call "the mulberry bush"—he removed it from circulation but left the information available for reference by other shifts.

"The slot" originally referred to the three or more copy desks arranged with a bay. The person sitting in the "slot" was the head copy editor, who distributed stories to copy readers "on the rim." But sometimes an assistant news editor coming in to relieve the day or night city editor was called the "slot man" because he sat at the copy desk horseshoe during the short transition period that allowed him to catch up with the day's news and stories still being worked on.

Machine Gun (Jack) McGurn, a possible plotter in the St. Valentine's Day massacre, was gunned down at a Near West Side bowling alley on February 15, 1936. Harry Romanoff protégé Joe Fay called in the scoop from a booth at the scene, at Grand Avenue and Halsted Street, and with his encyclopedic mind gave the rewrite all the background needed from memory. Then he crammed wet chewing gum into the coin slot to keep competitors from using the phone.[29]

Back in the twenties the *Tribune*'s George Woltman had been reprimanded for using copy from another paper when he was unable to reach a source about a lake sinking, and when something like that occurred on July 29, 1936, he was determined not to make the same mistake twice. Scorching weather had broken with a squall. On a beat check, a lighthouse keeper told him the motor barge *Material Service* was sinking just outside a South Side breakwater. Woltman excitedly told him, "Don't answer your phone until I get there."

"Don't worry," the keeper said, "we're still fishing around for survivors." Seven of the seamen were saved, but fourteen others drowned.

Woltman flashed a phony star at a saloonkeeper in red flannel underwear near the scene and asked him describe how the rescuers had borrowed his launch. Woltman next bought two "flagons" of bourbon for the shivering bargemen wrapped in blankets, tarpaulins, and old coats on the shore.

As the exhausted reporter was returning, his friend Adolph Wagner of the *American* stood in the comfort of a Coast Guard cutter deck and hollered through a megaphone, "Hey, George, what can you tell me?" According to Woltman, he cupped his hands and uttered the first obscenity of his life.[30]

Whatever that expression was, Woltman and Wagner remained so close they sometimes acted as a team. One time came when Woltman was in the detective bureau on the midnight shift and learned that a limousine had just pulled up at the Central District station. Police jurisdictions were no longer called precincts. He found Wagner in the station lobby with a similar interest. Working together, the rivals traced the license plate to someone in the millionaire row at Oak Street and Lake Shore Drive.

Captain John Prendergast had been sworn to secrecy, but a detective let out that there had been a big theft. A man in a tuxedo, his wife in furs, and their chauffeur refused to speak to the reporters as they left the station. So Woltman and Wagner waited for them to arrive home, undress, and go to bed—the time when they would be least wary.

Wagner then called the luxury apartment and identified himself as a detective, with Woltman moaning in the background. The *American* reporter said the policeman who had been carrying their statement had been shot while responding to a robbery in progress, and now blood was all over the pages and the statement could no longer be read. "Detective" Wagner asked the couple to repeat the gist of their statement, and that was how the two of them shared the story of a fur theft that readers no doubt took for granted.[31]

The *Herald & Examiner* had no education requirement and many of its reporters spoke like Damon Runyon characters, but single-fingered typist George Morgenstern was a Rhodes scholar. He was one of about thirty Illinois reporters who flocked to a downstate town where a man had killed his family and had been about to turn the gun on himself when a maid stopped him. The distraught husband happened to be a friend of the town mayor, and the mayor told the press throng that he would make a statement in the morning.

Morgenstern knew the mayor would be too upset to be articulate, especially since he would have had little sleep. As the other reporters were whiling away their time drinking or playing cards, Morgenstern called in not only an account of the shooting and arrest but also what the mayor's statement and his own questions would be. The story was set up in advance, with only the mayor's responses left blank. Morgenstern offered the statement to the relieved mayor in private, and while the other reporters were just beginning their stories Morgenstern only had to phone in the mayoral responses.[32]

Much of the fun went out of the two Hearst papers in Chicago when The Chief ran into financial difficulties in the thirties and bankers took over.

Accountants made regular visits to ask why an editor had sent a reporter to a scene rather than having a rewrite man cover it by phone, and why column length stories were not cut down to a third. Edward Doherty became so fed up with the slashing of his copy at the *American* that he headed for New York, leaving his five brothers behind for several years.[33]

Romance at around this time might have saved a woman's life. She was threatening to jump from a twenty-second floor balcony of the Morrison Hotel in the Loop. Despite the drama, *American* reporter George Murray wanted to end his ten-hour day so he could be with his girlfriend, but editor John Dienhart thought otherwise and ordered him to go there. Seeing the woman standing on the lip of concrete just past the railing, Murray and photographer Edward Tanker inched closer with fire department chaplain William Gorman.

"Go ahead and jump," Murray called out to her. "Get it over with. I've got a date and have to do a story while you make up your mind. No one really gives a damn, one way or another." The woman stared at Murray a moment and lunged at him, but the priest grabbed her from behind and Tanker took the shot.[34]

A story that may or may not be true is reminiscent of the Russian legend of a non-existent Lieutenant Kije. When an indolent *Tribune* rewrite man was asked to get the name of a witness, he made up one that was unlikely to be found in any phone directory, "Ignatius Z. Yelswo"; that is, Owsley spelled backward, and gave him the address of a vacant lot. Later other reporters for convenience or as a joke put Yelswo into their own stories, such as when they were unable to learn the identity of one of several people injured in a fire. The hoax lasted for some time, until an editor told his staff to get Yelswo's photo.[35]

Under Frank Knox, the *Daily News* was less literary than before but maintained a strong reputation. Knox had political ambitions and in 1936 unsuccessfully ran for vice president of the United States on a Republican ticket headed by Kansas governor Alf Landon. Democrat Franklin Delano Roosevelt was so popular in Chicago that an election night crowd burned copies of the *Tribune* in the Loop. FDR would appoint Knox his Secretary of the Navy in July 1940 as a consolation prize, and while in Washington the publisher kept in touch with his paper nearly every day.

The late thirties seemed a time when anything could happen in the news business. For example, Karin Walsh began as a copyboy for the *Herald & Examiner* and became city editor of the *Illustrated Times* at the age of twenty-eight. During his rapid rise, Walsh married Mina Breax, a reporter he met when their editor assigned them to an abduction.

While Edward Doherty was making six hundred dollars a week at the New York *Daily Mirror*, his brother Jim was working at the Chicago *Tribune*. Their stocky kid brother Bill quit college to find himself, rode boxcars for two months, and decided to follow his brothers' lead. He started at City News for fifteen dollars a week, less than half what Jim was making. But then he learned the *Illustrated Times* was looking for a young reporter, preferably the son of an Irish policeman since officers were more likely to talk with someone from a cop family.

Bill started at twenty-five dollars a week in 1937, when Buddy McHugh was the paper's roving reporter and New York import Louis Ruppel was the managing editor. Ruppel, fresh from his role as the U.S. deputy narcotics commissioner, had a droopy face and not even his glasses could hide the way he lifted an eyebrow at things he doubted or disagreed with. George Murray said the Republican Ruppel would be remembered for his headline when Roosevelt was elected for an unprecedented third term: "Fifty-Six Shopping Days to Xmas."

But Ruppel could feel the tremors of a developing news story, such as when he sent German-American real estate dealer John Metcalfe to upstate New York so he could be recruited by the *Volksbund*. Metcalfe's brother, a former FBI agent, and German-born reporter William Mueller then prowled around Chicago's Nazi enclaves for a series that begin on September 9, 1937, about "The Secret Nazi Army in the U.S." The exclusive was picked up by the AP, and U.S. Senator William Borah of Idaho used it to demand federal action against a suspected Fifth Column.[36]

Also under Ruppel, investigative reporter Frank Smith had himself hired as a Cook County Hospital orderly in 1939 and laid bare deplorable conditions. The institution was dropped from the American Medical Association's approved list until it could be reorganized.

Doherty brother Martin found work at the Chicago *Post* after City News training. He once approached a house to steal a photo, but an officer at the door stopped him and a captain remarked, "That's the way to handle those press punks." Behind the officer's back, the captain told Martin about an open window and helped him climb inside.[37]

Management at some of the papers failed to notice labor organizing in their buildings. With numerous layoffs nationwide in the Depression year of 1933, New York columnist Heywood Braun proposed a newspaper writers union and was elected its first president. Organizer Bill Davy arrived in Chicago in 1935 to create a local chapter at each newspaper.

Hearst had spent his adult life promoting unions until the stock market crash made him think of them as the enemy. He called the U.S. Wagner Act protecting such organizing "one of the most vicious pieces of class legislation that could be conceived—un–American to the core." The guild picketed both Hearst papers in the city, and demonstrators repeatedly were beaten by company goons. To make up his losses during a fifteen-month walkout, The Chief in 1939 merged the *Herald-Examiner* and the *American* into the *Herald-American*. To save even more money, the paper was written more for entertainment than information, and the old "Her-Ex" spirit disappeared, and reckless high jinks at the papers started being frowned upon.

At the *Daily News,* Knox avoided labor unrest by making concessions, and in time the paper operated as a virtually closed shop. He even gave employee Carlton Ihde a leave of absence to work full time for the movement. But the *Tribune* chapter operated underground before giving up.[38]

Colonel McCormick rode daily to his ivory tower in an olive drab bulletproof Rolls-Royce coupe, and at times seemed to be avoiding contact with the outside world, which he knew so little. As one critic put it, he had the "greatest mind of the fourteenth century."[39]

Columnist Virginia Gardner, who earlier had exposed a quack doctor and fake mediums, was dropped from the payroll when McCormick learned that she had joined the union. The National Labor Relations Board ordered her rehired with back pay, but McCormick said he never wanted to see her name in print again. He banished the experienced newswoman to North Side reporting as if she were only a cub. But this tough Protestant from Fort Smith, Arkansas, wreaked her revenge. Her beat included the cardinal's mansion and Holy Name Cathedral, and she became the top reporter for the doings and opinions of the Roman Catholic hierarchy. Her reporting was even honored by George Cardinal Mundelein in 1938. One of her scoops was the beatification of Mother Cabrini, finally returning Gardner's byline to the *Tribune* and leading to the newsroom quip that the saint had performed her first miracle.[40]

Just as rival reporters worked together, sometimes so did the newspapers. A fire at the *Illustrated Times* in 1938 forced the management to bring its copy to McCormick's tower, leading to the *Times*'s playful headline: HOT OFF THE PRESSES (THE TRIBUNE'S).

Reporters at the detective bureau press room sometimes wondered how Dick Dolan, a reporter at the low-paying City News, always had enough money for gambling. His secret came out when he was arrested for holding up a laundry and locking a driver and his helper in the basement, unaware that a window was open. Dolan was sent to prison, came out on parole, and tried to pull a robbery with two fellow ex-cons. Both accomplices were killed by the police, and as officers closed in on Dolan he avoided going back to prison by putting a bullet through his head.[41]

Few people were paying attention, but radio reporters at several stations in the U.S. were starting to display the energy and invention of newspaper reporters earlier in the century. One opportunity came as the raging Ohio River killed more than three hundred and eighty people from Pennsylvania to Kentucky in January 1937. Radio reporters went out in rowboats or reported from polluted water that almost topped their knee-high boots, and one climbed a telephone pole to deliver a story while protecting his microphone from the wind with his heavy coat.

Their first reports urged listeners to lend their boats to emergency personnel and notified drivers which bridges were closed. Later broadcasts relayed the human impact of the flood. Former Chicago *Tribune* foreign correspondent Floyd Gibbons made a fool of himself by fabricating the destruction of a Cincinnati radio station as he broadcast *Your True Adventure* from the scene. Despite all that was going on around him, Gibbons was bored.[42]

Usually radio news was flat—except for sports. Future actor and president Ronald Reagan was working at an Iowa station when he seemed to be narrating Chicago Cubs games live. Actually, he was sitting in a studio and excitedly imagining every pitch as he read transcribed telegraph messages coming in.[43]

Chicago radio station WLS, which emphasized folksy entertainment such as the "National Barn Dance," sent handsome thirty-one-year-old staff announcer Herbert Morrison to the dirigible port at Lakehurst, New Jersey, to try out some recording equipment. The pretext was the routine landing of the zeppelin *Hindenburg* on its way from Nazi Germany to Rio de Janeiro. On May 6, 1937, Morrison, with his dark hair parted in the middle, stood at a microphone outside the sound truck when the world's largest luxury airship exploded not far from the ground. Without training as a reporter, Morrison exclaimed:

> It burst into flames! It burst into flames and is falling! ... It's crashing! Oh my! Get out of the way, please! ... Oh the humanity! ... All the people are screaming around here! I'm going to step inside where I can't see it. I tell you, it's terrible. Folks, I must stop for a minute. I've lost my voice.... Ladies and gentlemen, I'm back again.... It's still smoking and flaming and crackling down there....

The disaster killed thirty-six of the ninety-seven people aboard. But Morrison's account had not yet been heard by anyone other than his sound engineer and people running around them. Agents from the German government followed the men to impound the recording at the huge, empty dirigible hangar just off the scene, but Morrison and his sound man hid for a few hours. They then ran out with the recording and hopped onto a Chicago-bound plane. WLS played the account by noon the next day. NBC bought the recording and aired it nationally three hours later.[44]

Street coverage in Chicago continued as usual as if militant governments were not leading Germany, Austria, Italy, and Japan toward war. Reporter and future prize-winning columnist Jack Mabley learned to gather an abundance of details after he started at City News in 1937. *Time* magazine said that once when the young man turned in an account of a traffic fatality, "he was sent back across town—five miles by streetcar—to get the middle initial of a survivor."[45] Maybe the middle initial was necessary, as with a John Jones, but more than likely the editor just wanted to teach Jack a lesson.

Mabley also once found himself being summoned by a hungover judge at the Gresham District station courtroom. The judge "asked me to sit beside him on the bench and help him dispense justice. All the winos took a walk that morning."

At the time Mabley went to the *Daily News*, he was said to be the only sober person in the news room. That must have been an exaggeration, but the paper did have its own Alcoholics Anonymous chapter.[46]

Breakthroughs in radio reporting helped prepare listeners for on-the-spot coverage that brought World War Two to their homes after fighting began in Europe in September of 1939. The low monotone of Edward R. Murrow and several other reporters made listeners feel they were in London as the bombs dropped. But the same events seemed distant in the newspapers, even though a few reporters like Robert J. Casey had learned to write with style.

Casey developed his flair at the freewheeling *American* before becoming unhappy with an editor and jumping to the *Daily News*. His Hechtian fondness for ironic description showed in his coverage of the trial of a woman who courted elderly men only to put arsenic in their beer: "Anna Marie Hahn's four old lovers came to court today—three of them in bottles and one in a blue serge suit."

With America likely to be pulled into the war, colorful characters in the city seemed like leftovers from another age—including robust alderman Paddy Bauler. After winning an election over a reform candidate in 1939, Bauler supposedly said, "Chicago ain't ready for reform." The quote was possibly a newsman's invention.

The *Defender* had been staunchly Republican under founder Robert S. Abbott, but after his death in 1940 the black-oriented paper passed into the hands of his nephew, John Sengstacke, and he began writing about the need for war preparedness. The reversal was part of a power shift in the city back to the Democratic Party.

What the city was ready for was entertainment. Radio programmer Louis Cowan had an idea for a "Quiz Kids" program on the Chicago-based NBC network and wondered how to contact several bright and likable youngsters. He went to the *Daily News*, where an editor pulled a few names from the paper's files. The long-running series began in June 1940.

Two months later Casey was sent to cover the air Battle of Britain and demanded to speak to Prime Minister Winston Churchill about the wartime censorship that was keeping him from speaking to officials. The *Daily News* reporter was forced to undergo an accreditation hearing attended by representatives not only of the British Army and Navy but also of Scotland Yard.

One of the men facing him at the long table asked, "Are you, by any chance, the Casey who is supposed to have told Secretary Knox he could 'Stuff the navy where it would do the most good'?" (Casey actually had said, "Could stuff his navy up his....")

"Yes," he answered.

The British officials glanced at one another, and one said, "I think you need not worry about accreditation, old man." A bottle of Black Label appeared, the king was toasted, and Casey was given authorization to communicate with His Majesty's forces.[47]

At the *Illustrated Times*, future alderman Roman Pucinski, of Polish descent, was troubled over the massacre of thousands of Polish officers in the Katyn Forest in 1940. He was one of possibly several reporters nationwide trying to convince their editors that according to reliable sources the soldiers had been killed by Russian troops and not the Germans, as Russian officials were insisting. Nothing came of their persistence until proof surfaced years later. If the editors had cared less about offending an ally, perhaps Joseph Stalin would not have been as successful in his post-war takeover of eastern Europe.

In June 1940, the *Tribune* latched onto its third highly popular comic strip, Dale Messick's *Brenda Starr*, star reporter. Soon after it began, the paper was flooded with mail from teenage girls eager to enter the profession. World events would soon give some women the chance.

The anti–Roosevelt *Tribune* had recently expanded its Washington bureau to undermine FDR support in Chicago, and put former street reporter Walter Trohan in charge. The news slants and the editorial vehemence riled Marshal Field III, liberal grandson of the department store magnate. To counteract McCormick, he launched the city's last entirely new major paper, the *Sun*, with a five million dollar investment after discussions with Samuel Emory Thomason of the *Illustrated Times*.[48]

The Chicago *Daily News* building (1929). The huge office building reflects the newspaper's expectations before declining readership trends. The *Daily News* was later absorbed into the *Sun-Times*.

The name for this new broadsheet (non-tabloid) was chosen in a five thousand dollar contest, and its offices occupied three vacant floors of the large *Daily News* building. For a society editor Field hired enterprising Sarah Boyden, who had dressed as a hotel maid in order to enter the suite of Queen Marie of Romania for an interview.

Knowing the first issue of the *Sun* would hit the streets on the morning of December 4, 1941, the Colonel ordered department heads to come up with a scoop big enough to overwhelm public curiosity about the upstart paper. And so, neutral America was jolted by the *Tribune* bannerline of F.D.R.'s WAR PLANS! U.S. Attorney Francis Biddle was so furious he wanted the paper prosecuted under the Espionage Act, but McCormick's U.S. Senate reporter, Chesly Manly, was able to keep his sources secret even though the White House was tapping phone lines at newspaper offices and even planting informants in some newsrooms.[49] The leak supposedly had come from a general who wanted to expose how the "Rainbow Five" defense preparation plan was slighting air power. But the brash headline promised more than it delivered, since all countries must keep plans for every conceivable emergency.

Just four days after the first issue of the *Sun* hit the stands, all the papers headlined the Japanese attack on Pearl Harbor. But most readers by then already knew about the overwhelming blow to the U.S. Navy from the radio.

For years City News boasted that it had trumped the local papers with the story, claiming a well-heeled off-duty reporter had heard initial accounts over his short wave radio. Some legends are better left alone, but the final chief editor of City News, Paul Zimbrakos, kept wondering about the story until being able to trace what really happened. The wire service was not first but the last to know.

Cub City News reporter William Rogers was idly going through the New York *Times* at a police station and asked an officer if anything was happening. "Don't you know the Japs bombed Pearl Harbor!" the officer answered. United Press had broken story.

Rogers' editor sent him to the Japanese consulate in the Wrigley Building, where representatives of the imperial government were believed to be burning documents. Next, Rogers hurried to Navy Pier a mile away, where he saw two "German-looking guys" in a rowboat with what to him looked like a bomb. With so many imagined dangers, Rogers' brother talked him out of the news business, so he was not around to keep the myth from snowballing.

WGN was able to carry the first news of the attack locally at 1:26 that terrible Sunday afternoon, and NBC broke into programming with an announcement at 1:31 P.M. The heads of nearly every department at the papers, hearing the radio or contacted by their supervisors, rushed to work hours early or on their day off, even the *Tribune*'s political cartoonist.

With so many people toiling at top speed, the *Tribune* was able to cram all the war news available into the first edition of Monday's paper by 5:05 P.M.

Sunday instead of the usual time of 6:10 P.M.[50] Before long, the Mutual Broadcasting system, with one of its studios in the Tribune Tower, was trimming programs to provide listeners with one-minute news updates every hour.[51]

It fell to Naval Secretary Frank Knox to give a crowded room of reporters details of the Japanese bombing. Knox, by now a grandfatherly-looking man, leaned back in a comfortable chair in his Washington office and spoke slowly enough for the newsmen to write down nearly every word. But Knox's service in the Roosevelt cabinet soon ended, and he returned as publisher of the *Daily News*, although he had been feeding navy scoops to the paper all along.

You would think the United States' abrupt entry into the war would have been a boon for the city's newest paper, but instead the *Tribune* nearly sank it. First, the Colonel jumped from his soapbox of isolationism to the soapbox of all-out war, completely undermining the *Sun*. Then McCormick applied pressure on other publishers to keep Field from gaining an AP franchise.[52]

The better-funded *Tribune* and *Daily News* could outshine the *Sun* on every major story. Knox, for example, sent Casey to Hawaii for the raising of ships sunk by Japanese planes, but Marshall Field III could publish only local news. Soon paper and ink were rationed, further straining his budget. McCormick even suspended his dislike of the English and tied up both the British News Service and Reuter's when Field increased his foreign staff. When the U.S. Supreme Court ordered the AP to serve the *Sun* in 1945, it was too late to make the once-promising paper truly competitive.

One might imagine McCormick as a martinet from his sometimes outrageous political stands and the way he could choke a competing paper. But he was approachable and felt like a proud father toward his workers. The Colonel was known to drop by the pressroom some days or join the pressmen in the lunchroom.[53] Even his eccentricities mellowed as the war progressed on three continents, but his paper continued to have the most personality in town.

In 1941, Richard Loeb, who had taken part in the Bobby Franks murder, died from fifty eight cuts at Stateville prison near Joliet. One theory was that his attacker, James Day, went at him with a straight razor because Loeb would not share more cigarettes and candy with him. But popular lore has it that Loeb had made improper advances to him. This inspired stumpy, rumpled Ed Lahey, the drunken wag of the *Daily News,* to write what may be the most famous lead in Chicago newspaper history: "Richard Loeb, who graduated from college with honors at the age of 15 and who was a master of the English language, ended his sentence with a proposition."[54] After going through Alcoholics Anonymous, Lahey redeemed himself as a top labor editor.

The manpower drain from the war meant that a number of competent news people were moved up. *Illustrated Times* editor Richard Finnegan was fifty-eight, but his managing editor and his news editor were both just thirty-three, and in December 1942, he made successful Sunday editor Karin Walsh his city editor at twenty eight. Unlike the *Tribune*, Finnegan's tabloid was aggressive, lean, responsive to the period, and appealed to younger readers.

The war was coming closer to everyone in the Heartland in one way or another. The Navy trained pilots off the Chicago-area shore of Lake Michigan and the *Tribune* was using the *S.S. Thorwald* to carry newsprint (paper rolls) from its Canadian paper mill. The ship had been refloated and its guns removed after the Germans sank it off Wales.

Although changing times gave the *Sun* a chance to try something different, it hired familiar faces such as reporter Walter Spirko, who worked through a cloud of cigar smoke under night editor Joe Fay. But one newcomer was Max Sonderby. The Danish immigrant and college graduate had been hired away from City News, the easiest thing in all journalism. He became the *Sun*'s first court reporter, and politicians who read Sonderby's anti-corruption stories referred to him as "Max the Ax." He later knew the federal building so well that new judges were advised to ask him for help.

Editors and reporters were becoming more professional, and Chicago newspaper work was turning into journalisms—except for occasional fake scoops at the *Herald-American*.

SIX. Field, McCormick, and Hearst

Trying to determine what's going on in the world by reading the newspapers is like trying to tell the time by watching the second hand of a clock.
—Ben Hecht[1]

Colonel Robert R. McCormick's response to the Chicago *Sun* was: "Now we are under attack! A government-subsidized newspaper [in that it supported Roosevelt], financed through tax dodging, is fired at us.... No newspaper rotten at its heart can succeed."[2] The "tax dodging" charge was a calumny.

Sniping about the *Sun*, Kansas editorial writer and noted author William Allen White said in a letter that "I happen to have no use for the rich man who, like Marshall Field [III], because he has money, thinks he can start a newspaper"—as if anyone else could.[3]

Whereas McCormick sometimes seemed to forget the boundary separating him from God, there was a streak of remoteness in Field at least since his father was found dead at the age of thirty-seven in what may or may not have been a gun accident. The first Marshall Field had operated the city's premier department store and was well known as a reactionary during the anarchist rallies. His grandchildren were raised by nannies while their unconcerned elders attended to business during the day and to civic and cultural events at night.

After an education in England, the third in the line was awarded for bravery in World War One and did well as a banker in addition to taking part in the family's business enterprises. But while in New York in the thirties he became a heavily drinking playboy. A psychiatrist convinced Marshall Field III that his sense of completion would be found outside of himself. He started the Field Foundation and in its first two years it distributed a fortune to charities, including those helping African Americans. Then he founded what he promised would be "an honest newspaper." Largely because its existence in Chicago was superfluous with the Colonel now promoting the war, the *Sun* lost ten thousand dollars a week. But Field continued living in the Ambassador East

Hotel near Lake Shore Drive and walked to work on the seventh floor of the huge Daily News Building on West Madison Street. Knox leased him space and the use of equipment at a modest rate to get back at McCormick.

At first Field put Silliman Evans, formerly of the Nashville *Tennesseean,* in charge but soon found him too cautious and took over the paper himself, with a noticeable improvement.[4] As one of the best all-round newspapers publishers Chicago has ever seen, Field would stay in the building from around nine in the morning until five or six in the evening, usually finding time to speak to workers in each department.

Yet Field coasted through the war years and at times seemed to be running the paper for the future benefit of his son, attorney Marshall Field IV, whom he placed in the Washington bureau. While Marshall IV was serving as a naval officer, he gained an international outlook that would be useful in his family's battle against the McCormick-Pattersons. But as if carrying a family strain, the young officer suffered from periodic depression.

As the *Tribune* had published Roosevelt's war plans just before the attack on Pearl Harbor, on June 7 the next year it disclosed the position of Japanese ships in the decisive Battle of Midway. The inference was that the Navy had cracked the Japanese code. A grand jury was convened to decide whether the apparent leak violated any laws, but the matter was shelved when it became clear the information would not affect the war.

The ossifying Colonel McCormick was still the soul of the Tribune Tower, as gothic as the lettering of its masthead, and if at times he seemed to have no grasp of current events, he saw his paper as the culmination of all history. On his orders, foreign corre-

Marshall Field, III. This liberal grandson of reactionary Marshall Field I founded the Chicago *Sun* in 1941 to combat the *Tribune*'s opposition to the Roosevelt administration. The paper evolved into the Chicago *Sun-Times* (Chicago History Museum, photographer—Chicago *Herald-American,* ICHi-31020).

spondents came back with chunks of historic European or Asian structures to be embedded in the outer walls, turning a personal hobby into a tourist attraction.

Projecting from the wall facing Michigan Avenue were bits of the Alamo, Cologne Cathedral, Taj Mahal, Arc de Triomphe, and Great Pyramid. Sometimes these fragments were legitimately obtained, such as when the assigned building was being repaired, but a number were stealthily chipped away by the Colonel's time bandits, including William L. Shirer, whose *Berlin Diary* would become a bestseller.[5]

To have sensed the excitement at big city newspapers in the forties, you would need to have been in the editorial rooms with their cork floors, spittoons, cigarette butts, and clacking typewriters, and felt the vibrations from presses rumbling several levels below. Today's library-quiet news offices at the Tower, with their four-foot-tall cubicle barriers, daily-dusted shelves, and regularly vacuumed carpets are not the same.

In the lower levels of most news buildings, crews handled two-ton rolls of paper, and rats were such a problem at the *Tribune*, just off the river, that pressman Ron Montalbano claimed he suspended his lunches on a rope to keep them intact. The basement levels had four noisy block-long press lines and a small foundry that cast forty-five-pound plates while machinists, electricians, and engineers kept the machines running.[6]

Edward Doherty returned from success in New York to work at the Chicago *Sun* while his brother James was at the *Tribune*. Edward had already sent several stories to Hollywood and would soon share an Oscar nomination for the basic plot of *The Sullivans*, a true account of five Navy brothers who gave up their life jackets aboard a sinking ship so that other sailors might live. There must have been a lot of Doherty background in depicting the chaotic childhood of the rambunctious Sullivans as they fought over food, over who was lying, and over who would be first. Edward left Field's paper to perform charitable work, and in his old age joined an Eastern order that admitted married priests.

From the thirties through the early fifties, Jim Doherty, as Edward had, worked at the *Record Herald, Tribune,* and *Sun;* Tom worked for *American;* Frank was on the *Inter-Ocean, Daily News, Sun,* and *Sun-Times;* Bill joined the staff of the *Tribune* and the *Times;* and Martin went from the *Evening Post* to the *Herald & Examiner* and then the *Tribune* before he too became a priest. Since the Dohertys worked for different papers, they did not let on what stories they were involved in while at family gatherings. Several of their sons and nephews would follow them into the news business but received less attention.

In 1942, James Doherty kicked a door open and handed the state's attorney a mob gambling ledger documenting payoffs to public officials. A *Tribune* photographer captured the moment to make sure the chief prosecutor no longer ignored the problem. In later years, James's reporting helped pass tougher narcotics laws and won a *Tribune* Edward Scott Beck award for expos-ing graft that had freed four hoodlums.[7]

Also in 1942, the papers brought horses out again because of gasoline rationing. *Sun* delivery driver Angelo Duarte twice went through the agony of seeing a horse killed in traffic.[8] As newsprint shortages became severe, the *Tri-bune* experimentally recycled copies by having them de-inked, returned to pulp, and mixed with sulfate and freshly ground wood.

At City News, reporters called in stories to a rewrite, usually a woman in the war years, and the rewrite "cut a stencil" on mimeograph sheets, that is, put special paper in a typewriter without a ribbon. Once the editor used a sty-lus instead of a pencil on the stories, they were placed in velvet-lined brass cylinders and sent through pneumatic tubes through the city's unique under-ground tunnels downtown and up to the newspaper editorial offices.

By the end of 1942, ten percent of the *Tribune* staff was in the armed serv-ices, and most of the vacancies were filled by women "for the duration." This ratio was probably about the same at all other news agencies in the city. The newly hired women were shocked to see judges and politicians passing out ten dollar thank-yous to reporters at Christmas and were handicapped when males could impersonate officials on the phone. But they were as eager as men to get into the action.

The best known of the "war gals" was five-foot-two Patricia Leeds, one of the first five women hired at City News. On her first day the slender blue-eyed brunette was sent to the sixth floor press room of police headquarters. She looked so uncertain that the elevator operator remarked, "You won't have any trouble finding it, it's the noisiest room in the building."

As always, the press room door was open. She stepped in and heard the pinging "fire joker," police calls, and newsmen exclaiming over poker. City News reporter Buddy Lewis was elsewhere in the building and could not show her around. Since all the chairs were taken, she sat on an unused desk and heard the newspapermen complaining about women invading their profes-sion. Leeds pretended to be studying the firehouse directory on the wall some-where near pinup pictures and nasty notations.

Slim, good-looking James Murray—not to be confused with reporter-writer George Murray—told the other players they had to watch their language because a lady was present, but soon an exclamation suggested the cards had turned against him. Buddy Lewis breezed in, largely ignored Leeds, and went to work on the story he had just picked up. Then he muttered, "Who the hell tears pages out of these phone books?" That is, someone had found that pock-eting pages was easier than writing the numbers down. Spirko tossed him a newer phone book, almost knocking Lewis's glasses off.

Leeds was picked up by the *Tribune* in 1943 and stayed on as the first woman in any major city permanently assigned to police headquarters. This did not mean she was deskbound—editors often sent her to breaking news near downtown. She once found herself in a flaming building after fire crews had withdrawn their ladders. She jumped to safety while holding onto her notes. Another time she asked a police detective how a teargas bomb worked. Officers liked to show off before attractive women, and he overdid it. The bomb went off by accident and the stench nearly evacuated police headquarters.

Officers easily remembered Leeds, but she often forgot their names from one story to another, so she would ask, "How do you spell your name?" One snarled back, "How many ways are there to spell Jones?" Leeds later encouraged a woman who had killed her husband to confess by talking to her about a photo taken of the couple at a happy time. Leeds won a five hundred-dollar award from Pall Mall cigarettes when the case was dramatized on *The Big Story* on national radio in 1953.

A career-long concern of hers was that many dangerous people avoided arrest because of jurisdiction conflicts among law enforcement agencies. Leeds pressured Congress to institute a clearinghouse for information about drunken drivers and eventually establish the National Crime Information Center, making it easier to trace pathological criminals such as serial killers.[9]

Taller and more outgoing than Leeds was Virginia Marmaduke from downstate Carbondale, who because of her name was called "The Duchess." On her first day at the *Sun*, "The city editor looked me up and down. He said, 'So, you don't want any society stuff, you won't do fashion and you can't cook. Well, then, be prepared to cover blood, guts and sex—not necessarily in that order.'" Marmaduke then took her place among forty men on the news staff.

For a story about a dying mobster, she and a photographer hid in a closet across a corridor from his hospital room. The lensman took a picture of any gangster leaving the bedside, but one man caught on and snatched the camera. Marmaduke beat him on the hand with a spike-heeled pump until he let go and security guards came running to investigate. Several Chicago reporters have fought with mobsters, but Marmaduke might have been the only one to win.

Her 1944 series on children with cerebral palsy led the state to found the Children's Home Hospital. After she moved to the *Tribune*, she was the first woman named Press Veteran of the Year, and her career was profiled on the 1950s network television show *This is Your Life*.[10]

Outsiders might have thought female reporters were out of place—as a frequently reprinted painting by Don Cornwell suggests—but they were fully ready to compete with men, as writer Kurt Vonnegut learned when he was just another City News reporter in the mid-forties. "The very toughest reporters and writers were women," he said.[11] A bosomy Chicago *American* copy clerk during the war years cringed when reporter Peter Reich out of habit cried "Copy boy!" She responded, "I'm a girl. Take *two* looks."[12]

But there were genuine fears that female reporters might be sexually assaulted at a scene. In general, they were sent to the homes of victims while their male counterparts covered the location itself. That was fine with men who, like Vonnegut, were uneasy talking to relatives of victims even though grisly crime scenes seldom bothered them. When women were about to rush to a scene, their editors might tell them the paper would not be responsible for anything that happened to them.[13] Sometimes women were sent out in pairs. If a neighborhood was considered hostile, male as well as female reporters were told to leave before the police and firefighters did.

Young City News reporter Beata Mueller was sent to the neighborhood of a man who had secured himself to a self-made cross by the elevated tracks before dawn on a Sunday. According to editor A.A. Dornfeld, Mueller's mother phoned their church to explain her daughter's absence and said, "her office called her on a special assignment. Beata is covering a crucifixion."[14]

Whether women went to strikes or disasters, people spoke more freely with them since men tended to keep an emotional distance. The greater numbers of female reporters, writers, editors, and cartoonists also made papers in the forties more inviting to families, increasing circulation and drawing additional advertising. The *Tribune* ran clothing patterns for women and had a special Sunday comics page for children.

Press rooms and newspaper offices were becoming unisex, with smocks hanging near where sexy photos of women used to be, hairpins working their way toward washbowl drains, and jars of cold cream occupying rewrite drawers along with pipe cleaners and tobacco pouches. Or, as *Time* magazine put it, newsrooms were "converting from profanity to perfumery."

The *Daily News* promoted Lois Thrasher in 1945 as possibly the first credited female editor of any metropolitan daily. Although most people worked ten-hour days, the thirty-two-year-old former South Dakota schoolteacher took over the shorter but undesirable "lobster shift" from two A.M. to nine A.M. She worked well under pressure and literally knew the news from the ground up. When an editor had sent her to cover a hotel murder case, she took a job as a chambermaid and scrubbed seven bathrooms on her hands and knees before picking up what she needed. Thatcher claimed that she kept muttering, "I wouldn't do this for the man I love. I don't know why I do it for the *Daily News*."[15]

Good-hearted but cranky editors were not found only in fiction. In the forties, stocky Clem Lane was an unremarkable city editor at the *Daily News* but was beloved for his whimsy, friendliness, and his work at Alcoholics Anonymous. One day when the bushy-haired newsman heard a staff member speaking harshly to someone on the phone, Lane told him, "Young man, do not be as irascible as I am."[16]

Quite unlike Lane was gravely-voiced ex-marine Louis Ruppel, late of the *Illustrated Times*. As executive editor of the *Herald-American* he unwisely cut the foreign staff in the middle of the war. Ruppel also swaggered like a Foreign Legion officer. Seeing copyboys eating at their desk, he swept their doughnuts and coffee cups to the floor. Photo editor Vern Whaley responded by ordering coffee, cake, and bowls of soup for everyone in his department. Ruppel realized he had been made a fool of and rescinded his order against eating on the job. He continued his "heads will roll" attitude when he took over the ailing *Colliers* magazine.[17]

In contrast to Ruppel's cuts at the *Herald-American*, the *Daily News* was gaining respect with its foreign reporting. A.T. Steele distinguished himself covering the Rape of Nanking, the Japanese invasion that killed thousands of Chinese in the winter of 1937–1938, and Helen Kirkpatrick turned in vivid dispatches from bombed-out London. *Tribune* war correspondent John Thompson pioneered jumping with paratroopers. He landed behind enemy lines in Sicily and became the first reporter awarded the Medal of Freedom.[18]

Harvard-educated *Daily News* reporter George Weller fled the fall of Singapore, escaped from burning in Salonika, Greece, slipped through Gestapo fingers in Austria, interviewed Free French leader Charles DeGaulle, and escaped on a ship that was under repeated attack. While Weller was holed up in Australia with no way to get back to the fighting, he saw American submariners glad to be back on land and asked if they had seen anything unusual.

The result was a Pulitzer Prize–winning article about how a pharmacist's mate had performed an emergency appendectomy aboard the submerged boat with crude instruments and a medical text at his elbow. The cook had created an ether mask from a gauze-covered strainer, and he gripped the scalpel with a small clamp called a hemostat. Bent spoons held back both sides of the incision, and oversized rubber gloves were sterilized with alcohol "milked" from torpedo tubes. The patient seemed likely to die, but thirteen days later he was manning his battle station.[19]

The Chicago *Defender* could not vie with the much better funded white press for breaking stories, but concentrated on political issues and encouragement of the arts. In 1941, poet-essayist Langston Hughes began writing columns and editorials that were twenty years ahead of their time. Another *Defender* writer was Ben Burns, a young Caucasian. When Burns entered journalism he knew his anti-establishment outlook would not fit into the established papers so he worked for the Communist press in New York and San Francisco. In 1942 Burns and black publicity agent John H. Johnson invested five hundred dollars on a hope and founded the successful Chicago-based *Negro Digest*.

In 1944, Colonel McCormick married Maryland Hooper, who was seventeen years younger but, like his late wife, Amy, was the quiet, mothering type. Maryland had two daughters from a previous marriage, but the Colonel would never have any children of his own to inherit the paper.

When Colonel Frank Knox died that year, his executors sold the *Daily News* for a little more than two million dollars to John S. Knight of the Akron *Journal* and the Scripps-Howard news service. With his banker's personality, Knight kept wages low and brought in bolder type and page one human interest stories to conceal his indifference to crusades, as unimaginative press barons would do with their papers decades later. His idea of news was to stage a race between a reporter in a new Ford and a homing pigeon from a downstate site to the bird's rooftop base in Berwyn. The pigeon won.

Knight also started cutting previously sacrosanct dispatches from foreign correspondents to help pay off the paper's eighteen-million-dollar debt. And yet inside the paper was still lively, as columnist-novelist Bill Granger described:

> The presses were fixed in short rows perpendicular to the river. ... [and] ran all day. They roared when they ran, and they shook the foundations of the building. Newsprint streamed in a river through the presses.... The half-circular plates cast by stereotypers from papier-mâché mats of pages were fixed on the giant rolls, and newsprint was threaded through the complex, and when it was time to go, bells rang and the presses started slow and built up until the roaring filled the room and the universe. Copyboys pushed crude wooden carts down to the pressroom and waited for their city-room loads.... The copyboys ... got their carts full of ink-smeary fresh papers and slammed them on every desk in the city room. Every edition, every hour, every day but Sunday.[20]

Radio producers in the mid-forties had learned that while daily five-minute newscasts read by a man in a monotone were dull, they had a guaranteed audience for any expected breaking news, such as a battle or, after the war, a major strike. News could be broadcast from any location to which a soundman might lug a twenty-pound amplifier in one arm and a thirty-pound power source in the other, and listeners were rapt whenever an announcer broke into a program.

In 1944, a nineteen-year-old policeman's son, Art Petacque, took his first step toward becoming a mob reporter when he sought a job as a *Sun* copy boy. His opportunity came when devious restaurant owner Ben "Zookie" Zuckerman was gunned down in an ambush and his partner, Benny Glazer, died of a heart attack upon learning the news.

Petacque rushed to Glazer's home to confirm the report, and after telephoning in the story he needed to come up with a photo of Zookie. He called the murdered man's restaurant, a hangout for dubious characters, from a nearby phone with a bogus tip that the police were on their way to question everyone. When Petacque arrived, workers and patrons were fleeing the premises and leaving everything behind, including the picture.[21]

Bill Doherty of the *Illustrated Daily Times* and his brother Tom of the *Herald-American* had a friendly rivalry, but they took the gloves off when competing with other reporters. Bill certainly was not going to let a part-time suburban reporter like Gladys Erickson top him. During the forties Erickson was a stringer—occasional reporter—for the *Herald-American* because in those days before expressways she could reach the outer suburbs from her home in Joliet faster than someone starting from downtown Chicago.

The desk called Erickson about a soldier who had left his eleven-month-old son and some money for a few minutes on an eastbound train in Kansas

City, and the train chugged off without him. The stringer boarded the train and took custody of the child possibly by claiming to be his aunt. Needing to stall for time until a Hearst photographer arrived, Erickson continued the pretense even when the train pulled into the Dearborn Street terminal. She told the stationmaster that she was being hounded by the press, and he protected her behind a locked door at the station's Travelers Aid office.

The two-hundred-pound Bill Doherty showed up with a pair of *Illustrated Times* photographers and told his companions to stand aside. As flashbulbs exploded, he shattered the glass door with his bulk. Police arrested him while his hands were still bleeding.

The soldier eventually caught up with his little boy and refused to let the *Herald-American* take pictures of them, apparently because of Erickson's deception. This let the *Illustrated Times* win the game with two center pages of photos.[22]

Newer reporters were less showy but were still resourceful. James Peneff, whose medical studies ended in the Depression, once crawled along a catwalk at a union hall on his elbows and knees to cover strike talks. He later became a *Sun-Times* city editor and then general manager of City News, where he improved the hours and working conditions.

Editors in the mid-forties might have been losing their excitement with makeshift staffs and the war eclipsing local news, but you never knew where you might find an important story. Sometimes stories were literally under your nose.

On October 10, 1944, the *Illustrated Times* carried this classified ad: "$5,000 reward for killers of Officer Lundy on December 9, 1932. Call GRO-1758." The reward would not have been surprising if it had been offered a year or even two after the murder. But why after nearly twelve years, and why offer a reward when Joe Majczek was serving a ninety-nine-year sentence in Stateville prison for the crime?

This was what bothered Terry Colangelo as she was reading virtually every word of her paper on a slow day in the city room. Terry, one of the City News "war gals" who had moved on to a paper, sensed the dramatic potential where her more experienced colleagues might not have even seen a story. She showed the ad to young editor Karin Walsh, and what happened next showed that the tabloid was as serious about investigations as the larger papers.

Walsh gave the ad to reporter James McGuire, a former private detective. He learned that Officer Lundy had been shot by two robbers at a delicatessen in the old Stockyards police district, and a witness "fingered" Majczek at a showup (not yet called a lineup) in the station basement. But the case fell apart under scrutiny. The public had demanded an arrest, and under bullying from Mayor Cermak the police went out of their way to arrest someone, anyone. Majczek's alcoholic lawyer took fifteen hundred dollars from the family but only went through the motions of a defense and an appeal. The prisoner's

Polish-American mother decided to clean floors at night in the downtown Commonwealth Edison building until she could offer a sizable reward for information that could free her son.

This much was turned over to *Illustrated Times* reporter John McPhaul, a slim man seldom without a fedora and pipe. McPhaul located the original arrest slip in a police warehouse and interviewed the delicatessen owner who had identified Majczek. She insisted that she had told the truth, but McPhaul learned that at the time she was selling liquor without a license. This meant she might have told the police what they wanted to hear to avoid being arrested. By now the judge was dead, but his son said the man had spent sleepless nights over the case. This jibed with Majczek's written account that after his conviction the judge brought him to his chambers and said he was certain of his innocence. The judge, however, was unable to do anything about it because the Democratic Party soon dropped him.

This was no longer a "sob sister" feature about a woman who scrubbed floors for her son, it involved police misconduct and underhanded politics. The *Illustrated Times* started printing developments two and three times a week. Then editors took the unusual step of hiring state Senator Walker Butler to prepare an application for pardon, which was signed by Governor Dwight Green. As a former reporter, Butler must have respected the paper's efforts.

The prison gates opened for Majczek on August 14, 1945, and the state legislature eventually voted him twenty-four thousand dollars in compensation. He became an insurance broker, and McGuire and Walsh were honored by the American Newspaper Guild and the national journalism fraternity, Sigma Delta Chi. The newspaper received an outstanding public service award from the National Headliners Club and, after the story was dramatized on radio's *The Big Story*, Jimmy Stewart played a composite-character reporter in the movie version, *Call Northside 777.*[23]

One day after Majczek was released, the war against the Japanese ended with signatures aboard an American battleship, and Chicago went mad with excitement. Women working in factories and newsrooms knew they would soon be out of a job.

Journalism always reflects the times, and people seeking openings in the field after the war may have been less competitive than old-timers but they brought a more worldly perspective. Newcomers must have viewed the news room as a nest of eccentrics, including Edward "Dynamite" Sokol, who was remembered more for his way of playing the office than for any story he ever worked on.

While Sokol was supposed to be covering county building offices in the Loop for the *Herald-American,* he was barreling around New York with former news great Walter Howey and the Hearst general manager. So he had his rival, *Tribune* county reporter Ray Quisno, tip him off about any major development. Dynamite then turned the *Tribune* story in as his own, probably adding background off the top of his head and making small changes so the article would not seem pirated. One day, when Quisno called Dynamite in New York to say the desk could not find him anywhere in the building, Sokol hung up, dialed his office, and asked, "Anybody looking for me?"

When the *Herald-American* was about to mention a lawyer Dynamite disliked, he ran from his beat through Loop traffic to the Hearst Building half a mile away and asked at the offices in every stage of development if the name could be removed. Each time he was told no. Sokol settled for having a stereotyper scrape the plate with a sharp tool so the identification would be printed as a blur. Dynamite gloated, "That son of a bitch ought to learn not to fool around with me!"[24]

In New York, Joseph Patterson's drinking made him seem dragged through life. The man who abandoned socialism to help run the conservative *Tribune* and then gave America its first successful tabloid, the New York *Daily News*, died in 1946 at the age of sixty-seven. By then, Chicago-style journalism was dying, too. With so many global developments, readers were finding ordinary local crimes and accidents less relevant. Street reporting started being considered a little passé, a job for beginners and people without ambition.

When tall, lean Walter Spirko returned from military service, he grumbled about how police reporters were being taken for granted. While at a newspaper hangout (the Billy Goat Tavern when it was next to the Chicago Stadium on West Madison Street), he mentioned that they should have their own organization. Editor Joe Fay and reporter George Bliss encouraged him to start one, and Andy Frain of the usher industry offered the use of his stadium clubroom.

The first event of the Chicago Police Reporters Association, later the Chicago Newspaper Reporters Association, was a banquet honoring all veterans returning to the newspapers. From then on the group held annual fundraisers and provided scholarships for bright sons and daughters of its members, making news work in the city seem even more like a family.

At the time, newspapers were paying more attention to the post-war activities of the crime syndicate as the city administration denied its existence. At the *Herald-American* suspended policemen Tom Connolly and ousted honest police Lieutenant William Drury, brother of *Daily News* writer John Drury, operated a "link room" in 1948 and 1949 to concentrate on crimes possibly connected to the mob, with phrasing coming from some of the six rewrites on the staff.[25] Drury's determination would later cost him his life.

2

One of the worst Chicago fires of the decade killed sixty-one people in the LaSalle Hotel on June 5, 1946. At the time, John Paster was the *Tribune*'s overnight reporter at the detective bureau. He and a few other reporters spent their entire shift at the morgue to record each name as the victim was identified. Paster said years later that when grieving loved ones came out of the identification room in tears, they vomited at the sight of newsmen eating lunch on a desk or a slab.

But it took the death of six-year-old Suzanne Degnan to shock the city. Suzanne had been kidnapped in her sleep from a North Side home on January 7, 1949. Police Commissioner John Prendergast let radio recording equipment be set up in the home so that Suzanne's father could beg the kidnapper not to harm his girl, and could assure him that he was doing everything possible to raise the money. The message was played at intervals on several stations throughout the day.

At the Chicago *Times*, which had dropped "Illustrated" from its name because all papers now carried photos on every page, city editor Karin Walsh was convinced the girl or her body was still in the neighborhood. He sent half a dozen reporters, including Bill Doherty, to talk to every person in every building "till we find her," although a hundred police officers were doing the same thing. Bill located a soldier who remembered seeing a suspicious dark haired young man, later identified as compulsive burglar William Heirens.

The ever chic Virginia Marmaduke stayed on the case and watched officers find Suzanne's severed head in a catch basin. Other parts of her body were pulled from elsewhere in the sewer system. Frank Winge of the *Tribune*, who once had bullied his way past bodyguards to interview Al Capone, found a knife that was later linked to Heirens. He received a Pall Mall cigarettes award when his story was re-enacted on the radio.

The most puzzling aspect of the case was a message written in lipstick on the wall of a previous murder victim, a woman:

> FOR HEAVENS
> SAKE CATCH ME
> BEFORE I KILL MORE
> I CANNOT CONTROL MYSELF

A persistent suggestion was that a reporter or photographer had written the message himself for a scoop, possibly at the direction of an editor. Spirko, who had worked on the case, said late in life that the only one who could have done that was Buddy McHugh, but that this was unlikely because the first police officer on the scene would have had to have been in on the fake. Maybe he was.

In the Suzanne Degnan kidnapping, her abductor left a bogus ransom note. After her dismembered body was found, a *Daily News* editor wanted part of the note blown up, but that would require retouching to clarify a few words. As newspaper artist Frank San Hamel traced the letters he noticed a faint impression left from when someone had written on a previous page. Under ultra violet light the impressions yielded the partial telephone numbers and the names of several students at the University of Chicago on the South Side.

Seventeen-year-old Heirens, a U of C student, was arrested during a routine North Side burglary, and evidence seemed strong against him in the Degnan and "Catch Me Before I Kill More" murders as well as that of a second woman. Over six days of intense interrogation without a parent or lawyer present, the brilliant teenager was given sodium pentothal (the truth serum) to encourage him to talk.

The *Tribune*—with mottoes about the responsibilities of the press adorning its inner walls—was determined to convince every judge and potential juror that Heirens was guilty. George Wright, the man who had secretly recorded grand jury testimony in the Leopold and Loeb case, now secured his second great scoop, a copy of the confession as soon as it was typed up by police stenographers. The questions and answers took up twenty-four columns in the sensational July 16, 1946, issue.

According to some accounts, Wright fabricated all the hours of questions and answers, as unlikely as that might seem. Perhaps the suspicion arose because the paper never disclosed how Wright had obtained the confession (although carbon copies seem plausible), and State's Attorney William J. Touhy denied there had been one until details were satisfactorily corroborated three weeks later.[26] The prisoner would say the confession was entirely fictional and that he had based his later incriminating statements on the *Tribune*'s account. Heirens, the first American to earn a college degree in prison, also insisted that he never wrote the lipstick message, and so its origin may never be known.

One of the reporters who saw action in Chicago after the war was James Murray of the *Herald-American*. In 1947 he talked a woman out of throwing herself off the Michigan Avenue bridge, and later that year calmed down a man who had drawn a gun in a North Side police station and threatened to shoot himself.[27]

But it was Edward Eulenberg of the *Daily News* who represented the new breed of journal-

Chicago *American* Reporter James Murray working at the press room of the former Chicago police headquarters in the early 1960s (courtesy Tom Yanul).

ists. He said you might not have to take your editor too seriously but you must always take your job seriously. While at City News he coined its motto, which originally was "If your mother says she loves you, kick her in the shins and make her prove it." A politer version emerged in the retelling, "If your mother says she loves you, check it." But this became "If your mother says she loves you, check it out," and years of efforts by Eulenberg and his editor friend A.A. Dornfeld could never change it back.[28]

Even as the papers were becoming more ethical, editors had a closet of tricks to keep an exclusive. Bill Doherty of the *Times* went to a bar and spoke to an alcoholic woman who had just killed her abusive husband in his sleep, and she showed Doherty the gun. Bill called his paper, and city editor Joe Fay instructed him to keep the self-made widow drinking so that she would be incoherent when other reporters spoke to her at the station.

But the Bill Doherty story that made radio's *The Big Story* started when editor Karin Walsh called him seven hours before he was scheduled to report for work and sent him to the scene of a deadly shooting at a midnight card game. A gunman disguised as a car hiker (valet parker) had entered an apartment during two games of rummy and a round of high stakes poker. A patron who worked as a court bailiff reached for his gun, and he and the robber were killed in an exchange of shots. The getaway car sped off at the blasts. In an unusual move, the police commissioner ordered that the case be handled entirely by detectives rather than district officers.

Doherty knew this meant authorities did not yet want reporters to learn something about the case. Then, while covering the robber's funeral, he wondered why the mother was absent. It turned out that the family was helping to hide the surviving brother, a seventeen-year-old boy who had recently been released from reform school. Even without confirmation, the *Times* rushed out a front page story suggesting that the teenager might have been the scared wheelman. A sister called the news office to say the teen would give himself up but was afraid the police would beat him, so Doherty gave her the name of a good lawyer and promised that the boy would be treated well. When the teenager came home, Doherty drove him to the newspaper office to turn him over. That sent a message to the detectives: if you lay a hand on him, you will be exposed in the paper. Bill later visited the boy in jail and learned that the police had been on their best behavior.

Harry Romanoff had been a good reporter, but his fame came as a telephone virtuoso at the *Herald & Examiner* and *Herald-American* city desks. Making a sport of competition, he might call the police chief of a town that had just seen a bank robbery and say, "Well, hello, chief. This is Commissioner [whatever name he felt like using]. Do you need any help down there?" The police chief would then fill him in. If "Romy" learned where a swindler might be hiding after jumping bail, he would call the building and say, "Let me talk to [the con man]. I gotta ask him what to do with these bum bonds he signed."

Any reporter could get hold of a policeman at the station, but from the comfort of the local room, "Romy" usually would reach one at the scene by knowing the number of what seemed like every drug store in the city. Someone there was sure to call out for one of the officers outside. Romanoff also might keep three newsroom phone lines open on a major story, all the while humming or singing to himself and bellowing malapropisms to his staff. He once said that the Illinois Bell Telephone Company should erect a statue of him for making a million dollars in phone calls over his long career.

Another of his tricks was having two reporters apply pressure to a crooked officeholder. The first would call anonymously and threaten to make his graft public. Some time later the second would phone for corroboration, making it sound as if the story were about to appear on page one. In his efforts at damage control, the scoundrel would give the story life.[29]

Some of the best reporters seemed like everyday people with no particular talent until news entered their blood. Seymour Hersh applied at City News in the forties because he no longer wanted to work at a pharmacy.[30] As a freelancer, he would win a Pulitzer for revealing the massacre at the Vietnam village of My Lai by American troops.

Anyone at the papers could work on a story. Alexander Katz was just a low-paid employee at the *Sun* clippings morgue when he saw a young mother being slashed with scissors on the street. Katz used his army training to tackle the assailant although it meant being severely wounded. He rose to become the *Sun-Times* ski editor and assistant picture editor.

News agencies might have seemed cold to outsiders, but most had at least one friendly woman who served as a greeter and helper for the staff. As a secretary from one department to another in the *Daily News*, Margaret Whitesides treated employees as if they were relatives. She kept their names and the names of their family, dates of marriage, and other data on cards in a recipe box at her desk and gave motherly advice whenever needed. Noting the small woman's calm in the chaos, editor Clem Lane called her "an angel among devils" and in 1944 brought her to the city desk, where she wrote a few stories for the temporarily short-staffed paper.

At the *Tribune*, Whitesides' counterpart was Clare Burke, a former Ziegfeld Follies dancer who was a secretary at the Neighborhood News and Metro sections. The greeter at the *American* was Anne Musial, and at City News in the sixties she was plump, white-haired switchboard operator Gladys Wherity, who sometimes rubbed backs and gave personal advice.[31]

After the war, Marshall Field III attacked McCormick on his strongest point, the comics. Since the creators of Orphan Annie, Dick Tracy, and Brenda Starr were happy with the Tribune Syndicate, the *Sun* lured away Milton Caniff, creator of *Steve Canyon* and *Terry and the Pirates*, by offering well more than the Colonel was giving him and guaranteeing him ownership of his strips.

With newsmen returning from the war, the papers had more reporters than they needed, and that led to mischief. Numerous reporters converged on a four-eleven fire at Randolph and Halsted Streets, just a good sprint from the newspaper offices. A hose broke away from a hydrant, drenching the lower half of a new reporter for the *Herald-American,* and for some reason the more experienced hands, possibly including Adolph Wagner of the *American* and George Bliss of the *Tribune,* decided to hoodwink his boss into paying for new clothes. So they took the cub to one or more bars and splashed him with more water. Wagner finally introduced the soaked reporter to his editor, who authorized a new suit for him.[32]

In 1948, *Sun-Times* investigative reporter Carl Larsen sniffed something foul about Preston Tucker's automobile company in Chicago. Larsen talked his way past guards at the South Cicero Avenue plant by using a fire department pass and secretly counted the few cars that actually were being produced after the showman-like Tucker received millions from investors. Larsen won the Chicago Newspaper Guild's Page One Award for the exposé and the auto plant closed for good. One of those cars, however, was sent to the Smithsonian Institution as an example of post-war ingenuity.[33]

In December 1948, the city named a small lakefront airport after erudite but not very interesting former *Herald & Examiner* executive Merrill Church Meigs, a flying enthusiast who had proposed building the single runway on a neglected manmade island a ten minute drive from the Loop. The city would turn Meigs Field into a park by surprise with midnight bulldozers in 2003.

Daily News reporters William Mooney and Fred Bird dressed as derelicts in 1949 for a feature on conditions along the Madison Street skid row near their news office. That also was the year its Springfield reporter, George Thiem, and Roy J. Harris of the St. Louis *Post Dispatch* shared a Pulitzer for showing that Illinois newsmen had been put on the state payroll for do-nothing jobs under Governor Dwight Green.

Letting reporters dip into the public trough would not have meant much in the twenties, but by now journalists and state politicians were expected to be beyond reproach. In 1957, Thiem and an investigative team including Mooney and Edmund Rooney would share a Pulitzer for articles showing that state auditor Orville Hodge had squandered two and a half million dollars in taxpayers' money on such hobbies as a yacht and two airplanes.

Rooney, a small and genial man, was known as a "door-kicking" kind of reporter, one who found a way to get comments from someone withholding information. "I don't think I ever kicked a door," he once said. "I might have leaned on a couple."

Thiem's suggestions for investigative reporters remain valid today:

—Assume your tip is true until you learn otherwise
—Enter an investigation with a plan for long-range inquiry
—Use the casual approach

—Be alert for any possibly guilty responses to questions
—Find ways to get around a stone wall
—Write only what can be proven
—Ignore possible accusations of politics or persecution
—Avoid being sidetracked by details
—Share your information and uncertainties with others in your office
—Never back down on your rights as a reporter.[34]

In the forties, Marshall Field III used a small radio station in the attic of the *Sun* headquarters at the Daily News building to introduce all-news programming to Chicago, but relatively few people could pull in the frequency. When that experiment failed, Field persuaded NBC to sell him fifteen minutes a day for news written and delivered by one of his newspaper reporters, future TV commentator Clifton Utley.[35]

Television newscasting was older than most people imagine, with announcer John Cameron Swaze reading copy cut from a newspaper on a Kansas City station in 1937. He had to paint his eyebrows black to keep them from singeing in the intense lights then needed to transmit pictures.[36]

Chicago's first television station, WBKB-TV (later WBBM), started transmitting in 1941, with its sole newscaster, Ulmer Turner, formerly of the *Herald & Examiner*, using the resources of the *Sun*. Giving up newspaper work for television might have seemed unwise, but the ham radio operator with the professorial face was excited about the possibilities of the new medium.

Also in the forties, Bill Ray of WNBQ-TV (later WMAQ) had sound engineers set up a couple of speakers in the newsroom of the Merchandise Mart to monitor police calls. He was the first TV official in the city to send reporters to scenes and report live or make transcriptions at events.[37] Eventually the NBC station would run a cable from a van to a camera that could record images to be fed into a studio camera.

The *Times* had been struggling ever since the 1944 death of its founder, Samuel Emery Thomason. Marshall Field III decided to buy the paper and move the *Sun* editorial staff into its Wacker Drive building. He also acquired a good crew from the *Times*, including editor Richard Finnegan. From September 7, 1947, to January 31, 1948, the *Sun* reached morning readers and Field put the tabloid *Times* out in the evening, and combination editions came out on Sundays.

The post-war period saw a number of strikes across the country as workers demanded better conditions and a share of the prosperity. The International Typographical Union launched a walkout at all Chicago dailies on November 24, 1947. As the potentially crippling strike continued until September 1949, each paper had to deal with the stoppage in its own way.[38]

Field's response was to combine the weekday editions of the *Sun* and the *Times* on February 2, 1948. The *Times* staff thought the new boss too liberal, and *Sun* readers disliked the lowbrow advertising for such things as false teeth and chewing tobacco.[39] But the merger produced the city's liveliest paper of the time, and years later it would call itself "The Bright One."

The *Tribune* reacted to the strike by adapting a cast iron Graphotype machine—normally used to emboss metal for such things as military dog tags—to stamp short takes of major stories into thin strips of metal. When a fire destroyed a downstate hospital in April 1949, the *Tribune* was able to set up a Graphotype bulletin in just fifteen minutes. Since its linotype machines were silenced, *Tribune* carpenters brought long tables to the fourth floor as the workspace of stenographers, typists, and secretaries using noisy VariTypers, typewriter-like devices that produced columns similar to ones from linotypes.

Herald-American assistant managing editor Paul Evenstad went around conferring with printing company executives about how he could carry on without the strikers. He learned that liquid lead could be replaced by printed type that was pasted on pages and photographed onto zinc photo-engravings. Evenstad showed rewrites how to use scissors and rubber cement for preliminary mockups of their own stories. Like many writers, they were not known for their mechanical ability, and one of them supposedly sliced eight inches off his tie.[40] Evenstad used extra typists and paste-up artists for the final mockups.

On April 5, 1948, the *Tribune*-owned WGN-TV played the city's first film of scenes, but the images were static because the cameramen used to be newspaper photographers.

That autumn, WMAQ scheduled its first ten-minute TV newscast. Weather reports were delivered by Clint Youle, who had been a downstate reporter and who trained in meteorology during the war. Personable Dorsey Conners was brought in to offer household tips and craft ideas for the final few minutes. Some viewers might have wondered why they were still reading newspapers.

As the chief newsman at WMAQ, Clifton Utley rode the streets in a mobile unit—a truck—while monitoring police calls. Hearing something promising, Utley would tell the driver, "Go with that." He covered some stories the newspapers would not bother with, simply because he could get there quickly. After all, unlike newspapers he needed only one or two sentences to tell his story. Reading Utley's news on the air was young Mike Wallace.[41] Utley would become a foreign affairs specialist in broadcasting, and Wallace developed into a television mainstay, especially for his interviews and work on *60 Minutes*.

3

Editors often took a gamble that early indications would prove the end result, at times to their regret—as happened with the November 3, 1948, *Tribune* bannerline of DEWEY DEFEATS TRUMAN. Because of the printers' strike, the deadline had been moved up to a time when only the New Hampshire early returns were in. Washington bureau chief Arthur Henning, who bragged that he had been wrong just once in twenty years, assured Colonel McCormick that President Truman had no chance of staying in the office he had inherited upon Roosevelt's death. Nearly one hundred and fifty thousand copies with that headline hit the streets before later tallies turned the early trend upside down.

Future columnist Bob Weidrich (pronounced we-drik) was a City News copyboy at the time, and one of his duties was to pick up newspapers at a nearby stand a few times a shift. On election night "I saw a big tug-of-war going on between the newsstand guy and the *Tribune* truck driver, who was trying to retrieve the early editions," Weidrich remembered. "The newsstand guy wouldn't give them up. I guess he thought they would be valuable some day."[42] They are.

Police officers were still usually accommodating to reporters, but firefighters were not. The city's deadliest surface level mass transit disaster occurred when a streetcar collided with a jackknifing gasoline truck at 63rd and State Streets on May 25, 1950, killing thirty-three adults and children, some trapped by safety bars over the streetcar windows. As Bill Doherty was calling in the particulars on a pay phone, a firefighter swung an axe to cut the line and get him out of the way so the bodies could be removed through the trolley trap.[43]

That year saw the city reach a population peak of more than three million six-hundred thousand. As the number declined with the move of homes and jobs to the suburbs, and then to burgeoning smaller cities, newspapers continued as if the fifties would last forever. In retrospect, 1950 seems a golden twilight at the papers.

A new reporter at the time, future *Tribune* architectural critic Paul Gapp, said that when he arrived from Ohio he found that "The *Sun-Times* was scrappy but sophisticated; the *Daily News* lean, hard and Pulitzer-heavy; and the [*Herald-*]*American* ... still Hearstian in some respects but tough to beat on local stories."[44]

Newspaper publishers in Chicago and other major cities had started seeing advertising money flow to broadcast stations back in the thirties, and for some time were able to keep them from having access to the AP and UP. In the long run, the papers did the stations a favor by forcing them to establish their own news cooperatives and contacts. From its newspaper-bound early days, broadcast information was evolving into a different kind of news.

Marshall Field, III, was well liked by his employees, but retired from publishing in 1950 and turned the *Sun-Times* over to his capable but somewhat reserved son, Marshall Field IV. He dropped the evening edition and began the tradition of concentrating on local news at the expense of national and international coverage.

Nineteen-fifty was also the year headline-grabbing U.S. Senator Estes

Kefauver of Tennessee announced that he would take his racketeering investigating committee to Chicago. Officials still denied that all those mob beatings and killings were connected. Former police lieutenant William Drury, who had worked as a *Herald-American* crime investigator rather than as an actual reporter, asked Kefauver if he wanted to see his files on cases the police department refused to delve into and his paper could not use because there had been no prosecution.

On September 25, the night before Drury was to testify at an open hearing, a shotgun blast killed him in an auto outside his Addison Street home, and his wife saw two cars speeding away. That also was the day attorney Marvin Bas was shot to death in another part of the city as he was gathering evidence against mob-connected "Millionaire Cop" Dan Gilbert, a candidate for sheriff.[45]

Whether Kefauver was alarmed by the murders or not, he was astounded by the way stories about his secret conferences with authorities wound up in the papers, unaware that reporters were eavesdropping through the mail slot in a door.

Ray Brennan, working for the *Sun-Times* after his AP scoop on Dillinger's escape, had been following the committee from city to city but was unable to get transcripts of Gilbert's testimony. Brennan flew to Washington and, passing himself off as an aide to a committee member, asked if he could pick up a copy. Sure! Before long, Brennan was flying back to Chicago with testimony and committee comments suggesting that Gilbert had made a fortune by ignoring illegal gambling. Brennan was arrested for impersonating a government employee, but the Justice Department saved him from six years in prison by finding that there had been no criminal intent. By then Gilbert, whom the papers snidely called "the world's richest cop," had lost the November election.[46]

The Illinois Crime Prevention Bureau had been set up a little earlier at the urging of the *Tribune*'s Jim Doherty, and heading it was pretty policewoman Lois Higgins-Grote. She had been told not to bother with the Kefauver hearings because they were being put on just "for show," but she took the stand and gave impassioned testimony about the growing drug menace, then a shocking subject.[47]

Local television stations were replacing news professionals like Utley, who controlled their own content, with smoother announcers who read Teleprompter copy and rehearsed their delivery. Teleprompters had been invented in the late forties by Irving Kahn, a nephew of Irving Berlin. Mounted just below the camera lens, the devices slowly rolled up paper with large letters printed with a special keyboard. Teleprompters were regarded as too confining for comedy shows and dramas, which still used hand-held cue cards, but they were a blessing to newscasters since they needed to sit or stand in one place.

Newsreaders—a more honest British term than the American "newscasters"—were scorned by considerably lower-paid print reporters. But the new medium knew where it was going. Less dependant upon continuing information sources such as the police department and what Illinois lawyer-poet Edgar Lee Masters called "the bribe of advertising," television news tended to be closer to the progressive spirit the papers once had. And as children of technology, TV staffs could change quickly with every advancement while the papers were still operating largely as they had just after the Civil War.

Serious broadcast news executives were more alarmed about the growing conservatism of America in the mid-fifties than were the newspapers, which either went along with Wisconsin U.S. Senator Joseph McCarthy's grab for attention or were afraid to denounce him. Few print reporters questioned his figures for the number of Communists in the United States as he shook pieces of paper in feigned rage.

In 1951, the *Tribune* and another paper even drove respected bio-nuclear scientist Martin Kamen to attempt suicide by suggesting he had passed information on to the Soviets merely because he had met two Russian officials at a cocktail party hosted by his friend, classical violinist Isaac Stern. Kamen recovered, and four years later won a libel settlement against that paper and the Washington *Times-Herald*.[48]

In contrast to the *Tribune*'s attack, radio and television newscaster Edward R. Morrow would contribute seventy five thousand dollars so that blacklisted CBS radio humorist John Henry Faulk could hire the best attorney possible in his suit against a group that had smeared him, Aware, Inc.

On August 14, 1951, the eighty-eight-year-old William Randolph Hearst died in California. He had shaken up journalism with exciting but not always accurate newspapers across the country and then, disappointed in his political ambitions and living with a wife who would not grant him a divorce, ran them largely by telegram. Without his goading, the chain rusted and broke apart.

Young women were still encountering difficulties getting into the news business after returning servicemen replaced their sisters and aunts, even though the media were becoming more open to minorities. In 1950, the *Daily News* hired its first African American reporter, Les Brownlee of the *Defender*. Two years later the paper wanted to hire another black reporter, Ben Holman of the University of Maryland, but thought he needed seasoning and had him trained at City News, a common practice then. When Holman worked on stories in white neighborhoods he had to prove to officers in patrol cars that he really was "the press."

The first black woman on the *Sun-Times* news staff was sugary-nice Lillian Calhoun, who won an Illinois Press Association award for her article "Why Didn't They Scream?," about Richard Speck's murder of eight student nurses. Calhoun later worked for a newsletter on racial issues and was a commentator for WBBM-AM before opening a public relations firm.

During this transition phase in the early fifties, broadcast stations often used print reporters for their newscasts. Brownlee recalled that a news magazine columnist would show up at a radio station during his lunch hour for a 12:30 P.M. daily newscast with a sandwich in one hand and some newspaper articles in the other. "Nobody's got any copyright on a murder or accident," the noontime moonlighter would claim.[49]

The speed of newsgathering was continually increasing. By July 1952, all *Tribune* reporters had two-way radios in their cars so they would not have to rely on land lines while at remote locations. And before long, print reporters returning from news conferences were telling their editors that TV crews with their film and sound equipment were making questions and answers go faster than they could write in their longhand.

Even the news emphasis was shifting. Partly inspired by Murrow, television network executives in New York were trying bold programming to transform the neglected stepchild of the information age into its Cinderella. WBKB in Chicago hired the first two-man team in TV newscasts, and in 1952 someone at the CBS offices in New York coined the term "anchorman" for Walter Cronkite's coverage of the national political conventions.

From his work on the evening news, Cronkite would be called "the most trusted man in America," something no one could say of Joseph Medill, Walter Storey, William Randolph Hearst, or Colonel McCormick. In fact, Cronkite's steady baritone and air of informed confidence became the standard for most newsreaders, possibly further delaying the advancement of women in front of the cameras. This meant viewers and newspaper readers were still getting information from only the male perspective.

In 1954, CBS bought a barn-like building at 630 North McClurg Court, just north of downtown, for its television studios in Chicago. The "cavern" had opened in 1922 as a stable for more than five hundred horses, and later became an ice skating rink and a bowling alley as entertainment tastes changed. The sheer space suggested that the network had big things in mind.

The emergence of one medium and the decline of another split some news families. M. W. Newman chose to work at the *Daily News* in the mid-forties, but his younger brother, Edwin, went into broadcasting and became a well known writer and authority figure on NBC. Luke Doherty, one of a dozen people in the second generation of his newspaper family, left the *Sun-Times* and signed on as the police headquarters reporter for the Radio News Service.

Other reporters thought they would stay in newspaper work but found themselves attracted to the here-and-now of broadcast news. When John Chancellor of the *Tribune* ended his military service he chose the new field and distinguished himself on NBC.

As a City News county building reporter, soft-spoken John Calloway kept running into television crews and would offer them a little help. WBBM cam-

Former WBBM-TV Studios. This converted stable saw the first John Kennedy–Richard Nixon presidential debate in 1960, and TV began seriously competing with newspapers for audiences.

eramen were so grateful they persuaded their news director to hire him.[50] At the time, the only woman on the staff was assignment editor Lu Barlow, but several men from the station in the mid-fifties went on to important positions in CBS national news.

Part of the excitement of street reporting for the papers was that you could never be sure what would happen next. One summer in the fifties, a horse-fancier on the desk at the *Herald-American* was upset over the death of at least fifty horses in a stable fire. He sent cub reporter Hal Bruno to determine such things as whether there had been enough exits. Bruno crawled over the dead horses and through manure as a July sun was keeping temperatures in the nineties. Bruno called in his story and received his next assignment, a luncheon at the posh Ambassador East hotel, without time for a shower or change of clothes. "It didn't bother me," Bruno said about his arrival, "but some of the people around me seemed to get pretty emotional." Bruno later directed nationwide political coverage for ABC.[51]

In 1953, the *Herald-American* became the Chicago *American*, but the name change and blatantly cheesecake photos of shapely young women could not compensate for a loss of investigative resolve.

The next year, Colonel McCormick, knowing he would not live much longer, sat through family gatherings that turned into discussions of his succession. He also permitted a certain relaxing of the newspaper's Daddy War-bucks outlook and gave editorial space to contrary opinions.

As the holidays passed, the January bareness outside his home must have seemed like a preparation for his departure, and McCormick said he was lonely. He had become so weakened by heart disease and cirrhosis of the liver that he needed a nurse to help him dress, and he was saddened by a nearly twenty per-cent drop in circulation since 1946. *Tribune* officials replaced one another at his side because he did not want to die alone. They called themselves the Watch-men of the Night. His wife was little comfort. Worn out by the ordeal, Mary-land said, "You know you are going to die—why make it so hard on everyone else?"[52]

Biographer Frank Waldrop wrote of the Colonel that "it was his most severe affliction that no experience of his life ever broke his spirit enough to free him from his vanities and fill the vacant spaces in his days that, in the end, became so bleak."[53] The final watch ended before dawn on April 1, 1955, when McCormick died at the same age as his grandfather Joseph Medill, seventy-five.

Despite McCormick's faults, he had guided the paper from a position of strength. The story of the World's Greatest Newspaper for the next fifty years would be one of out-of-touch management making ultimately wrong or insufficient decisions, which began with the first post–McCormick publisher, W.D. Maxwell, who was known for spiking stories that might adversely affect business or civic leaders.

In early 1958, the *Sun-Times* moved into its new building at 401 North Wabash. The squat, functionally angular structure looked as if it had been built without an architect, unlike the stately Tribune Tower diagonally across the way. The tabloid's four new Goss presses were lowered into the lower level by chains, and saw their baptism in ink that January 23. From then on, people walking in from the Michigan Avenue side could watch through glass walls as pressmen leaned over or reached up from platforms in their denim pants, blue work shirts, and quaint caps made from scrap newspaper pages.

United Press merged with Hearst's International News Service that year, creating the United Press International. A.J. Liebling said the action was "like a cat merging with a canary." But Charles Novitz noted that the effect in Chicago amounted to no more than "clearing a couple of desks" in the UP's offices in the *Daily News* building.[54]

Newspapers provided rather routine coverage of labor-racketeering hear-ings in Chicago in the mid-fifties, but television gave them saturation treat-ment. The sight of mobsters and underhanded union officials repeatedly claiming ignorance of illegal acts took the glamour away from corruption, and viewers understood that "sweetheart contract" was a cover phrase for extor-tion.

But television usually skipped over stories needing details and background, and newspaper reporters were invaluable for public officials wanting someone to do their work for them. In 1955, Jack Lavin and Frank San Hamel, the Austrian-born *Daily News* artist who had helped in the Heirens case, were sworn in as temporary deputy coroners so they could go through police files and other privileged documents in a child murder. They were unable to find any links to the killer but assisted in solving twenty-six other crimes against children.[55]

Sometimes a reporter could get more out of a non-answer than from a cautious reply, as when Chicago *Defender* Washington correspondent Ethel Payne confronted President Eisenhower, who was less concerned with race relations than Truman had been. Payne demanded to know whether Ike would abide by an Interstate Commerce Commission recommendation that he end segregation in interstate commercial travel. The President replied, "What makes you think I am going to make special favoritism to special interests," meaning minorities. The remark was picked up by papers nationwide.

The era of taking mayors at their word that there was no such thing as organized crime ended in 1956 when Chicago *American* reporter Edward Williams noticed U.S. Attorney Robert Tieken checking a name on a list. Tieken let him look over the list, and he saw information on one hundred hoodlums: their homes, their rank, and their suspected criminal activities. Williams obtained permission to reproduce the list and distributed copies to his press room rivals so everyone could use it for reference.[56] Entertained rather than horrified by the mob killings, newspeople enjoyed making up monikers such as "Jackie the Lacky" for John Cerone, a hoodlum boss who bristled at the name.

To outsiders, the cooperation of many reporters from competing papers might seem unusual, but this was how it often worked. If a reporter was seriously scooped he would endure a dressing down, possibly a suspension, and might be fired. This could lead to cutthroat tactics that would sour official sources for everyone. So if a press room reporter picked up a good story, he turned it in to his office and then told it to the others or allowed them to listen in and take notes. But the first reporter often left something out and later made a quiet supplemental call to a rewrite, assuring himself of some exclusivity. Likewise, the other reporters surreptitiously followed up various angles on their own to avoid being accused of copying the story.

None of the major newspapers or broadcast stations in the city paid attention when Mamie Till-Mobley asked that the casket of her fourteen-year-old son be kept open at a South Side funeral home so mourners could see what racists had done to him. Emmett Till had been visiting Mississippi relatives when he apparently made a flippant remark or whistled at a married white woman. On the night of August 28, 1955, he was abducted, beaten, and shot, and his body dumped some distance away.

The *Defender* and Chicago-based *Jet* magazine, a black-oriented Johnson publication like the *Negro Digest*, tried to help Mississippi authorities, only to learn that they were not investigating very hard. Photos of the battered body in both publications would help spur the civil rights movement of the sixties.

On October 21, 1956, the half-century of Hearst presence in Chicago disappeared when the *Tribune* bought the *American* for more than eleven million dollars, apparently to keep the *Daily News* from using its plant for a Sunday edition. The two Tribune Company–owned papers continued to be printed separately, but editors at the *American* seemed uninterested in using fresh news to increase circulation.

In some ways the United States had become more innocent than in the twenties and thirties, and so the public was shocked when the two Grimes sisters, ages twelve and fifteen, were found dead in a forest preserve that December after going to an Elvis Presley movie and possibly accepting a ride home.

Just a few days earlier, an unpromising Mike Royko was hired by City News after all the Chicago papers had turned him down. His bosses discouraged deception and did not issue badges, so Royko bought a toy one at a Woolworth's to get a foot in the doors of the Grimes neighborhood and talk with skid row bums about a possible suspect who turned out to have been lying for the publicity.[57] The case remains unsolved.

This is not the place to detail Royko's career, he declined to be interviewed and you can read about him in F. Richard Ciccone's biography. But, although everyone thought of Royko as a columnist, he always regarded himself as a street reporter. After being notified that his column had won a Pulitzer he called City News obviously drunk and told the night editor, "I just want to tell you I owe City News everything. You [City News] gave me my start, I owe everything to you, I mean that."

Mike Royko at the City News Bureau in 1958.   In August 1957, readers saw a little story about how a man who had lain in Cook County Hospital for fifteen years after a crash awoke and was married in a hospital wheelchair. Not allowed to interview bridegroom Bud Koster, hefty Bill Doherty posed as a city inspector checking the hospital fire escape. He sneaked up three floors in the dark, pried a window open, and passed himself off to other patients in the open ward as a messenger looking for Koster. The man consented to an interview and even turned on the television so Bill would have enough light to scribble notes by.[58]

The next year, the *Tribune* changed the Chicago *American* into *Chicago's American* and expected a surge in sales from the apostrophe. On July 26, all the press units of the World's Greatest Newspaper were put on twenty-four-hour-a-day, seven-days-a-week schedules.

That December 1 was one of the saddest days in Chicago since the *Eastland* had rolled over: three nuns and ninety-two children perished in a fire at Our Lady of the Angels School. "For months I woke up sobbing in the night," United Press International reporter Everett Irwin said about the aftermath of his interviews with the families. *Chicago's American* editor C. Owsley Sheperd went for a drink or two to get through the job of working with reporters at the scene, with the families, and calling from the morgue.

The real story of that disaster may not have made print. Whenever a fire kills that many, code infractions must have been disregarded. Someone who worked at an archdiocesan office confidentially said years later, that fire inspectors regularly ignored violations on parish property. Even when the state established fire laws that were stricter than city ordinances, parochial schools were exempted, as if saving lives were less important than keeping tuitions down.[59]

The city was stunned again when a "babbling burglar" told authorities in 1959 that police officers in the North Side Summerdale district were not only taking money to let him continue, they were placing orders for merchandise and sometimes helped carry the appliances out. Readers learned about the scandal because a reporter lived on the Southwest Side.

Sun-Times reporter Walter Spirko, who at eighteen had been the first newsman to learn about the St. Valentine's Day massacre, usually made his first beat stop at the nearest station, Chicago Lawn. On this day he wondered why state's attorney's people were inside. That might mean charges would be coming down in a major story involving the police, but no one would give him a straight answer.

A few hours later, Spirko talked this over with his easygoing, chubby counterpart from the *Tribune*, Joe Morang, who said he had heard there was something going on across the city "in Summerdale." Neither of them jumped on the case because in those days investigations involving an officer might take months before any news was released.

Still later in his shift, Spirko mentioned his itchy feeling to his editor, who told him, "You want to go there? Go there."[60] He did, and the bannerline story led to a reorganization of the entire police department. Reformer O.W. Wilson was brought in from California as the city's first civilian police superintendent, and disgraced Summerdale was renamed the Foster Avenue district.

The ailing *Daily News* under the Field Foundation was downscaling the kind of investigative work that had made it so readable for nearly a century, and its staff now concentrated on "done in a day" stories. Although both the *Daily News* and the *Sun-Times* were being printed in the stubby building at 401 North Wabash, with a glass wall separating their operations, the two staffs usually did not try to steal news from one another. But then came the 1962 case of "terror-and-torture bandits" Nicholas Guido and Frank Yonder.

As a car hiker at an exclusive hair salon, Yonder would tip off his gang about good pickings. During a police stakeout, two members were killed but both Yonder and Guido remained at large. Yonder sent a letter telling the *Daily News* he was afraid that he would be tortured if he gave himself up. The paper let him know the police had promised to treat him fairly.

The paper even installed a special phone line for him in its news room, with at least one detective standing by on each shift to pick up the receiver. The *Sun-Times* people watched some of the goings-on through the glass but could not hear what was happening. After an eavesdropping *Sun-Times* copyboy claimed he was just making a shortcut through the sister city room, the *Daily News* set a trap. An unseen staff member called the special number, the detective answered, and suddenly everyone in the room became animated. Someone shouted near the nosy copyboy "Eighty-Seventh and Loomis!" After the copyboy quickly left, the *Daily News* people prepared to razz the two *Sun-Times* reporters and three photographers who had been sent on a wild goose chase.[61] Yonder and Guido were eventually arrested in Michigan for a traffic violation and sentenced in Chicago to serve between sixty and one hundred years in prison.

There were still a few hotshot reporters around. These were aggressive men, and they always seemed to be men, who embellished personal anecdotes. Colleagues were suspicious about parts of their stories, but kept silent because the editors needed them for scoops or colorful writing. *Sun-Times* columnist Mark Brown knew a few hotshots and said they were given perhaps more freedom than the others. But by now more editors were demanding that reporters be able to prove their stories even if the sources remained confidential.

Despite the growing professionalism in the press since the thirties, no one in the business was prepared for what was about to happen to America as the Vietnam war dragged on. The violent clashes increased public reliance on broadcast journalism, and the newspapers were left wondering what had hit them.

SEVEN. Newsboys and Photographers

One greater than kings had arrived—the newsboy.—Mark Twain[1]

Reporters in newsrooms, police stations, city hall, and in the field were the heart of newspapers, but the stories were humanized by a child calling out headlines and photographers capturing a scene in a way words never could.

In the late nineteenth century, boys needing to supplement the family income, or who ran away from home or were abandoned, knew how to start themselves in business when no apprenticeships were available. All they had to do was "flip" (hop onto) a streetcar and get off at Newsboys Alley, narrow Calhoun Place behind the *Daily News*.[2]

The boys bought their papers from the office for a fraction of a penny for the *Daily News* or one and three-fifths of a cent for a two-penny paper such as the *Tribune*. From there the adolescents spent hours working on the streets, often wearing a secondhand cap and coat, suspenders, and knickers and knee socks, a newspaper bag slung over the shoulder and perhaps a coin changer around the waist. They commonly called out "Newspaper, newspaper for sale" and "Extry newspaper, extry news, read all about it." When special editions came down, the boys hollered themselves hoarse. Many grateful buyers gave the young hawkers a nickel.

Lacking a circulation staff at the time, the *Daily News* built a hall with a gymnasium on the second floor of its new building to accommodate up to one thousand boys on cold or rainy days. The hall kitchen served a couple of hot dogs on buns for a penny, a pork chop for two cents, and a "square meal" for a nickel, with some of the money going to the Newsboys Benevolent Fund.

In periods of waiting for their bundles of newspapers, the boys pitched pennies in the street. But not everything was so wholesome; there was a lot of smoking, some drinking, and a few boys mixed morphine into their beer.[3]

A boy known only as "Herman the Great" claimed to know all the gangsters and first-night theatergoers in the city, until he was killed by downtown traffic.

The average age of a newsboy when the *Daily News* was founded in 1875 was sixteen, but by the 1890s it was down to thirteen. Any who just stood around waiting for customers made only a few sales. But ones who shouted the news and gave a little information about the day's top story—even if he couldn't read it—might bring home five to ten dollars. Many ran alongside streetcars to sell papers through the windows. But conductors usually let the boys climb on for free to sell papers and jump off. The boys were not above a little larceny such as calling out nonexistent headlines.

The boys' home might be just the *Daily News* basement or some stairway to curl up in. A night watchman at the old opera house chased out a few he found sleeping in the private boxes.

You might have found skinny adolescent Walter Spirko selling papers under the Marshall Field's clock at State and Randolph before he became a well-known crime reporter. Enterprising ex-newsboys included Alderman Michael Hinky Dink Kenna, his nickname coming from local slang for a streetcar; the Reverend Paul Leahman and several judges; shady taxicab union leader Joseph "Joey" Glimco; and state representative William Lorimer. There were so many underage newspaper sellers that they had their own union.

Sometimes newsboys got into competition fights with one another. Millionaire newsman Joseph Patterson, while serving as commissioner of public works, had several newsboys pulled off the streets in 1905 until the publishers assured him it wouldn't happen again.[4] Some newsboys were trained to be tough, with the *Daily News* keeping a crew of men to back them up at the more desirable street corners.

The Newsboys and Working Boys Home on Jackson Boulevard, set up by five Irish priests, in time became the Mercy Boys Home.[5] The Newsboys and Bootblacks Association at 14th and Wabash, a privately funded charitable organization founded by respected attorney Wirt Dexter and others, provided baths, lodging, and meals along with Protestant religious instruction and strict rules against spitting, gambling, or indecent language. Some of the four hundred newsboys there were just seven years old.[6]

Care for newsboys by several agencies helped remedy what could have been a serious delinquency problem. Long before James Petrillo headed the national musicians union, he was one of the children who learned to play instruments in the *Daily News* newsboy band, which performed at charity events in exotic red and blue costumes.

Ventriloquist Edgar Bergen patterned the original Charlie McCarthy on a Chicago newsboy named Charlie, and comic book artist Charles Beck started out in the city by creating a fifteen-year-old Chicago newsboy named Billy Matson who could morph into Captain Marvel. When the black-oriented

Chicago *Defender* opened its own newsboys home, one of the youngsters learning to play music there was later jazz great Lionel Hampton.

Today we can log onto the Internet for the latest developments, but where is the excitement of hearing "Extry, extry"?

A few boys were lucky enough to work on the copy bench at the papers. Their primary job was to grab a story from a reporter and bring it to the editor. Their secondary job was to go for coffee for nearly the entire city room staff.

Each paper had its own way of initiating copyboys. At the *Times*, they were tricked into bending over in the mailing room, then their pants were yanked down and their posteriors were painted with a wide paste brush as older employees howled. Sometime afterward they might be sent to the composing room, where pressmen "accidents" splattered their young faces with ink. When future NBC newscaster John Chancellor was a copyboy at the *Tribune* in the mid-forties, gullible newcomers were told to clean typewriter ribbons, leaving the sink full of ink.

Office boys were copyboys with additional duties such as running errands and bringing in stories from reporters at scenes. It's not a myth that a good office boy could virtually run a paper. The most fondly remembered was Jimmy Aloysius Durkin, who worked at the *Times* until the paper merged with the *Herald* when he was around fourteen.

He returned to his orphanage but happened to pick up the phone when editor James Keeley wanted someone for menial chores at the *Tribune*. Durkin said he would send someone right over, and that someone was himself.

Soon the news room was alive with: "Durk, where's the pencil ... where's the telephone book ... who's the mayor of Cleveland ... get me a sandwich, ham. ... throw this bum out." A cub reporter knew his job was secure when Jimmy borrowed a quarter.[7]

The impish and vulgar blond teenager would answer a call from a reporter, assign it to a rewrite man without going through the city editor, seemed afraid of no one, and notified staff members when their watch was up by calling out "Thirty!" Durkin also was one of the few news people who memorized the fire department location code, tapped out on a moving strip of paper as a bell tinged at each stroke. Without looking at the tape, Durkin would call out "Three-eleven at Wells and South Water Street. Lot of shacks and granaries there." It was no wonder that in time he was boosted to city editor.

Keeley thought so much of Durkin that he sent the then-thirty-year-old reporter to London as a *Tribune* representative for the coronation of George V in 1911. When Durkin came back, he reported that when the new king shook his hand, he said to him, "Hi, yah, George! How's the king business?"[8]

The liveliest office boys might be promoted to flyboy, who would wrestle huge rolls of paper and drums of ink all the way to the presses. Flyboys or copyboys sometimes would jump into a cab with the first paper off the press to show the head man, who might be the managing editor or the publisher. The best ones kept their mouths shut about what they saw.[9]

Where are the copyboys today? They're little computer keyboard buttons marked "Send."

Newspaper photographers and video journalists usually were as street savvy as newsboys, but reporters usually ignored them and publishers took them for granted. "Photogs" sometimes seemed naive, but that was because they were in a business that demanded single-mindedness. Each picture had its own story, even though the photographer was usually the only one who knew what it was.

The first crude news photos appeared in the New York *Graphic* in 1880.[10] Ironically the technology was developed by a notorious hoaxer, photographer William Mumler of Boston. He made a career out of faking ghostly portraits of wealthy people by superimposing faint images supposedly of their dead loved ones comforting them, including Lincoln with his hands on the shoulders of his widow. While not fighting off skeptics, Mumler patented a process that allowed newspapers to reproduce photographs without having engravers adapt them.[11]

Picture clarity improved by 1911, when photographers seemed everywhere. But the magnesium powder they put into flashguns was twice as explosive as gunpowder. Although the "gun" was held over the head of the photographer, the *poof!* often singed the subject's hair or beard. The faces of early lensmen such as Gene Cour of the Chicago *Journal* were marred by burns and bluish spots.

In 1915, the *Tribune* sent photographer Fred Eckhardt to take a customary shot of Western Electric workers and their friends boarding three excursion boats in the Chicago River. But the middle one, the *Eastland*, began listing. In a minute and a half, Eckhardt was able to take a picture and run to his office with the first depiction of a tragedy that would claim more than eight hundred lives.

Chief *Tribune* photographer Lyman Atwell braved his way through the 1919 race riot, where he was caught between a mob of white hooligans and a black man running for his life. Atwell kept his shutter going even as a bullet grazed him.[12]

Although a reporter could get his start at City News, there was no such training ground for lensmen. Some began as messenger boys and others on the copy bench. When the editor told them to pick up a camera and go somewhere, they learned by guesswork and talking to experienced men on the street and in the developing room.

Harry Houdini had used trickery in his escape theatricals, but in the mid-twenties he went around the country exposing spiritualists. With Houdini's help, an unnamed Chicago *American* photographer sneaked into a séance where a Chief Blackhawk appeared to be communicating through a trumpet. In the exploding light of the flash gun, men and women at the table could see medium Minnie Reichart with a trumpet to her lips.[13]

A photographer thought to have been Norman Alley needed to take the photo of a certain gunman. Knowing that his criminal career would be over once his picture was in the mind of every policeman and future victim, the ruffian made his displeasure known to Alley or whoever it was. To satisfy his editor, the photographer supposedly knocked the mobster out cold and snapped him in repose.[14]

When Walter Howey and Hilding Johnson kidnapped witnesses or suspects, they needed a photographer to play up the coup. That meant lugging a twenty-pound tripod and five-pound Speed Graphic camera in addition to a heavy case for magnesium flares, flash powder, film holder, light meter, and several half-pound photo plates of specially treated glass.[15]

The keenest competition for pictures was during the tabloid era, from the end of the Great War to the 1940s. In the twenties the *Tribune* was waging a spite campaign against Governor Len Small and sent a photographer to follow him around until he could take a picture that would "make him look like a village idiot." It took three months, but the *Tribune* used that photo for years until Small's obituary.[16]

In New York, blonde Ruth Snyder had no trouble seducing a corset salesman into crushing her husband's skull with a window sash, a club-like metal weight. When that was not enough, Albert Snyder was chloroformed and strangled with picture wire in hopes of collecting a fortune from his insurance policy. The illicit couple's arrest and conviction caused a nationwide sensation.

New York newspaper photographers would not deign to take an illegal snapshot of the first woman being strapped into an electric chair. Besides, authorities would recognize them all, and there was no way to hide a Speed Graphic with its overhead flash cone and protruding lens. To get around this, the New York *Daily News* hired Chicagoan Tom Howard of the New York *Daily News*–Chicago *Tribune* picture syndicate. Howard strapped a pre-focused miniature camera he had made for the occasion to his right ankle and sat with spectators on the other side of the glass in Sing Sing's death chamber. At just the right moment he pulled a thin shutter-release wire and snapped the picture through a hole in his trousers. The image of Ruth convulsing with the electric current stunned readers who saw it splashed across the front page on January 13, 1928.[17] On its web site, the New York *Daily News* calls this "the most remarkable exclusive picture in the history of criminology." But New York *Herald Tribune* city editor Stanley Walker at the time condemned the photo as "a blot" on the history of journalism.

Years later Howard became the chief photographer for the Chicago *Sun-Times*. His grandson, comedian George Wendt, recalled racing with him to stories with the car radio tuned to the police frequency.[18]

If there ever were a boxing match between reporters and photographers, there was no doubt who would win. When photographer Tony Berardi of the *American* arrived at the scene of the St. Valentine's Day massacre he saw a policeman guarding the door. "Get the hell out of my way," Berardi snarled and walked in. He recalled there were so many flashgun explosions in the garage that from time to time, despite the cold, the photographers opened the door to "suck away the smoke from the flash powder" so they could take more shots.[19]

Bugs Moran had escaped being victim number eight by failing to show up at the garage when expected, and there is a possibility Capone or whoever else ordered the massacre might have tried to get him a second time. This comes from Berardi, an amateur boxer who hung up his gloves and picked up a camera for the *American*.

A little after the garage shooting, Berardi was climbing out of his car to take pictures for an unrelated trial when he saw a man with a familiar face walking across the hotel where Moran was staying. The pleasant-looking fellow was Ralph Pierce, one of the suspected machinegunners.

"I had photographed him at least a half dozen times," Berardi related. "And like a damn fool—I wasn't thinking—I said, 'What the hell are you doing here?' He said, 'Tony, if I was in Kansas City you'd be there.' He was going to kill Bugs Moran. No doubt about it. So I actually saved Bugs Moran's life. If I'd kept my mouth shut I could have gotten the —— pictures of my life."[20] Berardi later posed as an inspector to sneak into an Ohio prison following a deadly fire, and hid a camera under his coat in a federal courtroom to capture Capone's expression at his tax fraud trial.

Longtime *Tribune* photographer William Loewe told of how he and others sometimes climbed through back windows and sneaked along fire escapes for their shots. "Many times I had to run like crazy to the nearest police station, chased all the way by a bunch of hoods...," Loewe said. "We were all threatened and shot at, and had nothing to defend ourselves with but our powder-flash guns."[21]

At a Chicago restaurant in the twenties, Frankie Berger of the *Record Herald* was knocked down and had his camera destroyed by gangster Legs Diamond.

Baby Face Nelson was mortally wounded in a suburban highway shooting in 1934. Two photographers from the Chicago office of the Associated Press knew they would have trouble getting past FBI agents guarding the body at a Niles Center (now Skokie) mortuary. So one of the men, Ralph Frost, made a scene by weeping that his boss had ordered him to get a photo. While the unsympathetic agents handcuffed Frost to a car handle for trying to impede them, James Quinn slipped in, pulled the sheet down, and took photos of Nelson's face and death tag.[22]

Hearst was easy to mock but he led several advances in the newspaper business. When he learned in the late twenties that Nick McDonald of the Chicago

American had lost a hand to flash powder, he ordered that all photographers in his chain stop using the substance and sponsored research into how the illumination could be confined. Flash bulbs, a German invention, reached the American market a short time later, in 1930.[23]

From the time the McCormick-Patterson New York *Daily News* became the country's first tabloid in 1919, almost anything might be used as a picture. In 1936 the *Tribune* carried a front page photo of an individual supposedly picking up discarded Roosevelt campaign buttons from the street after an FDR rally in Chicago, but it turned out that the photographer had strewn the buttons himself and the paper hired someone to pose as a collector of memorabilia.[24] Larry Nocerino always carried a shoe and a broken umbrella to improve an accident picture by tossing one of them onto the street.[25] One reason for such fakes might have been the fun of imagining editors at other papers browbeating their "photog" for overlooking such a detail. If a photographer arrived too late he might re-stage the scene. Bob Kotalik of the *Sun-Times* could not get to the rescue of a little boy from a window ledge, so he had the mother put her son back up there. Only this time, she combed his hair.[26]

Two of the best known pictures of the home front during World War Two were of Montgomery Ward executive Sewell Avery being carried out in his chair by a pair of helmeted soldiers and dumped on the street in April 1944 for obstructing the war effort by cracking down on unions. Bill Pauer of the *Daily Illustrated Times* and Hartland Klotz of the Chicago *Daily News* snapped Avery's calm expression at different angles.[27]

In the later forties schoolboys were hired to clean pigeon cages on the roof of the *Illustrated Times*. Sports editors took the birds to Wrigley Field or Soldier Field and fitted their negatives of the baseball or football game into a leg capsule. The *American* did the same thing, and the inevitable happened, the pigeons became lovebirds. After being taken to a football game, the *American*'s "Nellie" flew home with the *Illustrated Times* bird. So the tabloid could thank the avian heart for being able to publish a day's work by a rival cameraman.

Photographer Sol "Dixie" Davis, a horse fancier, hated the messy messenger pigeons on the *Daily News* roof. Maybe it was the way each arrival sounded a bell in the fourth floor photographer's room. So before putting anything in their photo capsule at a Bears game, he fed them peanuts, knowing that birds flew straight only when hungry.[28]

Stealing pictures from a rival may have started with Frank Carson. When he worked at the *Tribune* he would also pick up *Herald & Examiner* photographic plates from trains passing through. He once took an elevated train, a bus, and then a cab to reach a train during a two-minute stop in a rural area.[29]

Immediacy was even more important to camera people than to the reporters riding with them through red lights. The Chicago Press Photographers Association elected a police liaison whose only job was to fix tickets for parking and moving violations.[30]

Lazy lensmen put fried eggs on sidewalks on hot days but a few, such as Arthur Fellig—later internationally known as Weegee—framed pictures to say something beyond the events, even if he had to stage it. Fellig once photographed society people entering an opera house with a seemingly impoverished woman looking on from off to the side. In his famed New York days, Fellig's car had a police radio, a typewriter, and extra underwear, along with chemicals and small trays that allowed him to develop his film in his opened trunk.

Some camera-slingers could be a little rude. Using a wartime analogy, newsman Benjamin Feldman said an ace photographer he identified only as "Mike" would throw his heavy satchel of equipment over his shoulder and barge in front of everyone with his Speed Graphic "as though he was in the first wave on the beach." On one assignment, Mike stopped off at a bookie joint and called his office to say he had reached the building of someone in the news. "Mike," the editor said, "I hope you're a good swimmer because the address we gave you was wrong. It is out in Lake Michigan."[31]

The best-remembered stunt of the usually mild mannered George Emme of the *Illustrated Times* was dressing as a priest to take the picture of a hospitalized crime figure. Earlier, Al Capone tipped Mike Rottuno of the *American* fifty dollars for showing the unscarred side of his face.[32]

In the thirties, photos from all over the country could be sent to Chicago in eight minutes through the Associated Press's Wirephoto, developed by papers including the Chicago *Tribune*. Starting on January 1, 1935, seven-by-nine-inch pictures were wrapped around a cylinder that slowly revolved as a light beam electronically scanned it. The destination machine received the picture line by line over its own cylinder.

Jack Spray of the *Herald & Examiner* once drove forty miles to photograph the execution of rapist-killer Gerald Thompson in Joliet state prison in October 1935. While Spray was hurrying back to Chicago a tire went flat in a country area, and he ruined the floppy tire driving to a gas station for a repair. As the tire was being replaced, a drunken driver jumped the curb and smashed into his car. The photographer left the wreckage and hailed a cab to take him to the Hearst Building halfway across the city. When Spray arrived hours late the editor refused to reimburse him for repairs or the cab fare. "Get away from me," he said. "You flopped on the assignment. You're lucky you aren't fired."[33]

In 1940, the *Tribune* had a circulation of a little more than one million and could afford innovations. The photo department rolled out a special truck with a raised perch for a lensman to photograph a scene from a distance or over a crowd, and three searchlights were attached to the roof for night shots. Inside the truck were an emergency darkroom and a black suitcase with a portable wire photo transmitter.[34] A few years later the *Tribune* city desk had a direct wire to the telegraph company's mobile operator, saving time when dispatching any of its twelve photographers.

Bill Doherty of the *Illustrated Times* accompanied photographer Bud Dailey in 1945 on a story about a bar that kept open after hours to serve a horde of soldiers and sailors. Doherty scooted out when the bartender menaced them with a baseball bat, but Dailey stayed behind until a patron pulled off the front of his camera. The "photog" hurried to the car with the portion holding the photo plate.[35]

Of course, reporters and "photografers" (in the Medill-McCormick spelling) were capable of tender feelings. In 1946 Frederick Griese of the *Tribune* saw a young man and his former wife waiting far apart in court for a child-support hearing. Griese decided to play cupid and asked them to sit together for a picture, and then to hold hands. The couple later remarried.[36]

President Harry Truman called photographers the "One More Club" for continually saying "Just one more." A former member was Luigi Mendicino of the *Tribune*, who noted that even though photojournalists of the nineteen-eighties had high speed film, strobe lights, and lightweight cameras, they did not have the access to jails and crime scenes that those of the thirties and forties enjoyed.[37]

Hefty Joseph Mastruzzo of papers including the *Herald-American* was overcome by tear gas taking pictures of a jail riot, and in an adultery trial found himself being hurled over two benches.[38] When a TV cameraman elbowed Mastruzzo out of the way as President Dwight D. Eisenhower arrived at Union Station, the press photographer responded in kind. Ike told his aides, "Let's stop and watch the fight."

In *Deadlines and Monkeyshines,* John McPhaul said a photographer went to the University of Chicago for a reunion of scientists who had built a secret nuclear reactor there as part of World War Two's Manhattan Project. Having no grasp of physics, the man told them, "Now, fellows, I got three pictures in mind. First, you guys putting the atom in the machine. Then splitting the atom. And finally all of you looking at the pieces." Sorry to ruin a funny story, but the photo just shows Enrico Fermi and two fellow physicists looking at a bottle of Chianti they had used to toast the atomic age.[39]

In the fifties, Charlie Chaplin said in *The King in New York*, "I hope you don't mind the press photographers—they're the curse of the Twentieth Century."

That same decade, chief Chicago *Defender* photographer Herman Rhoden, who was black, risked his life when authorities in a small Mississippi town tried to hush up a lynching. He hid in the trunk of a funeral car and lifted the lid just enough to snap a picture.[40]

While the western and southern suburbs were flooded by two days of storms in the mid-fifties, Mort Edelstein of the *American* was sent to write a feature with photographer Al Phillips. Edelstein took one step too many and started sinking into the rain-swollen Sanitation and Ship Canal until Phillips could pull him out. Edelstein called the city desk and editor Harry Romanoff asked, "Did Phillips get a picture of you in the water?"

"No, sir."

"What? Then go out and fall in again. We gotta have the pictures."[41]

After *Tribune* photographer George Quinn took a photo of a mobster's widow at a 1958 funeral, he was chased for two blocks and beaten by half a dozen mourners.[42]

Numerous photographers were sent to the devastation left by a fire that killed ninety-two children and three nuns at the Our Lady of the Angels School that same year. What many readers remembered was the face of a firefighter holding the body of a ten-year-old boy. Five-foot-five Steve Lasker of the *American* had waited on the step of a fire engine with his Speed Graphic aimed at a doorway, its shutter cocked, for some time until someone came out. At the newspaper office, chief photographer Tony Berardi ordered a portion of the negative blown up many times to emphasize the firefighter's drained expression.[43]

Press photographers were threatened and occasionally struck by rocks during the West Side racial clashes in the early sixties, and before going to anti–Vietnam War demonstrations in 1968 some of them threw helmets and shields into their car. The next year *Tribune* photographer Walter Neal moved closer than reporters dared to at the Southwest Side apartment building where "mad bomber" Frank Kulak was holed up. Kulak, who had just killed two officers, shot at Neal and exploded a grenade near him before a police official talked the disturbed World War Two veteran into surrendering.[44]

African American Hank Martin lost his tailoring job in the sixties and had no idea how he would make a living. Then he took a picture of a light pole that a car had knocked onto a parking attendant's office and sold it to the *Defender* for three and a half dollars, the start of a new career. Martin was working for the Chicago bureau of the Associated Press when he followed smoke and discovered rioting following the murder of Dr. Martin Luther King, Jr. "There was chaos all around me," Martin said, "but I was busy shooting what ever I can see."[45]

During the police assault on war protesters at a downtown rally in advance of the 1968 Democratic convention, *Sun-Times* photographer Bob Ringham could hardly believe what he was seeing. Officers had always been accommodating to the news media, but now a policeman was trying to run him down with a motorcycle. When he yelled a complaint he was assaulted by what seemed to him to be fifteen others.[46]

Getting to the scene early sometimes presents a humanitarian problem. Ringham and a supervisor went to the home of a woman whose husband had just died in a construction accident, but after a few words they could tell she was unaware what had happened. The two men apologized for supposedly having the wrong address, then had a neighbor break the news to her and ask if she would let the photographer take her picture.[47] Some time later, Ringham waited three hours in the cold and with snow falling on him before horses at a suburban farm came to the fence just the way he had envisioned.

Some shots could serve as one-click editorials, such as when *American* picture editor Vern Whaley and a photographer bought ten potted plants and placed them in potholes for what the paper claimed was Mayor Richard J. Daley's city beautification plan.

Phil Mascione, a second-generation *Tribune* photographer, took shots at a hospital where a wounded Chicago policeman lay in serious condition. After bringing the pictures to the Tribune Tower and seeing the negatives through the printing, Mascione drove back to donate blood for him.[48]

Just how would you be sent out if you were a *Tribune* photographer? You would receive a photo request form with an assignment date, time, and a statement such as "Needed By: 7/8/83 at 4:00 P.M." There would also be a notice whether a reporter working on the story would be at the scene, and farther down an assignment summary would briefly describe the story you were to illustrate and outline what kind of shot was expected. Driving directions were at the bottom.

When only four dailies were being published in the sixties—the *Tribune, Sun-Times, American,* and *Daily News*—photos tended toward the routine and television visuals became more arresting. WGN cameraman David DeWert saw an opportunity when International Amphitheatre security guards told news crews they could not use their heavy shoulder cameras during a 1964 Beatles concert. Noticing all the screaming fans taking snapshots, DeWert chanced that they were creating enough light and let his videotape run, earning him the honor of Chicago television cameraman of the year.[49]

After minicams were introduced in 1974, new challenges opened for TV crews. The handheld video cameras let photojournalists cover the scene of any disaster or political upheaval. In the eighties Cable News Network correspondent Chuck DeCaro used small video cameras while simultaneously reporting and filming stories of guerrilla fighting in Nicaragua.

Since video journalists and "videographers" need to stay light to keep up with the action, special vests and jackets have zippered sections not only for notebooks and pens but also replacement equipment and extra rolls of film. But household video cameras have given ordinary people the capability of being reporters, as the police beating of Rodney King in California showed. The problem, as always, is resisting the temptation for capturing a misleading detail.

But some things have not changed for wire service photographers. When an estimated three hundred thousand people thronged to the downtown Daley Center Plaza to denounce international terrorism following the September 11, 2001, attacks, Associated Press photographer Stephen Carrera took a bird's eye shot by leaning precariously out a high window, just as in the old days.[50]

Part 3: The Media

EIGHT. Upheavals

They [the newspapers] have vilified me, they have crucified me. Yes, they have even criticized me.[1]—Mayor Richard J. Daley

Comedian-actor George Wendt, who once worked at the *Daily News*, was applauded at the City News centennial dinner in 1990 when he introduced himself as the grandson of Tom Howard, the Chicago photographer who had secretly snapped the execution of Ruth Snyder. With pretended outrage Wendt looked the audience over and said, "Who let the electronic media in here? Get out," he told the TV people, "go bury more dailies!"

But television was only part of the problem. Many successful and educated people were leaving the city for the suburbs in the sixties and were no longer interested in the Chicago news, and workers who once brought a paper with them on a bus or train were now driving to work. The publishers might have held onto some of those readers as Chicago lost its "second city" status to Los Angeles, if they had known who they were.

A few years before, broadcast reporters had been no more than a nuisance to those from the papers, who liked to kick their cables out of sockets at a scene. But by the sixties the electronic rivals were a threat. After all, it was in the barn-like WBBM studios in 1960 that John Kennedy and Richard Nixon engaged in the first of their televised debates, which probably decided more voters than did newspaper endorsements. Especially because of editorial restraints on interpretation, the papers could report only the words of the two candidates and not relay how they were spoken or the candidates' expressions and body language.

But the cameras and special lighting could be cruel as well as revealing. CBS flew in a renowned make-up artist to help the men, but Kennedy and Nixon declined. Instead, each candidate let a personal adviser dabble with his face, and the coating of "Lazy Shave" over Nixon's stubble made him look as though he were scowling. Kennedy won.[2]

The convenience of evening television news and individualized radio formats during the "drive times" were also among the reasons for withering newspaper readership. WGN radio was a favorite station for rush hour drivers because of the city's first helicopter traffic reporter, Officer Leonard Baldy. But Baldy and his pilot, George Ferry, were killed in May 1960, when a malfunction made their rotor blade disintegrate.[3]

Also that year, Chicago *Tribune* court reporter Paul Holmes was trying to remain impartial as he typed out a book about the 1954 arrest and prosecution of Dr. Sam Sheppard for the sexual assault and fatal beating of his attractive wife in an upscale Cleveland suburb. But as Holmes delved into the evidence he had seen and heard while covering the trial, he became convinced of the doctor's innocence. No motive had been offered, no blood was on Sheppard's pants, information about the sexual assault had been withheld from the jurors, and the judge had allowed what Holmes considered "poisoned" news coverage.

Holmes conferred with popular crime novelist Erle Stanley Gardner, who had already reinvestigated a number of possibly wrongful convictions. The resulting national bestseller, *The Sheppard Murder Case*, helped free the doctor at a 1986 retrial, and the case inspired the TV series *The Fugitive*. Many people still thought Sheppard responsible for his wife's murder, but later DNA testing showed that he was not the man who had sexually attacked her.[4]

This was the latest in several well-publicized accounts of convicted men being proven innocent. Some people at establishment-biased news businesses began wondering how many other innocent people might be in prison. It was all part of the anti-authoritarian reporting emerging in the sixties, especially on television.

Not everyone was joining the trend. Former *Daily News* reporter Jay McMullen in later years would long for the days of reckless journalism, complaining that "reporters today are frustrated FBI agents," which he blamed on journalism schools.[5] Some of the *American* reporters in that paper's heyday had not even completed grade school.

Television news led the way in presenting both sides of issues, starting with a Federal Commerce Commission dictate that stations broadcast relevant views. Then the Kennedy administration required stations to air opinions opposing their commentaries. Newspapers tried even harder to present "simultaneous rebuttals" even if it meant holding stories up for a reasonable period until a response could be obtained.

One of the last of the fast-disappearing comic relief characters at the papers was non-writing *American* reporter Meyer Zolotareff, who drove around in a car littered with old newspapers and other junk, and turned in stories with a thick Yiddish accent. The story goes that Zolotareff greeted a labor official named Phil with "Hello, Feel. How you phel?" Another anecdote said he turned a story in to Basil Talbott about "a woman who was bit to death." Refusing to believe it, Talbott had Zolotareff doublecheck and get more from the police. Zolotareff called back with: "The lieutenant says she was bit to death with a club."[6]

Sunday *Tribune* editor Lloyd Wendt was reassigned to trash the last traces of Hearst at *Chicago's American*. He banned stories about sex, ordinary crime, and Hollywood starlets in favor of hard news. Wanting to do away with the past, executives at the transformed paper also decided that writers should work in color coordinated rooms with modern furniture. Columnist Jack Mabley was so peeved that he chained his armless oak swivel chair to a desk but was told, in effect, that it had to go. Mabley took the chair with him to the *Tribune*.

Step by step, the *Tribune* was becoming fresher after decades of pontificating in the dark. Under Tribune Company president J. Howard Wood, in the early sixties the paper created journalism scholarships for African Americans and conducted a study of how crime coverage affected trials.

Former reporter Clayton Kirkpatrick, who started at City News in 1938 and won a Bronze Star while serving in an Air Force intelligence unit during the war, was made *Tribune* city editor in 1961 and editor on January 1, 1969. His main task was to help the paper find its way in the absence of the guiding and sometimes misguiding hand of Colonel McCormick.

Reporter William Mullen said the turmoil during the national Democratic convention the previous summer "showed the hierarchy how much the paper had lost touch with its audience and the tenor of the times."[7] As one of his changes, Kirkpatrick removed "The World's Greatest Newspaper" from its masthead. A few years later he would explain why: it wasn't.

In an early editorial Kirkpatrick announced that "No political party should take the Tribune for granted," and in 1974 he angered several members of the board by calling for the resignation of Republican President Nixon after the Watergate disclosures. That same year, *Time* magazine called the *Tribune* one of the ten best American newspapers. But after Kirkpatrick retired as president of the Tribune Company in 1981, the paper would slide back into its narrow ways.

Street reporters still did their work the old fashioned way. In late 1961, Bill Doherty of the *Tribune* went to the home of syndicate loan shark Sam DeStefano since no one had seen the mobster for a week. Was DeStefano in some car trunk? Was he on the lam ever since his underworld muscleman William Jackson was tortured to death?

Mrs. DeStefano let the friendly reporter inside and her husband soon appeared in pajamas. Doherty had spoken to the emotionally volatile syndicate member before, and extended his hand in greeting. Instead of shaking it, DeStefano struck him in the face. Bill responded by knocking the mobster across the room. DeStefano headed for a revolver by a telephone table, and Bill ran out of the house so fast he dropped his car keys and did not pause to pick them up.

He called his editor from a drug store to report that the supposedly missing crime figure was very much alive. When Bill stepped out of the store, DeStefano drove up in his own car, pointed a gun at him through the lowered window, and said, "I'm going to kill you and I'm going to kill every member of your family." DeStefano never carried through on his threat, but he did smash the windows of Doherty's car before the police arrived.[8]

In the more liberal sixties, staffs were becoming increasingly critical of authority abuses and lapses. Jim McCormick of *Chicago's American* defied the stereotype of copy editors as being mousy. Topping his Fred Astaire frame was the long, flowing hair of a Wild Bill Hickock, and he *was* a little wild, or at least Bohemian. Jim, who was unrelated to the *Tribune* family, once put his career outlook this way: "In every story there's usually one fact that the publisher is afraid to read and the reporter is afraid to write. I feel it's my job to find that fact and make it the headline."[9]

The old *Herald-American* had leaned a little toward black readers, but this became less conspicuous under *Tribune* ownership. Little wonder that increasingly more African Americans were turning to radio for information. With the FCC requiring stations to provide fair employment opportunities to minorities, even Southern stations were now hiring black talent.

Chess Records had already launched Chicago's first black-format station, WVON, and hired columnist Wesley South away from the *American* as its news voice. When Medgar Evers, a leader of the National Association for the Advancement of Colored People, was killed in a Mississippi ambush on June 12, 1963, South played his tape of a recent interview with him. Telephone service was disrupted as the station received thousands of calls.[10]

2

In the graphics section of the *Tribune*, Raymond Shlemon was known for turning details of an unexpected event into a drawing approximating the moment, at times using his wartime experience with the Office of Strategic Services. He also rode along with reporters so he could work with the police on sketches of fugitives. In 1963, Shlemon was experimenting with a method that would become the MIMIC system of transparent overlays, each with a different type of facial feature.[11] Police departments across the country used the equipment until computers made composite sketches easier.

But the soul of a paper was the way it responded to emergencies. All too often the steps were left to instinct and individual experience, but Battle Creek (Michigan) *Enquirer* editor Ellen Leifeld shared her steps with other papers. Here is the list with a few paraphrases:

—If news happens, go for it. Everything else stops.

—Get people to the scene. Period. Round up more than enough help. Reporters. Editors. Photographers. Graphic artists. Editorial assistants. Call in help if need be.

—One person should immediately be put in charge and responsibilities clearly delegated, and this could be any editor or assistant editor. The person in charge should plan to be in place for the duration.

—Brainstorm on content. Get away from the desk, and plan.

—Assign a scanner listener to write down everything and attach times to what the person heard. This can be a secretary, a copy clerk, or an intern.

—Set up a separate command center. Assign a facts checker for each angle of the story. Build a chronology. Order food; little touches like that boost morale. Send at least one editor home early so that he or she is fresh the next day to get started on the second-day plan.

—Finally: meet the next afternoon to review how the procedures went. Each story teaches us something.[12]

No one can train a great investigative reporter; there is always something in the person's background that makes him or her sharper or more determined than others, as with George Bliss. Although his father had been a Hearst labor editor, the rugged, muscular son wanted to become a boxer rather than a newsman. But then a wallop ended his career in the ring and led him to the *Tribune*, where he rose from copyboy to reporter.

Bliss returned to the paper after being in the Navy during the war and was the first or second reporter at the Our Lady of the Angels fire. He was promoted to labor editor but knew from his father that the position was static, and maneuvered himself into investigations. As he worked simultaneously with the Better Government Association, George's 1963 exposure of corruption in what was then the Metropolitan Sanitary District won him his first Pulitzer.[13] But, as we will see, personal trouble would lie ahead.

The old ways were falling one at a time during the early sixties. The tradition of interviewing a man just before his execution ended after *Sun-Times* reporter Ray Brennan spoke in May 1962 to Vincent Ciucci. The grocer had killed his wife and three children because he felt obliged to marry another woman who had born him a child. Editors had started feeling that death row interviews cheapened the paper, but Ciucci was "news" because he had had won a dozen stays of execution on his insistence that his wife had shot their children and he killed her in self-defense. Ciucci told Warden Jack Johnson to skip the last meal—for some reason he was not hungry.[14]

Warden Johnson was a big man who in the Irish tradition liked reporters, and they let him keep a secret. Johnson would show newcomers four red levers behind the execution chamber and say that, as with a firing squad, four guards pulled the handles simultaneously without their knowing which wire was connected to the chair. In reality, however, he was the sole executioner but never wanted his young daughter to learn about it.[15]

President Kennedy warned in April 1962 of possible nationwide inflation because Inland Steel in Chicago had just announced a price increase. *Daily News* editor Max Schneider then noticed a wire story saying that Inland Steel executive Joseph Block was in Japan. No reason was given, but on a hunch he cabled the paper's correspondent there. Learning that Block was flying back to Chicago for a board meeting, Schneider took a gamble and put out a story saying Inland apparently had decided to abandon the increase. His guess was on the money, and other steel companies followed suit.[16] The economy stayed stable.

For years, TV news lacked immediacy because film taken at a scene had to be sent to a developer, missing one or two newscasts, and even then four people had to be in each crew, for reporting, sound, lighting, and camera. Things changed around 1959, when stations adopted videotape machines that let crews in the field send tape to the station by messenger or cab while moving on to another event.

The freeing of news staffs from their studios catapulted television over newspapers in breaking news, but reporters no longer returned from an assignment to work with an editor on the story. Without the backstops that print reporters had, TV reporters had to think fast at the scene while knowing that a wrong decision could jeopardize their careers. The excitement of the early sixties increased the dirty tricks stations occasionally pulled on their rivals, paralleling ones by the four remaining papers, the *Daily News, Sun-Times, Tribune,* and *Chicago's American.*

In September 1963, City News bulletined that an off-duty police officer had been injured while skydiving. The man apparently had some of the dive on film, and happened to mention at the hospital that reporter Mort Edelstein was a friend of his. Edelstein had left the papers for more lucrative work at CBS–owned WBBM (Channel 2). He told reporter Walter Jacobson, recently of the *Chicago's American,* to do a hospital interview and grab the reel. When Jacobson asked the injured officer for the film, the policeman replied, "A guy came in here earlier and said he was from CBS, so I gave it to him."

Edelstein had planned to use the film on the six P.M. newscast, and when Jacobson told him what had happened he was so furious he called every other station in town until his friend Dick Goldberg at WBKB (later WLS) admitted acquiring the footage.

"It's mine!" Edelstein exploded over the phone.

"Like hell it is," Goldberg said, "I bought it from a free-lance photographer."

After impolite words were exchanged, Edelstein learned the thief was really a WBKB cameraman. With no time for diplomacy, Edelstein told Goldberg over the phone, "I'll break both your legs and shoot you in the head" unless he handed over the reel.

Not wanting to wait for his rival to do the right thing, Edelstein learned the film was being processed in a color laboratory at 19th and California. Two of the huskiest WBBM employees took possession and brought it in. When relaying the story a few years later, Edelstein said he and Goldberg were still friends. They just no longer trusted each other.[17]

The "talking heads" phenomenon of television proved an advantage one night for newsreader Alex Drier ("Chicago's Man on the Go"), who would explain his slight limp by saying he had been beaten by Nazis near the Swiss border. Drier's mellifluous voice had been wasted at the UPI, and he was a natural for television although he was imposingly large. One story has it that after rushing to WBKB in a tuxedo and hastily changing at the station, he stood up during a commercial break and realized he was wearing just shorts from the waist down.[18] In time Dreier left the business and became an occasional actor in movies and television dramas.

Black hiring was more common in broadcasting than at the newspapers. William Matney, Jr., became the first African American correspondent for NBC when he joined its Chicago office in 1963. The next year local radio station WYNR hired African American Bernard Shaw to cover Dr. Martin Luther King, Jr.'s marches in Chicago, which the minister had called the most segregated major city in the North. Shaw worked the four P.M. to midnight shift while studying at the University of Illinois' Navy Pier campus. His father had been a railroad worker who read all four newspapers daily, and for the son journalism was an easy choice. From his work on the Cable News Network in the nineties, Shaw would be considered one of the best-known newsmen in the world, but after launching his career the radio station went all-music as part of a trend away from news.[19]

In 1966 the *Tribune* did not want to upset religious readers when it told the story of a jail chaplain caught smuggling contraband so mobsters could live as they had on the outside. So the paper changed "priest" to "jail official."[20]

Religion usually is not much of a factor in the news business, but it has provided some amusing moments. A Jewish reporter from City News attended the funeral service of a prelate at Holy Name Cathedral just before Easter and gave the details to a Protestant rewrite man. Reading that all the statues were draped in purple out of mourning, the editor burst out, "That happens every Holy Week!"

American reporter George Murray was vacationing in Rome in the sixties with Jewish artist Nate Steinberg (not to be confused with a columnist with a similar name). They were able to arrange a special meeting with the Pope because Steinberg had painted his portrait. The Pontiff left the Chair of Peter to greet them as part of a public ceremony that promised to last some time.

The artist could not wait and whispered to Murray that he needed to go to the men's room. From his knowledge of the general layout of churches, Murray told him where there might be a non-public one used by priests. When Steinberg returned, Murray asked if he had found it. Steinberg said he could not and so he relieved himself at an excavation. He was unaware that the Church at the time was carefully digging up and studying the Vatican grounds for the long lost bones of St. Peter.[21]

Before becoming the *Sun-Times'* mob expert, Art Petacque was known for turning every "no" into an opening. Denied access to Kennedy while the future president was staying in the downtown Drake Hotel, Art persuaded a manicurist—that probably meant bribed—to ask JFK a list of questions casually while working on his nails.[22]

Petacque seemed able to sniff out developments before his colleagues, and his contacts were among the best in the city. But he was never objective. He would make his stories favorable to people who helped him and could dig for dirt around those who did not. Rewrites made his rawness seem colorful, but he did not work well with fellow reporters.

The way gruff-looking, rough-sounding Petacque went about reporting "seemed, at times, like a kind of mania, primal, like a salmon struggling up river to spawn," *Sun-Times* columnist Neil Steinberg wrote. "He, in a way, represented something outmoded and embarrassing about journalism."

Petacque was so tough he once broke the arm of a would-be carjacker, but readers were kept uninformed about how little he knew beyond his specialty. Jon Anderson of the *Tribune* claimed Petacque was illiterate and that was why he always had someone go for him to the newspaper morgue for background copy.[23] A likely rumor had it that a number of his stories came straight from the FBI.

On July 14, 1966, drifter Richard Speck, high on drugs and alcohol, jimmied open a window of a South Side townhouse and methodically killed eight student nurses. The initial reporter at the scene was radio newsman Joe Cummings, one of the last people to have gone through City News without a high school diploma. Cummings worked at several stations before finding a permanent job at WBBM.

He was a tall, loud, ex-suburban photographer who loved dashing to hot spots. Only a few knew that his father had been murdered before he was born and his mother died when he was a baby. Cummings never had a real family until he entered the news business. When making beat checks in person he would walk into a police station with sweet rolls for the officers. He was called a "get your hands dirty" kind of reporter, but some found him pushy and a little crude. Yet after covering a fire that left a widow and her children homeless, he bought them some furniture to sleep on.[24]

But no reporter learned more personal information about Speck than *American* night city editor Harry Romanoff, who was famed for posing as officials on the phone. The only survivor was a Filipina who had stayed hidden under a bed during the murders, and so Romanoff adopted an accent as he made various calls as the Philippine consul. When he reached the killer's home, he identified himself as Speck's attorney. Speck's sister gave him a wealth of information about Richard's early life and troubled marriage, which may have provoked the attacks.[25] Romanoff was the last well-known newsman of the *Front Page* era. Even he modified his audacity as times changed.

The cooperation reporters received from the police came at the price of looking the other way whenever a prisoner was beaten. A City News reporter was ordered off the floor of a station when a suspected child molester was brought in, and when the inexperienced young man dared to go back, the detectives who had promised him the story "took me into *The Twilight Zone* and insisted that no one had ever been in custody." He never learned whether the suspect was innocent or the police had insufficient evidence against him.

Edward Eulenberg told of a time a police lieutenant questioning a man believed to be withholding the whereabouts of a cop-killer knocked him off a chair. Realizing he had done this in front of reporters the officer asked them "Did you see—" and they chimed in, "See what, lieutenant?" After the killer was found, the lieutenant gave them all the details except how his officers had learned where to look for him.[26]

Chicago's American investigative reporter Don Sullivan, working on the case of a judge who had disappeared after being accused of bribery, went so far as to pursue him through several states. Sullivan caught up with the judge and persuaded him to take a lie detector test in front of a photographer, but the story was pulled from the November 22, 1963, edition to create space for the Kennedy assassination.

City News had been writing "Negro" after names even when race was irrelevant, largely at the request of the *Tribune*, which tended to "cheap out" stories about minorities. After the wire service dropped the practice, a little girl was killed by a car. The *Tribune* city desk called and asked, "Say, is this girl white or colored?" When the night editor said she was black the newspaper editor replied, "Ohhh." After a pause he added, "But it's sad story, anyway." He spiked the story.[27]

With drugs making murder commonplace in low-income neighborhoods and the sexual revolution going on, editors were becoming less certain what was newsworthy even though their reporters generally knew. Here is a case in point:

Hollywood actress Linda Darnell, who had co-starred with Tyrone Power in *Mark of Zorro* and played the vision of Mary in *Song of Bernadette,* dropped out of films after being offered only mature-women roles. In April 1965, she was staying overnight in the suburban Glenview home of a friend and former secretary when a fire broke out before dawn.

The forty-three-year-old actress awoke to smoke and rushed downstairs possibly thinking her friend's sixteen-year-old daughter was trapped, unaware the girl and her mother had escaped. Darnell died from burns over eighty percent of her body. A *Chicago's American* editor said, "Linda Darnell? I never heard of her. We don't want any of that cheap melodrama on page one. Bury the story in the back of the paper."[28]

Five months later Marshall Field IV died in his North Side home after heading his father's paper for fifteen years. In the last few years he had shown mood swings and began drinking more and taking pills. Officially he succumbed to a heart attack, but some believed that his death might have been the second possible suicide in the family. The *Sun-Times* and *Daily News* were taken over by a Field Enterprises trust until Field's two sons by different wives could take command.

Neither of the half-brothers had strong ties to the city, with Marshall V growing up in the East and Frederick "Ted" Field spending years with his mother in Alaska before settling down in southern California. Marshall exercised his personal judgment in the editorial offices, but once Frederick turned twenty-five in 1977, all business decisions were made jointly. And yet the paper still energetically went after scoops and wrote them freshly.

The *Sun-Times'* respected city hall reporter of the sixties was Harry Golden, Jr. His bony features and wrinkled forehead even suggested someone looking for answers, and he wore flashy clothes like a reporter from another era. He never relied on help from his father, the homespun wit and publisher of the *Carolina Israelite*. When the son was starting out in Charlotte, North Carolina, he gave a city hall janitor a carton of cigarettes a week to leave windows unlocked so he could explore wastebaskets for news. In Chicago, Golden could brag that few of his stories ever prompted a contradiction. Whenever he was working on an exclusive, he seemed to dance through city hall. Then, as he tapped everything out on an old Royal portable, he would laugh in his gritty voice and utter some of the words as if giving himself dictation.

Golden said he was never sorry he turned down an offer to work for television. "The money would have been nice, but. ... half the fun is writing your own stuff." To stay disciplined, he never gave an opening sentence more than twenty-three words. At home he edited his father's writings for several top-selling books, in effect overshadowing himself. As he lay dying of cancer in 1988 at age sixty, Harry Jr. wrote out the details for his funeral. One honor he did not plan was that the city hall press room would be named in his honor.[29]

Some crime reporters still enjoyed the ruses of competition. Before going to the *Tribune*, City News reporter Frank Haramija (pronounced hair-ah-me-ah) arrived at a home to interview a witness. Before ringing the bell he removed her name from the mailbox slot, wrote a fictitious one on the reverse side, and slid the card back in to make later reporters think they had the wrong address.[30]

Reporters are not born, few are made, and some just happen. Consider Seafarer's Union organizer Joseph Longmeyer. He started his car in June 1966 and four sticks of dynamite exploded. Rather than have his legs amputated, Longmeyer underwent nearly two dozen operations. The religious man felt he had survived for a reason and so, although white, he became a crime reporter for the *Defender*.[31]

Reporter Phil Wattley went from City News to the *Tribune*, where he called police headquarters "the cop shop." You could tell he was having fun from the way he gave names to unknown criminals years before the FBI started doing it, such as "the Gentleman Rapist" and "the Pork Chop Killer."[32] He also might call his editor from the cop shop and begin with, "This is Wattley at the barricades."

Wattley's wry sense of humor fit the way he spoke from the side of his mouth. He hoped to work at police headquarters the rest of his life, but after twelve years the *Tribune,* in its mysterious ways, wanted him rotated. He protested so much that he was made an assistant night editor as a punishment and stopped caring as much about his work. He died at forty-four of a heart attack while packing for a vacation. Chicago *Reader* media expert Michael Miner said Wattley's widow wrote to the editor, Jim Squires, accusing the paper of killing her husband. But the *Tribune* was being taken over by the corporate mentality, and Squires had only been following company policy.[33]

After the blizzard of 1967 left the city under nearly two feet of snow, people could read about the disaster only because news employees had done everything possible to get to work, some even reaching their downtown offices on skis. The *Tribune* bought out a restaurant for a couple of days to feed employees unable to go home, and purchased snowmobiles so its reporters could reach some scenes. A few circulation drivers did not get home for days.[34]

What people were reading in the late sixties was not the kind of newspaper of a generation earlier. Its coverage was more balanced, its reporters more responsible, and the emphasis was on regional and national news rather than local crimes and accidents. A *Daily News* man told a *Time* associate editor in 1968 that "Police-beat news is what runs on a dull day."[35]

The papers at the time were trying to make sense of the escalating Vietnam war. One indelible disclosure was of a massacre of civilians by American soldiers at the village of My Lai. Following reports from the Dispatch News Service in 1969, *Sun-Times* editor James Hoge had reporter Bill Granger put a witness and his girlfriend up under phony names in the Executive House hotel and grill the man for a week. The *Tribune* needed to "cover" the scoop, that is, to do its own version. So reporter Paul McGrath tracked down a My Lai witness who conveniently worked in the paper's composing room, and repeatedly questioned him until the man confirmed everything in Granger's account.[36]

As the jungle war escalated, the country seemed to go off kilter. A blind resentment of authority by a few radicals was encouraged as liberalism. Good police officers were spat at and called "pigs," firefighters were hit with rocks as they made rescues, and a few small social organizations were taken over by people hungry for power. Calling for a revolution, with equality in education, housing, employment, and civil rights as its goal, the Black Panther Party was arming its members in Chicago and other cities, and white supremacists in the South thought they could halt the civil rights movement with murder.

On Thursday, April 4, 1968, the *Defender* staff was putting its weekend edition to bed when news came in that Dr. King had been severely wounded in Memphis. The women's editor, Theresa Fambro Hooks, ran stunned up from the lower level composing room and found her colleagues studying wire reports in the editorial department. Hooks said in a *Defender* feature years later that press time was suspended and a few staff members went to a restaurant close by so they would be ready for a long night. Their regular waitress walked to their booth and said, "He's dead." The restaurant owner then picked up their check and said, "No charge."

For hours, *Defender* reporters and editors were writing up whatever responses they could get by phone. Editorial employees also worked with the pressroom foreman to determine how much of the news could be shoehorned into the weekend edition. "We were all misty eyed," Hooks said, and "many of us actually cried."[37]

The next day the Chicago school board dismissed classes early out of fear of hallway fighting, and this sent thousands of angry black teenagers into the streets. As they gathered here and there, their outrage erupted into a devastation of looting and arson. As *Defender* publisher John Sengstacke flew in from Detroit he could see blocks in flames.

Many police officers at the time owed their jobs to aldermen, and there was suspicion that their psychological screening may have been purposefully inadequate. *Chicago's American* managing editor Luke Carroll declined a suggestion to investigate several fatal shootings possibly by district officers during the King riot, saying that this was not the function of a newspaper and everything would be solved if only Americans turned to God.[38]

3

Less than two weeks following the riot, WBBM-AM became the city's first major all-news radio station, after news director John Calloway was given only a month to increase and prepare his staff. The station kept motorists abreast of traffic conditions with Herbert Howard looking through binoculars on a perch in what was then the world's tallest building, Sears Tower, just west of the Loop.

A cowboy hat made the Boston-born Howard look like a smiling, overweight Southern sheriff in movies. He apparently coined "Hubbard's Cave" for the Kennedy Expressway underpass at that street and might have been the first to call a tangle of expressways near downtown "the spaghetti bowl."

Maybe not everyone had fifteen minutes of fame, but radio meant that almost anyone could be a one-shot reporter. Starting in 1976, WBBM as "Newsradio 78" offered seventy-eight dollars for the best hotline tip of the day, and amounts increased for the best of the week and month. In time the station would have forty-five staff members.

For years the FBI had been feeding information to receptive reporters in each major newspaper, and in the sixties some Central Intelligence Agency operatives even worked as non-staff reporters on at least two of the three networks and at some newspapers. At City News, right-leaning general manager Larry Mulay asked his editors to alert the FBI whenever they learned of any planned war protests, which would let federal agents photograph peaceful demonstrators and start dossiers against them.

Thousands of war protestors from around the country massed in Lincoln Park before the 1968 Democratic National Convention. The *Tribune,* returning to conservatism after Kirkpatrick left, prepared readers for attacks on the police by "revolutionary groups" through a Chesly Manly article. It turns out that this piece was based on an article written by his friend Alice Widener in the conservative biweekly *U.S.A.,* and which had been based on a March 24, 1964, New York *Daily News* article ghostwritten for FBI Director J. Edgar Hoover.[39] In other words, the domineering and manipulative Hoover might as well have been working for the *Tribune.*

Police Superintendent James Conlisk once said of police misconduct that "Brutality is in the eye of the beholder," and during protests he insisted that reporters were the ones "stirring things up." During the clashes, the *Tribune* assigned reporter Bernie Judge a bodyguard of two off-duty officers, but in a single day the police beat two dozen other reporters.[40]

Columnist Jack Mabley recalled that such attacks put reporters in a quandary. "Every instinct says protest, but if you did, you knew those clubs would come down on you." He estimated that about twenty percent of the officers on the scene took part in the attacks.[41]

Covering the convention for WBBM-TV was young reporter Bill Kurtis. He had passed the Kansas bar exam but preferred journalism to the law, and in 1966 had stayed on the air for twenty-four hours straight after a tornado devastated the Topeka area. What he saw at the protest in Chicago was an altogether different kind of destruction.

"Nightsticks rose and fell," Kurtis would write. "Protesters were dragged into police vans and peppered with blows. I puzzled about how to report the scene until I realized it didn't matter. The pictures captured by our television cameras carried messages.... With television, I realized, a new language of electronic images was being created."[42]

City News reporter Charles Lewis was clubbed on the head as he stood close to demonstrators outside city hall, and at least two of the reporters at the two-room wire service saw officers herding demonstrators onto the stairs of an elevated train station and battering them. But general manager Mulay refused to let any of this get into copy. "The police are the greatest cooperators with the news media in Chicago," he maintained. "We believe in respecting law and order however it is represented."

The *Sun-Times* even falsified its account of how its photographer Jack Lanahan was pummeled by officers, saying the police had stopped when he told them he worked for the press. The paper also decided not to use a UPI photo of the beating, nor did it have the courage to object and risk losing future police and city hall stories to the *Tribune*.

Daily News photographer Paul Sequeira continued taking pictures even after the police broke his hand.[43] His superiors later made the city's first newspaper protest against police misconduct, and from then on, as reporter-editor Bernie Judge said, "newspapers were no longer part of the establishment."[44]

The assaults drew attention away from what was happening inside the Hilton Hotel, where some reporters hid under tables or disguised themselves as waiters to cover discussions in a Democratic Party largely divided over the war.[45] The nomination of lackluster compromise candidate Hubert Humphrey amid this tumult made it easier for Nixon to win.

Official misconduct in the city continued the next year. Using a floor plan supplied by a government witness, State's Attorney Edward Hanrahan led a detail of officers on a December 4, 1969, weapons raid at the West Side apartment where state Black Panther leader Fred Hampton lay sleeping. There was need for caution because Panthers in several cities had murdered eleven police officers and the police had killed five Panthers. And so on this early morning, Hampton and another man in the apartment, Mark Clark, died in a barrage of shots.

At a news conference, Hanrahan said both men had fired through the door at the raiders, and as proof showed a photograph of what he asserted were bullet holes. The TV stations and the *Tribune* accepted every word, but *Sun-Times* editor James F. Hoge received a tip that things were not as they seemed. Hoge, reporter Joseph Reilly, and a photographer went to the building and found that the "holes" were only nail heads.

Although Hanrahan's police unit was disbanded, the *Sun-Times* would not publish Bill Mauldin's drawing of bullets being fired through a door in a swastika pattern. Instead he drew such scathing political cartoons for the one-year-old *Chicago Journalism Review* for free.[46] The next year, a coroner's jury, apparently influenced by the wave of hatred and violence sweeping the country, found the killings justified.

Some reporters were still favored for police tips, but lieutenants stopped leaving case reports in easy sight and sergeants no longer asked, "Okay, what do you want to know?" Certain police officers were designated as spokespeople, and the fire department stopped supplying news people with pocket booklets containing the phone numbers of every firehouse.

The *Tribune* still did not know what to do with *Chicago's American*. To compete with the *Sun-Times*, "the Trib" turned the Hearst acquisition into a tabloid called *Chicago Today* in April, 1969. To discard any remnants of the late Chief, Australian-born Maxwell McCrohon made it a virtual daily magazine because features were cheaper to go after than enterprise news.

Network television news executives, aware they were surpassing the papers in covering the Vietnam war, civil rights marches, and war protests, felt they must adhere to high standards. NBC president Robert Kintner set them down for employees:

> We must hold someone accountable for every piece of work that goes into the show [newscast].... We cannot know enough about where the information came from.... My job is news, reporting it and interpreting it.... I pray that I may bring honesty, integrity, and a respect for the public that I serve. The truth to me shall be precious ... I will strive to set aside prejudice.... Whatever talent I have, I will give to relating faithfully this day's events.[47]

But after a period of war and civil unrest, broadcasters were left without a ready-made audience, and idealism in local television news was starting to seem quaint.

Newspaper workers enjoyed belittling television staffs because of on-camera announcers such as WBBM-TV's short, red-faced Fahey Flynn, an agreeable actor who would open newscasts with, "How do you do, ladies and gentlemen." For a while he was teamed with nationally known cartoonist P.J. Hoff as the weatherman. Since Flynn's hair was white and he conservatively wore a bow tie, the station in time teamed him with a younger and less formal newscaster the marketed viewers could relate to, Joel Daly.

Hearing these two men lightening the news one night, the Chicago reporter for *Variety*, Morris Roth, derisively come up with the term "happy talk."

Flynn never wrote the news he delivered and perhaps never really understood it more than ordinary listeners did, but he was a showman. But he was no longer quite the same after falling off the stage and breaking his hip at the Auditorium Theatre during a work-related event in November, 1979. Four weeks later he went up to the anchor desk in a wheelchair and was shown from the chest up so viewers would not notice the difference. After Flynn's death from unrelated causes in 1983, his widow settled a suit over the fall with the owner of the theater, Roosevelt University.[48]

Floyd Kalber went from running a one-man TV news department in Omaha to reading news on WNBQ-TV (later WMAQ) in 1960. He was soon commanding a larger audience share than any other newscaster in the city. As with Cronkite, Kalber had an authoritative air without rigidity, and stayed with the station into 1976, when he left for work on the *Today* show in New York.

Kalber had been so popular in Chicago that he was brought out of retirement to revive WLS-TV's six P.M. newscast in 1984 even though—as viewers would not know until his death—he was suffering from severe emphysema. By the time he retired in 1998, Kalber needed to keep an oxygen container within reach at the anchor desk. He used it to revitalize his lungs during commercial breaks.[49]

A newscaster who probably would not be featured on television today was Len O'Connor of WMAQ-TV and WGN-TV. The large man with a slow delivery reminiscent of Sidney Greenstreet knew some of the ins and outs of city government. But he was balding, looked at the camera from only the upper half of his eyes, and could not be cajoled out of his mumbled monotone. What viewers appreciated were his street experience and confidence.

But television staffing was getting away from male domination and, although executives denied it, they obviously were looking for pretty faces. Fellow workers at WMAQ-TV described one of the newcomers, Oklahoma beauty queen Felicia Ferguson, as temperamental and an unenthusiastic reporter.

One cannot imagine a homely, gruff Art Petacque or a plain, slightly mocking Phil Wattley anchoring a newscast. But women without credentials from other cities went through the same ranks as men. "I don't mind being thought of as a cold-hearted, tough bitch," said WBBM-TV's first female general assignment reporter, Susan Anderson. "There were many years when I was intimidated by men in three-piece suits and buffed nails."

Paula Zahn, a 1973 Miss Teenage America Pageant finalist, was hired at the same station to fetch coffee and catalog each news story. In her third year she interned with newscaster Harry Porterfield and became a news producer. After earning a degree in journalism she went to New York and co-anchored CBS's *This Morning* show.

Before becoming a welcomed fixture in Chicago's WLS-TV, pretty Linda Yu, born in China, intended only to be a news writer. But in the sixties an official at the ABC station in Los Angeles noticed that Yu had a way of communicating through the camera, and she became the first Asian-American on-air reporter at a network-owned station.

Yu was a television street reporter in San Francisco before moving to Chicago's WMAQ in 1979, first as a general assignment reporter and weekend newscaster. The next year she and Carol Marin (pronounced mar-een) replaced two males at the anchor desk. Yu went on to become a long-time news announcer at WLS-TV. She said in a recent magazine interview that "you're not just reading a story off a Teleprompter. You're talking to people, and that is the important thing."[50]

Some women found success easier. When Jane Pauley lost out in an Indianapolis cheerleading competition, she joined her high school debating squad instead. She was later inspired by *The Mary Tyler Moore Show* to try television news. While Pauley was on WISH-TV in Indianapolis, she was noticed by an executive at WMAQ-TV in Chicago and hired as the first female co-anchor of a nightly news program. In time she rose to the prime time news magazine *Dateline NBC*.

Not all the attractive on-air talent were women. Newspaper reporters sometimes mocked the vanity of WMAQ-TV anchorman Ron Hunter. Detractors joked that the blow-dried newsreader took pride in never covering a story and his hobby was watching tapes of himself. Actually, he covered some stories but, in the opinion of former *Tribune* critic Gary Deeb, "his writing tends to be cloyingly dramatic." Hunter's career nosedived after his two years in the city ended in 1976 and Kalber replaced him to restore gravity to the news.

While Hunter was doing a radio talk show in New Orleans, his wife called in to bicker about their marriage. His supervisors thought Hunter should have cut her off as soon as he recognized her voice, but he let her continue. After hanging up she shot herself to death, and Hunter was fired eight days later, which the management must have considered a suitable mourning period.[51]

With glamour giving applicants an inside track in television news, ordinary-looking male reporters considered radio even though it meant undergoing a sameness process. One City News reporter changed his long name and continually practiced speaking in a lower voice at work before becoming a long-time radio newsman. Another, though with a perfectly decent name, kept making lists of possible broadcast pseudonyms on the order of Gary Taylor and Dan Powers.

The city's second fatal crash of a helicopter traffic reporter came in August 1971, claiming the lives of "Eye in the Sky" patrolman Irv Hayden and his pilot.

On October 30, 1972, one Illinois Central train slammed into another near the 27th Street station in the city's worst commuter train disaster, killing forty-five people and injuring three hundred and sixty. Hospitals across the area immediately called in extra personnel.

Chicago Today editor O. Owsley Shepherd—who had steadied himself with drink to get through the Our Lady of the Angels fire coverage—was in the Northwestern Memorial Hospital emergency room for a possible bleeding ulcer when some of the victims were wheeled in. As if he were a reporter again the white-haired Texan waved his doctors aside, asked all the questions he could of the injured, and went to the nearest phone to call everything in.[52]

In the early seventies, former *Daily News* copyboy Gary Lee was hired as a WBBM-AM traffic reporter. In 1979, Lee became an executive of Shadow Traffic, based in Sears Tower. Within nine years the service was delivering twenty-four-hour reports for numerous Chicago radio stations, using a helicopter, forty-five regular employees, and one hundred stringers to keep track of congestion and road conditions.[53]

Radio reporters remained aggressive as long as they had a grounding in the newspaper tradition, as with Joe Cummings of WBBM, the first newsperson on the scene of the Speck murders. One reason Cummings had such good police contacts was his reputation for never betraying a source, which may have helped him get the scoop on the 1975 fatal shooting of former top mobster Sam Giancana in his Oak Park home apparently by someone "Momo" had been having a late-night snack with. That case has never been solved.

In 1979, Cummings was the first to disclose a federal investigation into the police pension fund. What made the exclusive unusual was that he went on the air from his bed at St. Francis Hospital in Evanston, where he had undergone open-heart surgery.

For newspaper readers, the real interest lay in disclosures of inefficiency and bribery at the combined City Hall and County Building. Reporters had become so accustomed to looking for corruption and public ineptitude that in the seventies they seemed to overlook positive news. U.S. Senator Paul Simon, who had worked at a downstate paper, said in Chicago "When I was in the newspaper business, the great weakness of reporters was whiskey. Now it is cynicism."

Just as many crime reporters were part police officer, Chicago Police Officer Larry Schreiner was part reporter. The short, trim man had started by selling crime photos to newspapers while still on the force. He then worked as a freelance television newsman in his spare time, peddling his sixteen-millimeter videos to whichever station wanted them. In time, he quit the department to be an on-the-scene radio reporter, usually for WGN.

Schreiner would drive throughout the Chicago area in a Mercedes-Benz crammed with a handheld phone, a car phone, a siren, a public address system, five police scanners, a bulletproof vest, a pair of portable two-way radios, two video cameras, three video recorders, three still cameras, a tripod, fire-resistant coat and boots, a gas mask and breathing tank, an axe and, to help the police, two body bags.

The former officer lived near John Wayne Gacy's suburban home, and in December 1978, police radio chatter suggested that an important surveillance was being conducted nearby. Then he received a tip that something was going on inside Gacy's house. The "something" was that police who were looking for a fifteen-year-old boy found the first hints that Gacy had killed thirty-three adolescents and young men. Police not only refused to answer Schreiner's questions—they ordered him to stay on the premises because they did not want him calling the story in yet.[54]

For more than twenty years, WMAQ-TV employed police officer Howard McBride to deliver film or videotape from the scenes on his time off, freeing crews to go to their next assignment. Over at WBBM-TV, motorcycle courier John Novotny needed tight pants to get through close traffic, so he took to wearing authentic Western outfits as he transported film, tape, equipment, and sometimes people.

For decades, the city hall reporter for WBBM radio was Bob Crawford, who could find news even while newspaper reporters on the other side of the press room were whiling away the lull between news conferences and city council meetings. Crawford kept a list of about two hundred possible sources and made it a point to call each one at some time or other.

Public officials put aside their resentment of TV crews once they realized that potentially uncomfortable news conferences could be turned into one-way presentations, called "photo ops," for photo opportunities. Joseph Reilly, who had been an editor at the *Sun-Times* before becoming the general manager of City News, said print reporters started forgetting their roles. They would write only about what they saw and heard rather than asking questions or delving into the implications.

Once-vibrant newspapers had become so passive about social issues that John McDermott, formerly of the Catholic Interracial Council, assembled a multiracial staff to publish the *Chicago Reporter*, a monthly resource on the city's poverty and racial troubles. The noncommittal articles were on the order of what newspapers could have been writing. They were often quoted at length in the papers and sometimes influenced city policy.[55]

The Caucasian-centric nature of the local news business into the seventies meant that editors did not really see the city's racial splitting. Alderman Ralph Metcalfe, a former Olympic runner and Congressman, broke away from the regular Democratic Party to found an influential black faction.

At the *Daily News*, black columnist Lu Palmer quit in January 1973, because a white editor had altered his copy.[56] Palmer became a respected voice on African American–oriented radio stations, founded the Black Independent Political Organization, and along with Metcalfe helped pave the way for the election of Harold Washington, the city's first black mayor. Television was keeping abreast of shifting political strength partly because the Reverend Jesse Jackson of the South Side, who had headed Dr. King's Operation Breadbasket, was so easy to interview.

WBBM-TV (Channel 2) and WLS-TV (Channel 7) maintained a spirited competition for several years to see which could win the most viewers. But the nature of newscasts was changing, and soon they would no longer be treated as a public service.

As William Fyffe served as station manager at WLS and later as vice president for news at ABC, he introduced more stories about good deeds and paired male and female anchors for their viewership appeal as if he were a Hollywood producer. Fyffe, later a media consultant, also encouraged a lightening of newscasts. He apparently felt the Vietnam war was a downer, drug proliferation had resulted in too much crime, and even glamour was losing its sparkle. ABC ordered that news readers at all its stations be glib and ad lib.

A few newscasters stiffened at the directive but went along with the faked spontaneity—which the network masked as on-air candor—even though some listeners might have cringed at such inanities as "That's a sad story, Chuck." WLS-TV reporter Hugh Hill would remark that "I didn't like [John] Coleman standing on his head and doing the weather, and the silly banter back and forth on the air. It was all so shallow. It just sickened me."[57]

But attorney, actor, and newsreader Joel Daly of WLS-TV's "Eyewitness News" defended practices like happy talk as a way of making viewers more interested in the news. Daly had tried *faux*-folksy delivery in Cleveland before moving to Chicago in 1967. The station's longtime newsreader John Drury also supported the new style. No wonder: careful training had made this amiable former WBBM-TV staff announcer look and sound like a newsman following early complaints that his delivery was starched and unconvincing.

Tribune media columnist Phil Rosenthal said that after Drury switched to the *Tribune*-owned WGN-TV in 1967, an Atlanta-based consultant coached him on speaking a little faster and appearing more relaxed. From time to time the station cut to him asking questions as if he were actively involved in the news. The remodeled Drury moved to WLS-TV in 1970, and for the next fifteen years hosted, if not really anchored, the most-watched ten P.M. newscast in the city. From his perspective, he referred to other staff personalities as "performers."[58]

No one seems to have noticed that as WLS benefited from Drury and its happy newscasts, the station was reducing its news staff. Then, with competition declining, rival WBBM did likewise. Among the reasons for the cuts were the high salaries of newsreaders. By the nineties, television news in what had been the country's hottest news town was as bland as in Los Angeles and Las Vegas.

Once upon a time, everyone knew what news was, but cautious newspaper editors emerging in the late sixties spoke in holy terms of news judgment as if the standards were carved by the finger of God. Those not cowered by managerial pronouncements in an era of fading rivalry might have sensed that overall news judgment was largely the ability to second-guess editors.

Instead of even trying to one-up their electronic competition, newspapers still sometimes opted to pull back rather than offend a source. In 1969, Sheriff Richard Elrod, campaigning for state's attorney, was crippled for life while chasing a militant war protestor who had been fleeing arrest. Officials said the man had beaten Elrod in a struggle and they charged him with attempted murder. The *Sun-Times* and *Daily News* were suspicious, but did nothing until Elrod's opponent suggested to *Time* magazine that the injuries occurred when Elrod accidentally slammed into a building during the chase. The truth has never been established, but the jury found the war protester not guilty.[59]

In 1974, Art Petacque and his translator, Hugh Hough, won a Pulitzer Prize for digging into the murder of U.S. Senator Charles Percy's attractive daughter Valerie in their suburban Kenilworth home eight years earlier and identifying the possible intruder, although the case is still open. When the prize was announced, Hough was away and so Petacque remarked at a news conference, "I wish Hugh were here today so I'd know how I feel about winning."[60]

An allegation Petacque and Hough were able to report before an indictment, was that former *Daily News* and WLS-TV reporter Les Brownlee had become involved in bilking the Fair Plan insurance program while he was its director of community relations. Brownlee pleaded guilty and was sentenced to serve a year in federal jail.[61]

Unions in 1974 failed to realize how inflation, the rising cost of newsprint, and the slow erosion of readership were affecting newspapers nationwide, and they waged a strike against the industry. The deliberately uncompetitive

Chicago Today had only been going through the motions of being a newspaper, and the walkout killed it. The last edition came out that September.

Trying to meet competition from television, magazines, and the *Sun-Times*, the *Tribune* started hiring more minorities and a few white liberals. In September 1975, the paper even dropped the peculiar Medill-McCormick misspellings, prompting *American Heritage* to announce that "the nation's roster of English-language newspapers increased by one."

The modernization of the industry caught an old-time newsman who worked at the police headquarters press room by surprise. He was such an airplane buff that talking about his hobby took up much of his workday. When a small plane crashed in DuPage County in 1975, the reporter, whose name is being withheld at the request of the source, wanted the wreckage left just as it was for a photographer. Because of the delay, the old-timer called the sheriff's police and identified himself as the regional head of the Federal Aviation Administration. He said he would be flying in by helicopter to take over the investigation.

After a long wait, the police traced the call to the press room and turned the case over to the U.S. attorney's office for prosecution. Considering that this reporter was a holdover from the forties, he was astounded that *Front Page* ways were now considered illegal. But on his way to an interview with federal agents he died of a heart attack at the age of sixty-two.

Politics and crime were just as newsworthy as in the forties, but in an age of litigation editors had become homogenized in the name of professionalism, and no matter how sharp reporters were, they were wasted under timid supervisors, as was the case with *Tribune* investigative reporters Bill Jones and Bernie Judge. They were trying to explore the scope of the brutal Blackstone Rangers street gang, which was evolving into the Black P Stone Nation, but witnesses refused to testify. No one else on the staff seemed interested in what was happening to black teenagers. But when the UPI announced that Washington officials were looking into the gang's violence and witness intimidation, the *Tribune* unspiked the story and put it on page one.

The *Sun-Times* was still the leading paper for scrutinizing city and county officials. This was a specialty of the thirty-two-year-old new editor, handsome James Hoge, Jr. (pronounced hoag), grandson of a Methodist preacher and brother of a New York *Times* editor. Their father, a Park Avenue attorney, was a heavy drinker given to violent outbursts, and Jim understandably grew up a little humorless and uncomfortable in social situations.[62]

After Yale, Hoge took a sixty-eight-dollar-a-week job as a *Sun-Times* reporter and rose to the Washington bureau and then the city desk. He asked to be called Jim and kept his light brown hair in an offhanded, boyish style. Co-workers said he was never known to light the battered pipe that served as an adult pacifier.

His intelligence and, perhaps, lack of creativity, showed in how easily he became bored, which meant his staff had to stay busy to satisfy him. Hoge knew talent and, even though an outsider in the city, used it to go after the *Tribune*'s weak points. He showcased movie critic Roger Ebert and street-level columnist Mike Royko, and made the *Sun-Times* more aggressive with chosen targets even though it meant easing up further on national news.

Hoge's intention of waking up the *Tribune* gave excitement to his newsroom as if the lively days were here again. Royko said the editor gave the paper a "war room atmosphere." Detractors griped that he might have sidetracked the careers of some people at the executive level, but with the high standards he had set for himself it was hard to say whether Hoge was backstabbing or just being honest about them. A reporter who got drunk after work supposedly called him a first class newspaperman but a ninth rate human being.

To keep Hoge from a tempting TV offer in New York, he was named editor in chief of both the *Sun-Times* and the *Daily News*. Hoge's team took on the mayor's floor leader, Alderman Thomas Keane, as well as Circuit Court Clerk Matthew Danaher and county corrections chief Winston Moore. At times, Marshall Field V accused him of trying to turn a working- and middle-class paper into a more serious publication like the New York *Times*, but readers were not complaining.[63]

The *Tribune* did not respond to the competition, or even to the readership drain of broadcast news, leaving some visitors to the quiet news room wondering what all the staffing was about.

One of the first important tips phoned in to WBBM "all news" radio was picked up on the cold, still day of December 20, 1976. That morning, Richard J. Daley, one of the best-known mayors in the country, seemed in fine health and even threw a basketball with some young men. But the tipster said Daley had collapsed and died in his doctor's office while on a routine checkup. With no one groomed as a successor, aldermanic power struggles left newspapers guessing what would happen next. In earlier days, city hall reporters probably would have known.

Perhaps the most productive moment of Hoge's Chicago career came when he took a walk outside the newspaper building with investigative reporter Pam Zekman in February 1976. Hoge had snatched the five-foot University of California graduate away from the *Tribune,* where in her spare time she would scan classified ads for hints of fraud. Red-haired Pam was cute in her way and easy to underestimate, but, with all her energy, not for long. Hoge kept his paper open to suggestions, and now he asked what she would like to do. As they strolled down the usually windy North Michigan Avenue bridge between the newspaper office and downtown, Zekman replied that a dream of hers was to buy a run-down tavern and see which public servants would seek bribes to overlook violations.

A few years before, investigative reporter George Bliss had suggested a similar idea to his *Tribune* bosses, but the newspaper's lawyers turned the plan down as being impractical because of the cost, possibility of lawsuits, and because anyone charged might claim entrapment. But Bliss talked the idea over with Pam, who had helped him investigate police brutality, and now she was presenting the rejected *Tribune* idea to its rival.

Once all the clearances and budgetary questions were over, Hoge enlisted the help of William Reckenwald, chief investigator of the Better Government Association, and in 1977, the *Sun-Times* bought a tavern at 731 North Wells Street, in the Near North Side entertainment district. Every violation in the building was photographed before the grand opening, and Reckenwald named the business The Mirage because it was not going to be what it looked like.

Once the Mirage opened with only minimal repairs, two photographers hiding in a loft documented

Pam Zekman. As a newspaper reporter and investigative television reporter, Zekman has inspired numerous young women to enter the field. But economic realities have largely made enterprise reporting passé (courtesy Pam Zekman).

all the illegal transactions. The *Tribune* soon learned that its competitor was running a tavern in the Rush Street area and sent a reporter to bar hop on company time and find which one it was, but somehow he overlooked diminutive Zekman serving drinks.

After the expose began, related reader tips kept federal investigators busy. More than a dozen city and state employees were eventually fired, and more than thirty electrical inspectors were indicted. In response to the outcry, slow-to-act Mayor Michael Bilandic, who had succeeded Daley by vote of the City Council, set up the Office of Professional Review, and the fire and buildings departments also established internal investigation units.[64]

A further upshot of the Mirage scandal was that TV stations were trying to get the barely one-hundred-pound Zekman to cross over. She thought the stations did not realize all the time a major investigation would take. But WBBM-TV assured her that it would give her all the resources she would need for "enterprise stories," that is, stories that would study a situation that had eluded official scrutiny.

Zekman made the switch but soon took a behind-the-scenes role because television had made her identifiable. When she was leading an investigation involving the city colleges teachers union, the union president twice slugged her cameraman, and over the years Zekman received at least two indirect threats.

By now, public officials had become so accustomed to media inquiry that a facetious saying at the Illinois State's Attorneys Association was "Don't screw up on a slow news day."

Zekman's investigative team at WBBM worked out of a windowless room with four computers, a pair of typewriters, and file cabinets crammed with tips, statistics, and copies of letters sent under the Freedom of Information Act.[65] In 1982, they showed "that various Chicago administrations have made it a policy to lie to the public and the FBI about the city's crime statistics and have been covering up crime in order to make the police department look good and to improve the image of the city to attract conventions and business." The policy of "killing crime" had slipped by the papers for a decade or more.

As with police officers, some of the best newspaper reporters were deeply troubled. *Tribune* investigative journalist George Bliss behaved as if devils were compelling him to outdo his rivals. When some construction workers plunged fifty stories at a work site and other reporters were trying to get information from uncommunicative company officials, Bliss gave an employee ten dollars for the use of a hard hat and went down to the pit.

To Bernie Judge, who would work variously at the *Tribune, Sun-Times,* and City News, Bliss had a "tremendously engaging personality," never violated a confidence, and had an uncanny sense of news. After Bliss "ran" a story—that is, made an investigation with desk approval—he always felt he could have done more. He left the *Tribune* to serve as the lead investigator for the Better Government Bureau, and for a while pursued subjects the papers shied away from. After rejoining the *Tribune* he shared Pulitzers in 1972 for exposing Chicago police brutality and in 1976 for investigating waste and fraud at mortgage firms.

One editor thought Bliss infused stories with his energy to keep from being overwhelmed by depression. Emotional ups and downs are part of the creative process, but Bliss may have been in need of psychiatric help. If indeed he was manic-depressive, that would explain his heavy drinking on top of pill-taking. Bliss's wife and ten children and step-children must have found him difficult to live with. Yet a colleague called him "one of the nicest guys you'd ever meet."

A *Tribune* employee took him to a sanitarium for treatment, but in a few weeks the former boxer gave up rehabilitation and walked out as if willing himself cured. In September 1978, he critically wounded his wife and then shot himself to death in their home on 99th Street in Oak Lawn. *Tribune* editor Clayton Kirkpatrick called him "the victim of his own intense devotion to journalism."[66] Two years later, Bliss was posthumously entered in the Chicago Press Club Hall of Fame.

Bernie Judge covered the 1968 clashes of police officers and anti-war demonstrators and went on to serve on the news desks of the Chicago *Tribune* and *Sun-Times*, as well as head the City News Bureau (shown at the centennial of the City News Bureau) (courtesy Tom Yanul).

Journalism itself carried dangers. UPI Midwest bureau chief David C. Smothers, son of a Chicago newsman and father of two City News reporters, was shot during the 1975 Algiers Hotel fighting between blacks and Detroit police but was saved by a bulletproof vest. City News alumnus Larry Buchman was killed at the age of thirty-four while covering ethnic fighting in Lebanon for a Barbara Walters TV show. His chartered Learjet crashed on takeoff, and his widow won a one-million-dollar suit against the airline. Buchman twice won the Jacob Sher award for Chicago investigative reporting.

Smart as he was, Buchman was a little slow catching on to a joke. One way of hazing a new reporter was to leak information that the mother of the Unknown Soldier was staying at a downtown hotel. When Buchman excitedly called City News about the scoop, night editor A. A. Dornfeld told him, "All right, Larry, put the phone down and think about it. When you've got it figured out, call me back." Buchman apparently was too embarrassed to mention it again.

Getting the news may have contributed to the death of another former City News reporter, Bruce Ingersoll, a small, slender man with blondish hair, wire rimmed glasses, and a cheerful face. Although usually easygoing, Ingersoll could throw himself into stories. Since he loved flyfishing in Minnesota he was appalled at the dead Chicago River. While still in his twenties he became the *Sun-Times*'s first environmental editor.

In 1979, Ingersoll went dangerously close to the radiation zone at the Three Mile Island nuclear plant after the facility near Harrisburg, Pennsylvania, came close to a meltdown. He later gave up his environmental investigations and worked at the Washington bureau of the *Wall Street Journal* and then again for the *Sun-Times*. Ingersoll died in 2001, at the age of sixty, of a rare bone disease that his family blamed on his long-ago radiation exposure.[67]

Newspaper studies of readership decline were showing what anyone could have told the pollsters, that the largest drop was among young people in a time of flower children, the Beatles, and jaw-length sideburns. The *Sun-Times* tried bucking the trend by hiring an editor away from *Rolling Stone,* but it took an outside consultant in the late sixties for the *Tribune* board to realize it had allowed the paper to become dull and politically monotonous.

After Clayton Kirkpatrick became editor in 1969, the paper took on some writers that must have seemed peculiar working with men and women who had known the Colonel. The next year, writer, historian and broadcast commentator Vernon Jarrett, who covered a race riot on his first day as a reporter for the *Defender* in 1946, became the *Tribune*'s first African American columnist. He was the grandson of slaves and son of two teachers. In Jarrett's spare time he helped put together the National Association of Black Journalists and an NAACP–sponsored scholarship program.

In 1972, staff writer and columnist Joan Beck, who had joined the *Tribune* in 1950 when there was only a handful of women on the staff, became the first woman on the editorial board. Another person who did not fit the mold was writer Bill Curry, who would find places in the Tribune Tower that no one but the cleaning staff had seen for years and play his bagpipes.

Bruce Vilanch of the *Tribune*'s youth culture beat kept himself so hidden by hair and beard that he looked like a werewolf. Vilanch claimed that when he asked for Yom Kippur off his editors had to look it up. In time he decided to make jokes for a living and did well writing for Hollywood talk-show celebrities and propping up years of Academy Awards ceremonies.

And then there was Ridgely Hunt, a conservative Yale graduate. His Vietnam war stories won four Associated Press awards. Later, Hunt wrote a *Tribune* feature about learning scuba diving so that he could explore sunken wrecks. His magazine-inspired style weaned others off the inverted pyramid story-form, which executives thought resembled tabloid writing and newscasts.

Hunt had a wife and three children, and acquaintances described him as "tough talking, profane ... very macho." But halfway into his more than twenty-year career at the paper, he came to think more about damnation and screamed when an editor changed anything of his. After overcoming his personal demons, he grew his hair long, put on rouge and, during his second marriage, underwent a sex change. The *Tribune* kept quiet about this, but *Sun-Times* columnist Irv Kupcinet wrote about the operation in 1975. Because of the public attention, the *Tribune* decided to reassign (demote) "Nancy Hunt" to night copy desk.

Nancy Hunt married a man and retired from newspaper work. Not only did fellow employees have a pronoun problem when referring to her, so did she. Before she died of natural causes years later, Hunt wrote her own obituary but never mentioned Ridgely, as if he had never been a part of her life.[68]

The *Daily News*, with its literary past and fifteen Pulitzers, was still probably the best-written of the three remaining metropolitan dailies, but under budget cuts it lapsed into a moribund sameness. Despite the cartoon antics of Pogo and L'il Abner, circulation was dropping faster than for the other papers. News editor George Cullicott blamed the situation on "a flock of vice presidents" and cramming the news offices into the Sun-Times building, "where it had to share a composing room, and engraving room and a pressroom, causing many deadline problems. It was so cramped the illustrious Red Streak edition was crippled to make room for the Sun-Times bulldog edition.... The cruelest blow came when executives cut off circulation trucks."

By late 1977, the *Sun-Times* management debated whether to shut the *Daily News* down and let Chicago become a two-paper town. That is, Marshall Field V wanted to fold the sheet but his half-brother, Teddy, thought it should be given another try. Promotional offers and odd changes such as printing borders in black failed to stop the paper from losing between four and seven million dollars a year.

On February 3, 1978, a statement was read simultaneously to the two news staffs. At the *Sun-Times* side, Marshall Field V stood on a desk to be seen and heard by all and announced that "we will now have to pass above the *Tribune* alone, and I'm sure we can do it." A *Chicago* magazine article reported that Jim Hoge wept at the layoffs he would have to make.

Mike Royko and other staff members who happened to be off work or could be spared went to sulk at the nearby Billy Goat Tavern, now in the dank shadows of lower North Michigan Avenue across from the bowels of the Tribune Tower. At the tables and long bar the gathering resembled a wake. Looking down at the dispirited newspeople were photos of the personalities who had made Chicago journalism a spirit rather than a profession, such as William Randolph Hearst, Colonel McCormick, Ben Hecht, George Murray, Walter Spirko...

For the March 4 edition it fell to copy editor Tom Gavagan to write the final bannerline. After several attempts, he came up with So Long, Chicago.[69] But it was not a total departure. With many *Daily News* employees being absorbed by the Fields' other paper, the *Sun-Times* became more aggressive

The Billy Goat Tavern, where news people such as reporter-columnist Mike Royko would hang out, and are remembered in photographs and by-lines along the walls.

and vigorously written, and the paper now had two more presses for a total of six.

While the Fields were trying to top the *Tribune*, the half-brothers should have realized they had greater competition from radio and television, whose reporters were showing some of the zeal their print counterparts had two decades earlier.

An airliner crashed just outside O'Hare Airport on the Memorial Day weekend of 1979, killing two hundred and seventy three people, and WBBM-AM was determined to beat the papers to the scene. The station called newscaster John Hultman that afternoon in his company car although he had been working since five that morning. Hultman shot over to O'Hare and stayed at the scene until around nine o'clock that night.[70] The papers could not capture the drama of hearing someone reporting from near the calamity, and by the time the headlines reached the reader the basic story was old news.

Mayor Bilandic, a quiet former alderman with the personality of the jurist he would become, was overwhelmed when the blizzard of 1979 avalanched an administration that had ignored a ninety-thousand-dollar study on ways to improve emergency snow removal. His consumer sales commissioner, pint-sized Jane Byrne, waged a mayoral campaign against him by speaking to disgruntled firefighters and ward superintendents. When she was swept into office the next February, the regular Democratic Party was stunned by its own death.

Byrne had quietly married newsman Jay McMullen on St. Patrick's Day the year before. The likable McMullen never took himself seriously. He had been known around city hall for talking about his romantic prowess, and an unconfirmed report claimed he wooed Byrne by slipping her a note reading: "Great gams. How about lunch?" Shortly before their wedding, he told *Esquire* magazine: "There was a day when I could roll over in bed and scoop the *Tribune*."

McMullen left his job as *Sun-Times* real estate writer to work as his wife's press chief, and had to put up with reporters who were just as pesky as he had been. After a year, he became his wife's behind-the-scenes political advisor. Their biggest surprise was putting an emphasis on public housing by moving into an apartment in the notorious Cabrini-Green complex, where a woman had recently been raped and two police officers had been shot to death by young snipers a few years before. Although the mayoral couple lived in the projects only three weeks, crime in the area stayed down for years afterward.

Newspaper city rooms for more than a century were still just a number of desks and chairs, but you could see some of the news stories progressing at the TV stations. Before computerization, WLS-TV kept a board with color coded notations representing items lined up for each newscast of the day: stories where crews were still out, ones being kept in reserve, and others requiring further development.

If an item intended for a certain newscast turned out to be less interesting than expected, or if it would not be ready in time, a story in reserve was quickly scheduled in its place, provided it could be squeezed or expanded to fill the time "hole," and the script was rewritten accordingly. The anchors might ask questions to round out the story before going over the lines until they could read them off the Teleprompter in an easy tone between informational and conversational. The work was more difficult than it sounds.

In 1980, the Tribune Tower presses were trucked to the Freedom Center plant five-eighths of a mile west of downtown for greater efficiency. Without their rumble, the Tower became no more than a confusingly laid out office building. But imperial-looking CEO Stanton Cook was unconcerned about the romance of journalism. He was struggling to turn a formerly family-run paper into a professionally-managed enterprise.

Also that year, Marshall Field V decided to devote more time to real estate speculation and turned the *Sun-Times* over to Jim Hoge, who would carry on its solid city hall coverage, but could not win back readers who preferred two-sentence news on television and sound bytes over drivetime radio.

Nor could Hoge or anyone else capture the youth market, since that generation had gone through an adolescence of pabulum TV and highly promoted pop music, and by now could not understand the point of printed news except for disasters and elections. Thousands of these people started turning to the Cable News Network, which had begun on a tight budget in 1979 with the modest goal of informing people in areas not reached by major newspapers.

By the eighties, Chicago had two parties, white Democratic and black Democratic. The faction largely put in motion by Alderman Metcalfe could not reach every home in the predominantly African American neighborhoods, but radio could. WVON talk radio in 1982 and 1983 spread the word of empowerment and convinced listeners that in the upcoming mayoral election Harold Washington could beat incumbent Jane Byrne and regular Democratic Party candidate Richard M. Daley, son of the late mayor.

Washington's vigorous campaigning in white areas won enough support from independents to beat the odds. He was a popular mayor, but kept a barrier between himself and the press. He increased the mayoral public relations staff and ended interviews in the city council anteroom.

Starting in 1984, WBBM-AM's John Hultman co-anchored the morning news with Felicia Middlebrooks, who had worked in a Gary steel mill before doing a little reporting for a radio station there. The male/female, white/black team did well even though for Middlebrooks it meant getting out of bed at two A.M. for the five o'clock newscast. Explaining the difference in the way newspapers and radio presented a story, she told the *Tribune* that "I think people appreciate being talked to rather than talked at—especially in the morning."[71]

Women who were inspired to enter the business because of the Brenda Starr cartoon strip, female co-anchors, or Zekman's stories, sometimes were caught in a bind between succeeding in the media and putting plans for a family on hold. Some decided not to have children, and others gave up their careers in a sacrifice few males could understand.

Since the seventies, affirmative action had done much for increasing diversity in the media, even though it meant the papers and wire services were keeping some of their more experienced Caucasian males in place. African Americans who entered newspaper work during this period could not help but wonder whether they were there solely on their merits, and some of the more successful, such as Leanita McClain, felt uneasy about their high salaries.

McClain grew up "in the projects" amid poverty and street shootings. She suffered from depression much of her life but was idealistic and had a talent for expression. McClain was the first black woman on the *Tribune* editorial board and was picked as one of the ten outstanding women in America by *Glamour* magazine. But she was dismayed by her hate mail and the reaction of bigots to black leaders, and she committed suicide in 1984 with an overdose of pills at the age of thirty-two. Friends told *Time* magazine that she suffered under the strain of being an impossibly ideal role model.

Psychiatrist Carl Bell, an African American with his own radio program, remarked in a *Sun-Times* interview that McClain was disturbed by going to work with a briefcase and yet seeing her aunt get off a bus to clean houses. Bell noted that whenever successful black people returned to their old neighborhoods, they were taunted with remarks such as "Oh you think you're white now, huh? You think you're better than we are now, huh?"[72]

Black reporter Max Robinson seemed to have it all, and then lost it all for reasons not even those close to him could understand. When Robinson started broadcasting in Virginia, African Americans were paid less than whites and no one seemed to imagine there would be black anchors on national news. But in 1978, ABC experimented with racial balance to compete with the older, white newscasters at network news powerhouse CBS. Robinson reported from the national desk in Chicago while Frank Reynolds, formerly of Chicago stations WBBM and WBKB (WLS), manned the Washington bureau, and Peter Jennings spoke from the London foreign desk.

Then, Robinson plunged into alcoholism and started losing interest. He tried to resuscitate his career by working for WMAQ-TV (Channel 5) but was no longer at his best. He died of AIDS, even though he said he was not homosexual or bisexual and that he was not an intravenous drug user. His former wife, U.S. Energy Secretary Hazel O'Leary, declined to acknowledge their marriage in later interviews.[73]

All news agencies were covering the increased hiring of women in other industries, but not all of them were keeping up with the times. In 1978, seven female employees sued the Associated Press for gender discrimination and eventually accepted a two million dollar settlement. One of the plaintiffs, AP Washington correspondent Frances Lewine, was so disgusted with her employer that she went over to Cable News Network.

The corporate mentality taking over many papers across the country during the seventies and eighties was effective as long as it dealt with interchangeable products, because its nature kept it from evaluating. In a climate where he who hesitated was boss, editors started thinking like lawyers about all that could go wrong with an enterprise story. Collectively, facelessly, the executives buried the Chicago tradition of devil-may-care snooping.

Another reason fewer papers were doing as much enterprise reporting was that local and federal prosecutors were now going aggressively after criminals themselves. Authorized wire taps and hidden microphones made that kind of creative reporting almost obsolete.

One of the causes the Chicago papers could have taken up, but declined to, was the evident corruption of numerous judges who repeatedly twisted laws to set gangsters, rapists, and killers free. The story would have entailed only a listing of strange decisions from certain judges and their specious justifications for them. Royko went after one judge, and a City News editor was trying to put something together on a few others, but the papers seemed unconcerned.

Then, in 1983, courts reporter Peter Karl of WMAQ-TV "Action News" broke the story that an FBI mole was involved in "the largest undercover operation in the history of the Justice Department." The newspapers were surprised by what had been going on under their noses. Before Operation Greylord was over, more than fifty police officers, lawyers, and judges were convicted or pleaded guilty. Disclosures included that some judges were pressuring lawyers to pay up, and that assistant prosecutors were keeping quiet about it because they might become defense lawyers or did not want to ruin their chances of seeking a Party endorsement for judgeship.

The seventies and early eighties were the high point of broadcast journalism in the city. In the second half of the eighties, however, ABC, CBS, and NBC ownership changed hands. The new corporate owners required more profits from their news divisions, and advertising rates were tied not to viewer interest but to Nielsen ratings and the tested share of the product-buying age group.[74]

This decline in enterprise stories in both media in the decade after the Watergate scandal, prompted the American Bar Association to convene a panel on "Law, Ethics and Investigative Reporting" in the city on August 4, 1984. "Chicago used to have two papers and three TV stations doing thorough investigative reporting," said Zekman, referring to the *Sun-Times,* the *Tribune,* WLS, WMAQ, and WBBM. "Now one TV station has disbanded its investigative unit entirely. One of the papers (the *Sun-Times*) has, I think, entirely abandoned investigative reporting while the other (the *Tribune*) does short shots, which can be very effective but are still just short shots."[75]

Because of broadcasting deregulation in the mid-eighties, many stations dropped commentaries and radio listeners were hearing less news on stations with talk or music formats. This boosted the audience for all-news WBBM-

AM and then WMAQ-AM, when it switched over under Westinghouse ownership in 1988.

Also that year, Colleen Dudgeon became one of America's first female news directors at a network-owned station when she was hired at WBBM-TV. Her duties included discussing with news presenters their delivery, appearance, and wardrobe to make sure they resembled news anchors everywhere else.

Although television newscasts had expanded to half an hour, ABC news commentator Dennis Prager deduced that they contained only eighteen minutes of anything that might be regarded as news. This meant readers jumping from lead sentence to lead sentence in a paper could get ten to twenty times more news than viewers were able to pick up sitting through a thirty minute news show with all its commercials and fluff.[76] The ratio became less by the year.

Employees at newspaper research departments began coding current and past stories in the early eighties so they could be retrieved electronically from several computer data bases. Computers were also changing the nature of newsrooms. Reporters now did their own background studies, rearranged elements in their stories, and checked their spelling, making rewrite men and women as obsolete as boomers. But without their writing flair, ever more news stories came out rubber-stamped.

In the first few years of computerization, a reporter at the scene or in a police station had to telephone an editor and make sure each story came over, since at least one out of every six transmissions failed or was garbled. The papers continually changed software programs until they became reliable, and in time news staffs learned to love the machine. Reporters eventually used Web sites for statistical analyses and other research that would have been impossible or too time consuming before.

Eventually, an entire newspaper page could be assembled by computer and readied for printing. This process, called pagination, meant that the remaining copy editors worried more about the placement of articles and less about how they were written. Grammatical blunders started popping up not only in the Chicago papers but with some regularity on the front page of the New York *Times*.

Despite long-run savings from these mechanical advancements, the overreaching *Tribune* was about to be mired in debt and the *Sun-Times* would suffer at the hands of two publishers who were without sufficient understanding of American journalism.

NINE. The Pirates

Survival of that fittest, that's the way to run a newspaper. —Rupert Murdoch[1]

While the *Tribune* paid increasing attention to the suburbs, the *Sun-Times* continued serving Chicago from South Side barmaids to North Side independents. Its thirty-year-old newsroom was a mess with stacks of old newspapers and desks sporting phone books opened from the day before. Cold coffee was useful for putting out flare-ups from cigarettes carelessly discarded amid soda pop cans in trash baskets. Reporters and editors spoke over one another, and anyone overheard using an expletive to a lawyer over the phone was applauded by his peers.

Jim Hoge had been somewhat successful in upmarketing the energetic tabloid, but he was unable to snatch enough advertisers from the *Tribune,* and a figurative "for sale" sign was hung on the door in April, 1983. The paper at the time had no insurmountable debts, it was just that half-brothers Marshall Field V and Frederick "Ted" Field wanted to get rid of the only thing they had in common. This began what would become a more than twenty year time of troubles.

For clean-shaven Marshall, freedom from publishing meant real estate speculation, and bearded Frederick, a former race car driver whose hand had been mangled in a towing accident, was having fun producing Hollywood films and living at the sprawling estate of the late film comedian Harold Lloyd.

Word of the impending sale came as inflation was making publishing innovation dangerous, and a number of papers in the English-speaking world were lying adrift. At a time when newspaper chains needed leadership, they found only pirates whose personalities were quite different even though their paths sometimes crossed.

Australian Rupert Murdoch was looking for another American paper after purchasing three in San Antonio as well as the Boston *Herald,* the supermarket tabloid *Star,* and the sensation-seeking New York *Post.* He was now eyeing the *Sun-Times,* the country's seventh largest daily. Ralph Otwell, an Arkansan, had shepherded the paper to six Pulitzers during his fifteen years as managing editor and editor.

When Jim Hoge scurried to buy the paper from the Fields for sixty-three million dollars, and JMB Realty mentioned that it might raise one hundred million, Murdoch offered approximately ninety-three million. Cash.

Nothing Murdoch did was strictly for business. He was always jumping from project to project as if to keep ahead of someone unseen. His grandfather was a Scottish Presbyterian minister, and his father had owned a newspaper in southern Australia. At Oxford, Rupert was taunted because of his down-under accent and unexceptional grades. But he always sought his father's approval, and when Sir Keith died in 1951, his son wanted to top what the publisher had accomplished. "In Murdoch's world there are no rules," said *Esquire* magazine. "He is amoral."

Rupert showed a rough sense of fun as he bent or ignored rules to take something away from the established order, and he would say whatever he needed in order to project an image. Murdoch's triumph came in 1981 when he bought *The Times* of London and the Sunday *Times*. But he preferred the British Fleet Street tradition of titillating photos and exclamation point features passed off as meaningful news. "Americans don't know how to do journalism," he sneered.

As a young man, Murdoch had been excited by news and deadlines, but entering middle age he was interested only in acquisitions themselves, as if each were a seduction. His assertiveness seemed a coverup for what some saw as a lack of confidence. One indication of his private insecurity was the way he not only shrugged off but distrusted suggestions from his editors. He left the impression that if stripped of ambition, there would be nothing left.

The interplay of his moods sometimes kept his

Marshall Field V at a news conference. He and his half-brother Fred Field, ran the *Sun-Times* well but sold the paper to Australian press lord Rupert Murdoch and began its period of decline (Chicago History Museum, photographer — Jack Lenahan, Chicago *Sun-Times*, ICHi-31029).

staffs uneasy, and the only predictable thing about him was that he would be wearing a dark gray suit. Observers said one of his traits was to flatter people he wanted to use and then not put any confidence in them, as if punishing them. After spending millions for a paper, he would fire a number of editors and run it frugally. Murdoch claimed he started by aiming low; he would gradually improve the tone of his papers, but the *Star* and the *Post* still insulted their readers.

On November 1, 1983, Murdoch, Hoge, and Marshall Field V announced the sale of the *Sun-Times* as people in the back of the newsroom stood on desks to hear. At a later news conference in a Michigan Avenue hotel, Marshall Field V said he would have preferred to sell locally but that his half-brother wanted to hold out for the best offer.

The new owner promised to keep the paper substantially the same and added, "The yellow journalism of today is on TV."[2] As it turned out, his idea of keeping the tabloid substantially the same was to meddle for the sake of meddling.

Murdoch had a surprise coming when he took over in January: no one was around to edit the paper. Otwell had simply stayed away rather than serve under him. Murdoch had to call upon Scottish editor Charles Wilson of the London *Daily Mail* until he could find a steady replacement. When Wilson was needed in England, Australian Roger Wood of the New York *Post* sat in for him.

For his publisher, Murdoch summoned Robert E. Page, vice president of his News America group in New York. When Page arrived, Maryland McCormick sent him a letter inviting him and his fiancée to have a glass of champagne with her, "as I know the Colonel would have done if he were alive."[3] Page meant well, but a former employee said he did not really know what he was doing. "He was like a gambler put in charge of the river boat. Policies kept changing; people kept changing."

Fearing that the *Sun-Times* might turn into another New York *Post*, Mike Royko held a news conference to say that "No self-respecting fish would want to be wrapped in Murdoch's publications." He crossed the street on January 10, 1984, and began writing for the *Tribune,* although his heart stayed at 401 North Wabash. He still patronized the Billy Goat Tavern, a restaurant and bar in a world without sun on Lower Michigan Avenue.

At the *Sun-Times*, every major TV station—and even the *Tribune*—people being brought in from other cities did not really understand Chicago and its ways. News was seeming pre-packaged on the outside and bland inside. Royko biographer F. Richard Ciccone said Mike would grumble that he and other reporters used to gather at "the Goat" and play a game of recalling at least one business at any intersection someone had named, but that "Most newspaper people here today don't know anything about Chicago."

Murdoch tried to make Royko give up working for his Chicago rival, but a judge ruled that a provision in his contract against working for a competitor was too broad. Among the others who switched loyalties was nationally known advice columnist Ann Landers. African American columnist Vernon Jarrett accepted a buyout.

One of the most closely watched local news stories the wintry month of Royko's crossover came as bearish WGN cameraman Robert Whitmore was looking for a weather "visual" with a sound man and a reporter. When they reached Wilson Avenue beach the television team discovered that four-year-old Jimmy Tontlewicz had fallen through the ice and that his father had jumped in after him but was now drowning.

Whitmore pulled a heavy fifty-foot extension cable from the sound truck and threw an end to the father. The team taped firefighters arriving and rescuing Terence Tontlewicz, but when Jimmy was pulled out, the boy was regarded as being essentially dead because he had been under the ice for more than twenty minutes. Yet, after six weeks of intensive therapy, he was playing on his own and asking about his dog. The case taught many people about the survival capabilities of children, and Whitmore was awarded a local Emmy.[4]

At the Murdocked *Sun-Times,* narrowed columns let the front page feature a clutter of stories, some insufficiently checked, and a movie star's birthday was considered newsworthy. At times, headlines strained for cuteness, which can be seen in the headline: "[Cardinal] Bernardin Bops Bingo."

"The Bright One" was dimming with staff uncertainties arising from temporary editorial appointments and repeated department reorganizations. The Rupert effect might have been even worse but, as investigative reporter Charles Nicodemus said, he and several other experienced staff members "dragged our feet in pursuing the themes and the kind of writing that the Murdoch people wanted."[5]

Studies by the Medill School of Journalism at Northwestern found that de-emphasizing news at the paper lowered morale. But media critics waiting for eyepopping headlines or outlandish photo displays were disappointed. Hindsight shows that Murdoch was like a storm that was much dreaded in its approach but caused relatively little damage.

With Royko churning out his columns at a paper he detested and drinking more, the *Tribune* further competed with its rival across the way by increasing crime and accident news by more than a third. But with less access to reports, beat officers, detectives, and battalion chiefs than in the fifties, and with editorial judgment frowning on police news, such stories became largely a matter of filling in the blanks.

This coincided with a decline in enterprise stories directly relating to Chicago readers. For a while, an investors group was negotiating with the *Tribune* to print a new daily to be called the Chicago *Evening Post,* headed by a former advertising consultant to both metropolitan papers, sixty-eight-year-old John R. Malone. "Malone's the kind of guy you find building a spaceship in his back yard," *Tribune* editor James Squires told the *Wall Street Journal*, "but one day it might go up." Such a paper would wage a readership battle with the *Sun-Times*.

The editor in chief lined up was respected Harold Evans, formerly of *The Times* of London and now of Atlantic Monthly Press. Malone arranged for a temporary office but everything else was uncertain. "Heck," he noted, "the *Tribune* and the *Sun-Times* have more people sweeping the floors than we have in our entire staff."

Advertisers might have welcomed a third choice if Murdoch had made his acquisition as trashy as expected. But since the *Sun-Times* remained largely the same, Chicago *Post* backers were unable to raise the twelve-million-dollar start-up costs. All that Malone could show for his trouble was a sixty-four-page prototype that "wasn't quite what we wanted," and he reluctantly gave up.[6]

Murdoch became an American citizen in 1985 to pursue a new hobby, collecting TV stations. But the FCC pointed to a rule against owning newspapers and broadcast stations in the same market. So, after two and a half years of intruding in the city, he divested himself of the *Sun-Times*. Murdoch then acquired Metromedia as a fourth television network, Fox Broadcasting Company, and financed its station in Chicago, WFLD. After this he drifted out of the Chicago news world.

By then, Jim Hoge, the last major editor to show personal leadership at a Chicago paper, had gone over to the New York *Daily News*.

In the summer of 1986, the ever-optimistic Robert Page, known for speaking of the "big picture," bought the *Sun-Times* with one hundred and forty five million dollars provided by two New York firms, Equitable insurance and Adler & Shaykin investments. As if he were Citizen Kane, Page published a front-page pledge on July 3, 1986, that with its return to local ownership, the tabloid would be "unafraid in pursuit of the truth, yet, at the same time, fair and considerate," and fun.

But the absentee owners found themselves just moving debts around and were unhappy with Page's high spending. In 1988, he left the city and bought several small California papers, only to claim after being ousted from the chain that he had paid nearly two million dollars for a publication found to be worth only twenty-one thousand.

An international press baron who had no direct effect on Chicago but in a way pointed to what was happening in the industry was portly Robert Maxwell. He had enlisted in the British army after an impoverished childhood in Hungary, worked in the foreign office, and began taking over newspapers as downpayments on respectability. In 1984, Maxwell purchased the London *Daily Mirror* and later acquired the New York *Daily News* from the Tribune Company for an undisclosed sum while it was having labor problems.

Maxwell let Hoge stay on as publisher of the New York paper during its transition, but in time was overwhelmed by bills from his overextended holdings. His answer was to put his sons in charge and sail for Europe. In November 1991, Maxwell was found dead at sea in either an accident or suicide. An investigation showed that the Mirror Group's assets were overshadowed by its debts, and that millions of pounds were unaccounted for.

While the *Sun-Times* was floundering, morale was slipping away at the *Tribune*. James Squires of Nashville thought he could shake things up when he took over as editor and executive vice president, and under his leadership the paper tackled issues including failing education and the need for neighborhood development in the slums. Squires' apparent goal was to make the paper at least as influential as it was under Kirkpatrick, but his method was to change staff members so often that veteran reporters called his announcements "bloodbaths." Executives also reminded him from time to time that the days of the excited one-man chief editor were over.

In July 1985, *Tribune* mailroom employees, pressmen, and typographers walked out over the paper's transfer of workers to other departments whenever their jobs were taken over by technology. The next May, Georgia Demarest Lloyd, great-granddaughter of one of the *Tribune* founders, William Bross, gave the strikers fifteen thousand dollars to cover family necessities.[7] In August 1988, more than three years after the dispute arose, an arbitrator sided with management, but the paper was ordered to rehire forty-five workers.

The strike occurred while public reliance turned even more toward broadcast news. Studies found that in the decade ending in 1995, the general Chicago area television news audience grew at more than twice the rate of the area's population growth, while *Sun-Times* and *Tribune* readership fell by sixteen percent. With local news being de-emphasized at the papers, fewer reporters were showing the excitement and resourcefulness of some broadcast people.

When Gera-Lind Kolarik went from being a City News reporter to a WLS-TV assignment editor, she would hear of breaking stories, study traffic maps, and advise crews on how to reach the scene. In 1984, a policeman in a wheelchair pulled out a gun in a courtroom and started shooting. "We have a judge shot," came a message on the scanner. "Judge Olson is the complainant."

Kolarik pulled out the station's folder on judges and called Wayne Olson as he was hiding under a table in his chambers just behind the courtroom. As he was telling her about the wounded jurist, she heard a bang and Olson said a lawyer had just been shot as well. Her jump on other reporters won Kolarik a local Emmy.

Another feisty reporter was Susy Schultz, a small former lifeguard. She had covered the suburbs for the *Sun-Times* but happened to be in the office in 1986 when fifty-four-year-old editor Frank Devine turned bluish. Managing editor Ken Towers grabbed him as he was slipping off his chair and Shultz came over. She told Towers to lay Devine on the floor, then she and metropolitan editor Dick Mitchell thumped on the man's chest and gave him mouth-to-mouth resuscitation until he revived.[8]

The black-run *Defender* was in trouble for reasons all its own. Now that two of its goals since 1905, integration and equal employment, had somewhat been achieved, more African Americans were reading the *Tribune* or *Sun-Times* instead.

More black talent was being hired at television, but the Rev. Jesse Jackson launched an eleven-month boycott of WBBM in the summer of 1985 because all its local newsreaders and on-air reporters were white. Its African American general manager, Johnathan Rodgers, responded by integrating the visible staff. *Sun-Times* media critic Robert Feder said in later years that "managers who dare to tamper with the racial mix of their anchors and reporters do so at their peril."[9]

The *Sun-Times* continued to be written as if its staff were a happy family, but there was a lot of bitterness over the abandonment by the Fields, the meddling of Murdoch, and a parade of editors who in the opinion of some employees had lost sight of what the paper was for. Because the corporate mentality does not evaluate, it does not always know where to make the most effective "efficiencies." Reporters, not having to answer to bankers, naturally viewed Ken Towers as being scissors-happy.

The cuts rankled well-liked Bernie Judge, who, as metropolitan editor, was leading the paper's investigations. This "South Side Irish kid," as he described himself, had started as a City News copyboy and before long drew attention with his incisive reporting. At thirty-four he was the second-youngest city editor at the *Tribune*, and actor Ed Asner met him several times while working out the character of editor Lou Grant on the *Mary Tyler Moore Show*. After the retirement of James Peneff, Judge was chosen general manager of City News, where he held motivating talks with the staff for the first time in anyone's memory.

Murdoch, however, hired Judge away after he had headed the wire service for just a year and a half. Judge was perfectly happy with the freedom Rupert gave him. But when Towers took command and refused to authorize money for more enterprise stories, Judge quit to edit the Chicago *Daily Law Bulletin*. He always tried to sound upbeat, but a couple of employees said he missed being part of the action. Even a bottle of painkillers could lead to a prize-winning story. On September 29, 1982, twenty-five-year-old Adam Janus suffered chest pains and reached for an aspirin substitute in his suburban Arlington Heights home, only to collapse in a coma. Janus's younger brother, Stanley, told a doctor there was nothing in Adam's history to explain what had happened. Stanley and his wife then went to Adam's home to comfort relatives. Stanley was so upset he took some painkillers he found there and crumpled from oxygen starvation.

The medical examiner's office called the two deaths in to City News on separate lists a few hours apart, since the wire service transmitted all "M.E. cases" to the newspapers after correcting any misspellings or erroneous addresses. Adam's death was considered from natural causes, and Stanley's was put down as unknown pending an autopsy, which was rather common. Through an omission in the location, it appeared on paper that Stanley had died at his own home rather than at his brother's, and so the two cases seemed to have no similarity except the last name.

John Rooney, a young son of journalism professor and former door-kicking *Daily News* reporter Edmund Rooney, was at the police headquarters press room at around eleven o'clock that night when he received a call back from a hospital about the routine death of an elderly man. While the nursing supervisor was on the line, Rooney asked about the second Janus case, on a chance there might be a connection to the first. The nursing supervisor said she would switch him over to a spokeswoman. That alerted Rooney, who knew that such people did not work this late unless a major story was involved. The spokeswoman read him a newly prepared release stating that both Janus deaths were under investigation.

Calls to neighbors who were listed by address in a "reverse directory" rented by news agencies showed that the Arlington Heights home had been sealed by the medical examiner's office as a crime scene. Although several suburban police officers had been wounded in a shooting that day, John and his equally young editor, Rick Baert, kept on the case until it became clear a number of people were becoming seriously ill after taking Tylenol.

Investigations by several agencies were initially stalled because the outbreak concerned different hospitals, different suburbs, and even different counties.[10] But in time it appeared that someone was opening Tylenol packages in stores chosen at random and adding cyanide, possibly with an eyedropper, to kill strangers in what one doctor called "American roulette."

Authorities worked hundreds of hours to remove Tylenol from shelves and talk to store employees and customers, and the quick response kept the death count down to seven. The killer is still unknown, but the Associated Press named this the second most important national story of the year, following the economic recession, and City News received its first Lisagor award for wire service journalism.

In a smaller instance of news being sensed, a cab driver died when the Kinzie Street bridge near downtown was raised abruptly in April 1987. Print reporters apparently did not get near the veteran bridgetender, but WMAQ-TV newscaster Ron Magers pressed close enough to smell alcohol as the man declined to be interviewed, and the resulting scandal led to his firing.

With fewer reporters needed at a time when state agencies and suburban police were faxing their cases to news offices, the once-vibrant Chicago Press Club in the basement of the towering white Wrigley Building was fading away. By early 1987, its checks were bouncing.

In May the next year, babysitter Laurie Dann went on a one-day rampage in the upscale suburb of Winnetka. She mailed poison to people she hardly knew, set a fire at a school, and then entered another and methodically shot students. The first reporter on the scene was believed to have been Jim Gibbons of WLS-TV. Before long, there were so many newspeople around the police station that Chief Herbert Timm saw a fistfight between a camera crew and sound men from a rival station.

Since Timm lacked experience with violent crime, he tricked the news media into providing him with tips on how to conduct his investigation. When a reporter asked "Did you..." he would reply "We're looking into that," and after the crews left he told his people to look into it.[11]

The only child to die before Dann fatally shot herself in a nearby home was eight-year-old Nick Corwin, and all reporters were kept back from the synagogue where his funeral service was being held. There is an unverified story that a gentile cub reporter put on a yarmulke available at the temple, made himself look pious, and, when called upon to say something, memorialized what he could off the cuff. When the reporter called in the story, a rewrite man supposedly remarked, "It's a good thing that's all he had to do to pass inspection."

One of the Murdoch crossovers from the *Sun-Times* to the *Tribune* was a future managing editor for news, Hanke Gratteau. In time, her switch put Gratteau and her husband, *Sun-Times* columnist Mark Brown, in daily professional competition. "We cope by building a Chinese wall around what we can and can't talk about," Gratteau told *Chicago* magazine.[12]

With readership down since the late seventies, the *Tribune* published fewer editions, stopped staffing police headquarters overnight, and downplayed local crime. There seemed little point in TV stations chasing after local stories when newspapers were losing interest in the game.

CBS officials also thought WBBM-TV was losing too many viewers to "happy talk" WLS, and so they hired Bill Applegate as its general manager in 1991. Applegate had been a newspaper reporter in Fort Wayne, Indiana, and a TV reporter and newscaster in Detroit and Los Angeles. Perhaps thinking Johnathan Rodgers had been too high-minded, he increased the coverage of violence in the hope this would boost the Nielsen ratings. Employees muttered behind his back, "If it bleeds, it leads." But the station learned that many viewers were turned off by lingering shots of a bloodstained street.

At WBBM and other television stations, single reporters were now standing pointlessly in front of police barricades and talking into a camera from a few notes, rather than a team being sent to answer all the questions raised. The stand-up reporters were often inexperienced and sometimes were just being tested for future anchor spots.

The passing emphasis on mayhem was just what John Drummond must have been waiting for. When the street reporter was young, his favorite reading was the Jack Lait and Lee Mortimer exposé of city vice, *Chicago Confiden-*

tial, and WBBM-TV let him dress the part of a crime expert even though his porkpie cap, checkered sports coat, and twenty-five cent La Palina cigars were four decades out of fashion. When Sam DeStefano, the mobster who had threatened reporter Bill Doherty, was gunned down at his Northwest Side garage in 1972, "Bulldog Drummond" arrived in time to watch the police zip up the body bag.[13]

When the "if it bleeds..." craze ended, Applegate held private talks with attractive female anchors in Chicago and suggested that they start wearing silk blouses to display their figures. When he moved on after three years in the Windy City, he persuaded Cleveland anchorwoman Sharon Reed to be taped nude for a story about life as an artist's model. The story was held off for four months until the November ratings sweeps. Applegate later defended his downplaying hard news by saying, "The free press has no obligation to teach or preach or hold itself up as the arbiter of social issues or information."[14]

With more female reporters and news readers, the eighties saw subtle shifts away from officialdom and local coverage, and toward more human interest stories and consumer features. This came after studies provided statistics showing the obvious, that more American women than men bought products advertised on television.

One high-profile TV reporter was Russ Ewing, a soft-spoken African American who usually wore a beige trench coat. He had been raised an orphan, and as a teenager saw one of the musicians he performed with die from drugs. Ewing started as a WMAQ courier and was promoted to reporter, then took his skills and understanding of blacks struggling in a white world to WLS.

In 1970, a time when police brutality was still hushed up in the papers but was well known on the streets, Ewing offered to help a wanted man surrender as a way of assuring him that he would not be physically abused in custody. From then until his retirement in October 1995, Ewing helped bring in a possible record of one hundred and fourteen fugitives, including a jail escapee.[15]

The last rewrite at the *Tribune* was relaxed Jerry Crimmins, who, in a 1989 interview, said he had spoken to an intern who had gone through journalism school and had worked at a small paper without ever hearing the word "rewrite." One of Crimmins' stories was about being held up in a Loop subway station. Because he had no money, the robber threw him off the platform. In addition to his other injuries, his ankle was burned by the electrified third rail.[16]

An example of how a good journalist could be lost amid news business problems, Rob Warden was left without a job when the *Daily News* folded. The Mississippi native briefly worked at a paper in Washington, D.C., but returned and started the *Chicago Lawyer*, which kept two staff reporters looking into aspects of local cases for a readership of a few thousand lawyers, court buffs, and journalists. One thing dismaying Warden was that no one was checking up on possible misconduct in murder prosecutions. A 1981 letter started him on the case of four black men from suburban Ford Heights who were convicted of killing a white couple in a vicious highway robbery in another suburb.

More than seven years later, Warden sold his publication to the Law Bulletin Publishing Company, which shunned "muckraking" stories. Still haunted by the case, he later enlisted the help of Professor David Protess of Northwestern University's Medill School of Journalism along with a few students, a private investigator, and several volunteering lawyers. They uncovered political railroading, bribed witnesses, and double sets of police reports. The Ford Heights Four were finally exonerated in 1996, but the Chicago papers treated the case as an aberration of justice rather than evidence of what should have been clear from years of lawsuits and DNA tests: prisoners in Cook County were being railroaded in a systemwide malignancy.[17]

Clear-sighted professionalism, such as that shown by Warden's team, was taking some of the enjoyment away from police reporting. As Walter Spirko said, "Today's there's no romance in the business anymore—no glamour. In my day we had romance. Rough but good times."[18]

Soon after Richard M. Daley took office as mayor in April 1989, he ordered that public information from all city departments come only through his office. "We're not talking about taking away access," his press secretary said. "We're talking about coordination." It was just another part of press release journalism.

That was the year *Tribune* editor Jim Squires lost his final run-in with unbending executive officer John Madigan, not to be confused with a former WBBM radio commentator with the same name. Temper, an adjunct of enthusiasm, was no longer appreciated in news offices, although Royko said that when he entered the business in the fifties any editor without a short fuse was considered odd. Indeed, this history suggests that editors who lose excitement over individual stories turn their office into just another business.

Squires would later contend in his book *Read All About It! The Corporate Takeover of American Newspapers* that *Tribune* political endorsements were often determined by legal counsel Don Reuben rather than by its fourteen-member editorial board. He also charged that former publisher Stanton Cook, one of the few executives he got along with, had a "particularly cozy relationship" with the Defense Department.

In addition, Squires reported authorizing several projects to build readership only to see them undermined by nearsighted budget cuts. He traced what he considered the management decline to when the McCormick family trust expired in 1975 and stock was distributed to heirs. He claimed the Tribune Company "was headed for public ownership as soon as its profitability reached the levels to be termed a 'quality' stock investment."

The increased business orientation at such corporate-run papers meant that short-term thinkers had the loudest and sometimes the only voice, Squires added. He lamented that publishers consistently reshaped huge media complexes to a fifteen percent growth, since panic sets in whenever the stock drops to fourteen percent. "If you went to industry meetings," Squires wrote, "you would hear very little talk of journalism any more. They talk about business. Journalism is something our predecessors were involved in."[19] When the excitable Squires was forced out in late 1989, he took up the more rewarding field of Kentucky horse breeding.

Just as Squires had represented the enterprise-news side of the paper, Cook had been trained as an engineer and rose through the production side. No one watching the belt-tightening and creation of hierarchy after them would doubt that the background of new company president John Madigan lay in investments.

From now on, the newspaper would be treated as just a component of an overall Tribune Company product. Some employees felt they were being treated impersonally under a barrage of required forms, mission statements, and euphemisms. The paper still conducted well-researched series on aspects of Chicago life, but there were fewer stories that made people want to nudge someone and say "Did you read about...."

Most accident and crime stories were put in side columns as if the management were a little ashamed about printing them, and in a twenty-minute video the *Tribune* produced to impress employees with its operations, "reporter" was mentioned only once, in a passing reference to the sports department.

Squires was succeeded by Jack Fuller, a quieter man of unquestioned intelligence who had served as a special assistant to the U.S. attorney general after putting his time in as a City News reporter. In 1986, the cool-tempered Fuller won a Pulitzer for editorial writing. But during his years in the ivory tower, he was unable to put his personal stamp on the paper.

The post–Murdoch management crew that moved into the *Sun-Times* in 1989 was led by tall, lean, white-haired Sam McKeel. With his voice harking back to North Carolina, McKeel had earlier helped turn the Philadelphia *Inquirer* around. He considered the *Sun-Times* the most mismanaged major daily in America because of its hello-goodbye succession of editors and publishers following the departure of the Fields.

McKeel's editor was Dennis Britton, formerly of the Los Angeles *Times*. Without flamboyance or front-page pledges, they laid off workers, eliminated vacant positions, and tried to concentrate on what the paper did best rather than trying to provide a feature for every taste, as the *Tribune* had done for a century. After exposing one scandal after another in the Richard M. Daley administration, the *Sun-Times* for a while in the new century would brag that it was the "UNofficial paper of City Hall." But after another media baron took over, the paper would find itself fighting for its life.

Ever since 1973, the WBBM-TV ten o'clock news had a winning team of tall Bill Kurtis and shorter Walter Jacobson, who also served as its commentator. The station might have hoped a good thing could be split up into two good things, but things did not work out that way.

Jacobson was used to bolster an earlier newscast. Kurtis, after co-anchoring the studio desk at one time or another with Mary Ann Childers and Linda MacLennan, left to produce independent television documentaries. For a time, he filmed his lead-ins inside the long, narrow single-room office of City News when it was in an aging office tower at 35 East Wacker, sometimes changing clothes in a large alcove lined with file cabinets for newspaper clippings.

Kurtis's seat at the WBBM anchor desk was filled by handsome African American newscaster Lester Holt, a no-nonsense newsman installed to woo back viewers lost during the Bill "Slash and Trash" Applegate period. As an example of how appearances were important to newscasts, WLS-TV anchorman Hosea Sanders posed for *Playgirl* magazine in 1987 as one of "America's Sexiest TV Reporters."

Every now and then a person comes along who actually fits a stereotype, and for newspaper people making snide remarks about TV newsreaders, an example was WBBM's Giselle Fernandez. She tended to inject personal opinions into her somewhat theatrical newscasts, made snippy on-air remarks about her critics, and picked up the tab for a seventy-dollar pizza dinner for flashy drug lord John Cappas as she escorted the arrogant young man on his surrender. It also was rumored in print that Fernandez was romantically involved with her news director. Was she fired? Of course not. In 1991, Fernandez was promoted to CBS network anchor and correspondent.[20]

That year, Walter Jacobson, the million-dollar early evening anchor at WBBM, wore a fake beard and down-and-out makeup as he spent two days wandering the streets as a homeless man. The idea had long been tried by newspapers, but Jacobson was the best-known person to do it. During the six-part series he said, "I'm miserable. I'm really, really miserable." A shabby man recognized him and said, "You don't know nothin' about the homeless."

Under the pressure of simultaneously being a celebrity and a serious newsman in an ever more flighty business, Jacobson was said to have become harder to work with, and in one newscast even uttered the one unutterable word in the English language.

What might be called "conduct unbecoming..." cost *Sun-Times* reporter Ray Hanania (pronounced han-ah-nee-ah) his job in 1991 for having an affair with nice-looking City Treasurer Miriam Santos and possibly giving her political advice. Eleven years later, nationally syndicated columnist Bob Greene left the *Tribune* at the age of fifty-five after admitting that, as the paper put it, he had "engaged in inappropriate sexual conduct" with a female high school student he had met at work years before.

With Chicago television people largely concerned about ratings and presentations rather than the basics of news, they drifted toward clichés and silliness. A WBBM-TV reporter who arrived too late to catch a 1991 story interviewed a neighbor about where he was when he did not see anything. And this is a CLTV lead-in to one of its later newscasts: "She suffered an unspeakable tragedy, and now she will speak about the murder..."

A WGN-TV newscaster once said on the air that FBI agents were going in and out of a suburban home and that revealing its name would jeopardize the investigation. As he spoke, the station put a sign below his image: "Glenwood."

Of course, broadcast news staffs denied having less background than their print counterparts, but newspaper people knew better. A fledgling City News reporter went to WLS-TV reporter Bob Petty before a news conference and asked, "Mind if I stand by you to make sure I understand it right?"

"I don't have to understand it," nice-guy Petty told her, "I just play a sound byte."[21]

TV and radio newscasters have told us such things as there was a fire at a mental institution "but none of the patients were disturbed," "a composer of note," and, about a girl rescued by helicopter from the Great Smoky Mountains during a storm: "she isn't out of the woods yet."

On May 2, 1991, a WLS-TV reporter talking about a fourth prosecution in the murder of nine-year-old Jeanine Nicarico in an outer suburb years before gave listeners this mind-boggler: "If Jeanine were alive now she'd be old enough to serve on the jury of her own trial."

Unlike newspaper reporters, who could write in relative comfort, TV reporters often must speak into a camera after just glancing at a note card, leading to some regrettable utterances. A WGN reporter once said, "The issue of right turn on red is no longer black and white."

But some news writers just don't think. Another WGN reporter apparently meant that guns caused half the deaths of children who had died by accident or violence in the city. But she smoothly read these carefully typed words from a teleprompter: "Bullets killed half of Chicago's children last year."

With television cable news networks using satellite transmissions, the national wire services were in trouble. United Press International became like a child's top running out of spin. In 1988, it was saved from bankruptcy when Mexican press lord Mario Vazquez Rana bought it for forty-one million dollars, but after much infighting the UPI was believed to be losing twenty million dollars a year, and both the *Sun-Times* and the *Tribune* threatened to cancel the service.

In May 1991, after years of keeping its national broadcast offices in Chicago, the UPI laid off eight workers in the city and moved the operation to its headquarters in Washington, D.C. That August, the eighty-four-year-old national wire filed for bankruptcy protection. After televangelist Pat Robertson backed away from his offer to buy the wire service for six million dollars, it was taken over by News World Communications, a global mixed media company founded by the Reverend Sun Myung Moon of the Unification

Church. But it was no longer a serious competitor of the AP in national coverage.

In 1989, WMAQ employees and tons of equipment were moved from the Merchandise Mart to the ground floor of the forty-story NBC Tower on redeveloped land a little behind the Tribune Tower. But after a heyday in the seventies, broadcast news staffs were having some of the same problems the papers and wire services were facing.

Walter Jacobson was overstaying his welcome at WBBM-TV, where his rebellious spirit and longing for newspaper-style features was a poor fit, and in April 1993, he accepted a sizable pay cut to work at WFLD (Channel 32). WBBM had no one with a definable personality to replace him.

In 1992, the *Tribune* started trimming its national coverage but not its international stories, keeping eleven foreign bureaus over the *Sun-Times*'s none. As managing editor F. Richard Ciccone explained, "The day of sending a reporter to cover a hurricane is gone when people can watch it on CNN."[22] The war between the media was ending in a capitulation.

That April, cracking walls in a tunnel carrying downtown electrical wires led to massive flooding in sub-basements of the Merchandise Mart and several Loop buildings. The *Tribune* treated the story as a breaking emergency, that is, leaving a "hole" (blank space) for last-minute updates while preparing the rest of the edition.[23] Electrical service to seven downtown buildings was shut off for repairs, forcing City News to bring its paper and clipboards across

NBC Tower, home of station WMAQ-TV.

Wacker Drive to unused space at the *Sun-Times* building. Without the use of computers, the agency had to fax typewritten copy to all thirteen of its newspaper and broadcast clients.

An all-news radio format proved too costly for WMAQ-AM, but executives decided to blend in unrelated features gradually, then pink-slipped two midday anchors in 1994. The news format stopped only in 2002, when most of the forty staff members were let go and the city's oldest radio station was replaced by sports-talk WSCR.

Newspaper people tended to grouse about the highly publicized salaries of national television news anchors, ranging from two million for Connie Chung to seven million for Peter Jennings. Journalism professor Peter Herford observed that "It is precisely the same system that is used to pay [top movie stars] ... it has nothing to do with journalism whatever."[24] But the smooth delivery and pleasant appearances of glamour-casters in Chicago were worth their salaries for the number of people tuning in, even though the local news they delivered was no longer the type of solid, detached reporting that viewers had watched during the competitive seventies.

In 1992, TV critic Rick Kogan quoted an unnamed longtime local TV reporter as saying, "When I started up in this business, there was a sense of serving the viewers. We had a mission to inform. We were relevant. Now, we're mostly just show biz."[25] A WLS radio reporter put it another way in a conversation a few years later, "It's unusual to find ethics in the broadcast news business." He meant any longer.

Deciding which happenings were news had been easier in the twenties and thirties. Editors knew by instinct, and so did readers. But after the public became more divided and critical, newspaper editors and their broadcast counterparts, news producers, thought they could solve the problem with formulas, such as that individual tragedies in drug-ridden neighborhoods were not newsworthy.

When the *Tribune* announced that it had received an award for a series on the shooting of children in gang areas, the executives did not mention that the paper had been spiking the problem for so long a writer had to go to City News for back copy. The broadcast stations' explanation for not looking into the impact of street crime was that they covered only issues affecting their readers. In other words, many viewers thought such crime was a turn-off, and residents in low-income neighborhoods did not buy the products advertised.

Contrast the concept of gearing news to what the public presumably wants to this 1976 statement of standards for CBS news: "We in broadcast journalism cannot, and should not, and will not base our judgments on what we think the viewers and listeners are 'most interested' in, or hinge our news judgment and our news treatment on our guesses or someone else's surveys as to what news the people want to hear and see, and in what form."[26]

The calm that viewers saw in newscasters never reflected the often hectic nature of story scheduling. About a dozen reporters, producers, and editors would meet each morning for about an hour to discuss which developments to pursue in any major story that happened in the last twenty-four hours, sometimes taken from newspapers. Ideas that sparked the most interest would provide visuals yet not be too costly to cover.

A reporter, sometimes an anchor, might breeze by the assignment editor and say "we're rolling to..." a certain address. The reporter would keep in touch with a producer or assistant by cell phone on the way, and, if a story looked promising, would ask that it be given two or three minutes of air time rather than the usual sixty seconds or less. If the story was a feature or part of a series, the reporter might record the narration in the station's small soundproof announcer's booth.

At the time, an anchorman might be getting a rubdown at a downtown gym and a female anchor would be applying cosmetics in front of mirrors. After the "show," the anchors would meet with the news director for a debriefing, a going over of how the delivery went and how it could have been improved.[27] Unlike the freewheeling fifties, in the high-pressure nineties crew members no longer tried to rattle a newscaster with pranks such as a dead mouse next to a coffee cup.

Former WMAQ-TV reporter Ray Suarez in 1993 explained why he gave up the news business for work in public radio. He said NBC's concern for profits had led to a decline in local news, and that with satellites beaming stories from around the world producers would pick dramatic images even if they were irrelevant. "There are no gatekeepers," he complained. "You just download the stuff and put it on the air."[28]

Electronic Media columnist Ron Aldridge said TV's covering individual events without looking into their causes could be a disservice. "It is the resulting narrowness of local television's news judgments that most explains its all-too-common sameness and shallowness," he said.[29]

In 1994, Walter Cronkite told a Los Angeles audience that he was "afraid we're breeding a generation of electronic reporters whose thinking is as truncated as the format in which they must work. They aren't interested in news except as it resembles show business."[30]

With the papers wrestling with economic realities, news-gathering awards were going to such small publications as the *Windy City Times*, a gay weekly, for fact-checking mayoral candidates to show their hypocrisy, and the neighborhood *Lakefront Outlook/ Hyde Park Herald,* for pointing out questionable dealings involving an alderman and the city's main public library. These were the sort of things the dailies used to go after regularly.

After Charles Brumback became president and chief executive officer of the Tribune Company in 1990, he accelerated its acquisition of publications and broadcast stations across the country. His conclusion after a year of study was that "making a newspaper, literally putting ink onto newsprint, is not our core business [any more].... We needed to start thinking of ways we could take these news and entertainment products and leverage them across a number of distribution channels."[31]

This moderately stocky man with a friendly face called his plan "visionary," but as events turned out it was the wrong vision for a time of worsening financial conditions throughout the news industry.

While the *Tribune* was jeopardizing its future on further expansion, the wobbling *Sun-Times* fell into the hands of its second foreign owner, Conrad Black, the pushy son of an aggressive Canadian brewery executive.

At the age of eight, Black had invested his savings in a share of General Motors. At fourteen he broke into a school office to alter the grades of students he despised. He was later expelled for selling the answers to final exams. Black eased out of his shyness when he realized women found power alluring. After reading a biography of Hearst, he was eager to publish newspapers but without gaining first-hand experience with news.

After his father died, he suffered anxiety attacks that eased with both psychoanalysis and early success with mining and newspaper investments. He developed a patrician manner and threw into conversations words more suited for crossword puzzles.

The only time Black's practices were questioned during his rise came when Toronto police opened a file on him because his financial lines of conduct were so complex. Nothing came of the inquiry. He went on to establish Hollinger Incorporated, a Vancouver, British Columbia, public company that sometimes acted as if it were separate from him. His two-pronged approach made it easier to buy controlling stock in the London *Daily Telegraph*. With this control base he purchased scores of small papers and transferred holdings into the U.S.–based Hollinger International, an entity separate from Hollinger, Incorporated.

After federal regulation forced Murdoch to sell the *Sun-Times*, chairman Leonard Shaykin of the Adler & Shaykin investment company mulled over Black's interest in the paper and gave him a call in 1991. But Black did not acquire the *Sun-Times* and its suburban papers until February 28, 1994, when they went for one hundred and eighty million dollars. He purchased them through his local tentacle, the American Publishing holding company based in West Frankfort, Illinois, and did not bother to attend the contract signing. At the time, American Publishing owned ninety-seven dailies and seventy-one weeklies.

Everyone seemed happy about the purchase because Black was less of a meddler than Murdoch, and he promised to make no changes other than to modernize the tabloid. That was good news because *Sun-Times* reporters at the time did not even have a direct link to the Internet.

As the new *Sun-Times* chairman, Black's shady right-hand man, F. David Radler of Vancouver, was despotic with the newspaper guild and his own editors. Executive news editor John Dodge quit and moved to WBBM-TV. In the next months, the *Sun-Times* newsroom staff was slashed thirty percent, as if Black and Radler were not really interested in Chicago coverage.

For more than a century the heart of the city had been the Loop, but now financial interests were more interested in the two hundred acres of underused land immediately north of the river. With all the construction nearby, the new owners of the *Sun-Times* were well aware that their stumpy, unattractive building was occupying prime real estate. Black put the building up for sale in 1999, and two years later found a buyer in flashy real estate developer Donald Trump, who would build the tallest residential building in North America.[32]

Also in the nineties, fewer local TV executives were concentrating on news, with cable television surpassing their capabilities on national stories. Some station managers considered enterprise reporting a waste of time, or at least not a profitable part of the product. By early 1993, Pam Zekman's WBBM-TV investigative team was reduced to just her, although it would later be increased.

An unidentified radio station news director told *Chicago* magazine at around the same time that at WLS-TV, "They've forgotten how they got to be number one. There's no direction." The station made up for a shrinking news staff by using "satellite-feed video," generic stories that stations across the country may use in any way they want. The source said the station no longer had commentators or an investigative unit, but it did lead the others in restaurant reviews.[33]

WMAQ-TV newscaster Ron Magers justified the diminishing importance of news on television this way: "We've got 23 minutes. We try to give everybody something. There used to be a 'common view' of what the news was. We would try to lead with what was going to be Page 1 of the paper the next day, but not anymore. Our lead may not even be *in* the paper the next morning."[34]

In 1997, WMAQ-TV's serious-minded reporter Carol Marin quit after refusing to anchor a newscast using syndicated talk show host Jerry Springer, who on his show encouraged circuslike antics such as shouting matches among his guests and suggested that female guests bare their breasts to the audience. Marin called him, "the poster child for the worst television has to offer." In response to her widespread support, WBBM station manager Hank Price experimentally hired her as a solo anchor, but the underfunded news show had the effect of someone reciting magazine articles, and before long it was canceled.

1997 also saw the death of the Chicago *Defender*'s publisher for fifty-seven years, John Sengstacke, leaving Sengstacke Enterprises in a trust for his six grandchildren. In addition, they inherited a printing debt of seven hundred and fifty thousand dollars, and a three million dollar property tax bill.

After five more years of financial uncertainty and management by well-meaning non-news people, the *Defender* was sold to Tom Picou, nephew of Sengstacke's late wife and head of the Real Times media company.[35] The transaction kept the nation's last black-owned daily in the hands of the extended family.

Picou, a man with a lined and grave face, started reducing what he regarded as whip cream on the news pages, but the *Defender* was only hobbling along. Some stories were still pounded out on typewriters, and its few computers were not hooked up to the Internet. Staff members at times even competed with one another for telephones, and employees later occasionally stole local stories verbatim from the Internet without attribution.

Then a Chicago news tradition died. After one hundred and nine years of uninterrupted service and the production of hundreds of reporters and editors for newspapers and broadcast stations, the City News Bureau shut down on February 28, 1999. The wire service had been owned by all of the major dailies. After the *Daily News* and the *Chicago Today* folded, this meant the *Sun-Times* and the *Tribune* had to finance it themselves, augmented by radio and TV subscribers. But, amid its turmoil, the *Sun-Times* was no longer able to keep up its share.

At virtually the last minute, the *Tribune* bought the wire service and made room for up to three editors in a single glass-enclosed fourth floor office just a forty-second walk from its own city room. But what had been an around-the-clock staff of forty-eight was reduced to nineteen, with some of the loss being made up through pagers and cellular phones.

The renamed City News Service opened on March 1, 1999, with just a twenty-minute pause in service as the midnight crew crossed the river from Wacker Drive to North Michigan Avenue. The *Sun-Times* tried to replace it with Alliance, carrying features by Medill journalism students, but the service closed in less than two years.

The *Tribune* could still have a team of reporters spend months working on an issue that had been hushed up. A series by courts reporter Maurice Possley and others detailed prosecutorial misconduct in numerous criminal cases, but even then it took the Ford Heights Four and the Jeanine Nicarico cases for editors to realize the problem. Governor George Ryan cited the series as a factor in his headline-making decision to impose a moratorium on death sentences in 2000 and to commute all Illinois death sentences three years later.

The financial troubles in the news business might suggest that reporters were glum, but they usually kept their sense of humor. Not long after City News nestled into the Tribune Tower, one of its reporters, James Janega, became the paper's obituary editor. He instituted the Yorick Award for well-written sendoffs. Winners were allowed to keep on their desk for one month a small plastic skull "which," Janega admitted, "my wife said gives her the creeps." Suburban winners were sent a faxed photo of the skull.

The *Tribune*'s buying City News and keeping all the same broadcast subscribers allowed the wire service to continue its annual baby derby, in which reporters called dozens of hospitals late each New Year's Eve and asked that

Final home of the City News Bureau, before the wire service was downsized and moved into the Tribune Tower as the City News Service. In the middle distance is a statue of *Sun-Times* celebrity columnist Irv Kupcinet.

someone notify the agency of any birth that occurred from midnight to about 12:20 A.M. A Cook County Hospital nursing supervisor once called about a delivery clocked at around twelve-ten, but the editor had to inform her of a child who entered the world at 12:04. The nursing supervisor paused and said, "Oh, we made a mistake, the baby was born at exactly 12:01."

In 2000, Machelle Tulipano and her lover pleaded guilty to offering an undercover agent twenty-five hundred dollars to kill her husband, John.[36] It turned out that John Tulipano owned FireNet Chicago, a service that monitored numerous police and fire scanners to alert news clients about blazes and major accidents. FireNet probably saved newspapers and broadcast stations on staffing, and the downsized City News could not have functioned without its beeping, palm-sized plastic notifier.

Some of the increasing coldness and bitterness in the modern news business came from managerial detachment and budget cuts, leading to layoffs, increased demands, and pay freezes. Several people at the papers complained that they seldom heard mirth in their newsrooms any more. "I remember the *Daily News*," Royko said. "If you didn't hear someone burst out in laughing every few minutes, Bob Rose, the city editor, would say 'Laugh!'"[37]

Within fifteen months in 2000 and 2001, two employees committed suicide at the Tribune Tower, but neither of them was from the news side. The first was an advertising systems manager who jumped from a fifth story window. The other was a woman who "fell to her death" from the top of the nine-story annex. Wanting to avoid a third instance, the management issued this statement to all employees: "If you are concerned about a coworker, contact your supervisor...or [the] Tribune's medical director...."[38]

Just as the quieter, less bustling newspapers hid a world of backbiting, office politics, and petty revenges, television stations could be cruel to their staffs. Seven years after retiring, Russ Ewing was accused of threatening three WMAQ officials he blamed for the fatal heart attack of his niece, Margaret Salmon, several weeks after she was fired as an assistant assignment editor. Ewing said he never personally threatened anyone but that the management had treated her viciously.[39]

Such edginess was bound to carry over at work. The founder of Mothers Against Gangs, Frances Sandoval, was holding an outdoor news conference when a press reporter protested being elbowed out of the way by a TV cameraman. The cameraman then grabbed the reporter by the collar and shoved him down the sidewalk. The fight might have continued, but Sandoval shouted, "Please stop. We're here against violence!"[40]

The reasons TV people were often more physical than newspaper reporters could be anything from internal pressures to a smugness that sometimes is part of the job. A Cook County Hospital administrator tried to make a WMAQ cameraman stop following the gurney of an eight-year-old gunshot victim into the emergency room. Bushy-blond reporter Rich Samuels scuffled with the administrator to the point of being charged with misdemeanor battery and was later fired.

Samuels had earned a doctorate in history and once worked as a Better Government Association investigator. But, as Ron Magers said, his temper was "something he has struggled with for years."[41] Perhaps Samuels would have learned self-control if he had gone through newspaper work—not that print reporters were gentlemen. From time to time, the police would ask one of them to stand in a lineup with suspects. When hefty City News reporter Marty Walsh stood against a wall in a police station he asked the others, "Which one of you guys did it?"[42]

In time, technology allowed newspapers to print single moments from video cameras rather than having photographers go "click click click." This further erased the line between broadcast and print, and made police-beat reporters with their pens and notebooks a little old fashioned.

The terrorist attacks on September 11, 2001, required so much background, involved so much tragedy, and would have so many repercussions that television could not top newspaper coverage apart from the videos of the smoldering ruins and the rescues. The *Tribune* had all its reporters and editors working with its national and international bureaus, but the *Sun-Times* had to rely heavily on wire service copy.[43]

2

Conrad Black's Hollinger International was selling a number of Canadian and downstate Illinois papers to shuck off labor trouble and make him more acceptable as a member of the British House of Lords, a distinction he was about to achieve now that he had renounced his Canadian citizenship. Detractors said his wife, Amiel, a former television journalist, longed to become Lady Black.

Confident but not grounded by any core values, Black seemed driven by no clear constant other than his love of acquisition and divestiture, as if wishing to write his name large even though it meant leaving nothing behind. According to a documentary, Black dismissed Robert Maxwell as an "amateur" and, as if forgetting what century he was in, spoke about the "rights of nobility." He even chose to attend a costume party as the aloof French schemer Cardinal Richelieu.

As someone who loved orbiting the powerful around him, Black chose for his board of directors such people as former secretary of state Henry Kissinger and ex-Illinois governor James Thompson, now an influential attorney. The board refrained from objecting whenever Black gave himself a "noncompete" fee for selling a newspaper. But in the eyes of the U.S. government, fees accepted for not opening a competing publication belonged to the stockholders.[44]

At the time, *Tribune* editor F. Richard Ciccone was having his staff use a magazine approach to daily stories as an alternative to the two-sentence local stories on television. Readers often waded through paragraphs of background and local color only to discover that the bloated pieces were commonplace. Ciccone admitted in a farewell note as he was clearing the way for his successor that "I should have...[made] it clear that great writing can occur only after great reporting."

In February 2001, Ann Marie Lipinski, who had won a Pulitzer for articles showing conflicts of interest in the city council, rose to the top of the masthead, making this slender daughter of a schoolteacher and a Michigan barber possibly the most important journalist in the city. As an investigative reporter rather than someone with a business background, Lipinski promised to be a revitalizing force.[45] But some of her plans were curtailed by the first wave of economic setbacks that would batter the paper over the next few years. Much of it was the paper's own fault.

The Tribune Company, America's second largest newspaper conglomerate, had just absorbed the Los Angeles-based Times Mirror Company, operator of the Los Angeles *Times* and Baltimore *Sun* as well as five other dailies and the Long Island area's *Newsday*. The company now had more than twenty-one thousand employees in newspapers and broadcast stations from New York to Seattle, not to mention owning the Chicago Cubs. Its television station, WGN— since 1978, one of the country's few "superstations"—reached sixty million households through cable and direct broadcast satellite.

But in their eagerness to become what an internal publication called America's "premier major-market media company," executives in the Tower seemed unaware that insiders did not trust the present L.A. *Times* owners. Not that the Chandlers had started that way.

The Chandler family had operated the paper for decades, and the troubles did not begin until Otis Chandler took over as Times-Mirror chairman in 1981. He took some of the editorial bite out of the *Times,* and ambitious company president Robert Erburu, a lawyer, began handing positions over to his friends.

In 1985, Otis was deposed in a coup organized by Erburu's brother-in-law, also an attorney. The board, dominated by other Chandlers, then started selling company assets to make up for TV and radio news losses, as well as a drop in readership to the younger reader-oriented *USA Today* of the Gannett newspaper chain.

Chronicler Dennis McDougal said the Los Angeles *Times* management became "ruthless" in hacking away at competition from suburban papers. By 1992, overreaching had left the board wondering how to pay off more than sixty-six million dollars in overdue bills. Some observers claimed the Chandlers were using financial sleight-of-hand to keep Times-Mirror going despite its healthy appearance in an art-deco office tower that was one of the attractions of downtown Los Angeles.

On January 1, 1996, General Mills vice chairman Mark Willes stepped in as chairman and said he would get rid of any division not equaling the sixteen percent profit enjoyed by *USA Today*. Willes liked people who said yes to him, and morale was not improved by his firing of seven hundred and fifty employees in a single day, a hundred and fifty of them in the editorial department, including reporters and editors. When Willes became publisher of the L.A. *Times*, he thought he could make up for his lack of a news perspective by using focus groups. He ran the fourth largest newspaper in the country as if there were no difference between its content and Cheerios.

In 1999, Chicago *Tribune* executives bought the L.A. *Times* and Times-Mirror directly from the Chandlers, bypassing Willes and the Times-Mirror board, and despite some doubts about the company's finances.[46] The U.S. Tax Court ruled in 2005 that the Times-Mirror's tax liability, now grown to one billion dollars, was carried over in the merger. That was two hundred and fifty million dollars more than the *Tribune* had set aside for an adverse ruling. Even worse, the *Tribune* needed to give the Internal Revenue Service as much of the amount as possible to reduce potentially crushing interest.

This came at a time when mergers and consolidations reduced the number of North American newsprint companies from thirty to seventeen in just six years. As a result of the reduced competition and other factors, newsprint prices jumped thirteen percent in a single year—and kept increasing.

The Chicago *Tribune* responded by narrowing its width slightly and going from a five-story front page to six. The management sent messages asking reporters to write "crisper ledes" (leads) because of the narrower columns, and editors squeezed some institutional stories—largely those involving city hall or the county building—into news briefs instead of featuring them as the *Sun-Times* was doing.[47]

Newspaper executives may have been experimenting to cut costs, but journalism was still exciting and potentially dangerous at the street level. In 2001, *Sun-Times* sports reporter Larry Hamel was covering a boxing match in suburban Rosemont when the promoter scolded him about an article written by someone else. Next, a man with a shaven head entered the "media room," smashed Hamel's computer, threw him to the floor, and growled while kicking him, "Do you think what you do is funny?"[48]

Rookie City News reporters Patricia Troumpoucis and Tania Ralli were sent to a Dan Ryan Expressway chemical spill that August. They avoided the traffic snarl by walking through the newly evacuated neighborhood. Below the bridge they were crossing, fumes were igniting upon contact with the air. Firefighters strongly advised Troumpoucis and Ralli to shower immediately for their own safety, but the young women had an assignment to finish.

Only after conducting a few interviews, did the women go under a numbingly cold firehose-shower, fully clothed, where they were scrubbed down and hosed off again top to bottom. Firefighters advised them to put their clothes in a dryer at the station, but instead they stayed behind, still soaked, to interview the last emergency workers on the scene.

In December 2002, about seventy people rushed into the *Defender* offices at 24th and Michigan over a story about the fatal shooting of a man suspected of wounding a police officer. Claiming the accused had been a bystander, the protesters overturned desks, destroyed potted plants, and struck a couple of reporters on the head. News photographer Robert Sengstacke curled into a ball to protect his camera until several employees, including his daughter, pulled the intruders away from him—but not before they tore off his flash unit.[49]

Economic realities were even harsher to the *Defender*, whose readers were now generally middle aged and therefore of little interest to major advertisers. The *Sun-Times* and the *Tribune* were also unable to re-think themselves at a time when local news, once so scandalous and fascinating, was seeming less pertinent.

With papers everywhere failing to gain readers from sixteen to thirty-four, the *Tribune* in 2002 developed its RedEye mini edition, a few pages loaded with pop celebrity tidbits, large photos, nightlife features, and several shortened news stories. The *Sun-Times* beat its giant rival by a few days in rushing out its similar *Red Streak* edition. Both sold for twenty-five cents from red street boxes to attract "socially active" (product-buying) adults. But three years later, the *Tribune* grabbed the entire market by providing its RedEye every day for free at a giant loss, and forcing the *Sun-Times* to give up its experiment. The gamble worked, and the mini-paper started showing a profit from ad sales in 2005 as two-hundred thousand copies were reportedly picked up on weekdays.

As children of technology, television stations were always faster to adopt new ways than newspapers. Stations that had cut their news staffs were now encouraging viewers to submit audio tapes, video camera footage, and even cell phone videos of news happenings. The CNN term for such people was "I-reporters." There could be fifty-five million such instant reporters, the number of Americans owning cell phones with video capacity.

Wounded by staff reductions, by 2003 Chicago papers were doing what had been forbidden a few years before, substituting some of their own reporting with news stolen off the television set. The *Sun-Times* apparently started it, sometimes printing whole articles "according to broadcast reports." The *Tribune* followed as if conceding that newspapers were now unnecessary for on-the-spot coverage.

Yet television crews were no longer feeling the excitement of reaching a scene before print reporters. Mike Flannery, who had worked at the *Sun-Times* before joining WBBM, said TV news assignments had to be decided by committee since a number of people including a reporter, a camera operator, a videotape editor, and news producers were now involved.[50]

There also was an increasing sameness at the stations, partly because executives were listening to the same advisers, such as Frank N. Magid Associates, with offices in New York and Los Angeles. In 2003, Magid Associates advised clients that covering protests against the war in Iraq turned off viewers. Media expert Lee Abrams remarked, "It's almost as if Frank Magid has hypnotized every news director in the country."[51]

At least at the downsized City News, its low-paid employees still acted as in the old days, even though it sometimes meant reckless behavior. A reporter had just covered a Chicago appearance by the Chinese premier and wanted to get the story out before the dignitary left O'Hare Airport. He kept trying to send the copy from his laptop in his car as he soared sixty miles an hour, but each time the file garbled. As a solution, he drove single-handedly while keeping one eye on his screen and one eye on traffic, and with his free hand he held a cellular phone to dictate the copy to an editor.

With much of network programming tailored for women by the start of the twenty-first century, four TV news operations in town were headed by females, and at the two others women were second in command. The increased attention to features about home life and schools was neither good nor bad. The concept of news had just evolved from its blood-and-thunder political days and the muckraking and scandal sheet eras.

The *Sun-Times* staff left the low-rise, roughly rowboat-shaped home in

Present home of the Chicago *Sun-Times*. After years of turmoil of management changes and declining advertising, the paper moved to the 9th and 10th floors of the huge Apparel Mart.

Above: WLS-TV in the heart of the Loop conducted a spirited competition with WBBM-TV in the 1970s, before entertainment dictates emphasized "happy talk" and "news you can use" features. The news set is behind this bulletproof glass wall. *Below:* WBBM-TV Studios with a giant screen facing Daley Center Plaza and the Picasso statue. The office tower replaces the 19th century Newspaper Row.

2004 and plugged their computers into the ninth and tenth floors of the Apparel Center, a huge office and hotel building at 350 North Orleans Street. The next year, crews tore down the seven-story pride of Marshall Field IV to make way for the ninety-story Trump International Tower and Hotel. That left the Tribune Tower just across Michigan Avenue the last Chicago building designed for newspaper offices.

The lofty Tower seemed to hold mysteries, but most TV news stations in the city were becoming fishbowls for passersby to gawk at. After WMAQ followed the trend toward street-level newsrooms, WLS-TV set up its anchor desk on the other side of bulletproof glass at State and Lake Streets. In the summer of 2008, WBBM moved its news staff from the decrepit McClurg Court building just north of the river to the ground floor of a new office building at Washington and Dearborn Streets, the former site of newspaper row.

3

A tremor was felt on November 16, 2003, when F. David Radler stepped down as *Sun-Times* publisher and director of Hollinger International. Lord Black resigned as chief executive officer the next day, but he remained chairman despite suspicions of self-dealing. A New York investment firm and brokerage soon accused Black, Radler, and two other officials of pocketing more than thirty-two million dollars in unauthorized payments.

Cardinal Capital Management, Hollinger's largest shareholder, sued the board that December, and the U.S. Justice Department began a criminal investigation of Black after he declined to testify before the U.S. Securities and Exchange Commission. Following an uneasy stillness, Hollinger International officials unsuccessfully sought a meeting with Lord Black before a sale of shares in January 2004. This was a week after Black rewrote the company's bylaws to keep the board from meeting without his approval.

In an unrelated scandal, the *Sun-Times* announced on June 16, 2004, that officials had inflated circulation figures for several years. "Very few people were involved," said Radler's successor, John Cruickshank, former editor of Hollinger's Vancouver *Sun*. In October of that year, the paper disclosed that the circulation had been inflated by up to fifty thousand copies a day. With subsequent lawsuits mounting, Hollinger International said it was setting aside twenty seven million dollars to compensate advertisers that had been cheated.

The audited circulation was brought down to four hundred and thirty thousand, well below the *Tribune*'s six hundred and fifteen thousand. But before long, the Tribune Company admitted that since 2002, a number of managers and circulation workers had lied to executives about the daily sales of its Spanish-language publication in Chicago, *Hoy,* and *Newsday,* the tabloid serving Long Island and the Queens borough of New York City. By mid–2006, nine Tribune Company employees had pleaded guilty to fraud in New York federal court. Paying back the advertisers was expected to cost ninety million dollars on top of the company's other financial burdens.

Allegations continued against the parent company of the *Sun-Times*. Hollinger International stated in a civil action that Radler, Black, and others had plundered five hundred and forty-two million dollars from the company. The SEC filed its own suit, charging that Black and others had defrauded Hollinger International out of eighty-five million dollars.

On August 18, 2005, a federal grand jury indicted Radler on charges that a series of secret transactions had allowed him to siphon off the initially alleged thirty-two million dollars in corporate funds. "This was a systematic fraud on the shareholders," U.S. Attorney Patrick Fitzgerald said. By then, Radler was already cooperating with the government in its investigation of Black, but not all he was telling may have been the truth.

At the end of the month, a Hollinger report charged that executives possibly stole more than four hundred million dollars over seven years, and no local paper carried more details of the accusations than the *Sun-Times* itself.

On September 20, Radler pleaded guilty in Chicago for taking part in the scheme to steal the thirty-two million. The sixty-two-year-old defendant refused to comment outside as he walked past a swarm from the American and Canadian news media. (He would later be turned over to Canadian prison authorities.)

On November 17, 2005, Black was indicted on eight counts of mail and wire fraud, and on December 15 was named on additional counts of racketeering and obstructing justice. The last count stated that after the media baron was ordered to preserve his records for the SEC, a security camera showed him, his chauffeur, and another man suspiciously taking thirteen boxes from a Toronto office building and putting them into a Cadillac.

As Black awaited trial, the *Tribune* announced in late 2005 that the downscaled City News Service would fold on December 31, allowing the paper to put more money into Internet ventures. The mood in the little office was glum over the holidays, but the on-the-spot news service had become an anachronism.

The *Sun-Times* was struggling to get out from under losses arising from the circulation fraud and from profit margins demanded by Black and Radler, as well as a tax encumbrance from the Sun-Times Media Group's unloading of assets under them.

Opening statements in Black's trial began the following March in the tall steel-and-glass Dirksen Federal Building in the Loop. Prosecutors told a crammed courtroom that "Black did not make a distinction between his money and that belonging to a public company," Hollinger International.

In a case involving financial dealings that would give some people a headache, the most striking evidence was the videotape of Black and others removing the boxes. But defense attorneys turned the proceedings into a virtual trial of Radler, who they said was trying to drag his former employer into what the government was calling a massive "fleecing."

Black's team also claimed that Radler conducted his own schemes without conferring with him or Hollinger International. Indeed, under cross-examination Radler admitted lying to conceal his role in a coverup of financial irregularities.

Jurors on July 13, 2007, acquitted Black of the major charges but found him guilty of obstructing justice and three counts of mail fraud. With a steady drizzle outside that December 10, the graying aristocrat of the press was sentenced to serve nearly six and a half years in federal prison. Judge Amy St. Eve also ordered him to forfeit more than six million dollars he was believed to have acquired illegally. Before his sentence was pronounced, Black expressed regret not for any alleged crime but that one billion, eight hundred million dollars in shareholder value had "evaporated" after he was forced out.

A week later, Radler was sentenced to serve nearly two and a half years in prison and pay two hundred and fifty thousand dollar fine. The government noted that he had already paid back more than sixty million dollars as settlements in suits filed by the SEC, Hollinger, and others.

The *Sun-Times* never sufficiently recovered from the Black-Radler era and competition from television and the Internet. The publishers reduced the number of pages, made major cuts in the news department, stretched routine photos across the front page and, while looking for a buyer, began making further layoffs. Readers noticed withering investigations and increasingly dull coverage even of city hall and the criminal courts.

Financial conditions were also worsening at the other daily. In just two years, the Tribune Company stock price declined by more than forty percent. Conceding that it was under a "punishing debt load," the paper in May 2006 took the extraordinary measure of offering to buy back a quarter of its outstanding shares for more than two billion dollars.[52]

That same year, the Chandler family tried to oust the Tribune Company management team with a complaint to the SEC. The Tribune Company responded that the California family was putting its interests above those of stockholders, and no action was taken.

In 2007, the Chandlers tried to buy the *Tribune*. But with burned fingers the Tribune Company sidestepped them and grabbed a thirty-four-dollar-a-share offer from Chicago developer Sam Zell, who operated from an office in the large former *Daily News* building. The Tribune Company went private that December 20.

Zell, a balding man with a small beard, exuded confidence and energy as he held news conferences in jeans and open-neck shirts. Taking over after the eight-billion-dollar deal was approved by federal regulators, he declared, "I'm here to tell you the transaction from hell is gone" and urged employees to "shed all the things that tied us down in the past." By this he meant the corporate structure that had prevented the conglomerate from exploring new approaches. Conceding that he expected to make mistakes, Zell remarked "I don't think, frankly, that the newspaper business has ever been subjected to that kind of clear thinking."

But in subsequent months, Zell showed that drawing upon people with entertainment backgrounds might not be the best way to run a newspaper. Ann Marie Lipinski quit as editor and senior vice president in July 2008, saying she no longer fit in with the new leadership. Thanking the staff, she said, "Newspapering is the ultimate team sport."

A few days later, longtime *Tribune* courts reporter Maurice Possley joined several other employees volunteering to be laid off, and soon the managing editor for features, James Warren, left and the recently named managing editor for news, Hanke Gratteau, accepted a buyout. Forty-one-year-old Jane Hirt was chosen the single managing editor after bringing the free RedEye edition into profitability. Before then she was the foreign and national news editor.

Zell contended that reporters and editors remaining at the paper should be more productive. That was the kind of thinking that had weakened papers in the fifties. But has anyone come up with better ideas?

Conrad Black remained in a Florida federal prison, but in late 2008 Radler was paroled after serving ten months of his twenty-nine-month term for helping to cripple what had been a great newspaper. A Canadian parole board took into account that this was a first offense.

In December of that year, Zell's paper filed for Chapter 11 bankruptcy during a national recession and eliminated eleven more jobs in the newsroom. In the following January, the *Tribune* appeared in tabloid size for weekday street sales, although home subscribers still received the full-sized paper. The Tribune Company also closed its three-year-old, ten million dollar Freedom Museum adjacent to its Tower, which from the start had been more of a vanity project than cultural enrichment, and went ahead with plans to sell Wrigley Field and the Chicago Cubs.

But the newspaper continued to serve as a political gadfly. Before Governor Rod Blagojevich was impeached in early 2009, prosecutors claimed that he threatened to withhold state money for renovations to Wrigley Field unless the *Tribune* fired editorial board members opposing his administration.

For years, WBBM-TV had planned a news fishbowl in a soaring office building that replaced the Loop vacant lot called Block 37. But by early 2009, just four months after the station cleared out of its headquarters in a former stable, new executives started using a less showy studio on the second floor.

All local TV stations were still grappling with an erosion of viewers, with WMAQ having its news producers, writers, and editors reapply for new "platforms" (divisions), such as mobile devices and the Internet. A single "content producer" would screen video, do the editing, arrange any graphics, and write a script for it, along with other duties.[53] Employees throughout the business were multi-tasking to keep up with the reality that news was now less a part of people's lives.

In this survey of a century and a half of people in the Chicago news business, it is easy to overlook what all these moments add up to. There was a time when editors would virtually chain themselves to their desks, and a time a century later when reporter Charles Nicodemus told his wife after covering two murders on his first night at City News, "Ginny, it can't get any better than this."[54]

News other than business, marriage, and death reports began not to inform people but to manipulate them for political and moral goals. As cities expanded, newspapers exposed worsening social conditions until law enforcement agencies could go after those responsible. With newspapers losing some of their relevance for readers, editors became satisfied with just reporting events rather than finding the news behind the news, or at least showing the consequences of these events.

Newspaper timidity and a trend toward paternalism inadvertently increased rivalry among local television stations. Soon after television crews began transmitting events from the scene, print editors stopped trying to compete. Strikes and the increasing price of newsprint further weakened the papers while their readership base withered under suburbanization and the opening of jobs in smaller cities. An increase in crime in the sixties, especially in minority neighborhoods, contributed to an uncertainty at the editorial level over what news is.

Competition that bred great scoops could exist only when there was sufficient money to free reporters to go after individual stories and possible follow-up angles. But the newspapers and television stations were forced to reduce their staffs until investigative local reporting became sporadic.

During this mutual decline, television newscasts, once considered the "moneymaker" of local stations, were absorbed into network entertainment programming and a showbusiness mentality led to a colorless sameness. Staff cuts then led stations more toward "news you can use" features.

At a time when fresh approaches were needed, newspaper publishers and boards of directors made unsound financial decisions. Some, including the Chicago *Tribune*, became dominated by corporate thinking without fully realizing the consequences, and others, like the *Sun-Times*, fell victim to media barons who conducted business more as bullies than as leaders.

Many intangibles were also at work in the downslide, such as the way the papers sloughed off their individuality in the cause of impartiality and professionalism. No wonder people only casually interested in the news preferred the friendly voices of radio and television. As Arlene Morgan of the American Society of Editors told an Illinois convention, "TV has personality that you don't. And it's going to get worse."[55]

News in Chicago began with the certainty of self-driven publishers who devoted their lives to their work, and deteriorated until executives thwarted their staffs or converted news to merchandise governed by the presumed market, only to see that readers and viewers were no longer interested.

With the emergence of the Internet, front page stories become stale by the time they reach the reader. Cyber items are updated or replaced regularly, sometimes with video, bringing computer users close to the action. Another elusive factor in the war between the newspapers, and between newspapers and broadcasting, has been the fading relevancy of local interests. From the political broadsheets before the Civil War through the early 1950s, readers had a focal point, something they equally cared about, and that was the city itself.

But the adage that all news is local has not been true for some time. Suburban sprawl, waves of immigrants from as far away as Russia and Africa, and the outsourcing of industries have meant that cities have lost their specific meaning in the minds of readers and newscast listeners. We may not feel the changes in ourselves, but every day we are becoming more a part of the world. The diminution seems to be encouraging escapism over information.

Necessity has made news in what had been America's greatest news town an amalgam, with the once rival fields of newspapers and newscasts finding ways to use one another. Their real foe has been the escalation of individual choice in news as well as music and movies. People turning to the Internet want information of interest only to them, told in lean sentences without style or judgment getting in the way. Yet no one is sure where Internet will go as a news medium.

As this was being written, no one in the business could say what it will soon be like, not publishers, not station managers, and surely not the reporters. Jeff Bordon observed in *Crain's Chicago Business* that "almost anyone with a personal computer and a modem can reach the same audiences [the] *Tribune* has spent decades and millions of dollars building."[56] *Tribune* development director Lisa Wiersma told Bordon that at the paper these days "You have to be comfortable with uncertainty."

The *Sun-Times* returned to profitability in 2008, and the Sun-Times Media Group rid itself of control by Hollinger, Inc., in March of that year when six directors who had been appointed by Black's holding company agreed to step down as part of a litigation settlement. But the paper continued making newsroom layoffs as it waited for a buyer to sweep in and come to the rescue.

The *Defender* went back to being a weekly in February 2008, and executives at the *Tribune*, whose Standard & Poor's credit rating was lowered to B-minus at around the same time, shrank the paper to a compromise between a broadsheet and a tabloid. In August of that year, Fitch Ratings lowered the credit category of the company owning the once-flourishing *Tribune* to "junk" status.

At the same time, television stations were struggling against what Chicago

Tribune Tower, as seen from below. The building symbolizes the vigor and dedication of Chicago journalism in its heyday.

media expert Robert Reed cited as a thirty-eight percent drop in viewership for local news since 1988.[57] While pouring more money into the Internet and high definition transmission, some stations cut staffs at the top. In early 2008, WLS-AM laid off news director Jennifer Keiper and respected City Hall reporter Bill Cameron.

That April, WBBM-TV made headlines by letting go of Diann Burns, said to be the city's highest-paid newscaster at two million dollars a year, as well as top sportscaster Mark Malone and former longtime anchor Mary Ann Childers, who was then the station's health reporter.[58] And in August, Cable News Network began reducing its Chicago staff.

The public is getting some of what it regards as news not only from web sites but also from blogs, amateur comments posted on the Internet. News video can now come from a neighbor as well as from a professional. Geneva Overholser of the New York *Times* editorial board has said, "Journalism as we know it is over."[59] In June 2008, Sam Zell said he was exploring options such as selling the Tribune Tower, the last Chicago symbol of newspaper times gone by.

Some reporters would like to be transported back to the days when papers pulled everything they could get away with for a story, and editors practically jumped up and down with excitement. But as an editor told Edward Doherty long ago, "Well, kids grow up. And adventure dies."

Chapter Notes

Introduction

1. *Inside Page One*, (1945): 11.
2. Quoted by Jack Willner of the *Chicago Daily News* in *Behind the News* (1960): 4.
3. Quoted by Clarence Petersen, *Chicago Tribune*, May 23, 1988.
4. Martin Mayer, *Making News*, 46.
5. William Shakespeare, *A Winter's Tale*.

Chapter One

1. Richard Digby-Junger, "A New Version of the Founding of the *Chicago Daily News*," *Illinois Historical Journal*, 28.
2. Don Fehrenbacher, *Chicago Giant*, 19.
3. For details about early papers in the city, see Edwin O. Gale, *Reminiscences of Early Chicago*, 343–46.
4. Adoption of AP objectivity is from the *AP Broadcast News Handbook*. The AP formerly believed it was founded in 1848 but in recent years has come across documents tracing it to 1846, *Chicago Journalists Newsletter* (Spring 2006).
5. Reporters in 1850, Rick Kogan, "How We Got the Story," *Chicago Tribune*, June 8, 1997.
6. Scripps and Ogden bringing the railroad to Chicago, etc.: William Bross, *History of Chicago*, 51–58. Information about Scripps, Philip Kinsley: *The Chicago Tribune, Its First Hundred Years*, 10–11.
7. Don Fehrenbacher, *Chicago Giant*, 16, 30.
8. Ray's introductory letter from Horace Greeley: "The W-G-N," *Tribune*, June 10, 1922, 21. Details of how Medill and Ray met and later inspected the office, and the condition of the city are from Jay Monaghan, *The Man Who Elected Lincoln, a Biography of Dr. Charles Ray*, 47–49. The pony is mentioned in Philip Kins-

ley, p. 14, and a sketch of the animal at work is in "The W-G-N," 39. *Tribune* buyers, from "The W-G-N," 17–18.
9. "the great unwashed": Elmer Gertz, "Joe Medill's War," 11. Regarding Medill's and Ray's prejudices: in later years, Medill advocated spiking broth given to tramps with poison. Ray's hatred of Catholics was expressed in a "bitter article," mentioned in Franc B. Wilkie, *Thirty-Five Years of Journalism*, 18.
10. John Tebbel, *An American Dynasty*, 17, and Jay Monaghan, *The Man Who Elected Lincoln, a Biography of Dr. Charles Ray*, 49–50.
11. Bernard A. Weisberger, "Celebrity Journalists," 20, and Allan Churchill, *Park Row*, 139.
12. Carl Sandburg, *Abraham Lincoln*, Vol. II, 27.
13. Renaming the Ohio paper the *Republican*: Frank Luther Mott, *American Journalism, A History: 1690–1960*, 284. New name of the party: Jay Monaghan, *The Man Who Elected Lincoln*, viii, 14, 61, 62.
14. Lincoln's "lost speech": Frank Luther Mott, 285; description of Majors Hall and Scripps' remark: Jay Monaghan, 74–76; Lincoln's demeanor and Medill having only notes from the introduction: Philip Kinsley, 56. That Lincoln's notes were in a lost hat box is from a news release by Martin E. Janis & Co. for Plaza del Lago, Feb. 9, 1989. This would not seem a solid source, and the anecdote is not found in *Lincoln's Lost Speech* by Elwell Crissey, but Lincoln sometimes kept notes in his hat and the account is plausible. The first speech quotation is from the *Illinois Guide and Gazeteer*, 83, and the second is from Sandburg, 274.
15. Greeley's suggestion for a debate, and Medill's sending "floating voters" downstate: Elmer Gertz, "Joe Medill's War," 4. Lincoln's letter of gratitude: Wayne Andrews, *Battle for Chicago*, 51.

16. Frank Luther Mott, 281.

17. Gertz, "Joe Medill's War," 2.

18. Medill telling Lincoln "Give him hell" is from an Associated Press article in the *Daily Herald* on Feb. 22, 2000, about a new web site. Ray's quote, "Hold on Lincoln," is from Gertz, "Joe Medill's War," 3. Medill's and Ray's revisions of Lincoln's speeches, Sandburg, 210 and 215.

19. Sandburg, 337.

20. "The W-G-N," 29.

21. *Chicago Tribune*, Feb. 12, 1993, Section 5, p. 3.

22. The design and name of the Wigwam: "Site of the Sauganash Hotel and the Wigwam," a brochure at the Chicago History Museum. On the delegates, see Theodore J. Karamanski, *Rally 'Round the Flag*, 17–18.

23. Medill printing tickets: Sandburg, 345. Lincoln telling Medill and others he would not allow deal making: Gertz, "Joe Medill's War," 5. Medill changing the Ohio vote: Sandburg, 345.

24. Reaction to Lincoln's convention victory: Monaghan, 172. Halstead's description: Sandburg, 345, and "Lincoln in Chicago," a brochure at the Chicago History Museum.

25. John Tebbel, *An American Dynasty* 22–23.

26. Ray explaining why Scripps should be postmaster: Wayne Andrews, 51. Medill's remark about the two thousand dollars: Gertz, "Joe Medill's War," 6. Medill, "We shall permit no nation to abuse Mexico but ourselves": (ibid., 8). Recruitment and armed guards: *Chicago Tribune*, June 8, 1997.

27. *Tribune* circulation and Medill delivering papers: *Chicago Tribune*, June 8, 1997.

28. Medill sending his own reporters to the scene: Richard A. Schwarzlose, *The Nation's Newsbrokers*, Vol. I, 240. The *Tribune* printing stories of Grant's intoxication, Gertz, "Joe Medill's War," 7. The *Tribune* buying the *Morning Democrat*: Henry Justin Smith, "A Gallery of Chicago Editors," lecture.

29. John J. McPhaul, *Deadlines and Monkeyshines*, 36.

30. Justin E. Walsh, *To Print the News and Raise Hell*, 17.

31. Storey's background: Ibid., 156; Wilkie, 106; Robert S. Harper, *Lincoln and the Press*, 258. Penny paper and ninety-nine cent sales: Melville E. Stone, *Fifty Years a Journalist*, 60 and McPhaul, 71.

32. Gertz, "Joe Medill's War," 11.

33. Wilkie, 105.

34. Henry Justin Smith, "A Gallery of Chicago Editors," lecture.

35. About Vallandigham: Bruce Catton, *Never Call Retreat*, 164 and Catton, *Glory Road*,

244. Vallandigham's suggestion about dividing the country: Philip Kinsley, 169. Storey's editorial: Walsh, *To Print the News*, 173; Kinsley, 273; and a footnote in Edwin Emery, *The Press and America*, 293.

36. Ferdinand Cook, *Bygone Days of Chicago*, 52–53, Walsh, *To Print the News*, 3, 4.

37. "will be no *Tribune*": Emery, 300. Details of the federal seizure are in Walsh, *To Print the News*, 182; Emmett Dedmon, *Fabulous Chicago*, 65; Gertz, "Joe Medill's War," 11.

38. Medill calling for "exercise of arbitrary power": Gertz, "Joe Medill's War," 11. Greeley's response: Mott, 358. Meeting Burnside in Indianapolis: Wilkie, 101.

39. Cadwallader's experience: Sylvanus Cadwallader, *Three Years With Grant*, v-vi, 104–110, with additional information from Dan Bauer, "The Big Bender?," *Civil War Times* (December 1988). The article carries a third account, which tends to confirm part of Cadwallader's version but says the general had stocked wine, not whiskey, aboard the steamer to celebrate the expected victory at Vicksburg. (Cadwallader's editor mistakenly believed Wilkie was from the New York *Times* instead of the Chicago *Times*.) Dana's news background: Richard A. Schwarzlose.

40. McPhaul, 187.

41. Theodore J. Karamanski, 177.

42. Chicago reporters possibly inventing the term "scoop": Cook, 251. "Beat" is this author's own inference.

43. The infamous caption "Jerked to Jesus" appeared in the Nov. 27, 1875, edition but Storey apparently did not write it. He did write similarly flippant headlines.

44. *Encyclopaedia Britannica*, 11th edition, Vol. 27, 543.

45. Mott, 466–67.

46. Ownership of the *Republican*: Henry Justin Smith, *It's the Way It's Written*; Dana information: Elmer Gertz, "Charles A. Dana and the Chicago Republican," 124–35. Dana at the *Republican* and his suit against the paper: McPhaul, 57–58.

47. Joseph Medill, "An Easy Method of Spelling the English Language," *Chicago Tribune*, 1867.

48. Glimpses of Medill and his brother Sam at work: *Times-Herald*, March 17, 1899. Other details are from Andrews, 49–50 and Tebbel, 65–69. "Minion" and "nonpareil": Kenneth E. Olson, 63. White's promotion of Chicago as a transportation hub: *Chicago Tribune*, Dec. 1, 1865, and Harris L. Dante, "The Chicago Tribune's 'Lost Years.'" Edward S. Beck's remark about Medill and the state constitution is from his talk, "Recollections of the Early Days at the Tribune," 12.

49. New York AP and Western AP: Charles Dennis, *Victor Lawson*, 186–187. Details are in Oliver Gramling, *AP, the Story of News*, 61–73.

Chapter Two

1. Lincoln Steffens, *Autobiography of Lincoln Steffens*, 63.
2. The gutted buildings partially left standing: Bessie Louise Pierce, *A History of Chicago*, Vol. III, 6. Information about the *Times* building, Stubbs' death, Storey's quote, Medill and the *Journal* sharing a crude press, and the donation of old type: Robert Cromie, *The Great Chicago Fire*, 169–179, 258–261. Most of the *Tribune* information is from Tebbel, 49–50. Other details about Storey are from Henry Justin Smith's lecture. Information about White came from Louis L. Snyder and B. Morris, *A Treasury of Great Reporting*, 182–183. Recovery of the *Tribune*: *Chicago Tribune*, June 8, 1997.
3. Bross urging men to go to the fire-devastated city: Karen Sawslask, "Smoldering City," 84–85. Medill's house: Annie M. Nicholas, his niece, *Reminisces of Journalism in Chicago*, 271.
4. *Chicago Sun Times*, Showcase section, p. 24, year unknown.
5. Donald L. Miller, *City of the Century*, 165. Reporter John Kelley said in 1911 that the three newsmen had told him the story. For accounts of the fire from the *Journal* and the *Times*, see Mel Waskin, *Mrs. O'Leary's Comet*, 65.
6. Kenneth E. Olson, 60.
7. Richard C. Lindberg, *To Serve and Collect*, 39.
8. Medill's resignation and resting in Europe: Tebbel, 51. Medill buying back into the *Tribune*: Wayne Andrews, 7.
9. Andrews, 91.
10. John Tebbel, 70.
11. William C. Patric, *American History* (June 2003): 41.
12. Andrews, 165.
13. Medill on communists and tramps: Tebbel, 8. The arsenic remark seems to have been a joke.
14. Tebbel, 4.
15. Paul Selby, *Illinois State Journal* (Feb. 13, 1879), from the unnumbered clippings in a Chicago History Museum scrapbook related to Chicago newspapers.
16. For details about boomers, see Allen Churchill, 55. Lanigan, the drunken reporter: John J. McPhaul, 46. That Medill sent drunks to Dwight: *Illinois Guide and Gazetteer*, 230.

The quotes from Stone about drunken journalists and the Washingtonian Home are from his autobiography, *Fifty Years a Journalist*, 61. That some papers extorted advertising and other details are from Stone, 51–60, but his account lacks objectivity.

17. For a more detailed version of the first year of the paper as well as information about newsboys and the relationship of Stone and Meggy, see "A New Version of the Chicago Daily News," Richard Digby-Junger, *Illinois Historical Journal* (Spring 1993): 27–33.
18. Lloyd at the *Tribune* and the *Daily News*: Lloyd Wendt, *Chicago Tribune*, 261; Melville E. Stone, *Fifty Years a Journalist*, 61.
19. Bross' loan to Stone and plan to take over the *Daily News*: Henry Justin Smith, *It's the Way It's Written*, 14–16. Stone breezes over this period in his autobiography, always a sign he was hiding something. Lloyd's stress-related mental problems are found in Chester MacArthur Destler, *Henry Demerest Lloyd*, 154–171. That Lloyd was the first American muckraker is given in several sources, including Walter J. Cooper, *Dictionary of American Biography*, and *Webster's Biographical Dictionary*.
20. Percy English breaking the story of Lincoln's remains: *Chicago Tribune* January 5, 2008, a review of the book *Stealing Lincoln's Body*. English was used as a police stenographer on the Haymarket case. On the McMullens trap: Stone, 63–64; Mott, 467. Henry Justin Smith, *It's the Way It's Written*, working from memory, gives a mangled account on page 37. The *Tribune* trap: McPhaul, 74–75.
21. The reason for acquiring the *Post and Mail*, and that the McMullens sold the paper to the Willards: Bessie Louise Pierce, 418. (Henry Justin Smith, on page 37 of *It's the Way It's Written*, mistakenly states the brothers sold the paper directly to Frances Willard.)
22. That Parsons had been a printer at the *Times*, and that reporters covered the strike on horseback and some were arrested: McPhaul, 67. Parsons and Medill quote: Tebbel, 53. Details of the railroad strike: Ray Ginger, *Altgeld's America*, 36–37. "Hordes" of newsboys and the circulation increase: Henry Justin Smith, 15. The meeting with Stone and Lawson: Robert V. Bruce, *1877: Year of Violence*, 236.
23. On the influence of the *Police Gazette*: Gene Smith, "The National Police Gazette: A Little Visit to the Lower Depths," reproduced over the Internet on AmericanHeritage.com. On the new kind of reader: Norman Howard Sims, 15.
24. The Spencer case: James Harland Ball, *A Study of Typical Crusades Undertaken by Chicago Newspapers, 1833 to 1930*.

25. Mackin's conviction: the *Daily News's* role is briefly mentioned in Henry Justin Smith, and his background and prison term are in Wendt and Kogan, *Lords of the Levee*, 19 (including the footnote). Details of the *Daily News* in the early years came from Fred A. Chappell, *The Daily News Building Yesterday and Today*, 3–4.

26. Cramped conditions at the *Herald*, Steger at the typewriter, and Fred Rae: *Chicago Tribune* May 31, 1943, an obituary of reporter John Kelley. Buck McCarthy anecdote: Slason Thompson, *Way Back When*, 253–4.

27. Why the *Herald* folded: Charles Dennis, *Victor Lawson*, 75–76. Scott information: *Chicago Tribune* April 15, 1895, an obituary of James W. Scott. Information about Reilly: Dennis, *Victor Lawson*, 88; McPhaul, 98. Reilly resigned in 1891 to serve as secretary of the Illinois State Board of Health. The *Daily News* staff working seven days a week, and the besotted Col. Reed: Dennis, *Victor Lawson*, 79.

28. The Vanderbilt story, including quotations: Dennis, *Victor Lawson*, 79–80. A briefer account says the astute editor was Charles Ham. The Stone version is from his autobiography, 116–118, and is discussed in John Steele Gordon, "The Public Be Damned!," 18–20. Gordon offers a version by Vanderbilt's favorite nephew, Samuel Barton, which essentially confirms the quotation given by Dennis.

29. Helen de Freitas.

30. Andrews, 70.

31. Invention of the linotype and the company formed to produce them: Olson, 98–99. Stone erroneously says the second shipment went to his paper. Dennis's quote: Dennis, *Victor Lawson*, 177. White impressed by the line drawings in the New York paper: Dennis, 87.

32. The Dr. Cronin murder: Barbara C. Schaaf, 13–16; Richard C. Lindberg, *To Serve and Collect* (which goes into detail about the case), 81–84. The newspaper article about the alleged embezzling: *Chicago Tribune*, June 2, 1889.

33. Norman Howard Sims, 9.

34. About Eugene Field's work habits: Slason Thompson, *Eugene Field*, 193, 218- 219; Charles H. Dennis, *Eugene Field's Creative Years*, 189. Details, including Gladstone: Geoffrey Johnson, "Mr. Fields Rehabs His Dream House." Field seeking a raise: McPhaul, 87. Prison uniform story: Elmer Ellis, *Mr. Dooley's America*.

35. That the *Times* and *Daily News* carried advance stories about dynamite and bombs: Carl S. Smith, "Cataclysm and Cultural Consciousness: Chicago and the Haymarket Trial"; Lindberg, *To Serve and Collect*, 65. The *Daily News* quotation about socialism: Barry C. Nel-

son, "Anarchism: The Movement Behind the Martyrs," 4. That reporter Hull was nearly shot: Dennis, *Victor Lawson*, 94.

36. Melville Stone writes out the coroner's jury verdict: Stone, *Fifty Years a Journalist*, 171–172. Stone's golden parachute: (ibid., 179); McPhaul, 82. Stone's explanation sounds hollow. The crying out of newsboys: adapted from *Chicago* (Summer 1986). Chapin speaking in headlines: Churchill, 250.

37. Bross disinheriting Jessie: Carolyn Ashbaugh, "Radical Women: the Haymarket Tradition," part of the Lucy Parsons Project on the Internet, under "Jessie Bross." This is somewhat verified by an article giving Lloyd's estate at $250,000, although Bross was at least a millionaire from his real estate speculation.

38. The Palmer House bulletin board message: Pierce, 287. That the *Daily News* sold 482,843 copies, the most ever: Royal J. Schmidt, "The Chicago Daily News and Illinois Politics," 155.

39. That an unnamed Chicago newsman popularized the term "ragtime": John Shepherd, *Tin Pan Alley*, 26, 31. Since the book was written by a Canadian and printed in Great Britain, there is no local bias. A new style of sports writing: Elmer Ellis, 27. Calling in someone from the sports department: Jerome Holtman, "In Grange's Golden Age of Sports...," *Chicago Tribune*, February 3, 1991, sports section.

40. Yerkes' background: Emmett Dedmon, 259–260. Yerkes' conversation with a Dunlap reporter: Andrews, 36.

41. About Bell and Yerkes and Debs' quote: James D. Startt, 19, 11. Tanner and the traction bill: Ginger, 179.

42. John Wilkie and the "Indian rope trick": Peter Lamont, 77–88.

43. Theodore Dreiser, *Newspaper Days*, 46–47.

44. About McDonald: "The Unlucky Love Life of King Mike McDonald," Wayne Klatt, *Chicago Reader*, Sept. 23, 1983. The raids: McPhaul, 90. (Dreiser in his autobiography misidentifies McDonald as John.)

45. John Burke, *Duet in Diamonds*, 44, 60.

46. For bannerlines, see Churchill, 83. Early telephone subscribers, from an Illinois Bell Telephone Company reproduction of its 1878 directory. That there was a single telephone in the *Tribune*: Edward S. Beck, *Recollections of the Early Days at the Tribune*, 21.

47. The United Presses of Illinois, etc.: Dennis, *Victor Lawson*, 186–7; Joe Alex Morris, *Deadline Every Minute*, 18. The anecdote about UP stealing from the AP: McPhaul, 82. A good but biased account of Walsh's switching from the UP to the AP is in the *New York Times*, July

4, 1894, and is available on the Internet under "John R. Walsh."

48. Ferdinand Lundberg, *Imperial Hearst*, 152.

49. Margaret Sullivan and women in the city room: Ishbel Ross, *Ladies of the Press*, 20, 550, 554. Edna Wooley's almost being fired: Ross, 554. Schaack closing down the *Times* and West being convicted: Lundberg, 97–98. A somewhat inaccurate account is in William Adelman, *Haymarket Revisited*, 56.

50. Henry Justin Smith, 17.

51. Theodore Dreiser, *Newspaper Days*, 38–39.

52. John France, "The Opposite Side of the Barricade," *Chicago History* (Summer 1995): 46.

53. Chapin chases down McGarigle: John Kelley autobiography in the Harpeal scrapbook, February 1926. A shorter version is in Michael Miner, "A Bare-Knuckle Journalist Who Ended Up in Sing-Sing," *Chicago Reader*, February 20, 2004. The shootout at the Round Bar and Kelley's exploits: *Tribune*, April 6, 1927.

54. John Kelley autobiographical writing, May 1926, 8.

55. James Weber Linn, 15–30.

56. The Johnson County War coverage: Linn, 46–51; Peter Clark MacFarlane, "Explaining Keeley," *Colliers* magazine reprint. The *Herald* reporter is from Paul Trachtman, *The Gunfighters*, 210.

57. Keeley's vow, which sounds as if he were claiming a distinction the origin of which is lost to us: Linn, 64. What "putting the paper to bed" meant at this time: Lloyd Wendt, *Chicago Tribune, the Rise of a Great American Newspaper*, 279.

58. Baker's career: John Semduch, *Ray Stannard Baker*; David Grayson, *Ray Stannard Baker, an American Chronicle*. His work hours are from Grayson. Casey's account of *Inter-Ocean* drunks and fabricating stories: Robert J. Casey, *Such Interesting People*, 52–57. Kohlsaat's buying up the *Record*: Henry Justin Smith, 18. On Fred Hall and Charles Chapin: Churchill, 262.

59. The fighting between Scott and Walsh: Dennis, *Victor Lawson*, 300–302. "No quarter": *Tribune*, April 6, 1927. Information about Scott's death is from John Kelley in the Harpeal scrapbook.

60. James Harland Ball, *A Study of Topical Crusades Undertaken by Chicago Newspapers*, 67.

61. Faye's advising an open shop: Schmidt, 159–160. Three days without news: "The Chicago Journal as It Was," *Chicago Journal*, April 22, 1904.

62. Matthew Pinkerton, "The Luertgert Case," in *The Chicago Crime Book*, 203; also Richard Digby-Junger, *Journal of Illinois History* (2004), a review of *Alchemy of Bones* by Robert Loerzel; Digby-Junger in the Associated Press, Oct. 2, 2003.

63. Linn, 18. See also Richard Smith, 130–132.

64. Robert J. Casey, *Such Interesting People*, 59, referring to a somewhat later time.

65. The *Tribune*'s idea of a "gentlemanly reporter," Dedmon, 126.

66. Details of the Whitechapel Club: AP story on June 6, 2002; anonymous account in *Behind the News* (1963): 56–57; Sims, 221–222; and Digby-Junger, "The main rendezvous for men of the press," 81–85.

67. John Tebbel, 76.

68. Frank Luther Mott, 561; Richard Smith, 65.

69. Circulation information in 1899: Andrews, 200.

70. The fire department's yearly reports are in the Chicago History Museum library. Developments in Kiolbasa's career and the succession of fires come from daily newspapers over this period.

71. An alternate version of Howey and the Iroquois Theater fire is in Doug Fetherling, *The Five Lives of Ben Hecht*, 74. The *Tribune* obituary of Howey on March 21, 1954, gives a somewhat different version and omits City Press. Howey's account is in A.A.Dornfeld, *Behind the Front Page*, 80–81. Harrison's attributing the blaze to fate: Anthony P. Hatch, "Inferno at the Iroquois," *Chicago History* (Fall 2003).

72. The *Tribune*'s coverage of the fire: Wendt, *Chicago Tribune*, 355.

Chapter Three

1. Ben Hecht chapter quote, from his novel *Eric Dorn*, 17.

2. The reason Hearst set up the *American*, and the quote about novelty and facts: Roy Hoopes, "The Forty-Year Run," *American Heritage* (November 1992); Christopher Ogden, *Legacy*, 43. Cavalho's "we'll have to shoot our way in": Ogden, 44. Hearst's clothes in 1902: Churchill, 162–3. The other papers threatening to stop accepting ads: George Murray, 65.

3. This author saw "new miracle" twice at City News and read about another instance at a newspaper. Other examples are from Myron Weigle in *Behind the News* (1964): 20. Doherty's list of bloopers is in *Crime Reporter*, 168–169. Baumann's story of James

Murray is from a letter to this author dated April 3, 1989.

4. Ferdinand Lundberg, *Imperial Hearst*, 139–141.

5. Information on the *American*: Andrews, 232–5. Chamberlain saying, "Get excited": George Murray, 58–9. Hearst's paid tipsters: (ibid., 39).

6. Robert A. Carter, *Buffalo Bill Cody: The Man Behind the Legend*, 393. (An erroneous account elsewhere claimed that Pratt had met a prostitute who claimed she was Annie Oakley, and he believed her.)

7. Pratt and Lait absconding with photographs from a deputy coroner: George Murray, 19–20. The Lait election fraud case: (ibid., 99–101). The mocking cartoon is from Francis X. Busch, *In and Out of Court*, 79–80. George Murray says an editorial caused the outrage.

8. June Sawyers, "The Way We Were," *Chicago Tribune Sunday Magazine*, March 22, 1987.

9. Berns sleeping among the rolls of paper: "Press Vet" (Summer-Fall 2002). Hearst shoving the form off the table: George Murray, 88. Max Annenberg and the *Morning American*: (ibid., 41–3).

10. Tuttle inventing the world's busiest corner: Harpeal scrapbook, Chicago History Museum.

11. Larzer Ziff, *The American 1890s*, 152. "A stinking, treacherous game": Dreiser, *A Book About Myself*, 59.

12. Car Barn Bandits story: George Murray, 19–24.

13. The *Lancet* series on the stockyards area: Andrews, 343. The issues were on January 7, 14, 21 and 28, 1905.

14. Max Annenberg and the Marshall Field's demonstration: John Cooney, 32.

15. Moe Annenberg's threat to circulation manager: Ogden, *Legacy*, 56.

16. Robert Abbott information: William Best, "The Chicago *Defender* and the Realignment of Black Chicago," Chicago History (Fall 1995), 6–7; "A Love for Children," Chicago *Defender*, August 11, 2001.

17. Jack London's hasty marriage: Richard O'Connor, *Jack London*, 239.

18. Keeley at the bank meeting: Wendt, *Chicago Tribune, the Rise of a Great American Newspaper*, 355, with some details from Linn, 75–9.

19. Charlie Johnson and the Black Hand: Washburn, 58–9.

20. Koeningsberg catching Hoch and the delay in the red signal: George Murray, 8–14. Details of the execution are from Ed Baumann, *May God Have Mercy on Your Soul*, 130–33.

21. Howey and the McKinley scoop: George

Murray, 108. Howey writing stories in advance: Burton Rascoe, *Before I Forget*, 237. This author saw the late John Noonan do this at City News.

22. Howey at the Everleigh Club: Washburn, *Come into My Parlor*, 46. Charlie Johnson and the millionaire: same, 59. An editor calling Calumet 412: McPhaul, 257.

23. Kelley explaining how reporters got to look at the "squeal book": Harpeal notebooks, p. 9, under "Kelley." The Armory Station and the reporters who worked there: Lindberg, 115–16.

24. Richard Smith, 137.

25. George Murray, 63–4. For an example of the gas company falling in line, see Lundberg, 144.

26. The decline of Joseph Medill McCormick, Shaffer's offer, the quotation from Nellie Patterson, and the assessment of Kate McCormick as "coldly manipulative": Richard Smith, 126–9.

27. Keeley addressing reporters in the third person and rejecting all of Patterson's ideas, Burton Rascoe, 240–2.

28. The Little Red Book and the breach between Joseph Medill and Robert McCormick: James Weber Linn, 141; Richard Smith, 125–7.

29. The *Tribune* wooing Howey and Annenberg: George Murray, 50–1.

30. Andrews, 236–8.

31. George Murray, 50–51.

32. Moe Annenberg threatening the circulation manager: Ogden, 30. The fatal shooting of a man named Clark: same, 51. The circulation wars reaching the gunfire stage, McWeeney's helplessness, and falsifying facts: Lundberg, 153–4; George Murray, 51–2. Battle involving sixty men, and that Altman was killed in the hotel, Andrews, 234.

33. Edward Doherty, *With Gall and Honey*, 50–67.

34. Mark Twain obituary: Edward Doherty, 44.

35. Doherty and the stockyards fire: Edward Doherty, 33. (Writing from memory, he mistakenly gave the number of deaths as twenty-six instead of twenty-three.)

36. The *Tribune* declaring itself "the World's Greatest Newspaper": Wendt, *The Chicago Tribune*, 361.

37. That no one was arrested for the major crimes: Annenberg testimony, Andrews, 234. Briggs House as a newspaper haunt: Cooney, 36.

38. Assassination attempt on Teddy Roosevelt: Henry F. Pringle, *Theodore Roosevelt*, 398–9. X-ray story: Robert J. Casey, *Bob Casey's Grand Slam*, 121–3.

39. Waldrop's "aqueous assault": Kelley, Harpeal notebooks, June 1925, 8.

40. John J. McPhaul, 240.

41. Keeley's testimony about an unreported murder attempt in the *Tribune*'s old building and the "gangs of murderers": Andrews, 236–8.

42. Rascoe, 241–2, 255.

43. Richard Smith, 148, 151.

44. Burke, 214–15.

45. Strike against Hearst: Dennis, *Victor Lawson*, 402–4; Lundberg,167–8.

46. The proxies: Rascoe, 242–3. Patterson going to the *Record-Herald*: Richard Smith, 148–9.

47. Keeley going over to the *Record-Herald*: Linn, 184, but the biography sheds little light. A fuller account of a complex series of events is in the *New York Times*, May 8, 1914.

48. Patterson's editorial about putting the infirm to death: Rascoe, 255.

49. Pegler information is largely from Russ Lane, *Behind the News* (1961): 32.

50. Snippets from Doherty's career are from Edward Doherty, 50–67.

51. "And adventure dies": Edward Doherty, 50.

52. Wallace Smith eavesdropping on deliberations and Smith's advice on writing: Edward Doherty, 115, 114.

53. The Christmas Ship: Lilian Bell, *The Story of the Christmas Ship*, with details from the *New York Times* Oct. 19 and Nov. 10, 1914, and July 20, 1929. For the voyage, see the *London Times*, Nov. 26, 1914, and Dec. 2, 21, 26, and 31, 1914.

54. Information on Gibbons: Louis L. Snyder and Richard B. Morris, *A Treasury of Great Reporting*, 338–9; and Rudolph Unger, *The Chicago Tribune News Staff 1920s-1960s*. Gibbons' desire to be on a ship likely to be torpedoed: Phillip Knightley, *The First Casualty*, 124. Information on the Paris Edition: here-and-there details from Waverly Root, *The Paris Edition*. Gibbons' work for NBC: Edward Bliss Jr., *Now the News*, 27.

55. Details of how the Versailles treaty was smuggled out comes from Seldes' letter to the editor in *Time Magazine*, January 19, 1968.

56. That Gibbons could deliver two hundred and seventeen words a minute: John Dunning, *On the Air, The Encyclopedia of Old-Time Radio*, 380. Gibbons in Spain: Bliss, 75.

57. Walter Trohan, *Political Animals*, 24.

58. Richard Smith, 263.

59. Reutlinger and Mother Cabrini: George Murray, 290; McPhaul, 121. Background on Mother Cabrini: Pietro Di Donato, *Immigrant Saint*. Background on Reutlinger is from George Murray, *Behind the News* (1981). News commentator John Madigan, who knew Reutlinger, said he was Jewish.

60. Robert J. Casey, *Such Interesting People*, 78.

61. Yellow Kid Weil: *Prohibition Era Times* (August/September 1995). His autobiography does not mention his newspaper days, but it was long part of City News lore.

62. Mencken quote: John Chancellor, *The Chicago Experience*.

63. Brisbane quote on "yellow journalism": Francis Hackett, 177. Information about Marquis and Bessie James: Wendt, *Chicago Tribune*, 450; Ross, 593. Hackett's Chicago experience comes from his autobiography, *American Rainbow*, 171–7.

64. Ben Hecht, *A Child of the Century*, 238–9.

65. McPhaul, 252–3.

66. Doherty, *With Gall and Honey*, 65.

67. Background on the *Eastland* disaster may be found in George W. Hilton, *Eastland: Legacy of the Titanic* (Stanford, CA: Stanford University Press, 1995). Other sources include Doherty, *With Gall and Honey*, 97; Lowell Thomas, *Good Evening Everybody*, 66–7; George Murray, 114–16; Ishbel Ross, *Ladies of the Press*; *Chicago Daily News*, July 24, 1915; *Chicago Daily Journal*, June 7, 1921; *Chicago American*, Aug. 12, Aug. 17, Aug. 24, 1915; and *Chicago Tribune*, Aug. 24, 1915.

68. Lowell Thomas, 67–8.

69. George Murray, 260.

70. Details about Howey are from George Murray, 170–8. In *Chicago Tribune, the Rise of a Great American Newspaper*, Lloyd Wendt says the break came when Patterson barked at Howey about writing a puff piece for filmmaker D.W. Griffith (p. 462). This does not seem like Howey, and could be one of the inaccuracies in the official *Tribune* history. Howey tricks Patterson with an actress: Rascoe, 246.

71. "Profane romanticist": *Time* magazine, June 17, 1935. A description of Howey is in Ben Hecht, *Charlie*, 49–50.

72. Howey being empty inside: George Murray, 170–8; "Good for a column," Doherty, *With Gall and Honey*, 65, 84.

73. George Murray, 180–5.

74. Romanoff and the flood pictures: *The Late Edition* (Spring 2002). Westbrook Pegler's description of him: *The Late Edition* (September-October 1990).

75. The 1919 race riot: William M. Tuttle Jr., *Race Riot*; Carl Sandburg, *The Chicago Race Riots*. Sullivan quotation: Lundberg, 163.

76. Carson and the tornado relief photo: McPhaul, *Inside Page One*, n.d.

77. Anonymous, "Thank You for Smoking," *The History Channel Magazine* (May/June 2008): 36.

78. Early newscasts in Detroit, Newark, and New York: Jim Cox, "Storytelling in a Box: the Evolution of Radio News," *Nostalgia Digest* (Winter 2008).

79. Richard Smith, 237.

80. Dwight Green and the portrait: Casey and Douglas, *The Midwesterner*, 73–7.

81. The Dempsey-Carpentier story: McPhaul, 142. McPhaul admitted he heard the story second hand. Details of the fight: Clifton Daniel, ed., *Chronicle of the 20th Century*.

82. Edward Doherty, 44–6. Since this was only an approximation of a conversation, if indeed it occurred at all, I moved Jack Lawson's remark a little higher. Doherty had placed it last.

Chapter Four

1. Duffy's remark is in several places, including William MacAdams, *Ben Hecht, The Man Behind the Legend*, 17, and the front page of the Tempo section of the *Chicago Tribune*, March 25, 1980.

2. Hanlon and the murder-suicide: Robert J. Casey, *Such Interesting People*, 104–6. (Ben Hecht changed the story around and used it in his autobiographical novel *Gaily, Gaily*.)

3. The Gera-Lind Kolarik quote is from an address she gave for the City News Bureau centennial dinner on October 6, 1990.

4. The detective bureau press room: George Woltman, *Behind the News* (1958): 58.

5. Typical scene at the *Daily News* in 1918–1920: Henry Justin Smith, *Journalism Day to Day*, 13–14. Why Lawson paid on Tuesdays: Dennis, *Victor Lawson*, 175.

6. Casey, *Bob Casey's Grand Slam*, 22

7. Allen Churchill, 86.

8. Mildred Frisby Doherty and the dirigible tragedy: McPhaul, 131. (Apparently working from memory, he said ten were killed.) Details of the crash are from Richard Lindberg, *Return to the Scene of the Crime*, 36–47.

9. George Murray, 178.

10. Romanoff uses a doll to get Fitzgerald's confession: Baumann, *May God Have Mercy on Your Soul*, 167–8. Romanoff on the phone: *Behind the News* (1984).

11. The 1919 White Sox scandal: Leo Katcher, *The Big Bankroll*, 139–150; Robert I. Goler, "Black Sox," 42–69. The telegrams between Casey and Eastman: Casey, *Such Interesting People*, 87–8. Reutlinger getting a confession from Felsch: Rascoe, 256.

12. That Fullerton apparently fabricated "Say it isn't so": Paul Halloway, *Chicago Tribune* Tempo section, October 20, 1988, 1–2.

Hathaway and the Landis order: William T. Moore, *Dateline Chicago*, 144.

13. *Chicago Tribune*, December 1952, in the Harpeal scrapbook.

14. The Carl Wanderer case: mainly from Snyder and Morris, 374–7, and some from George Murray, 232–41.

15. Martin, *Cissy*, 180–4, 133.

16. Carson fakes a collision to obtain Ruth Randall's diary: George Murray, 189–91.

17. Carson's use of phony badges and documents: George Murray, 210; McPhaul, 16.

18. Harvey Church and the Packard: George Murray, 194–201; Baumann, *May God Have Mercy on Your Soul*, 212–16.

19. Almy's speech at the feast: Kelley, Harpeal scrapbook, p. 8.

20. Luce's work for Hecht: W.A. Swanberg, *Luce and His Empire*, 48–9.

21. The *Tribune* and the KKK, see Gini Graham Scott, *Homicide: 100 Years of Murder in America*, 82–3, and *Tribune* articles over the period. The *Tribune* carrying a full-page ad and calling the KKK a "romantic" response: Tebbel, 150–151.The Bell series was reprinted in book form as *Creed of the Klansmen* in 1924. The second *Tribune* editorial quoted appeared on June 8, 1927. It should be noted that the northern Klan did not make racial remarks in the recruitment period in Chicago, where African-American votes were needed for the local Republican Party. Stephenson was released from prison in 1956.

22. Maurine Watkins and the origin of the play *Chicago*: *Chicago Sun-Times*, December 27, 2002; *Chicago Reader*, July 22, 2005; *Chicago Tribune*, April 7, 1986.

23. The typewriter scoop in the Loeb and Leopold case: Karen Rothmyer, *Winning Pulitzers*, 27–8.

24. George Wright using the false ceiling for the Loeb-Leopold grand jury hearing: his obituary in the *Chicago Tribune*, May 29, 1960. A brief account is in *Chicago* magazine, June 1972. That the ceilings varied from fourteen to nineteen feet: Harry Golden Jr., *Chicago Sun-Times*, June 6, 1984, an article about the former courthouse.

25. George Murray, in pages 340–342, said the judge had tipped off Carson but, like Paul Higdon in *Crime of the Century*, this author does not believe it.

26. Joseph Medill McCormick's suicide: Richard Smith, 240–51.

27. The card game description and quotation are from the published play, 1940 edition. The extensively revamped courthouse building is now used for commercial offices.

28. Most of Ben Hecht's background is from: Doug Fetherling, *The Five Lives of Ben*

Hecht; William MacAdams, *Ben Hecht: The Man Behind the Legend*; and Ben Hecht, *Child of the Century*, 73. Hecht's bouts of depression: MacAdams, 33.

29. Most of MacArthur's background is from William Hoffman, *The Stockbroker*, a biography of John D. MacArthur, 35–6, and Gene Fowler, *Skyline*, an autobiography, 36–7. Some of their details may not be accurate, because their subject was a fabricator.

30. Hayes' comment about her husband's falsification of his life: Helen Hayes, *On Reflection: An Autobiography*, 75.

31. Ben Hecht: *Charlie*, 103; Kenneth Barrow, *Helen Hayes*, 82–3; and Hayes, *My Life in Three Acts*, 48.

32. Hayes' remark about the influence of Chicago on Hecht and her husband is from a talk she gave at the Newberry Library in Chicago in October 1980.

33. William T. Moore, 59–60.

34. Robert J. Casey, *More Interesting People*, 113–14; George Murray, 296–7.

35. The McSwiggin case: George Murray, 297; Curt Johnson, *The Wicked City*, 206–9; and Wendt, *Chicago Tribune*, 509–10. Johnson being beaten in court by a state's attorney official: George Murray, 297. Johnson stayed on the criminal court beat until his death in March 1931.

36. Casey on Sherman Duffy: Casey, *Such Interesting People*, 98–9.

37. Hayes' account of how MacArthur proposed: Barrow, 96–7. Hayes gave less detailed versions in *My Life in Three Acts*, 56–7, and in her Newberry Library talk.

38. Big Tim Murphy tips off Peggy Doyle: Ross, 490. First known use of a Tommy gun in a gang shooting: Robert J. Schoenberg, *Mr. Capone*, 141, and *Prohibition Era Times* (October/November 1995). Vern Whaley calling news people "freeloaders": *Chicago Journalist* (June 1991). Details of McEarlane: *Prohibition Era Times* (October/November 1993). Capone apparently crushing a delivery drivers' strike: Schoenberg, 303.

39. For the beating of Robert St. John and abduction of his brother, see John Kobler, *Capone: The Life and World of Al Capone*, 141–3. Robert St. John's obituary on February 6, 2003, said he had been "left for dead," but this seems an overstatement considering the medical profession at the time and his recovery in a few days.

40. WGN covering the Scopes Money Trial: Bliss, 19–20.

41. McCormick lying about the circulation wars: Rick Kogan, "How We Got the News," *Chicago Tribune*, June 8, 1997.

42. Capone averting a newsboys' strike:

McPhaul, 265–6; Wendt, *Chicago Tribune*, 512. About his also allegedly averting a drivers strike: Richard Smith, 273–4.

43. Murphy and the accident reports: Walter Trohan interview in the *Chicago Reader*, February 13, 2004. (In the interview and his book, Trohan misspells Paster's name as "Pastor.")

44. Cagney drops in at the *Tribune: Cagney by Cagney*, 31. That Bright's partner burned down his shop so they could go to Hollywood: Charles Higham, *Warner Brothers*, 93.

45. Dornfeld and the sinking of *The Favorite: Behind the News* (1979), at the Chicago History Museum; A.A. Dornfeld, *Behind the Front Page*, 130–2. A more accurate account is in William Lafferty, "Excursion on the Lakefront," *Chicago History*, (Fall and Winter, 1991–1992). This author heard Dornfeld say a few things about the day, such as his use of a megaphone.

46. Dornfeld, 238; several other sources.

47. Walter Trohan, 147.

48. Mose Lamson tracking down the rapist: Rudolph M. Unger, 46–7.

49. WGN installing a police radio system: anonymous, "First Hundred Years," 15, and a feature in the Tempo section of the *Chicago Tribune*, November 8, 1993, which said the police calls were not aired until March 1929.

50. Spirko's scoop on the St. Valentine's Day massacre: "Press Vet" (Fall 1991); *Tribune* obituary, November 27, 1995; Dornfeld, 139; this author's interview with him on June 27, 1988. That "Gersh" sent Trohan to the scene by streetcar is from Trohan, 25. The line "It runs every five minutes": Trohan's obituary in the *Tribune*. That Gershman dictated the story is from the Trohan interview in the *Chicago Reader*, February 13, 2004. Murphy posing as a deputy coroner and stealing notes: Dornfeld, *Behind the News* (1981). Vern Whaley claiming he kidnapped rival photographers: "Press Vet" (Fall 2000).

51. Chamberlain and Lyle going after Capone: Judge John H. Lyle, *The Dry and Lawless Years*, 237–44.

52. Wendt, *Chicago Tribune*, 537.

53. Green's life is traced in Casey and Douglas, *The Midwesterner*, 69. His downfall comes from the obituary of reporter Carl Baldwin, *Chicago Sun-Times*, December 14, 1994.

54. Knox acquiring the *Daily News*: Harold Ickes, *The Secret Diary of Harold Ickes*, Vol. III, 88. The suspicious relationship between Knox and Allard: Trohan, 49–50. More on Allard: Ross, 548.

55. Thomason information: Alfred Augustus Crowell, "History of the Chicago Daily Times," i–36; *Time* magazine, March 23, 1932.

56. Hecht and MacArthur lamenting the passing of the freewheeling reporter: the printed edition of *The Front Page*, 31.

57. Drop in murders: Albert Halper, ed., *The Chicago Crime Book*, 97.

Chapter Five

1. chapter quote, McPhaul, *Deadlines and Monkeyshines*, 115.

2. Lloyd Lewis, *Inside Page One* (1945): 45.

3. *Chicago Sun-Times*, April 1, 1979.

4. *Chicago Sun-Times*, April 1, 1979.

5. The Lingle case: mostly from Albert Halper, ed., 97–110. That Boettiger found fourteen hundred dollars and that the official story of his inheritance was increased: McPhaul, 265. (He mistakenly said the inheritance was from Lingle's father.) On the meeting of McCormick and Wilson, see Richard Smith, 291. (Previous accounts had claimed that McCormick never heard of Lingle.) Details of the shooting: "Who Killed Corrupt Newsman?," *Chicago Sun-Times*, April 15, 2001; June Sawyers, "Way We Were" feature, *Chicago Tribune Sunday Magazine*, June 10, 1988; and Frank Pasley, *Al Capone*, 37, 267. That Thomason looked into the Clearing House Association records: Richard Smith, 293.

6. Wayne Andrews, 146–7.

7. McCormick's meeting with Thomason over the Sunday edition, and the newsstand compromise: *Time* magazine, March 28, 1932.

8. Reutlinger and the Lindbergh baby: George Murray, *Behind the News* (1971).

9. *Sun-Times*, November 6, 1985, obituary of Gus Talbott.

10. For a description of "Reutlinger rats" and hiring the city's first radio street reporter, see Len O'Connor, *A Reporter in Sweet Chicago*, 225–36.

11. *The Late Edition* (January-February 1990): 5.

12. For these and other Buddy McHugh stories, see *Behind the News* (1953, 1955, 1970 and 1974).

13. Avery anecdotes: George Murray, 303, 366; Moore, 31–2, 91. (Moore gives an apparently less accurate account and says the loss was an even one hundred dollars.)

14. Cermak's remark after being shot: George Murray: 374–5.

15. William E. Doherty, *Behind the News* (1958).

16. The Wynekoop case: Walter Spirko, *Behind the News* (1955); Halper, 242; and Moore, who does not name the family, 53.

17. Frank Devine's secret drinking: George Murray, *Behind the News* (1975).

18. Victor Watson anecdotes: Churchill, 164; Moore, 15, 38–40.

19. Harold Cross's fictions: Moore, 57.

20. John Madigan, "Half a Century of Words...," in *The Chicago Experience*, 63.

21. City News covering a triple execution: Walter Spirko, *Behind the News* (April 1984).

22. Ray Brennan learning of Dillinger's escape: Bill Doherty, *Crime Reporter*, 18

23. Details of Dillinger's escape and killing: John Toland, *Dillinger Days*, 201–6, 303–9. Foust at the scene: Bill Doherty.

24. Ross Lane, *Behind the News* (1984): 16.

25. Norman Ross Sr.'s broadcasting the news: Bob Herguth, *Chicago Sun-Times*, July 22, 1984.

26. Murray suspects a Nazi plot: George Murray, *Behind the News* (1967).

27. The *Tribune* courting Nazism: Andrews, 286.

28. The City News party: *Behind the News* (May 1964): 34. This writer has heard that reporters used binoculars at the Clark Street location, and the same switchboard caught fire a couple of times when it was at 188 West Randolph, so the story is plausible.

29. Joe Fay and the Jack McGurn scoop: George Murray, *Behind the News* (1972): 13.

30. Woltman and the barge sinking: George Woltman, *Behind the News* (1958): 28.

31. Woltman and Wagner posing as policemen to get a burglary story: Woltman, *Behind the News* (1962) 16.

32. Morgenstern giving the mayor a statement: George Murray, 304.

33. Edward Doherty leaves the *American*: George Murray, 71. He said Edward's description of a Mexican town, "Half a dozen 'dobe huts and half a hundred hounds," had been changed to "Six clay huts and fifty dogs."

34. Murray and the woman on the balcony: George Murray, *Behind the News* (1968–1969).

35. The creation of Iggy Yelswo: John Danovich, *Behind the News* (1955): 34. He said the gag lasted two years.

36. About Louis Ruppel: *Chicago Tribune*, January 25, 1958, obituary of Louis Ruppel; Bill Doherty, *Crime Reporter*, 47–8; George Murray, *Behind the News* (1978): 56; Alfred Augustus Crowell, 44–5, 131–3. Ruppel left the *Times* in December 1939 for a public relations job at CBS radio but worked as the *Herald-American* executive editor in 1944–1945.

37. The early careers of Bill and Martin Doherty, see Bill Doherty, *Crime Reporter*, 18–33, 84.

38. The newspaper guild: *Chicago Tribune*,

October 31, 1988, Smyth obituary; George Murray, 388–9; W.A. Swanberg, 560.

39. "Greatest mind of the fourteenth century," quoted by Mary Watters, "Illinois in WWII," *Illinois State Historical Society* 29.

40. Virginia Gardner and Mother Cabrini: George Murray, 293–6. Gardner's background: Ross, 544–5.

41. The short life of Dick Dolan is from Russ Lane, *Behind the News* (1984): 15–16.

42. Chris Chandler, "The Whole World is Listening," *American History* (August 2007): 53.

43. Anne Edwards, *Early Reagan: The Rise to Power*, 136–7; *Time* magazine, Sept. 29, 2003.

44. Morrison and the *Hindenburg*, and the Nazis trying to impound his recording: Herbert Morrison obituaries in the *Chicago Tribune* and *Sun-Times*, both on January 11, 1989; Edward Bliss Jr., 36. That Morrison and his sound man hid for a few hours is from the WLS Radio Web site. After the war, Morrison worked in Pennsylvania.

45. *Time* article on Mabley is from 1965 and is in the City News centennial booklet, 66.

46. "Press Vet" (Summer 2004): 7.

47. Casey at the two papers and in England: George Murray, 327–332.

48. For details of Roosevelt's possible help starting the *Sun,* see Richard Smith, 410.

49. Manly obtains FDR's secret war plans: Thomas Fleming, "The Big Leak," *American Heritage* (December 1987).

50. Department heads rushing to the papers after the Pearl Harbor attack: Harpeal scrapbook, *Tribune*, December 1941.

51. War updates: Todd Nebel, "Pearl Harbor Week on the Radio," *Nostalgia Digest* (December/ January, 1999–2000).

52. The *Tribune* keeping the *Sun* from getting an AP franchise: Andrews, 306; McPhaul, *Deadlines and Monkeyshines,* 295.

53. McCormick in the lunchroom: *Tribune,* Nov. 17, 2007, obituary of pressman Edward Earl Pertl.

54. Ed Lahey's lead for Loeb's death: *Daily News,* December 23, 1975, 5. The other possible motive for the killing is from Thomas O'-Gorman and Lisa Montanarelli, *Strange But True Chicago,* 94.

Chapter Six

1. Ben Hecht, *Child of the Century*, 308.

2. Wayne Andrews, 296.

3. John J. McPhaul, *Deadlines and Monkeyshines*, footnote, 294.

4. Field's work day: Andrews, 306. Firing Evans and taking over: "Battle in Printer's Ink," *Colliers* magazine, June 30, 1945.

5. For more about the *Tribune* rocks, see *Chicago Tribune*, July 20, 1999.

6. Two-ton rolls of paper and Montalbano hanging his lunch on a rope: "Inside Chicago Today," (May 28, 2001): 6. The four press lines: *Chicago Tribune,* December 9, 2004, obituary of Fred Pawlikowski, press engineer.

7. Edward Doherty returning to Chicago and James Doherty giving a gambling ledger to the state's attorney's office: Unger, *The Chicago Tribune News Staff*, 19.

8. *Sun-Times*, March 1, 2002, obituary of Angelo Duarte.

9. Pat Leeds information: *Behind the News* (1959), her City News obituary on January 23, 1985, and *Tribune* obituary, January 24, 1985.

10. Virginia Marmaduke anecdotes: *Sun-Times*, August 22, 1986; *Sun-Times*, November 11, 2001, obituary of Virginia Marmaduke; the Illinois Press Association publication, November 30, 2001.

11. Kurt Vonnegut on women in the news field appears in an excerpt from *Slaughterhouse Five* in the City News centennial booklet, 62.

12. The copy girl anecdote is from Russ Lane, *Behind the News* (1954).

13. About women being warned that anything happening to them would not be the paper's liability: this author believes the precaution was general, but it is given in the case of Virginia Gardner in McPhaul, *Deadlines and Monkeyshines*, 120.

14. Dornfeld's story of the "crucifixion": *Behind the News* (1975). The event was also covered by John R. Thompson and Buddy McHugh. The two other self-crucifixions this author knows about came just before Easter, so perhaps this one did, too.

15. "...from profanity to perfumery": *Time Magazine*, April 18, 1945. Lois Thrasher working as a chambermaid: same. That she was believed to have been the first female editor: Jack Hemstock, *Behind the News* (1971).

16. Anecdotes about Clem Lane: his obituaries in the *Daily News* and *Tribune*, both on October 28, 1958.

17. Vern Whaley defies Ruppel: "Battle in Printer's Ink," *Collier's* magazine, June 30, 1945.

18. The *Daily News* war correspondents: Snyder and Morris, 520, 578, 614. Thompson's parachuting is in his obituary, City News Bureau, December 15, 1995.

19. *Sun-Times*, December 22, 2002, obituary of George Weller. The emergency operation in a submerged submarine was used in the fictional film *Operation Tokyo*.

20. *Daily News*, October 15, 1988.

21. The Art Petacque story is from his obituary, *Sun-Times*, June 7, 2001.

22. Gladys Erickson story: Bill Doherty, *Crime Reporter*, 70–2. (McPhaul, apparently getting the story second-hand, erroneously said she was working for the *Times*, and that the baby was accidentally left by a woman.)

23. The *Call Northside 777* case: the main source is McPhaul's *Deadlines & Monkeyshines*, 191–200. Some information, including pressure from Cermak, is from a *Chicago Tribune* article on March 19, 1989. Details are from a *Tribune* article on Jan. 9, 1995. The circumstances of the shooting are found in Richard Lindberg, *Return to the Scenes of the Crime*, 407.

24. Both Dynamite Sokol stories are from *The Late Edition*, May-June 1990.

25. William Drury and the link room: Len O'Connor, *A Reporter in Sweet Chicago*, 234. A "link room" was where one or more reporters worked exclusively on links between one crime and another or linking several crimes to a particular hoodlum or gang.

26. The reporters in the morgue after the LaSalle Hotel fire: Paster told the author this. The Heirens case: Lucy Freeman's *Catch Me Before I Kill More* has the complete confession, interviews, and psychiatric evaluations. Freeman, a Hearst journalist who clung to Freudian theory, believed the message was crucial to understanding Heirens. This author cannot recall a convincing similar case and believes a newsman wrote the message on the wall. That the state's attorney's office initially denied the confession: *Chicago Reader*, August 25, 1999. Frank San Hamel's role is from his obituary, *Sun-Times*, March 29, 1990.

27. *Tribune*, November 21, 1997, obituary of James Murray.

28. On Ed Eulenberg: Dornfeld's conversations with this author as well as these obituaries: City News, January 11, 1988; *Sun-Times* and the *Tribune*, both on January 12, 1988.

29. Romanoff on the phone: several sources including Moore, 27–28. Using two reporters to squeeze a story out of a politician: Frank Sullivan, "And the Beats Go On!: The Ben Hecht Era," *Avenue M* (May 1987).

30. How Seymour Hersh began at City News: *Rolling Stone* interview, April 24, 1975, excerpted in the City News centennial booklet, 1990, 74.

31. *Tribune* and *Sun Times*, both August 28, 2002, obituaries of Margaret Whitesides.

32. The drenched reporter story: George Selgrat, *Behind the News* (1971); Russell Raciti, *Inside Page One* (1946).

33. *Sun-Times*, August 3, 1993, obituary of Carl Larsen.

34. Thiem's two Pulitzers: anonymous, "Chicago Daily News, 1876.... Today." Thiem's rules for investigative reporters: George Thiem, *The Hodge Scandal*, 234–5.

35. Marshall Field III and NBC: Len O'Connor, *A Reporter in Sweet Chicago*, 199200.

36. Ritchie, *Please Stand By: A Prehistory of Television*, 89–90.

37. Information on WNBQ: *Sun-Times*, April 11, 2004 and *Tribune*, April 12, 2003, obituaries of TV cameraman Gene Cartwright; WNBQ Web site.

38. The starting date and ending month of the strike: City News Bureau copy on November 1, 1983.

39. The *Sun* and the *Times* merging: Becker, *Marshall Field III*, 393–5.

40. The printers strike and a rewrite man cutting off his own tie: *The Chicago Experience*, 44; *The Late Edition* (Spring 1993). *Tribune* response: Richard Smith, 471.

41. Early Chicago newscasts: largely from O'Connor, *A Reporter in Sweet Chicago*, 198–200, 252.

42. "Press Vet" (Winter 1998).

43. Bill Doherty anecdotes, including the CTA crash: Doherty, *Crime Reporter*, 108–87

44. Paul Gapp's appraisal of the papers: *Chicago Sunday Tribune Magazine*, date unavailable, 1989.

45. The Bas and Drury murders: George Murray, 407; Lindberg, *Return Again to the Scene of the Crime*, 161; Madigan, *The Chicago Experience*, 85; newspaper articles September 27–29, 1950.

46. McPhaul, *Deadlines and Monkeyshines*, 202–3; Walter Oleksy, "Front Page," 51.

47. *Sun-Times*, June 4, 2004, obituary of Lois Giggins-Grote.

48. Kamen's attempted suicide and libel suit: New York Times News Service, September 4, 2002, obituary of Martin Kamen.

49. Les Brownlee on the moonlighting reporter: "Inside Page One" (1952): 17.

50. The history of the McClurg Court studios: Chuck Schaden, *WBBM Radio Yesterday & Today*, 54. Robert Feder's column in the *Sun-Times*, June 16, 1998, calls it "the cavern." Calloway goes into TV: *The Chicago Experience*, 46.

51. Hal Bruno and the stable fire: *Behind the News* (1962).

52. The nearly twenty percent drop in circulation and Maryland McCormick saying "You know you're going to die": Richard Norton Smith, 518–22.

53. Frank Waldrop, *McCormick of Chicago*, 284.

54. The International News Service: two mentions in *The Late Edition* (January-Febru-

ary 1990): 4. It was fictionalized in the *Kolchak* TV series.

55. *Sun-Times*, March 29, 1990, obituary of San Hamel.

56. The secret FBI list of mobsters: *Behind the News* (1960).

57. Mike Royko and the murder of the Grimes sisters: F. Richard Ciccone, *Royko: A Life in Print*, 65–66.

58. Bill Doherty and the Bud Koster story: Doherty, *Crime Reporter*, 162–3, and newspaper articles on the case.

59. That the state codes exempted parochial schools: *Tribune*, April 28, 1992, a feature on tragic blazes. Irwin crying afterward: *Sun-Times*, May 17, 1989, obituary of Everett Irwin. Shepherd needing a drink: *The Late Edition* (July-August 1991).

60. The Summerdale scoop: this author's interview with Spirko.

61. The *Daily News* tricks the *Sun Times* in the Guido-Yonder case: James Mann in *Behind the News* (1967).

Chapter Seven

1. Mark Twain, *A Connecticut Yankee in King Arthur's Court*.

2. Details of the *Daily News* and the newsboys: Chappell, 7–9.

3. "Read all about it," extract from private memoirs by Lucille E. Block, *Chicago Tribune*, October 21, 1990. Newsboys taking morphine: June Sawyers, "Way We Were" feature, *Chicago Tribune Sunday Magazine*, January 3, 1988.

4. Shadow Nyquist, hopping onto streetcars, and how much the boys paid for their papers: Jim Bowman, "The Way We Were," *Chicago Tribune*, date unknown. Lorimer from Lindberg, 143. Other notable former Chicago newsboys were Continental Bank executive Vincent Lizzo, Italian-born choreographer Vincenzo Celli, Statistical Tabulating Company head Michael Notaro, Norman Stone of the Stone Container Corporation, and St. Valentine's Day Massacre victim Earl "Hymie" Weiss. Millionaire W. Clement Stone started his fortune at the age of 13 at a news stand at 31st and Cottage Grove. Patterson yanking newsboys off the street: Andrews, 224.

5. The *Daily News* keeping tough newsboys at certain corners: Cooney, John, *The Annenbergs*, 32.

6. Conditions are from "Report and Statement of the Board of Managers of the Newsboys and Bootblacks Association, 1890," Chicago History Museum.

7. Durkin on the job: Linn, p. 106, and articles in the "Newspaper" file at the Chicago History Museum, volumes 6–10, the *Tribune*.

8. Durkin and the king: Rascoe, p. 235. Rascoe did not say who started the story, but it was probably Durkin himself.

9. About flyboys: *The Late Edition* (Spring 2002).

10. First newspaper photo in the *NY Graphic*: March 14, 1880; Madeline Rogers "The Picture Snatchers," *American Heritage* (October 1994).

11. "The Mumler process": Charles Case, "The Ghost and Mr. Mumler," *American History* (April 2008). Flash powder singeing hair: William T. Moore, 30.

12. Atwell at the 1919 race riot: Harpeal scrapbook, *Tribune*, 1932.

13. "When Houdini Came to Town," *Chicago Tribune Sunday Magazine*, October 23, 1988.

14. Alley knocking out a hoodlum: Casey, *Such Interesting People*, 242.

15. Mike Rottuno in a Mount Pleasant, S.C., newspaper article he sent to this author. Date unknown. The article was excerpted in *The Late Edition* (March–April 1988).

16. The bad photo of Governor Small: Ray Brennan, "Fun with Photogs." *Chicago* magazine (May 1954): 47.

17. The Ruth Snyder photo: Madeline Rogers, "The Picture Snatchers," *American Heritage* (October 1994); Snyder and Morris, 438–45; and Walter Oleksy, "A Funny Thing Happened...," *Chicago* magazine (January, February 1972). The murder was the basis for the novel *Double Indemnity* and subsequent films.

18. George Wendt speaking at the City News centennial dinner in 1990.

19. Berardi at the St. Valentine's Day garage: "Chicago Profile" feature, *Chicago Sun-Times*, February 26, 1993; *The Late Edition* (Summer 2005). About Legs Diamond and Berger, and Hearst and McDonald: Rottuno, Mount Pleasant article.

20. Berardi and Capone: *The Late Edition* (Fall 1995). Berardi's quote about Ralph Pierce: *Sun-Times*, February 13, 1994 (omitted word is as found in this original source).

21. *Chicago Tribune*, November 21, 1986, obituary of William Loewe.

22. The photographers and Baby Face Nelson (real name, Lester Gillis): Ray Brennan.

23. *The Late Edition* (March–April 1988).

24. Graham J. White, *FDR and the Press*, 97.

25. John Conroy, "Getting the Picture," *Chicago Reader*, February 5, 1988.

26. McPhaul, *Deadlines and Monkeyshines*, 147.

27. The circumstances of Avery's removal: Robert Henderson, *The Grand Emporiums*, 230. The names of the photographers: Bill Doherty, *Crime Reporter*, 70.

28. Pigeons at the *Daily Times*: *Sun-Times*, May 27, 1986; McPhaul, 145–6. Sol Davis versus pigeons at the *Daily News*: Bill Doherty, *Crime Reporter*, 157–8. More Sol Davis stories are found in Kevin Davis (the photographer's grandson), *CityTalk*, (May 10–23, 2002).

29. Carson stealing plates: McPhaul, *Deadlines and Monkeyshines*, 142; McPhaul, *Inside Page One*, 45.

30. The photographer association's police liaison is from Joe Reilly, then general manager of City News, in an interview with this author on May 22, 1985.

31. Mike the rude photographer: Feldman, *Behind the News* (1966).

32. Capone tipping Rottuno: Feldman, *The Late Edition* (Winter 2003). Rottuno was so well liked he must not have been the rude photographer "Mike."

33. Brennan, 46.

34. The circulation of 1,076,866: Graham J. White, *FDR and the Press*, 172. The *Tribune* photography "car": Harpeal scrapbook, *Tribune*, March 1940, 3. The direct line to the mobile operator: Harpeal scrapbook, *Tribune*, March 1949.

35. Bill Doherty, 75.

36. *Tribune*, May 30, 1946.

37. *Chicago Tribune*, November 15, 1985.

38. *Sun-Times*, September 21, 1995, obituary of Joseph Mastruzzo.

39. The atom-splitting story: McPhaul, 148; O'Connor, *Behind the News* (1956); and a *Tribune* story and photo, September 26, 1988.

40. *Sun-Times*, February 12, 1991, obituary of Herman Rhoden.

41. *Behind the News* (1955).

42. *Chicago Tribune*, April 25, 1992, obituary of George Quinn.

43. Lasker's photo at the school fire: *CityTalk* (January 17–February 27, 2004).

44. *Tribune*, April 2, 1999, obituary of Walter Neal.

45. On Hank Martin: Chicago *Defender* feature, December 20, 2003.

46. John Conroy, "Getting the Picture," *Chicago Reader*, February 5, 1988.

47. John Conroy, same.

48. *Sun-Times*, April 14, 1995, obituary of Phil Mascione.

49. DeWert and the Beatles concert: *Chicago Tribune*, February 7, 2006, obituary of David DeWert.

50. The bird's eye AP photo of the anti-terrorism rally: Steven Rhodes' Media column in *Chicago* magazine, November 2001.

Chapter Eight

1. Daley's remark is in several sources, including *Time* magazine, July 18, 1969.

2. The cosmetic factor in the Kennedy-Nixon debate: Theodore T. White, *The Making of the President 1960*, 344; "Make-up Moment": *History Channel Magazine*, (May/June 2008): 38, adapting an excerpt from the book *The Greatest Presidential Stories Never Told*.

3. Dan Kening, *Chicago Tribune*, January 26, 1993.

4. Paul Holmes, *The Sheppard Murder Case*; Holmes, *Retrial: Murder and Dr. Sam Sheppard*.

5. *Avenue M* magazine, May 1987.

6. Meyer Zolotareff anecdotes: *The Late Edition* (May-June 1989).

7. *Chicago Tribune*, August 24, 2008, metro section, 6.

8. Sam DeStefano threatening Bill Doherty: *Chicago Tribune*, November 13, 1961.

9. Jim McCormick's background came from his second wife, Edie, after his death, in *The Late Edition* (Spring 2002). Jim's outlook as a copy editor: *The Late Edition* (Spring 2000).

10. Wesley South and the Medgar Evers interview: *Chicago Tribune*, Tempo section, February 15, 1994, 2.

11. *Tribune*, June 6, 2001, obituary of Raymond Shleman.

12. Ellen Leifeld sent "The Drill" to the American Press Institute's city and metro editors seminar, September 16–26, 1990.

13. George Bliss's background: Basil Talbott, *Behind the News* (1962). His donning a hard hat: this author's interview with Bernie Judge, August 30, 1988.

14. Ciducci's execution, Baumann, *May God Have Mercy on Your Soul*, 419. That Brennan was the last reporter: this author's interview with Walter Spirko.

15. That Johnson was the only executioner: *Tribune Sunday Magazine*, December 10, 1990.

16. hunch about Inland Steel: *Sun-Times*, May 16, 2002, obituary of Max Schneider's.

17. Edelstein and Goldberg fight over a film reel: *Behind the News* (1968–1969).

18. Alex Drier without pants: his obituary, *Sun-Times*, March 14, 2000.

19. Bernard Shaw's background: *Tribune*, Tempo section, February 27, 2001.

20. Author's interview with Bernie Judge after he left the paper.

21. George Murray's story about Nate Steinberg and the Vatican: *The Late Edition* (March-April 1990). For background, see *The Bones of St. Peter*.

22. *Sun-Times*, June 7, 2001, obituary of Art Petacque.

23. Anderson's claim that Petacque was illiterate is from a letter to the editor in the *Chicago Reader*, July 13, 2001. Neil Steinberg on Petacque: Steinberg's column, *Sun-Times* June 10, 2001, p. 12 A.

24. On Joe Cummings: his obituary, *Sun-Times*, December 10, 1999; "Press Vet" (Winter 1999–2000).

25. How Romanoff scooped the other papers on the Speck case: *Time* magazine, May 31, 1968.

26. Ed Eulenberg on the beating of a witness: *Behind the News* (April 1984): 8, 41.

27. The racial issue is discussed in a report "'John Smith, Negro' in the Tribune," delivered to the City Club of Chicago, September 12, 1950, and located at the Chicago History Museum. "Spiking" a story: When an editor decided not to run a story that had already been written, he would put it on a spindle—a long, pointed needle rising from a metal base. The next editor might look at the story and decide to assign someone to work on another aspect, or an item that seemed minor could turn out to be important hours later. In a broader sense, when a newspaper "spiked" City News copy, such as the wounding of children in drug-related gunfire, it meant that the editors decided not to follow up on them. Spiked stories were usually thrown out after 24 hours or so (at City News, whenever the spindle was full), but sometimes they were kept on file for awhile.

28. Joe Reilly's comment on laziness at the newspapers since the mid-sixties: interview with this author on September 12, 1988. The *American* putting Linda Darnell's death on the back page: George Murray, *Behind the News* (1978).

29. Harry Golden information. Bribing the janitor: *Sun-Times*, May 5, 1988. Dancing through city hall: *Chicago Reader*, May 6, 1988. Talking and typing: *Chicago* magazine, July 1988. Turning down a television offer: his obituary, *Sun-Times*, May 2, 1988. Twenty-three words: late edition, *Sun-Times*, May 2, 1988. Writing his obituary: *Sun-Times*, May 6, 1988. Press room named in his honor: *Sun-Times*, October 13, 1988.

30. Frank Haramija writes a fake name on a mail box card: Walter Oleksy, 51. This author remembers Haramija talking about it.

31. *Chicago Tribune*, March 25, 2005, obituary of Joseph Longmeyer.

32. Jaye Slade Fletcher: *Deadly Thrills*, 255–6.

33. *Chicago Reader*, May 14, 1993.

34. "Inside the *Chicago Tribune*," May 28, 2001, and August 8, 2001.

35. Ray Kennedy, *Time* Magazine, May 31, 1968.

36. *Chicago Reader*, December 4, 1987.

37. Theresa Fambro Hooks recalling the night King was shot: Chicago *Defender*, January 19, 2002, 24.

38. Luke Carroll declines to investigate possible killings by the police: James Allen Flannery, "Chicago Newspapers' Coverage of the City's Major Civil Disorders of 1968," 255.

39. Tribune article based on a *U.S.A.* article based on a Hoover article: Flannery, 250.

40. Flannery, 659–660.

41. *Tribune Sunday Magazine*, July 24, 1988, 21.

42. Bill Kurtis: *Bill Kurtis: On Assignment*, 9.

43. "...the police are the great cooperators...," quoted by Flannery. The Lanahan beating and the *Sun-Times* not using a UPI photo: Flannery, 707–708. That police officers broke Sequerira's hand: (ibid.).

44. The *Daily News* protests the beating of newsmen at Michigan and Balbo: Flannery, 769. "...no longer part of the establishment": this author's interview with Bernie Judge.

45. Michael Miner, "Jim Hoge and His One-Horse Chariot," *Chicago* magazine (May 1979).

46. Mauldin's cartoons: Adrienne Drell, ed., *20th Century Chicago*, 151; Michael Miner, "Mauldin on the Attack," *Chicago Reader*, Jan. 21, 2003, Hot Type column.

47. The broadcaster's credo is given at length in Curtis Mitchell, *Cavalcade of Broadcasting*, 194.

48. Morris Roth coins "happy talk": his obituary, *Chicago Tribune*, June 13, 2008. On Fahey Flynn: *Sun-Times*, August 12, 1983, and October 11, 1989.

49. *Sun-Times*, May 14, 2004, obituary of Floyd Kalber.

50. Linda Yu's background: interview with Cassandra A. Gaddo, "Lights! Camera! Linda!" *Today's Chicago Woman* (January 2008).

51. The rise and fall of Ron Hunter: *Tribune*, July 1, 1990; Richard Roeper's column in the *Sun-Times*, March 2, 1993. Deeb's opinion is from Hunter's obituary, *Chicago Tribune*, June 28, 2008.

52. Shepherd reporting train crash victims from a hospital: "The First Edition" (March-April 1988).

53. Dan Jedlicka, *Sun-Times*, June 13, 1990, auto column.

54. On Larry Schreiner: Michael G. Glab, "Trouble is His Business," *Chicago Reader*, August 23, 1991. The equipment in his Mercedes: Bill Brashler's column in the *Sun-Times*, May 18, 1987, 37.

55. John McDermott and the *Chicago Reporter*: Associated Press, February 15, 2002.

56. *Sun-Times*, September 13, 2004, obituary of Lu Palmer.

57. Hugh Hill against happy talk: *Sun-Times*, Oct. 6, 1988, Television & Radio page.

58. Joel Daly supporting happy talk, and John Drury calling fellow news people "performers": interview in the *Daily Herald*, Feb. 21, 2002, Suburban Living Section. Drury's training as an anchor: Rosenthal, *Tribune*, Nov. 27, 2007.

59. Details of Elrod's injury and the trial: Bryan Smith, "Sudden Impact," *Chicago* (December 2006). That the papers sat on the Blackstone Rangers and the Elrod stories: this author's interview with Bernie Judge.

60. *Sun-Times*, April 17, 1986, obituary of Hugh Hough. One suspects that Petacque said "was here."

61. *Tribune*, November 6, 1979.

62. Details of Jim Hoge's career: Joshua Hammer, "The Agony of Jim Hoge," *Chicago* (September 1991); Edward Klein, "Front Page Drama," *Vanity Fair* (October 1989); Miner, *Chicago* (May 1979)

63. The story of the tavern exposé: Zay N. Smith and Pamela Zekman, *The Mirage*.

64. For Zekman's TV work: Christina January Adachi, "Pam Zekman," *Today's Chicago Woman* (May 1987) 10–12. The description of her work: Linda Witt article in the *Sunday* magazine of the *Tribune* around 1986.

65. Bliss's career: Unger, 8.

66. Bruce Ingersoll's exposure at Three Mile Island, his obituary, *Sun-Times*, December 4, 2001.

67. On Bruce Vilanch: *Tribune*, September 22, 1999, Tempo section. About Hunt: *Tribune* obituary, July 11, 1999; Marcia Froelke Coburn, "Final Edit," *Chicago* (September 1999).

68. "...Red Streak edition was crippled...": George Cullicutt letter to the editor, *Tribune*, September 19, 1990, 16. The death of the *Daily News*: City News Bureau February 3, 1978; *Tribune*, same date; *Sun-Times*, September 19, 1997, obituary of Tom Gavagan.

69. Chuck Schaden, 82.

70. Hultman and Felicia Middlebrooks interview, *Chicago Tribune*, September 10, 1991, Tempo section.

71. The downfall of Leanita McClain: *Sun-Times*, December 9, 1992.

72. On Max Robinson: *Tribune Sunday Magazine*, May 18, 1989. That O'Leary refused to acknowledge him: *Sun-Times*, February 28, 1994, 12.

73. All three networks changing ownership, and judging profitability by Nielsen ratings: "the scorecard showing how many households had someone watching each newscast," Ryan Ver Berkmoes, "89 Hours," *Chicago* (April 1995).

74. *Editor & Publisher* (Aug. 25, 1984): 14.

75. Readers spending two or three hours with a paper: Dennis Prager, *Moment Magazine* (1991): 14. A similar estimate was in Michael Miner's column, Hot Type, in the *Chicago Reader*, November 20, 1987.

Chapter Nine

1. Michael Leapman, *Arrogant Aussie*, 37.

2. Background information on Murdoch: Leapman; Harold Evans, *Good Times, Bad Times*; Thomas Kiernan, *Citizen Murdoch*; and three City News Bureau stories. Royko's news conference is from F. Richard Ciccone, 339. Information on temporary editors at the *Sun-Times*: Michael Miner, "Murdoch's Man in Chicago," *Chicago Reader*, February 24, 1984.

3. *Sun-Times*, July 22, 1985, obituary of Maryland McCormick.

4. Jimmy Tontlewicz: *Tribune*, June 7, 2002, obituary of Robert Whitmore.

5. Charles Nicodemus and others dragging their feet: Michael Miner, *Chicago Reader*, December 1, 2000.

6. Malone's failed *Post*: Jack Star, "Post Time?" *Chicago* (April 1984); *Chicago Tribune*, Charles Storch, May 15, 1984; Joe Beck, and Deborah Nathan, "The Evening Post, John Malone's Last Hurrah," *Chicago Journalism Review* (July 1983); Michael Miner, *Chicago Reader*, January 26, 1989.

7. Georgia Lloyd donating money to strikers: *Sun-Times*, May 6, 1986. Background is from City News Bureau copy on July 19, 1985. Figures for newscast audiences and newspaper readers: Ryan Ver Berkmoes, "89 Hours," *Chicago* (April 1995): 73.

8. Susy Schultz helps save Frank Devine: Michael Miner, *Chicago Reader*, February 28, 1986.

9. The Jesse Jackson boycott of WBBM: Robert Feder, *Sun-Times*, August 20, 2002.

10. "John Rooney Breaks the Tylenol Story": City News centennial booklet, 1990. 68.

11. That Jim Gibbons was the first person at the Laurie Dann case: his obituaries in the *Sun-Times* and *Tribune*, both on January 17, 1994. Timm using a news conference for tips on how to proceed: "Community Crisis: the Laurie Dann Case," a television documentary.

12. Hanke Gratteau and Mark Brown: Marcia Froelke Coburn, "Sleeping with the Enemy," *Chicago* (Jan. 2001).

13. John Drummond profile: Bill Brashler,

"Bulldog's Beat," *Chicago Tribune Magazine*, November 10, 1995.

14. Robert Feder, *Sun-Times*, November 19, 2004; Pat Widder, "Live! Exclusive!" *Chicago Tribune Magazine*, July 18, 1993, 18.

15. Russ Ewing background: Bob Herguth, *Sun-Times*, April 20, 1988. The number of fugitives had reached one hundred by October 1992. See the Robert Feder column in the *Sun-Times*, October 30, 1995.

16. Michael Miner, *Chicago Reader*, December 13, 1989.

17. Details of the Ford Heights Four case: David Protess and Rob Warden, *A Promise of Justice*.

18. Richard C. Lindberg, *Quotable Chicago*, 200.

19. Squires is quoted in the *Washington Journalism Review*, June 1990. Passages from, and paraphrases of, Squires' book: *Chicago Reader*, February 13, 1993.

20. Giselle Fernandez at WBBM: Robert Feder, *Sun-Times*, September 19, 1991.

21. Bob Petty's remarks about not having to understand an event: the City News reporter told this to this author.

22. *Tribune* downscaling: *Sun-Times*, May 8, 1982, 42.

23. *Chicago* (June 1982): 90.

24. TV anchor salaries and Peter Herford's comment: *Electronic Media* (February 14, 1994).

25. Rick Kogan, *Tribune*, February 3, 1992.

26. CBS standards statement: Tom Fenton, *Bad News: the Decline of Reporting the Business of News and the Danger to Us All*, 58.

27. A typical day at a TV news department: Pat Widder, "Live! Exclusive!" *Chicago Tribune Magazine*, July 18, 1993. The article followed Carol Marin and others at WMAQ, but the experiences were similar to those of people at other stations.

28. *Daily Herald*, March 30, 1993, Showcase section.

29. *Electronic Media* (February 14, 1994).

30. *Near North News*, January 8, 1994.

31. Gretchen Reynolds, "Tower of Power," *Chicago* (September 1994).

32. Conrad Black's background: Richard Siklos, *Shades of Black*.

33. The reduction or elimination of investigative teams at WBBM and WLS: Gregory Hinz, "Identity Crisis," *Chicago* (March 1993). WLS's reliance on satellite-feed video: Ryan Ver Berkmoes, "89 Hours," *Chicago* (April 1997).

34. Pat Widder, "Live! Exclusive!" *Chicago Tribune Magazine*, July 18, 1993.

35. Sale of the *Defender* to Tom Picou: Associated Press, June 25, 2002.

36. The Tuplipano murder plot: City News Service, June 22, 2000.

37. Richard Digby-Junger, "The Chicago Press Club," *Journal of Illinois History* (Winter 1998): 93.

38. City News copy and a *Tribune* internal memo.

39. Michael Sneed, *Sun-Times*, May 8, 2002.

40. City News Bureau copy, April 15, 1988.

41. Rich Samuels' firing: *Sun-Times*, July 26, 1990, Radio & Television section. The confrontation was on July 10 of that year.

42. As told to author by Marty Walsh.

43. Steven Rhodes, *Chicago* (November 2001).

44. Conrad Black information: Richard Siklos, *Shades of Black*, and a television documentary on Conrad Black.

45. Problems with a features approach to hard news and Lipinski's elevation: Steven Rhodes, "Ann Marie's World," *Chicago* (April 2001). Getting away from anecdotal leads: Michael Miner, *Chicago Reader*, March 9, 2001, 8.

46. The *Tribune* buying the L.A. *Times* behind Willes' back: Dennis McDougal, *Privileged Son*, 451.

47. Newsprint price increases: "Tribune News," an in-house publication, June 19, 2001. The *Tribune*'s changes in the size of the paper and number of columns: Steven Rhodes, *Chicago* (November 2001).

48. *Sun Times*, March 25, 2001.

49. The attack on the *Defender*: City News copy December 10, 2002.

50. Mike Flannery's comment about newspaper and TV news assignments: Robert Feder, *Sun-Times*, June 2, 2000.

51. Phil Rosenthal, *Tribune*, March 16, 2008.

52. The *Tribune*'s crushing debt load: *Tribune*, May 31, 2006, Business section; *Tribune*, June 11, 2006.

53. *Chicago Tribune*, Rosenthal's column, January 29, 2009.

54. Nicodemus: "it can't get any better than this," his obituary, *Chicago Tribune*, November 1, 2008.

55. Arlene Morgan address: "TV has personality..." *Illinois Presslines*, October 15, 2002.

56. "...can reach the same audience...": Jeff Bordon, "A Collision of Media," a *Crain's Chicago Business* extra: "Chicago 2000 and Beyond."

57. A thirty-eight percent drop in viewership: Robert Reed, "Changing Channels," *Chicago* (February 2008).

58. *Chicago Tribune*, April 1, 2008, 1, 13.

59. Scott Gant, *We're All Journalists Now*, 13.

Bibliography

Many gaps in the story of the news were filled in by insider publications, such as *The First Edition* and *The Late Edition*, for veterans of the Hearst papers in Chicago; the Chicago Newspaper Guild's *Inside Page One*; *Behind the News*, a Chicago Newspaper Reporters Association fund-raising periodical of reminiscences; *Prohibition Era Times* of the Merry Gangsters Literary Society; and *The Trib*, a monthly house organ 1919–1985. The dates of each issue used as well as minor references from newspapers and magazines were given in the "Notes and Sources" section. Sources conveniently found only in the Chicago History Museum are marked CHM.

*Reference works that were especially useful are noted with an asterisk.

Books

Abbott, Willis J. *Watching the World Go By*. Boston: Little, Brown & Co., 1933.

Adams, Rosemary K., ed. *A Wild Kind of Boldness: The Chicago Historical Society Reader*. Chicago: Erdmanns Publishing company, Chicago Historical Society, 1988.

Adelman, William. *Haymarket Revisited*. Chicago: Illinois Labor History Society, 1978.

*Andrews, Wayne. *Battle for Chicago*. New York: Harcourt, Brace and Company, 1946.

Asinof, Eliot. *Eight Men Out*. New York: Holt, Rinehart and Winston, 1963.

Baker, Ray Stannard. *American Chronicle*. New York: Charles Scribner's Sons, 1945.

Bannister, Robert C. *Ray Stannard Baker, the Mind and Thought of a Progressive*. New Haven, CT: Yale University Press, 1966.

Barnouw, Erik. *A Tower in Babel, a History of Broadcasting in the United States to 1933*. New York: Oxford University Press, 1966.

Barrow, Kenneth. *Helen Hayes: First Lady of the American Theatre*. Garden City, NY: Doubleday & Company, 1985.

Beasley, Norman. *Frank Knox, American*. Garden City, NY: Doubleday, Doran & Co., 1936.

Bell, Lilian. *The Story of the Christmas Ship*. Chicago: Rand McNally & Company, 1915.

Bliss, Edward, Jr. *And Now the News, the Story of Broadcast Journalism*. New York: Columbia University Press, 1991.

Boettinger, John. *Jake Lingle, or Chicago On the Spot*. New York: E.P. Dutton and Co., 1931.

Bonham, Jeriah. *50 Years of Recollections*. Peoria, IL: J.W. Franks and Sons, 1883.

Bross, William. *History of Chicago*. Chicago: Jansen McClurg & Company, 1876.

Bruce, Robert V. *1877: Year of Violence*. Chicago: Ivan R. Dee, Inc., 1989.

Burke, John. *Duet in Diamonds*. New York: Manor Books, 1975.

Cadwallader, Sylvanus. *Three Years With Grant*. New York: Alfred A. Knopf, 1955.

Carter, Robert A. *Buffalo Bill: The Man Behind the Legend*. Edison, NJ: Castle Books, 2005.

Casey, Robert J. *Bob Casey's Grand Slam*. New York: Bobbs-Merrill, 1962.

_____. *More Interesting People*. New York: Bobbs-Merrill Co., 1947.

_____. *Such Interesting People*. New York: Bobbs-Merrill Co., 1945.

Casey, Robert J., and W.A.S. Douglas. *The Midwesterner, the Story of Dwight H. Green*. Chicago: Wilcox & Follett Co., 1948.

*Churchill, Allen. *Park Row*. New York: Rinehart & Company, 1958.

Ciccone, F. Richard. *Royko, a Life in Print*. New York: PublicAffairs, 2001.

Cook, Ferdinand. *Bygone Days in Chicago*. Chicago: A.C. McClurg & Company, 1910.

Cooney, John. *Annenbergs, the Salvation of a Tainted Dynasty*. New York: Simon and Schuster, 1982.

Crissey, Elwell. *Lincoln's Lost Speech: the Pivot of His Career*. New York: Hawthorn Books, 1967.

Cromie, Robert. *The Great Chicago Fire*. New York: McGraw-Hill Book Company, 1958.

Daniel, Clifton, ed. *Chronicle of the 20th Century*. Mount Kisco, NY: Chronicle Publications, 1987.

Dedmon, Emmett. *Fabulous Chicago*. Enlarged ed. NewYork: Athenaeum, 1981.

De Freitas, Helen. Biography of N.K. Fairbank, her grandfather. Privately printed, 1981.

Dennis, Charles. *Victor Lawson, His Time and His Work*. Chicago: University of Chicago Press, 1935.

Dennis, Charles H. *Eugene Field's Creative Years*. Garden City, NY: Doubleday, Page & Co., 1924.

Destler, Chester MacArthur. *Henry Demarest Lloyd and the Empire of Reform*. Philadelphia: University of Pennsylvania Press, 1963.

Di Donato, Pietro. *The Life of Mother Cabrini*. New York: Dell Publishing Co., 1962.

Doherty, Bill. *Bill Doherty: Crime Reporter*. New York: Exposition Press, 1964.

Doherty, Edward. *With Gall and Honey*. New York: Sheed and Ward, 1941.

Dornfeld, Arnold A. *Behind the Front Page, the Story of the City News Bureau of Chicago*. Chicago: Academy Chicago Publishers, 1983.

Drell, Adrienne, ed. *20th Century Chicago: 100 years—100 Voices*. Chicago Sun-Times/Bannon Multimedia group, 2000.

Dunning, John. *On the Air, The Encyclopedia of Old-Time Radio*. New York: Oxford University Press, 1998.

Ellis, Elmer. *Mr. Dooley's America: A Life of Finley Peter Dunne*. New York: Alfred A. Knopf, 1941.

Emery, Edwin. *The Press and America, an Interpretive History of Journalism*. 2nd ed. Englewood Cliffs, NJ: Prentice Hall Inc., 1962.

Fehrenbacher, Don. *Chicago Giant: A Biography of "Long John" Wentworth*. Madison, WI: The American History Research Center, 1957.

Fenton, Tom. *Bad News: The Decline of Reporting, the Business of News, and the Danger to Us All*. New York: Regan Books, 2005.

Fetherling, Doug. *The Five Lives of Ben Hecht*. Toronto: Lester and Orpen Limited, 1977.

Fink, John. *WGN, a Pictorial History*. Chicago: WGN, 1961.

Fletcher, Jay Slade. *Deadly Thrills*. New York: Penguin Books, 1995.

Fowler, Gene. *Skyline: A Reporter's Reminiscences of the 1920s*. New York: Viking Press, 1961.

Gale, Edwin O. *Reminiscences of Early Chicago*. Chicago: Fleming H. Revell Company, 1902.

Gant, Scott. *We're All Journalists Now: The Transformation of the Press ad Reshaping of the Law in the Internet Age*. Tampa, FL: Free Press, 2007.

Gibbons, Edward. *Floyd Gibbons, Your Headline Hunter*. New York: Exposition Press, 1953.

Ginger, Ray. *Altgeld's America.* New York: New Viewpoints, 1973.

Golden, Harry. *Carl Sandburg.* New York: World Publishing Company, 1961.

Gramling, Oliver. *The AP, the Story of News.* New York: Farrar and Rineholt Inc., 1940.

Gross, Ben. *I Looked and I Listened: Informal Recollections of Radio and TV.* New York: Random House, 1954.

Hackett, Francis. *American Rainbow: Early Reminiscences.* New York: Liveright Company, 1971.

Halper, Albert, ed. *The Chicago Crime Book.* New York: Pyramid Books, 1969.

Harper, Robert S. *Lincoln and the Press.* New York: McGraw-Hill Book Company, 1951.

Hayes, Helen. *On Reflection: An Autobiography.* New York: M. Evans and Company, 1968.

Hearst Strike News, Vol. 1. Hearst Strike Committee, January 1939. (CHM)

Hecht, Ben. *A Child of the Century.* New York: Signet Books, 1955.

Hecht, Ben, and Charles MacArthur. *The Front Page.* New York: Coivici-Friede, 1940.

Higham, Charles. *Warner Brothers.* New York: Charles Scribners Sons, 1975.

Hoffman, William. *The Stockbroker.* New York: Lyle Stuart, Inc., 1969.

Holmes, Paul. *Retrial: Murder and Dr. Sam Sheppard.* New York: Bantam Books, 1966.

_____. *The Sheppard Murder Case.* New York: David McKay Co., 1961.

Ickes, Harold L. *The Secret Diary of Harold L. Ickes.* Vol. III, *The Lowering Clouds: 1939–1941.* New York: Simon and Schuster, 1954.

Johnson, Curt, with R. Craig Sautter. *The Wicked City: Chicago From Kenna to Capone.* Da Capo Press, 1998.

Jones, Louise Seymour. *Horatio Seymour.* Typewritten biography, 1948. (CHM)

Karamanski, Theodore J. *Rally 'Round the Flag, Chicago and the Civil War.* Chicago: Nelson-Hall Inc., 1993.

Katcher, Leo. *The Big Bankroll.* New York: Cardinal Books, 1961.

Kiernan, Thomas. *Citizen Murdoch.* New York: Dodd, Meade & Company, 1986.

Kinsley, Philip. *The Chicago Tribune, Its First Hundred Years.* New York: Alfred A. Knopf, 1943.

Kurtis, Bill. *Bill Kurtis: On Assignment.* Chicago: Rand McNally & Company, 1983.

Lamont, Peter. *The Rise of the Indian Rope Trick: How a Spectacular Hoax Became History.* New York: Thunder's Mouth Press, 2004.

Leapman, Michael. *Arrogant Aussie: The Rupert Murdoch Story.* Secaucus, NJ: Lyle Stuart inc., 1985.

Lindberg, Richard C. *Quotable Chicago.* Chicago: Wild Onion Books, 1996.

_____. *Return Again to the Scene of the Crime: A Guide to Infamous Places in Chicago.* Nashville: Cumberland House, 2001.

_____. *Return to the Scene of the Crime: A Guide to Infamous Places in Chicago.* Nashville: Cumberland House, 1999.

_____. *To Serve and Collect.* New York: Praeger, 1991.

Linn, James Weber. *James Keeley, Newspaperman.* New York: Bobbs-Merrill Co., 1937.

*Lundberg, Ferdinand. *Imperial Hearst, a Social Biography.* Westport, CT: Greenwood Press, Publishers, 1974.

MacAdams, William. *Ben Hecht, the Man Behind the Legend.* New York: Charles Scribner's Sons, 1990.

Martin, Ralph G. *Cissy.* New York: Simon & Schuster, 1979.

Mayer, Martin. *Making News.* Garden City, NY: Doubleday & Company, 1987.

McDougal, Dennis. *Privileged Son: Otis Chandler and the Rise and Fall of the L.A. Dynasty.* Cambridge, MA: Perseus Publishing, 2001.

McPhaul, John J. *Deadlines and Monkeyshines, the Fabled World of Chicago Journalism.* Englewood Cliffs, NJ: Prentice-Hall, 1962.

Miller, Donald L. *City of the Century, The Epic of Chicago and the Making of Amer-*

ica. New York: Simon and Schuster, 1996.

Mitchell, Curtis. *Cavalcade of Broadcasting.* New York: Benjamin Co., 1970.

Monaghan, Jay. *The Man Who Elected Lincoln, a Biography of Dr. Charles Ray.* New York: Bobbs-Merrill Co., 1956.

Moore, William T. *Dateline Chicago, a Veteran Newsman Recalls Its Heyday.* New York: Taplinger Publishing Company, 1973.

Morris, Joe Alex. *Deadline Every Minute: The Story of the United Press.* Garden City, NY: Doubleday & Company, 1957.

Mott, Frank Luther. *American Journalism, A History: 1690–1960.* 3rd edition. New York: The Macmillan Company, 1962.

Murray, George Jessie. *Madhouse on Madison Street.* Chicago: Follett Publishing Co., 1965.

O'Connor, Len. *A Reporter in Sweet Chicago.* Chicago: Contemporary Books, 1983.

_____. *They Talked to a Stranger.* New York: St. Martin's Press, 1959.

Ogden, Christopher. *Legacy: A Biography of Moses and Walter Annenberg.* Boston: Little, Brown and Company, 1999.

O'Gorman, Thomas J., and Lisa Montanarelli. *Strange But True Chicago: Tales of the Windy City.* Guilford, CA: Insiders' Guide, 2005.

Olson, Kenneth E. *Typography and Mechanics of the Newspaper.* New York: Appleton-Century Co., 1940.

Pasley, Frank. *Al Capone, the Biography of a Self-Made Man.* New York: Ives Washburn Publishers, 1930.

Pierce, Bessie Louise. *A History of Chicago.* Vol. III, *The Rise of a Modern City, 1871–1893.* New York: Alfred A. Knopf, 1957.

Protess, David, and Rob Warden. *A Promise of Justice.* New York: Hyperion, 1998.

Rascoe, Burton. *Before I Forget.* Garden City, NY: Doubleday, Doran and Co., 1937.

Root, Waverly. *The Paris Edition.* San Francisco: North Point Press, 1989.

Ross, Ishbel. *Ladies of the Press: The Story of Women in Journalism by an Insider.* New York: Harper & Brothers, 1936.

Rothmyer, Karen. *Winning Pulitzers, the Stories Behind Some of the Best News Coverage of Our Times.* New York: Columbia University Press, 1991.

Sandburg, Carl. *Abraham Lincoln.* Vol. I & II, *The Prairie Years.* New York: Harcourt, Brace & Company, 1926.

Schaaf, Barbara. *Mr. Dooley's Chicago.* Garden City, NY: Anchor Press/Doubleday, 1977.

Schaden, Chuck. *WBBM Radio Yesterday & Today.* Chicago: WBBM Newsradio 78, 1988.

Schoenberg, Robert J. *Mr. Capone.* London, England: Robson Books, 1993.

Schwarzlose, Richard A. *The Nation's Newsbrokers.* Vol. 1. Evanston, IL: Northwestern University Press, 1989.

Scott, Gini Graham. *Homicide: 100 years of Murder in America.* Los Angeles: Roxbury Park Books, 1998.

Seldes, George. *Witness to a Century.* New York: Ballantine Books, 1987.

Semonche, John E. *Ray Stannard Baker, a Quest for Democracy in Modern America, 1870–1918.* Chapel Hill: University of North Carolina Press, 1969.

Siklos, Richard. *Shades of Black: The World's Fastest Growing Press Empire.* Toronto: Reed Books, 1995.

Smith, Henry Justin. *It's the Way It's Written.* Chicago: Sterling North of Chicago, 1934.

*Smith, Richard Norton. *The Colonel: The Life and Times of Robert McCormick.* New York: Houghton-Mifflin, 1997.

Smith, Zay N., and Pamela Zekman. *The Mirage.* New York: Random House, 1979.

Snyder, Louis L., and B. Morris. *A Treasury of Great Reporting.* 2nd edition. New York: Simon and Schuster, 1962.

Startt, James D. *Journalism's Unofficial Ambassador: A Biography of Edward Price Bell.* Athens: Ohio University Press, 1979.

Steffens, Lincoln. *The Autobiography of Lincoln Steffens.* New York: Harcourt, Brace and Company, 1931.

Stone, Melville E. *Fifty Years a Journalist.* Garden City, NY: Doubleday, Page & Co., 1921.

_____. "*M.E.S*" *His Book*. New York: Harper & Bros., 1918.

Swanberg, W.A. *Citizen Hearst, a Biography of William Randolph Hearst*. New York: Bantam Books, 1967.

*Tebbel, John. *An American Dynasty*. Garden City, NY: Doubleday & Company, 1947.

Thiem, George. *The Hodge Scandal*. New York: St. Martin's Press, 1963.

Thomas, Benjamin P. *Abraham Lincoln, a Biography*. New York: Alfred A. Knopf, 1952.

Thomas, Lowell. *Good Evening Everybody*. New York: Avon, 1977.

Thompson, Slason. *Eugene Field, a Study in Heredity and Contradictions*. New York: Charles Scribner's Sons, 1901.

_____. *Way Back When, Recollections of an Octogenarian*. Chicago: privately printed, H.G. Adair Publishing, 1930. (CHM)

Trohan, Walter. *Political Animals: Memoirs of a Sentimental Critic*. Garden City, NY: Doubleday & Company, 1975.

Unger, Rudolph M. (compiler). *The Chicago Tribune News Staff 1920s–1960s*. Privately printed, 1991.

Waldrop, Frank. *McCormick of Chicago*. Englewood Cliffs, NJ: Prentice-Hall, Inc., 1966.

Walsh, Justin E. *To Print the News and Raise Hell*. Chapel Hill: University of North Carolina Press, 1968.

Washburn, Charles. *Come Into My Parlor: A Biography of the Aristocratic Everleigh Sisters of Chicago*. New York: National Library Press, 1936.

Waskin, Mel. *Mrs. O'Leary's Comet*. Chicago: Academy Chicago Publishers, 1985.

Wendt, Lloyd. *Chicago Tribune, the Rise of a Great American Newspaper*. Chicago: Rand McNally, 1979.

Wendt, Lloyd, and Herman Kogan. *Lords of the Levee: The Story of Bathhouse John and Hinky Dink*. New York: Bobbs-Merrill Co., 1943.

White, Graham J. *FDR and the Press*. Chicago: University of Chicago Press, 1979.

Wilkie, Franc B. *Thirty-Five Years of Journalism*. Chicago: E. J. Schulte and Company, 1891.

Articles and Other Sources

Abramoske, Donald J. "The Founding of the Chicago Daily News." *Journal of the Illinois State Historical Society*, Winter 1966.

Ball, James Harland. "A Study of Typical Crusades Undertaken by Chicago Newspapers, 1833–1930." Master's thesis, May 1930. (CHM)

Beck, Edward S. "Recollections of the Early Days of the Chicago Tribune." *Chicago Tribune*, December 13, 1939. An address to the advertising department of the Chicago *Tribune*.

Bell, Edward Price. "Creed of the Klansmen." *Chicago Daily News Reprints*, 1924.

Best, Wallace. "The Chicago *Defender* and the Realignment of Black Chicago." *Chicago History*, Fall 1995.

Brashler, Bill. "Bulldog's Beat." *Chicago Tribune Magazine*, November 10, 1995.

Brennan, Ray. "Fun With Photogs." *Chicago*, May 1954.

Chappell, Fred A. "The Daily News Building Yesterday and Today." *Chicago Daily News*, December 30, 1927. (CHM)

"Chicago *Daily News*, 1876.... Today." *Chicago Daily News*, 1959. (CHM)

The Chicago Experience. Convention pamphlet with various contributors. Chicago Headline Club National Convention Fund, 1987. (CHM)

*Chicago History Museum Harpeal and Newspaper scrapbooks.

Cox, Jim. "Storytelling in a Box: the Evolution of Radio News." *Nostalgia Digest*, Winter 2008.

Crowell, Alfred Augustus. "History of the Chicago Daily Times." Master's thesis, August 1940, Northwestern University. (CHM)

Dante, Harris L. "The Chicago Tribune's

'Lost Years,' 1865–1874." *Journal of the Illinois State Historical Society*, Spring–Summer 1965.

"Deal Frees *Sun-Times* from Hollinger Control." *Sun-Times*, March 26, 2008.

"Decision to Go Public in U.S. Set Stage for His Downfall." *Sun-Times*, November 18, 2005.

Digby-Junger, Richard. "The Chicago Press Club: The Scoop behind *The Front Page*." *Chicago History*, Winter 1998–1999. (CHM)

_____. "'The main rendezvous for men of the press': The Life and Death of the Chicago Press Club, 1880–1987." *Journal of Illinois History* 1, no. 3 (Winter 1998).

*_____. "A New Version of the Founding of the *Chicago Daily News*." *Illinois Historical Journal* 86, no. 1 (Spring 1993).

Duffy, Jim, et al. "The *Sun-Times* Before and After Murdoch." Newspaper Study Project, Medill School of Journalism, Spring 1984.

"Elsewhere in the News." *Sun-Times*, March 14, 2008.

"Ex-Publisher Hit with Fraud Charges." *Sun-Times*, August 19, 2005.

"Ex–*Sun-Times* Boss Charged with Racketeering." *Sun-Times*, December 16, 2004.

"Ex–*Sun-Times* Boss Radler Sentenced to 29-Month Term." *Chicago Tribune*, December 18, 2007.

"Ex–*Sun-Times* Publisher (Radler) Pleads Guilty." *Sun-Times*, September 21, 2005.

"FBI: *Sun-Times* Ex-Boss Chose to Steal with Both Hands." *Sun-Times*, November 18, 2005.

Ferris, William. "Knight of the Short Sentence." *Chicago*, November 1955.

"The First Hundred Years: Some Highlights of the First Century of the Publication of the *Chicago Tribune*." *Chicago Tribune*, 1947. (CHM)

*Flannery, James Allen. "Chicago Newspapers' Coverage of the City's Major Civil Disorders of 1968." Doctor's thesis, Northwestern University, 1971. (CHM)

Flemming, Thomas. "The Big Leak." *American Heritage*, December 1987.

"Former *Sun-Times* Publisher Indicted." *Chicago Tribune*, August 19, 2005.

Gertz, Elmer. "Charles A. Dana and the Chicago Republican." *Journal of the Illinois Historical Society* 1, 1952.

*_____. "Joe Medill's War." *Lincoln Herald* 47, no. 3. Lincoln Memorial University, Harrogate, TN.

Goler, Robert I. "Black Sox." *Chicago History*, Fall and Winter 1988–1989.

Gordon, John Steele. "The Public Be Damned!" *American Heritage*, September–October 1989.

Hanson, Harry. "And the Chicago Daily News." *Journal of the Illinois State Historical Society* xlv, no. 1 (Spring 1952).

Hatch, Anthony P. "Inferno at the Iroquois." *Chicago History*, Fall 2003.

"The Hollinger Upheaval and the *Sun-Times*." *Sun-Times*, November 26, 2003.

Hoopes, Roy. "The Forty-Year Run." *American Heritage*, November 1992.

"John Smith, Negro, in the *Tribune*." An address to the City Club of Chicago, September 12, 1950. (CHM)

Johnson, Geoffrey. "Mr. Fields Rehabs His Dream House." *Chicago*, June 1989.

Keeley, James. "Newspaper Work." Address at the University of Notre Dame, November 26, 1912. (CHM)

Klatt, Wayne. "The Unlikely Love Life of King Mike McDonald." *Chicago Reader*, September 23, 1983.

Lafferty, William. "Excursion on the Lakefront." *Chicago History*, Fall and Winter 1991–1992.

"Lincoln in Chicago." A brochure published by the Chicago Historical Society (now the Chicago History Museum), no date.

"The Looting of the *Sun-Times*." *Sun-Times*, September 1, 2004.

MacFarlane, Peter Charles. "Explaining Keeley." Reprint from *Colliers*, private information for the Chicago Historical Society staff. (CHM)

Medill, Joseph. "An Easy Method of Spelling the English Language." *Chicago Tribune*, 1867. (CHM)

Miner, Michael. "Jim Hoge and His One-Horse Chariot." *Chicago*, May 1979.

Moriarity, Frank Thomas. "Life and Public Service of Joseph Medill." Master's thesis, Northwestern University. (CHM)

Murray, Gart. "Chicago's Mutest Trumpets." *Saturday Review*, October 13, 1962.

Nelson, Barry C. "Anarchism: The Movement Behind the Martyrs." *Chicago History*, Summer 1986.

Oleksy, Walter. "A Funny Thing Happened...." *Chicago*, January, February 1972.

"Paper Sales Inflated up to 50,000 a Day." *Sun-Times*, October 6, 2004.

"Paper Trail: 100 Years of the Chicago Defender." Public television documentary. WTTW-TV, Chicago (aired February 15, 2007).

Patric, William C. "Custer's Expedition." *American History*, June 2003.

"Radler: Black in on All Discussions." *Sun-Times*, May 9, 2007.

"Radler et al Charged." City News Service, August 18, 2005.

"Radler: Mistakes, Anti-Jewish Sentiment in Report." *Sun-Times*, September 2, 2004.

Rosenthal, Phil. "*Sun-Times* Now Gets to Pay for Black's Crimes." *Chicago Tribune*, December 16, 2007.

Sawslask, Karen. "Smoldering City." *Chicago History*, Fall and Winter 1988–89.

Schmidt, Royal J. "The Daily News and Illinois Politics." Doctor's thesis, University of Chicago, June 1957. (CHM)

Selby, Paul. "Genesis of the Republican party in Illinois." Paper read to the Illinois Republican Editorial Association in Decatur, IL, September 14, 1904. (CHM)

Sims, Norman Howard. "The Chicago Style of Journalism." Doctor's thesis, University of Illinois-Urbana-Champaign, 1970. (CHM)

"Site of the Sauganash Hotel and the Wigwam." A brochure published by the Commission on Chicago Historical and Architectural Landmarks, June 1975.

"6 Plead Guilty in Circulation Scandal." *Chicago Tribune*, May 27, 2006.

Smith, Bryan. "Sudden Impact." *Chicago*, December 2006.

Smith, Carl S. "Cataclysm and Cultural Consciousness: Chicago and the Haymarket Trial." *Chicago History*, Summer 1986.

*Smith, Henry Justin. "A Gallery of Chicago Editors." *Chicago Daily News*, 1930. Lecture delivered at the University of Chicago and published by the *Daily News*.

Strevey, Tracy Elmer. "Joseph Medill During the Civil War Period." PhD diss., University of Chicago, June 1930. (CHM)

Sullivan, Frank. "And the Beat Goes On, the Ben Hecht Era." *Avenue M*, May 1987.

"*Sun-Times* Ex-Publisher Pleads Guilty to Fraud." *Sun-Times*, September 21, 2005.

"*Sun-Times* Parent CEO Conrad Black Steps Down." *Sun-Times*, November 18, 2003.

"*Sun-Times* Parent Seeks Answers." *Sun-Times*, January 26, 2004.

"*Sun-Times* Publisher Radler Steps Down After Eight Years." *Sun-Times*, November 17, 2003.

"The Telephone Journal." A reprint by the Illinois Bell Telephone Company on the 100th anniversary of exchange telephone service in Chicago, October 1978.

Ver Berkmoes, Ryan. "89 Hours." *Chicago*, April 1995.

Walsh, Justin E. "Radically and Thoroughly Democratic: Wilbur Storey and the Detroit Free Press, 1853 to 1861." *Michigan History* (a publication of the Michigan Historical Commission), September 1963.

Weisberger, Bernard A. "Celebrity Journalists." *American Heritage*, March 1989.

"The W-G-N" (World's Greatest Newspaper). *Chicago Tribune*, June 10, 1922.

Index

Numbers in **bold italics** indicate pages with illustrations.